Walking

Black-eyed Susan

Minnesota

by Mary Jo & Jim Malach
Contributing Writers—Mary Steffl and Martha McNey
Illustrated by Karen Berry
Design & Typography by Mary Walstrom/JEZAC Type & Design

Voyageur Press

ACKNOWLEDGMENTS

Over two hundred people contributed their ideas to this book. Special thanks to Jill Johnson who suggested we write a book on walking; to Tom Lebovsky who helped turn a general concept into a book; to all the Minnesotans, especially park personnel, who shared their time and thoughts about walking; to John Dillery and Dan Murray who helped with transportation routes; to the patient employees in the downtown Saint Paul post office who helped us determine individual postage rates for all the review packets; to all the people who helped us identify walking resources; to friends, family, and co-workers who were supportive during the entire project; to Olivia and her friends for their sustaining laughter; and most importantly, to Bob and Pat Wagoner who inspire from a distance.

PHOTO CREDITS

Front cover photo copyright © 1991 by Joel W. Sheagren, Viewfinders.

Back cover photo, p. 364 photos: R. Lincoln McNey

Printed in the United States of America
91   92   93   94   95   5   4   3   2   1

Library of Congress Cataloging-in-Publication Data

Malach, Mary Jo
Walking Minnesota/Mary Jo and Jim Malach.
p.   cm.
ISBN 0-89658-147-0
1. Walking—Minnesota—Guide-books. 2. Hiking—Minnesota—Guide-books.
3. Minnesota—Description and travel—1991-   —Guide-books
I. Title.
GV199.42.M6M35   1991

917.76'0453—dc20

90-23893
CIP

Published by Voyageur Press, Inc.
P.O. Box 338, 123 North Second Street
Stillwater, MN 55082 U.S.A.

In Minn 612-430-2210   Toll-free 800-888-9653

Voyageur Press books are also available at discounts for quantities for educational, fundraising, premium, or sales-promotion use. For details contact the marketing department. Please write or call for our free catalog of publications.

CHAPTER 1

Introduction

Walking is a way to get back to the basics in life, to plant both feet on the ground, and to move ahead, one step at a time. Walking sets the body, mind, and spirit to an internal rhythm unique to each person. It is, perhaps, the key that unlocks and releases the best in all of us.

It's not as easy to walk as it used to be. Years ago, people could step outside their tepee or cabin and walk for miles and miles. Today, people who are ready to "get back on their feet" find themselves in an almost antipedestrian environment. Walkers are forced to play Rushin' Roulette at intersections. Sidewalks have disappeared from some of the newer residential developments. Walking has become a fitness sport with players confined to malls and hiking trails.

Like a treasured find in the attic, the simple act of walking deserves to be honored for its ageless splendor and everlasting value. As individuals, and as a culture, we need to understand what we gave up when we decided to speed through time and space toward singular rather than collaborative destinations. We also need to explore ways to bring walking back into the home, the neighborhood, the classroom, and the workplace so that physical exercise is integrated into daily routines and not segregated into "workouts."

Minnesota already has a significant number of programs and resources in place to encourage walking. In fact, according to a 1985 survey prepared by the Minnesota Department of Natural Resources and published by the Minnesota State Planning Agency, walking is the most popular recreation activity for Minnesota residents, accounting for 18 percent of time spent in outdoor recreation activities. By the year 2000, state planners predict that this figure will increase to 29.1 percent. Health professionals, artists, employers, and school administrators are beginning to realize the important role of walking in maintaining a healthy, productive, and creative life. Walking tours are becoming one of the most popular ways to promote local tourism. Planners from all levels of government are working together to create an even more efficient network of city, county, state, and federal trails.

Minnesota is one of the most walkable states in the country because it offers over 4,000 miles of paved and turf trails that vary in length from one-third of a mile to over 100 miles. If you walked

3 miles a day, every day of the year, it would take you more than three years to walk every trail in Minnesota at least once, and by the time you finished, there would be a couple hundred miles of new trails to discover.

The Twin Cities metro area is known worldwide for its extensive greenway system. Charles E. Little, author of *The Greenways of America* (Johns Hopkins University Press, 1990), developed the following comprehensive definition of *greenway:*

> **Greenway** *n.* 1. A linear open space established along either a natural corridor, such as a riverfront, stream valley, or ridgeline, or overland along a railroad right-of-way converted to recreational use, a canal, a scenic road or other route; 2. Any natural or landscaped course for pedestrian or bicycle passage; 3. An open-space connector linking parks, nature reserves, cultural features, or historic sites with each other and populated areas; 4. Locally, certain strip or linear parks designated as a parkway or greenbelt. (American neologism: green + way; origin obscure).

An extensive 90-mile network of paved greenways through the cities of Minneapolis and Saint Paul link area lakes, rivers, and woods with downtown and neighborhood areas. During an interview, Little stated, "From the standpoint of local greenway development, the Twin Cities rank high if not among the highest in the country—especially in terms of age (turn of the century) and elaboration!"

In June 1990, *National Geographic* devoted a significant amount of space to an article titled "Greenways: Paths to the Future." During an interview for this book, author Noel Grove commented on Minnesota's walking heritage. "Philosophically, Minnesota is ahead of the nation regarding trail development," he stated. "In the 1900s, an extensive trail system was developed in the Twin Cities that connects city parks with a trail along both sides of the Mississippi. When you visit Minneapolis or Saint Paul, you experience a very outdoor, physical climate. Minnesotans don't need to make the philosophical shift that is needed in some states to support trail development, because trails have always been an important part of the state's history."

Others share Grove's enthusiasm for the healthy lifestyle that has become synonymous with Minnesota. According to a 1990 study conducted by the Institute for Southern Studies, Minnesota ranked third in the nation as "one of the healthiest places to live." A "green index," the basis for the rating, considered factors such as public health, politics and policies, worker health, and poisons (air and water pollution, pesticide use, and waste disposal).

Why does walking continue to be the most popular recreation activity in Minnesota? Three reasons: people, pavement, and pine needles.

PEOPLE

There is a strong tradition of walking in Minnesota. The Ojibway and Dakota Indians developed wonderfully efficient trail systems along rivers and streams. Many of those same trails were also used by the European traders and farmers as they moved their wagons and ox carts from one town to another. Some of the trails were made into roads. Others are still foot trails that wind their way through cities and parks. The earliest residents of Minnesota literally cleared the way for future trail development.

In the late 1800s, as the towns of Minneapolis and Saint Paul along the Mississippi River were well on their way to becoming cities, a small group of residents and city planners began acquiring land around the metro lakes, creeks, and rivers to ensure public access to these natural bounties. Thanks to these citizens, there is an abundance of public parks and walkways in the metro area.

In addition to Minnesota's earliest residents and turn-of-the-century public land advocates, a third group of people deserve the gratitude of walkers—the people in Minnesota who from 1920 until now participated in the acquisition of Minnesota parklands, who designed or built the paved walkways, who donated private land to become state parks, or who managed and maintained the parks. There are so many incredibly beautiful places to walk, thanks to their efforts!

The fourth group of people who make the state walkable are the people who use the sidewalks and trails. Walkers, by their gentle presence, continue to influence and shape the development of urban and remote trail systems.

Although the ideas and viewpoints of walking advocates and program developers are not typically included in guidebooks, they are highlighted in the beginning chapters of this book because they are just as important and worth exploring as the trails themselves. Furthermore, these issues and programs may be of interest to walkers from other states.

PAVEMENT

There is a remarkable relationship between people and pavement in Minnesota. Visitors to the state are amazed at how many people use the paved greenways for walking, running, biking, skating, and skiing, during all seasons, during all hours of the day, during the hot spells when the temperature climbs into the high nineties, or during the cold spells, when the windchill reaches forty below zero. Greenways have made it easy for visitors and residents to experience and enjoy the natural beauty of Minnesota.

In addition to the outdoor greenways, Minnesota has an extensive indoor system of skyways that makes it possible to walk around the downtown areas of Saint Paul, Minneapolis, Duluth, and Rochester without ever going outside! The square-tunneled skyways have windows along both sides so you can watch the activity below as you move from building to building.

In addition to greenways and skyways, there is a third form of "paved" walkway in Minnesota—shopping malls. The first enclosed, climate-controlled shopping mall in the United States, Southdale, opened in 1956 in Edina, Minnesota. Today, Southdale, and just about every other shopping mall in Minnesota, opens its doors early in the morning to walkers and provides monthly seminars. The Mall of America, scheduled to open in 1992 in Bloomington, Minnesota, will be the largest indoor mall in the United States. One lap around each of the four floors will give walkers a 3.5-mile workout!

PINE NEEDLES

The very best way to explore Minnesota is on foot, using your senses. You can experience the trickling of water over a rock, the telltale smell of mint, and all the subtle variations of greens and browns only when you're walking. To truly have a "Minnesota experience," you need to walk among towering, fragrant pines and feel a soft cushion of pine needles underfoot. There's simply nothing quite like it.

You don't have to go very far to experience Minnesota pines. Parks and nature centers within 5 miles of the Twin Cities offer the spirit of the woods in the heart of the city. Beyond the metro area, in greater or outstate Minnesota, there is an incredible variety of walking experiences, from the prairies in the southwest and northwest sections of the state, to the river bluffs in southeastern Minnesota, to the big woods in the central part of the state. The internationally known Superior Hiking Trail extends for 130 miles along the rugged North Shore of Lake Superior. The North Country Trail, Minnesota's segment of the National Scenic Trail, will eventually extend 390 miles across Minnesota. By the end of the decade, it may be possible to walk from one end of Minnesota to the other, and to walk from Minnesota to just about anywhere else in the United States!

HOW TO USE THIS BOOK

This book is designed to make it as easy for you as possible, whether you're visiting Minnesota or living here, to have not just a plain old walk, but a walking adventure—or, to be more specific, a "walk keen" adventure. To walk "keen" is to enhance your life through walking in any number of ways—to learn about the environment, history, or art; to improve your health by strengthening your muscles, bones, and cardiovascular system; or to create necessary solitude that nurtures thoughts, feelings, and relationships. Walking is a three-dimensional activity that can be used to invigorate the mind, body, and spirit. So slip on a pair of good support shoes and let the walking paths in Minnesota become your university, your health club, or your sanctuary.

Many of the barriers between you and the walking path have been removed. Maps from over 125 state, county, and city parks and other points of interest have been collected and reproduced so you can get a sense of the types of trails that are available in both the metro and outstate areas. Information about the availability of restrooms, water, and public telephones will make it easy for you to plan your trip to each walking site. A recommended route has been developed for each site that will introduce you to some of the area's highlights.

One thing to keep in mind when you use this book is that it is just a small sampler, not a comprehensive list of all the walking opportunities and resources in the state. This is an unrated guide to a variety of walking adventures through some of the state's parks, downtown areas, industrial parks, cemeteries, suburban neighborhoods, and nature centers. We hope these few selections will entice you to get out and explore all the other incredibly beautiful walking sites in this state.

There is comfort in the familiar, and with it a tendency to walk the same trails over and over again. But every so often it's important to push comfort aside and challenge yourself by trying something new. When you limit yourself to walking the same route over and over, you are missing the magnificence of Minnesota. If you are in a walking rut and are ready for an adventure, scan the sites and select one that is somewhat similar in length and terrain to your current route, but located in a different area. You may want to set a goal to explore one new walking site each month, or each week.

Wherever you walk, be conscious of your personal safety and walk with a partner whenever possible.

Another point to keep in mind as you use this book to explore new walking sites is that the trail systems in Minnesota are always being upgraded and expanded. Although most of the information in this book will be useful through 1993, be sure to pick up a current trail map at each site so that you are aware of current trail segments that have been changed or new trail segments that have been added.

Change is an important part of the walking experience. The trails change in length and direction. From one week to another trees, grasses, and flowers adapt to weather and growth cycles, changing their colors and textures. And the more in touch you become with your internal rhythm, the more you will change.

Walking changes your reference points. Cities on a map are fondly recalled not by their relationship to interstate freeways, but by the way they're nestled in a valley or perched on a river bluff. Parks are recalled by the faces of people you meet on the trail, the first sighting of a white-tailed deer, or the spotting of a late-summer wildflower. The more you walk, the more difficult it becomes to give directions to people in cars because you think in terms of pathways, not roads, and you know your way by curves, hills, creeks, and willows, not by street signs. All the things you've ever read about in biology, geography, or history classes are animated and understandable.

Walking also makes you aware of the issues surrounding trail development. As you will see, some of the walking sites in this book are well known, well financed, and well tended. Others are struggling for survival.

In recent years, with increased interest in the environment, there has been an increase in the use of parks and trails. Minnesota, like other states throughout the country, is faced with the challenge of having more trail users than ever before, with fewer tax dollars available to maintain or expand current facilities.

As you walk some of the trail segments that have been completed and those still in progress, think about becoming involved in trail development in your own community. The challenge facing all walkers is to give back some of what we've received from the trails, and to help create a plan for the next century that will continue to restore the simple act of walking to the place it deserves in all of our lives.

CHAPTER 2

Footwork, Friends, and Other Necessities

The phrase "let's walk" means different things to different people.

For some people, it means let's walk instead of taking the bus or driving the car. It means carrying groceries home from the store, or wearing sneakers to the office, or pushing a stroller to the daycare center. Walking is a major form of transportation for those who don't own a car and for those who do own a car but prefer to use it only on special occasions.

For some people, "let's walk" means let's relax—let's work off the day's tensions, listen to crickets, or watch the last brilliant remnants of sun straddle the horizon. Walking for many people is a way to step out of a sometimes mechanical daily routine and stay in touch with life on a much larger, more natural scale.

And for some people, it means let's get off the couch, turn off the television, and burn some pie. Like a sailboat gliding over the lake, the smooth, gliding rhythm of a walker in motion is something to behold. More and more people are walking at a clip to maintain their strength, stamina, and stability.

There are, then, at least three types of walking that serve different purposes: *transit walking, pleasure walking, and fitness walking.*

TRANSIT WALKING

The purpose of transit walking is to get from one point to another to accomplish a daily task or responsibility. A lunch hour walk to the post office, an evening stroll to the corner grocery store, or a weekend jaunt to the library are good examples of transit walking. How fast or how long you walk really doesn't matter. Once you accomplish your task, the walk has served its purpose.

Transit walking is becoming an important alternative form of transportation for people who are concerned about gas prices and the long-term effect of emissions on the environment. A growing number of people are starting to take pride in using their own footwork to power themselves around town. Transit walking gives people a chance to get some fresh air while accomplishing errands. Furthermore, hip packs and backpacks make it very easy and comfortable to walk and carry items at the same time.

In order to walk to the day-to-day functions that require a car, you need to live in a community that is designed for walking. In most urban areas it's usually possible to step out the front door and walk to a drug store, school, park, hair salon, or cafe. In some of the newer suburban areas, that's not possible, because stores are usually located in malls clustered around highway interchanges. People often find it easier to transit walk when they're at work, because small stores are usually located within walking distance of office and industrial complexes.

Some city planners and architects are beginning to design small, "sustainable" communities that are built to human scale (no building is over four stories high) with natural forms of transportation in mind so that people can accomplish most of their daily tasks within walking or biking distance of where they live or work.

Transit walking is an easy way to boost your activity level and burn a few calories. Just keep a comfortable pair of walking shoes and a backpack within easy reach so that when the weather's fine, and the mood strikes, you're ready to walk. Unfortunately, the stop-and-go nature of transit walking makes it difficult to obtain the aerobic benefits associated with fitness walking. If you own a car and are trying to use it less often, you'll need to ween yourself from the car slowly. Once you start walking, your car, no matter how old it is, will become a luxury to be savored on special occasions.

Transit walking is a great way to observe people's faces, details on buildings, and merchandise in windows. Take some of the less-busy side streets and savor the smell of freshly baked bagels, the silence of a historic chapel, or the budding flowers at a farmer's market. And, if you find your practical walks to the dry cleaners or hardware store enjoyable, there are lots of ways to extend the pleasure.

PLEASURE WALKING

The purpose of pleasure walking is to enjoy walking for the sake of walking, without any particular destination or purpose in mind. Pleasure walking involves wandering, meandering, and dawdling. As with transit walking, how fast or how long you walk really doesn't matter. Once you're enjoying yourself, the walk has served its purpose.

Pleasure walking is a relatively new phenomenon, according to Philip Larson, art historian and sculptor, and former curator of the Walker Art Center in Minneapolis. "People didn't walk for pleasure until there were places to walk, such as the formal gardens of the seventeenth century," he explained. "Elaborate formal gardens surrounded European chateaus and that's how the concept of 'artificial forests' or parks evolved. Hiking for the sake of pleasure, fresh air and nature study came about the same time—the late eighteenth century. The Paris plan of the late nineteenth century introduced boulevard plantings on sidewalks and this was really the beginning of walking for the sake of walking."

Pleasure walking is growing in popularity. People take pleasure walks on sidewalks, paved trails, and dirt or grass trails for many different reasons—to be alone, to learn, to socialize, to think, to grieve, to reduce stress, to celebrate. Your definition of "pleasure" will define how, when, and where you walk.

Wood Lily

If you find very little time during the week to be alone with your own thoughts, then a pleasure walk may involve a private walk in a safe place, where you won't be disturbed. Paved, circular trails or limestone linear trails are ideal because you don't have to watch your step or be interrupted with trail junction decisions.

If you find pleasure in learning, then you'll enjoy trails with self-guided tours and information posts along the way. You may want to carry a guide-book so you can learn more about nature. Walking tours through nature centers, cities, and historic sites are a great way to walk and learn. Walking tours vary in length from twenty minutes to extended walking vacations that last from five to seven days.

If you find pleasure in the company of friends or family members, then you may want to plan to walk together through a favorite park or historic area of town. If you want to have an adventure together, then try one of the longer turf trails with all kinds of twists and turns. Facing a new challenge together can add quite a spark to the relationship.

If you are grieving and need to work through a loss, walk in a safe, controlled environment like a cemetery where you can cry without feeling self-conscious, where you can get lost in your feelings without becoming physically vulnerable. Walking can become an important and necessary part of the grieving process.

Walking is also a great way to reduce stress. After about an hour on the trail, you will probably feel and think differently about the stressful parts of your life. Add some puddle-jumping, rock-skipping, bubble-blowing moments and life seems more manageable.

Pleasure walking is slowly working its way into traditional celebrations. Families walk together through the woods on Thanksgiving Day; friends celebrate New Year's Day together with an early morning walk along the river; children name their favorite trail and take a birthday walk with friends and family.

Sometimes the only difference between a thumbs-up and a thumbs-down day is a walk. If you want to turn something ordinary into something extra-ordinary, something simple into something profound, something intolerable into something you can manage, keep your feet and arms moving. And once you get into the swing of things, you may want to pick up the pace a bit and try one or more forms of fitness walking.

FITNESS WALKING

The purpose of fitness walking is to strengthen the cardiovascular and skeletal systems and tone muscles through regular aerobic exercise. Fitness walking includes activities such as aerobic walking, water walking, and competitive racewalking. Just as the number of transit and pleasure walkers has increased dramatically over the last ten years, so too has the number of fitness walkers. More physicians are recommending aerobic walking programs for their patients because of the health benefits and minimal injuries associated with the activity. More and more people of all ages are beginning to discover and enjoy the competitive sport of racewalking.

As with any other form of aerobic exercise, before starting any type of fitness walking program you should schedule an appointment to discuss the following information with your physician: 1) your target heart rate (based on your age and condition); 2) your weekly workout schedule (including number of days and time spent exercising); and 3) any special considerations or limitations based on your health history. Ask a health professional to show you how to measure your resting heart rate and your active heart rate so that you can stay within a safe exercise range and measure your progress. Based on the recommendations of your physician, you can then design a fitness walking program based on your abilities and health needs.

Variety is an important factor in any lifelong fitness program. Your chances of maintaining a year-round walking program increase when you cross-train with other walking activities or other sports such as cross-country skiing, biking, swimming, aerobic dance, or yoga.

Aerobic Walking

Aerobic walking involves 1) a five- to ten-minute warm-up period; 2) an aerobic walk (starting with ten minutes, working up to thirty minutes); and 3) a five- to ten-minute cool-down period.

Frequency. How often should you do aerobic walking? The frequency you want to achieve (and it may take you a year or longer to accomplish this) is to walk at least three times a week, for at least thirty minutes, within your target heart range.

Target heart range. Your target heart range is the rate at which your heart needs to beat per minute to strengthen the heart muscle. To figure out your target heart range, talk with your doctor. Some athletes suggest that you subtract your age from 220, and then multiply the number by .60 (60 percent), and then .80 (80 percent). To strengthen your heart muscle, maintain your heart rate within your target heart range for approximately thirty minutes during an exercise session. Check your pulse every ten to fifteen minutes to make sure you are within your target heart range. To check you pulse, walk slowly, find your wrist or neck pulse, count your pulse rate for ten seconds, multiply by six to calculate beats per minute, then adjust your pace accordingly. You'll eventually want to get your heart beating at the upper end of your target heart range when you exercise. The more you walk, the stronger you'll get. Don't rush the process. Take your time and enjoy each workout. You should feel invigorated and refreshed, not tired or depleted.

Where to walk. For aerobic walking, you'll need a flat, paved surface. Shopping malls are ideal for aerobic walking. A number of city and county parks are also ideal for learning the correct form and picking up speed.

How to learn the correct walking form. Aerobic walking and racewalking involve the same, efficient body movements. The only difference is that racewalking is done at a much faster pace.

The best way to master the correct form for aerobic walking is to take a racewalking class through your community education system. Community groups and health clubs also offer racewalking clinics with instruction and individual analysis. Like yoga, dance, tennis, or any other activity with refined movements, it's best to learn from people who know what they're doing, and who can provide you with the feedback you need to develop an excellent racewalking form. If you teach yourself the technique, you may learn some bad walking habits and injure yourself in the process. Here is a brief overview of some of the things you'll learn in a racewalking class:

Warm-up exercises. Starting is easy—just walk slowly for five or ten minutes and give your muscles and heart a chance to get going. To vary your routine, you may want to do some basic stretching exercises such as rotating your ankles in alternating directions, rotating your knees in alternating directions, or extending both arms against a wall, moving your body a few steps backward, and bending one knee at a time as you stretch alternate calf muscles.

Aerobic walking. If you are just beginning a walking program, take it easy during this portion of the walk. You should always have enough breath on reserve to talk or sing. If you can't carry on a conversation, you're walking too fast.

ARMS. Bend your arms at the elbow, alternately bringing your hand up to a point in front of the center of your chest, and then back down again, to an imaginary belt loop at the side of your waist. Keep your elbows close to your body—do not swing them out to the side. (You may want to stand and practice this movement for a while before you begin.) Do not leave your arms extended as you walk, because you'd be wasting energy. Bent arms will allow you to gain momentum and enhance your cardiovascular workout; straight arms will "drag" down your time.

LEGS. Don't worry about your leg movements until your arm movements are comfortable. Once you can walk easily with your arms bent close to your body, you can begin to refine your leg movements to gather speed. To get a feel for the movement, stand still for a moment with both legs touching. Bend one knee and then the other (you'll be bending your ankle but keeping your foot in the same place). Notice how your hip swivels to accommodate the movement. Keep doing this movement for a while to get the feel of the racewalking hip swivel.

Correct racewalking form takes a long time to master, but you can begin with some of the basic movements so you can increase your speed as you walk. Here are the basic movements: 1) Walk with one foot in front of the other, as if you were walking on a straight line. Try this movement for a while. Walk along the line in the middle of a paved walkway, or go to a shopping mall and walk along the lines on the floor. The movement feels awkward at first, so keep practicing when you walk. 2) Roll your weight to the outer edge of your foot as it touches the ground. 3) Push off with your big toe as you change from one foot to another. This push will eventually evolve into a fluid, streamlined movement. 4) Keep your knees straight when they are directly beneath your body. 5) Always have one foot in touch with the ground. Keep contact with the ground as you pick up speed. Imagine your legs are the spokes of a wheel, and your feet are the rim that keeps gathering momentum.

Walk as fast as you can, keeping your elbows bent and close to your body as you walk in a straight line, pushing off with your big toes, placing one foot after the other on the ground with ease, and swiveling your hips.

Cool-down exercises. At the end of your walk, gradually slow down and resume a casual walking speed. You may want to add some stretching exercises to give your muscles one final workout.

Water Walking

Water walking is ideal for 1) people who are very overweight; 2) people who have problems with their back, hips, legs, knees, or ankles that would be aggravated by walking on pavement; 3) pregnant women; 4) people with physical disabilities; and 5) people who are looking for an indoor winter walking activity.

The safest and best way to learn water walking is to take a water walking class at a local pool. If there isn't a water walking class offered, suggest that they start one.

There is little or no risk of injury in water walking, and the resistance offered by the water is excellent for upper and lower body conditioning. In the water, bodies are 10 percent lighter than they are on land. Water walking is very simple. You start walking slowly in the water (using the racewalking form described previously) just as you would on land, and then you gradually pick up your speed, ending with a slower-paced, cool-down walk. Do not lean forward when you water walk or you may experience neck strain. There's a tendency to float between steps and spring from your toes so be sure to keep your feet in contact with the floor of the pool, just as you would on the trail.

Racewalking

Racewalking, a track and field event, is still a relatively unknown sport in Minnesota but it is gaining in popularity every year. There are more judged races, more competitors, and more trained judges than ever before.

If you're interested in becoming a competitive racewalker, there are a number of organizations in Minnesota that offer racewalk instruction and coaching. Once you've mastered the basic form, you can start working on your time.

Like any other sport, participants must pass through a hierarchy of sanctioned events before they can enter national competitions. Walkers need to qualify for regional and national competitions by achieving a certain time in a local race and this time changes every year as people get faster and faster. In 1990 the qualifying time for an indoor 3,000-meter race was 14:45 and an outdoor 10,000-meter race was 52:36. Meets vary in distance, but championship meets are always 3,000 and 10,000 meters.

There are a number of judged racewalking competitions in Minnesota including the St. Patrick's Day Race in March, the Star of the North Games in June, the Hennepin-Lake Classic in August, and the Racewalk Classic in September. The best way to begin competitive racewalking is to enter a local event sponsored by The Athletic Congress (TAC). (See chapter 8 for more information.)

Once racewalkers achieve those times, they are eligible to compete in regional and national events. Members of the U.S. Racewalking Team enjoy the benefits of training with other racewalkers and having their expenses to national and international meets paid for by TAC, the International Amateur

Athletic Federation (IAAF), or the United States Olympic Committee. International racewalking events are by invitation only.

Mary Howell, exercise physiologist and coordinator of Melpomene's WALKS program (see chapter 8), has an eye on the 1992 summer Olympics, in hopes of becoming a member of the first Women's Olympic Racewalking Team. She has been a member of the U.S. Racewalking Team since 1985 and finished in eighth place in the 1990 national championships.

Howell, who can walk a mile in 6:55, became involved in the sport of racewalking almost by accident. "I was running with a club team in Detroit," she explained, "when one of the coaches asked me if I'd be interested in *walking*. I didn't know what he meant, and he had to explain the sport to me. I worked with him for three weeks learning the technique, and then he entered me in a mixed race with men and women. It turned out that it was the Alongi Race, an international competition. I was the top U.S. finisher, the top female finisher, and placed third overall.

"After winning a race with so little preparation, I thought I was a natural," she laughed. "But now that I've been in competition for a while, I know that I really didn't know what I was doing, and that it takes a lot of work to develop a consistent, winning form."

She has been working with Martin Rudow, one of the men's Olympic racewalking coaches, since 1984, and Bob Kitchen, a coach from International Falls, Minnesota, since 1988. Cross-training has been effective in preparing Howell to successfully compete. She varies her hard "quality training days" (three days a week) with less rigorous practices. Her workouts include fast- and slow-paced racewalks that usually average 6 to 10 miles, and workouts in which she simulates the fast and slow surges of a particular course. On other days, she works out with upper-body weights and she swims almost daily for relaxation. Every three weeks she takes a day off. During the fall, she runs five days a week and walks the other two. In the winter, she rides a bike to build strength.

Her coaches guide her training from a distance. "I've learned to abdicate the responsibility for my training, to let go and let someone else focus on the whole picture. We discuss what I'm doing and why," she added, "but basically they tell me what to do. It takes some of the responsibility away from me so that when I go to the track I don't have to think, I just 'do.' I have total confidence in the fact that what they are asking me to do is in my best interest and will help me race better."

She wears regular walking shoes when she trains, but "racing flats" (the same shoes runners use) when she competes. During the course of a year, she needs at least four pairs of walking shoes, three pairs of indoor track racing flats, and four pairs of roadracing flats.

Howell values her place on the U.S. Racewalking Team. "The other members of the team are like a family. We understand each other's strengths, and we support each other. The team manager is an integral person," she continued. "I don't have to worry about anything because he deals with tickets, hotels, airlines, food, money. All I have to do is sleep, eat, train, and race. They make sure that I have the right uniform and shoes, that I have the right food to eat. I worry about all those things in my 'normal' life, but I don't have to deal with those things when I'm competing."

Howell is thrilled at being one of the first women racewalking competitors in the United States. "It's such a new sport that men and women are starting at the same point, and that's exciting. There aren't many stereotypes attached to the sport yet so it's not a woman's sport or a man's sport, it's just a sport." She hopes that someday Minnesota will host a national and an international racewalking championship.

WALKING PARTNERSHIPS AND CLUBS

If you enjoy walking and you'd walk more often if you had someone to walk with, then you should consider starting or joining a walking partnership or club.

Walking Partnerships

If two or more people live, work, or shop in the same area, are available at the same time during the day, and walk at the same pace, then it makes sense to start a walking partnership. Walking partners don't have to be friends—all they need in common is a fondness for walking and a similar walking pace.

The best way to find a walking partner is to join a local walking club. You also may want to approach walkers you see on a regular basis and discuss the possibility of forming a walking partnership. Community education programs that sponsor fitness and racewalking seminars also provide an opportunity to meet other walkers. Apartment or condominium buildings are ideal settings for walking partnerships.

All it takes to form a partnership is two people, but a walking partnership with four to six members has a greater chance of survival because there is a built-in backup system to cover the absence of one or more members. When the group gets a few members, it's helpful to establish some simple group operating norms about walking schedules, schedule changes, no-shows, pace, talk walks, and think walks. Keep the rules simple though because in order for a walking partnership to succeed, participation has to be very easy and pleasurable for all the partners.

It's important for walking partners to identify if they want to talk, and what they want to talk about. If you are taking a pleasure walk with a coworker, you may or may not want to talk about work. If you are taking a fitness walk with a friend, you may or may not want to talk about problems at home or on the job. Walking partners should be able to take quiet think walks together during which nobody says anything except hello and good-bye. Some walking partners choose to walk a few hundred feet apart, but always within view of each other.

There are a number of built-in benefits for walking partners. People who walk and shop together can help each other carry packages. People who are afraid to walk alone can provide each other with physical security and companionship. Fitness walkers can carpool to the mall and walking events.

Don't be afraid to initiate a walking partnership. You'd be surprised at how many people would walk more often if they only had a partner.

Walking Clubs

There is a definite need for more neighborhood-based walking clubs that provide walkers with 1) walking partners on a daily or weekly basis; 2) information about local walking events; 3) access to walking-related resources (racewalking clinics, health screenings, fitness assessments); and 4) group transportation to walking sites throughout the state.

Walking clubs make it easy for members to share car and gas expenses, or club-owned and loaned binoculars, tape recorders, walking sticks, compasses, and cameras. Some clubs have even been able to secure group discounts on shoes, shirts, hats, and socks.

Walking clubs can be inclusive (they actively recruit and include people without regard to race, color, creed, religion, national origin, disability, sex, or status) or exclusive (they only attract or selectively recruit members from the community who share the same demographics). The strength of an inclusive walking club is the diversity of its membership. International walking tours have proven that walkers don't even need to speak the same language to share a walk in the woods.

One of the most recently formed walking clubs in the metro area, TC Walkers, had its beginnings at a community walking event. Sue Minor, director of the Racewalk Classic for Autism, an annual fund-raising event for the Twin Cities Society for Children and Adults with Autism, Inc. (TCSAC), explained, "The Racewalk Classic for Autism is a judged racewalking event and fun walk which draws several hundred walkers ranging in ability and interests from eight-minute-per-mile racers to twenty minute-per-mile strollers. At the close of the 1989 classic, one participant, Bob Lindsey, approached race management and asked about racewalking clubs in the metro area; we didn't know of any. When we mailed the results of the race we included a short note asking anyone interested in forming a walking club (not solely racewalking) to contact TCSAC. At the end of two weeks we had forty-four names!

"We held the first meeting at another community walking competition," she continued. "After that race we went to a restaurant and decided to meet at a member's house the following Saturday. We continued meeting at a member's house until we settled on a permanent location and time: every Saturday at 9 A.M. at the Linden Hills Community Center.

"We had a potluck supper after one of the first meetings so that everyone could meet each other," she added, "and that was fun and built a sense of community. We also invited a local sports store to talk to us about winter walking gear after one of the walks. The store offered discounts on walking clothes and shoes as well as an informative talk. It was well attended.

"The group has met weekly since October 1989. Having a regular meeting place and time allows members to go on vacation or otherwise miss meetings, come back, and know exactly where to find the group without having to call around.

"Anyone can join," she continued. "There are beginning walkers and advanced racewalkers. When we walk around the lake together, the fast walkers will go ahead, and then circle back to chat a bit with the slower walkers, then walk ahead and circle back again. Some walkers prefer not to socialize when they walk, they want a hard, fast workout, and that's fine. The great thing about the group is that people learn from each other. The advanced racewalkers help the beginning walkers work on form. It's great fun."

What other advice would she give to people who wanted to start a walking club in their neighborhood? "Recruit members at community walking events," she advised, "because people there share a common interest in walking, and that's a good starting point. It's also a great way to recruit people from different areas of town.

"Don't hold business meetings," she added. "People join walking clubs to walk, and to meet other walkers. They don't want to sit around and talk so don't schedule meetings, schedule walks. If you keep it walking-centered, you don't need to charge dues, but if you get more formal than that, and want to plan group activities or have a newsletter, then you'll need to charge membership fees, elect officers, and have occasional business meetings so that the club can respond to the needs of its members."

Another way to ensure the longevity of a walking club is to affiliate the club with a neighborhood community center or park facility. The Minneapolis Municipal Hiking Club, a walking club sponsored by the Minneapolis Park and Recreation Board, was started in 1925 and maintains an annual membership of over three hundred people per year. (For more information about walking clubs, see chapters 8 and 9.)

WALKING CLOTHES AND EQUIPMENT

Although advertisers would like you to think otherwise, there's no need to go out and spend a fortune on new walking clothes or equipment. Most of the essential clothes and equipment can be purchased new for a reasonable amount of money. In fact, one of the best ways to purchase walking clothes is to go to a thrift store (preferably one that is the bread and butter of a local charity) and stock up on used cotton shirts, pants, and hats. You'll find some great bargains and you might be less apt to worry about grass and dirt stains.

The best way to learn about new products for walkers is to read magazines and newsletters designed for walkers and to periodically browse through camping, travel, and sports stores.

Essential Clothing

Whether you are walking in the city or hiking in the forest, you will need some essential pieces of clothing that will make your walk healthier and more enjoyable.

Walking shoes. There are more walking shoes available on the market than ever before. Walking shoes, like any other pair of shoes, will wear out after about 300 miles, so if you're an avid walker who walks at least 3 miles a day, four times a week, you'll need at least two pairs of walking shoes per year.

Before you invest your life savings in a pair of shoes, talk with other walkers. Ask them what they like and don't like about their shoes. The styles and models of walking shoes change from year to year, so go to the library and read newspaper and magazine articles that compare walking shoe features and prices. From an orthopedic point of view, all you need is a solid, flexible, level cushion between your foot and the pavement. Shoes should be comfortable. Your toes should have plenty of room so they're not crowded or pinched against the top of the shoe. Your shoes should be laced to provide adequate ankle support.

If you are a fitness walker, get a light, flexible shoe that will let you work up some speed. If you are a pleasure walker who enjoys the trails, get a shoe that is flexible enough to bend as you walk up steep hills, and durable enough to keep your foot stable as you walk over gravel and rocks. If you belong to a walking club, try to get group discounts on shoes from a local sports store.

For winter walking, you may want to purchase a shoe in a size one width wider than usual to accommodate the layers of socks you'll be wearing to keep your feet warm.

When you buy a new pair of walking shoes, remember to keep your old pair to wear on muddy days.

Socks. If you walk, you will need more pairs of socks than you ever imagined, so buy them on sale and in bulk. When selecting a sock, choose a style with a cushioned sole, and a medium to long (elastic if you can stand it) cuff, since you'll be pulling the cuff up around your pant legs when you walk on grass or dirt trails. Your socks should be a light color so that you can easily spot and remove insects or thistles that hop on board as you walk. Cotton socks are recommended for summer use.

For winter walking, you'll need a thin "liner" sock made of polypropylene that will keep your foot warm and "wick" the moisture away to the next layer, a wool sock that will cushion your foot, keep the cold air at a distance, and keep the moisture away from your toes.

Hats. One of the best ways to protect yourself from the sun is to wear a hat that casts a shadow over your face and neck. You'll want a hat that has a medium to wide brim and fits snugly around your head so that it can be worn on windy days. Some hats have convenient chin straps that can be tucked into the brim when not in use. Select a hat that has small holes for ventilation. You may want to purchase an all-season waterproof hat that will keep the rain off your face as you walk. In addition to protecting you from the sun, hats sometimes keep hovering insects at bay.

During the winter, you will need layers of clothes that protect your face and neck from the sun, wind, and cold. You especially need to protect your breathing passages from the cold air by covering your nose and mouth. Some jackets come with hoods that provide face and neck protection, but you may want more flexible clothing arrangements that can be added or removed in response to changing body and weather conditions. During the beginning and end phases of a winter walk, your body will be cold and in need of more clothes. During the peak of your walk, you will probably have to remove some clothing as your body generates more heat.

Although a warm cap and scarf will provide sufficient warmth and sun protection, they can become bulky and uncomfortable if you walk outdoors on a regular basis. Some of the newer alternatives in outerwear include the thermal face mask (balaclava) that fits snugly over your head with openings for your eyes (and in some styles, openings for your nose and mouth). If the thought of a face mask gives you claustrophobia, consider wearing a ski cap and a neck gaiter (a fabric cylinder that slips over your head, covers your neck, and can be pulled up to cover your mouth and nose as needed). Make sure the clothing you buy to cover your face and neck is washable because there is a continual build-up of moisture that should be routinely removed from the fabric.

Street Clothes vs. Trail Clothes

Now that both extremes of the body have been discussed, what about all the clothes in between? Walking shoes, socks, and a protective hat are essential elements for all types of walking, but where you walk will determine what other pieces of clothing are needed.

Street clothes are just what the name implies—comfortable clothes that you wear when you take transit, pleasure, or fitness walks in urban areas with sidewalks or paved paths, or in shopping malls or skyways. You can wear shorts and sleeveless tops because you won't be coming into direct contact with insects or plants. Any exposed areas of skin should be protected with sunscreen. Light, comfortable cotton clothes are ideal for walking in most urban areas.

If you walk to work, there are a number of ways to adapt your clothing so that you're comfortable as you move between indoor and outdoor environments. During the summer, keep one or two neutral suit jackets or sweaters at work so that you don't have to wear or carry them while you're walking. You may want to talk with management about adding some dressing room features to washrooms such as shelves, hooks, and a closet or locker area for hanging wet clothes to dry or storing excess clothing such as long underwear in the winter.

If you are walking early in the morning or late at night when it's dark, wear reflective clothing.

Trail clothes are different. Whenever you walk in the woods, or on dirt, grass, or wood-chip trails, you need to wear protective clothing. Long-sleeve, light-colored cotton shirts and long cotton pants offer protection from the sun, insects, and poisonous plants. When you walk in the woods, pull your socks over the cuffs of your pants to keep insects away from your skin. Tuck your shirt into your slacks. In some areas, you may need mosquito netting over your head. Reasonably priced, easy-to-carry head nets are available in most fishing and camping supply stores. They slip over your head and are secured with a loop that passes under each arm. They look outrageous, but if you're walking through a mosquito-infested area, they will provide the peace of mind you need.

If the insects are very bothersome, you may want to spray your clothes with insect repellent. However, if you use both sunscreen and insect repellent on a regular basis, you may begin to feel like a hazardous waste site. Think twice about attending social events immediately after a walk in the woods, because most people don't savor the blended aroma of sweat, sunscreen, and insect repellent.

You (and the environment) may be safer in the long run if you wear a couple of thin layers of cotton clothing to keep the insects and sun away from your skin. Most forests are naturally ten degrees cooler than other areas of town, so you won't notice the extra clothing. However, if the trails wind through open and forested areas, you'll probably have to opt for sunscreen and insect repellent.

Underwear and outerwear. If you enjoy walking in the rain, purchase a wide-brimmed, waterproof hat to keep the rain off your face, and wear a loose waterproof poncho that can fit over your backpack or hip pack. Wear an old pair of walking shoes, since rain boots are not comfortable for long-distance walking.

If you walk in the winter, you will need to layer your body, just as you layer your head and your feet. Start with a layer of polypropylene long underwear, topped with a fleece or wool shirt and pants (sweatshirts and sweatpants are great), and covered with a water- and wind-repellent jacket and pants. Outer clothing is expensive, so you may want to find mix and match segments at a thrift store, or wait for off-season sales.

What Not to Wear When You Walk

Do not wear headphones. No matter where you walk, you'll be surrounded with interesting and sometimes pleasurable sounds. Use your walk time to listen to people's voices, or birds, or invisible animals as they skitter when you approach, or the wind. You need to hear if a biker is coming around the corner, or if a person is approaching you on the trail, or if a car is approaching you along a dirt road. The more you walk, the more you'll begin to rely on your sense of hearing for both pleasure and safety. There are a number of walking tapes available on the market, but unless they are part of a walking tour, they're not recommended.

Do not wear jewelry. Jewelry serves no purpose on a walk. Rings become uncomfortable as your hands swell with retained fluids. Necklaces and watches become glued to your body with perspiration. Another reason not to wear jewelry is that valuable objects, within easy reach, invite robbery. If you have an emotional attachment to an expensive ring with a stone, turn it on your finger so that the stone touches your palm and only the band shows.

Do not wear scented fragrances or hair sprays. The quickest way to gather insects is to smell like a flower. Remove your fragrance before you walk with a nonscented towlette.

Essential Equipment

Hip pack, backpack, or cart. Although hip packs are sold in discount retail stores and drug stores, you may want to visit a travel supply or camping store to compare prices and features. Make sure it's waterproof—some of the cheaper models bleed in the rain! Look for lots of separate, easy-to-open and -close compartments, one for keys, ID, and change; one for your insect repellent and sunscreen; one for a notebook or guidebook and pencil; and another for your handkerchief or tissue. When purchasing a backpack, try it on with weight in the back to make sure it feels comfortable in the shoulders. If you walk to the grocery store, you may want to invest in a pull cart. Change hands frequently to evenly distribute the weight of your grocery bags.

Water bottle. If you're going to be walking more than a mile, you should always carry water. There are a number of light plastic models on the market that hold up to twelve ounces of water and slip on the belt of your hip pack or clip onto your waistband.

Sunglasses. Wear sunglasses with protection from ultraviolet rays whenever you walk, during all seasons, to protect your eyes from harmful radiation and to prevent cataracts. During the winter you may want to wear ski goggles that offer protection from both the sun and cold temperatures.

Identification, keys, and money. It's always smart to carry a photo ID when you walk so that, in the event of an accident or medical emergency, you can be quickly identified and receive the help you need. In addition to carrying your house or car keys, it is recommended that you carry enough money to make a few phone calls or buy a refill of water or soda. When you're transit walking, slip a checkbook and credit cards into your hip pack.

Watch and compass. Unless you own an expensive, waterproof watch, the perspiration from your wrist will eventually damage your wristband, so it's better to carry your wrist watch or stop watch in your hip pack. Always carry a compass. Most camping or sports stores sell inexpensive compasses on key chains. Two-in-one, waterproof watch/compass instruments are available, but they're quite expensive.

White cotton handkerchief. This handy, collapsible item serves as a brow wiper (on those hot, humid days when your brows can't hold any more water) and an insect chaser (when swarms of mosquitoes or gnats start buzzing around your head).

Small package of white tissues and a metal spoon. You may find yourself on a dirt trail with no restroom in sight. A small package of tissues and a spoon will come in handy in such situations. (More about the spoon later.)

Sunscreen. The best way to protect your skin from the sun is to wear protective clothing. If any of your skin will be exposed in the sun as you walk, wear level fifteen suncreen.

Insect repellent. Mosquitoes and ticks are a fact of life in Minnesota, and they can be quite bothersome in the woods. The best way to protect yourself from insects is to wear protective clothing (including face nets) and use an insect repellent. Wear old clothes, because most insect repellents leave grease stains on fabric.

Tweezers. If you happen to be hosting a tick, a tweezers will make it easy to quickly remove it.

Sound alarm or mace. Until an effective, economical personal alarm is developed, you may want to carry a safety device such as a sound alarm (a canister of compressed air that sends a high-pitched sound 900 feet) or mace (a canister of tear gas that can be used to defend yourself.) It is recommended that you take a basic safety and self-defense class through your community education system or police department to learn how and when to use personal safety devices, as well as the advantages and hazards of carrying and using such devices.

Optional Equipment

Notebook, pen with waterproof ink. Small, spiral notebooks that fit into your slacks pocket or hip pack compartment are ideal for the trail. Use waterproof ink to protect your thoughts from fading into oblivion when the paper becomes moist with sweat, humidity, tree droppings, and rain.

Guidebooks. One way to learn as you walk is to carry a small pocket guide to help you identify butterflies, grasses, wildflowers, trees, insects, birds, cloud formations, or mushrooms. Be sure to select guides that are specific to Minnesota or the central United States. Large photos and brief descriptions that include the biological and historical or cultural significance of the species are particularly useful.

Walking stick or staff. Some walkers believe this should be in the list of essential equipment, and this is true if you regularly walk on grass and dirt rather than paved trails. A walking stick is just a bit longer than an umbrella, and is usually used for balance. A walking staff is longer and helps you maintain balance when you are walking up or down steep hills.

By using a walking stick or staff you can increase your upper-arm movement by about 10 percent. You can also use a walking stick to protect yourself.

Tape recorder. When you can hear something but can't see it, and want to identify it, record the sound on a portable tape recorder. If you have a favorite place to walk, you may also want to record the sounds so that you always have them with you, in case you need to escape to that place for a meditation break during the day. Portable tape recorders are expensive, so you may want to share the expense with walking partners or borrow one through a walking club.

Binoculars, monoculars, and magnifiers. One of the best ways to respect wildlife is to observe it from a distance. If you're a birdwatcher, then you may want to consider investing in a pair of binoculars. If you have only an occasional need to see things in the distance, then you may want to share the expense with your walking partners or borrow a pair through a walking club. Monoculars are easier to carry, have the same field of view and are more reasonably priced. Binoculars can be used with eye glasses, but monoculars can't. You may want to carry a magnifier to closely examine a mushroom or flower. Again, if you're going to be observing something up close, take a course through community education or a nearby nature center so that you learn how not to disturb or harm what you are observing.

Camera. If you are going to photograph animals, you should take a wildlife photography course and learn how and when to use a camera in the presence of animals. Flashing lights can upset and disorient an animal.

TRAIL ETIQUETTE

Whether you're walking in the city or out in the country, there are some basic trail courtesies that, when practiced, demonstrate a respect for other trail users and the environment.

Keep to the right. Allow plenty of room for other walkers and bikers to pass. If you're walking on the road, face oncoming traffic. If you're passing a walker, warn them with a simple "passing on your left" so that they aren't startled.

Leave no trace of your visit. If you carry a can of water or soda, carry it home to recycle it, or drop it off at a local restaurant and they will recycle it for you.

Leave rocks, flowers, moss, and mushrooms in their place. Do not disturb natural vegetation or wildlife as you move through an area.

Respect the solitude of other walkers. If you see someone you know, establish eye contact before you speak. They may be deep in a "think" walk or a "work" walk and need the time to concentrate.

Learn about the pet ordinances. Animals are not allowed in nature centers or wildlife refuges. Most cities and parks require that pets be on a leash no longer than six feet and that owners remove and dispose of animal feces. Call the walking site and ask about their animal ordinances.

Rocks and spoons. Even though you may have relieved yourself before you started walking, you may reach a point where you need to relieve yourself again. What do you do if there's no restroom in sight?

The book *Soft Paths*, by Bruce Hampton and David Cole, published by the National Outdoor Leadership School, offers some environmentally sound alternatives. If you need to relieve yourself of liquids, urinate on a rock or in a nonvegetated area so that the liquid evaporates quickly. If you need to relieve yourself of solid waste, make sure you are at least one hundred feet away from a major water source (creek, river, or lake). The book advises that you "choose a level spot, and dig a hole several inches deep in the organic layer of soil, where microorganisms are abundant. When you're done, take a stick and mix the soil with your feces for quicker decomposition. Then cover your cathole with at least an inch or two of topsoil. Finally, camouflage the surface."

The metal spoon, one of the "essential pieces of equipment," will come in handy when you need to dig your hole, and the small package of tissues will serve you well. As for mixing and camouflage tips, some things are better left to the imagination.

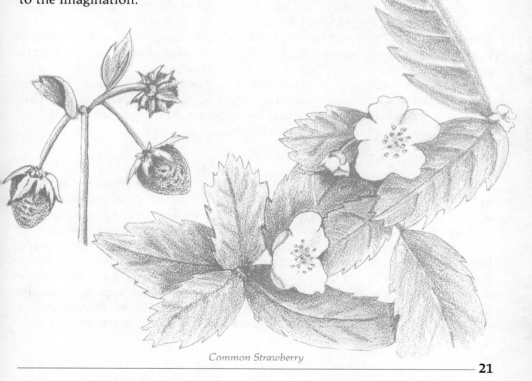

Common Strawberry

CHAPTER 3

The Health Benefits and Risks of Walking

Sedentary Positive Intenders (SPI). That's a research term for people who know they should exercise, and fully intend to exercise, but never quite fit it into their schedules.

There are so many reasons *not* to walk. During the summer it's too hot. During the winter it's too cold. And on those "just right" days there's always something more important to do. But the consequences of a sedentary lifestyle are well documented. The heart muscle atrophies. Bones become fragile twigs. Precious thoughts wait in line as oxygenated blood tries to make its way through a labyrinth of arteries plugged with past indulgences. Disease often visits ten, twenty, sometimes thirty years early. Even the most brilliant mind, the most indomitable spirit, cannot survive in an abandoned body.

For most SPIs, exercise has to be more than a one-dimensional experience. It has to engage the imagination and replenish the spirit, like a page-turner novel, a haunting piece of music, or an engaging film. Walking is slowly becoming the activity of choice for people who don't find much pleasure in organized sports, health clubs, or exercise classes, because it is a multidimensional activity that involves not just the body, but the mind and spirit.

Even though "health" may be at the bottom of the list when it comes to why SPIs walk, Minnesota health professionals recommend it to their patients because it is a low-cost, low-injury, high-pleasure activity that can benefit people of all ages, in very poor to excellent condition.

How will walking improve the body? What is the relationship between walking and heart disease, osteoporosis, and weight management? What precautions should walkers take to prevent injuries? What precautions should walkers take to maximize their personal health and safety?

HEART DISEASE

Dr. Arthur S. Leon is a professor in the Division of Epidemiology and director of Applied Physiology and Nutrition at the University of Minnesota. He is also a Fellow of the American Heart Association Cardiovascular Epidemiological Council and a Fellow of the American College of Sports Medicine.

Dr. Arthur Leon has been studying the relationship between exercise and heart disease. As past president and current member of the Minnesota Heart Association's Hennepin County Affiliate, he continues to share his clinical research findings with the community by reviewing and approving public information about exercise and heart disease to be sure it is accurate and does not misrepresent or distort data that have been clinically tested and proven.

His initial research, began twenty-five years ago, focused on the effect of exercise on the coronary circulation of dogs and rats. His studies concluded that through exercise training, the number of capillaries and size of coronary arteries can be increased, thus improving the heart's blood supply.

As one of the co-investigators of the MRFIT and LRC Coronary Prevention Trials conducted at the University of Minnesota from 1973 to 1984, he was able to further define the impact of exercise on the cardiovascular system. "In the MRFIT trials, we studied over 12,000 men and concluded that even moderate, self-selected physical activity (such as gardening, walking, housework) can reduce risk from premature death from heart attacks."

He went on to state, "What this means is that moderate physical activity will not prevent heart attacks, but it will increase your chances of surviving a heart attack. People who exercised moderately for thirty minutes or more per day had one-third fewer deaths than those who didn't exercise at all and over time the group that exercised lived approximately two years longer than those who didn't exercise at all."

The study corrected for factors such as weight, smoking history, diet, income level, and stress factors. "Physical activity was an independent factor that made a difference," Dr. Leon confirmed.

Another finding of this longitudinal study was that heart disease is not related to stress. "In fact, on the average, men with Type A personalities, the hard-driving workaholics, actually had lower rates of heart attacks."

Women were not included in the original study because "before menopause, women have one-tenth the number of heart attacks as men." Women have been included in more recent clinical trials and the results indicate that there are substantial differences in the way exercise impacts men and women.

"The difference we see between men and women is the impact of exercise on body composition and blood lipid response," Dr. Leon stated. "In one of our research projects, men who exercised moderately for ninety minutes or longer five times or more per week lost a 25 percent level of body fat and improved their levels of 'good' (HDL) cholesterol. We've never been able to demonstrate similar results with women. Even rigorous physical activity such as running on treadmills has not been successful in changing the body composition or HDL cholesterol levels in women."

Dr. Leon speculates that the differences may be linked with reproduction function. "In animal populations, similar results have been reported," he stated. "The males are able to change their body composition through exercise, but the females retain their pre-existing levels of body fat to use during reproduction by increasing food intake."

Another finding is that vigorous exercise can strengthen the heart so that it beats more efficiently. "However, to achieve any change of this sort," he advised, "you'd have to be walking at a *very* fast racewalking pace. Most people can't walk that fast, so they don't achieve this benefit. The average American's heart rate is eighty beats per minute. People on a vigorous exercise program can bring their heartbeats down to sixty beats per minute. The heart of a professional athlete works at forty beats per minute."

Based on his findings, what are his recommendations?

• Talk with your physician before starting any strenuous exercise program. Your doctor should determine your current level of fitness and prescribe an appropriate amount of exercise.

• Do some physical activity at least thirty minutes a day.

• Whenever you are going to be walking in high heat, drink at least an eight-ounce glass of water ten to fifteen minutes before you walk, and carry water with you . "As your body temperature rises," he explained, "more blood is sent to the muscle and skin so the heart is under a great deal of stress. As you lose more and more water, the heart loses its ability to function, so avoid dehydration at all costs. The body is able to signal when it is tired or hungry, but it won't signal that it needs more water until after the dehydration process has started. If you are walking with children, make sure they don't get dehydrated."

• If you feel faint, dizzy, or lightheaded while walking, sit in the shade and drink water. If you feel chest pains on the trail, sit down so that your body can stabilize. Send someone for help so that you can be evacuated to a medical center as soon as possible. Death usually occurs within three hours of the first symptoms of a heart attack so it's important that you get medical attention as quickly as possible.

• Condition your body to walk up hills. "Walking uphill increases the demands on the heart," he advised. "Get in condition by walking up slight hills. Gradually work up to walking the steep hills. If you experience shortness of breath, you're moving at too fast a pace for your body."

• During periods of illness, consult your physican about your exercise program. "Some respiratory viruses can invade the heart," he warned. "So you need to be very careful about exercising during periods of illness. Your doctor will advise you on whether or not to modify or temporarily discontinue your program."

• The best way to lower a dangerous cholesterol level is to modify your diet. "There's plenty of literature available on the value of low-fat, high vegetable, fruit, and fiber foods," he continued. "Don't depend on walking to lower your blood cholesterol level, because it won't. You can only achieve significant results with a low fat-diet."

• Encourage children to participate in a moderate exercise program. "Many of the health problems associated with a sedentary lifestyle can be prevented by turning off the TV and getting kids involved in track and field programs," he advised, "or volleyball, soccer, anything that will keep the kids moving. In Finland, all the children are involved in a school athletic program and the best athletes in each event are honored at a nationwide gathering in Helsinki. It's important to establish a regular physical activity pattern early in life."

OSTEOPOROSIS

The Melpomene Institute, founded in 1981, is an independent, nonprofit research center located in Saint Paul, Minnesota. The Institute is unique in that it focuses on how exercise impacts the health of women. Melpomene began an osteoporosis study that continues today. In Melpomene's *The Bodywise Woman*, published in 1990, the subject of osteoporosis is explored in depth.

"Osteoporosis," explained Judy Lutter, president, "is an age-related disorder that is characterized by decreased bone mass with increased susceptibility to fractures. It is a fact that one out of every four postmenopausal women has osteoporosis, that the disease accounts for one million hip, wrist, and spine fractures annually in U.S. citizens over age forty-five, and that women are eight times more likely than men to develop osteoporosis.

"The women in our study continue to be followed to determine the relationship between their physical activity and bone mass fluctuations," Lutter stated. "Our goal in this study is to provide factual information that will encourage women to incorporate good exercise and nutrition into their lifestyle. The underlying hypothesis is that women who have engaged in physical activity throughout their lives will have significantly denser bones (more bone mass) than their peers who did not engage in physical activity. Indeed, this belief turns out to be true."

What has Melpomene learned about exercise and osteoporosis?

• The average bone density of physically active women is 25.6 percent higher than the average of the women in low-activity groups.

• Exercise does increase bone density and/or decrease significant bone loss in postmenopausal women.

• Walking can maintain and in some instances improve the amount of bone mass in the hip, spine, and legs. Melpomene further advises: "Begin continuous walking ten minutes a day. Gradually increase to thirty minutes a day. Always warm up first and use static stretching before and after activity. Be sure to wear cushioned, low-heeled walking or jogging shoes. Legs, hip, and spine benefit from working against gravity."

• Women with osteoporosis are most likely to fracture a bone in the upper arm at the shoulder, the forearm at the wrist, and the thighbone at the hip and spine. Only the hip and spine can be strengthened by weight-bearing exercises such as walking or running; the arms must be stressed by other specific exercise.

For strong bones in the shoulders and arms, Melpomene recommends 1) weight-loading exercises: tension, torsion, compression, bending; and 2) resistance exercises (with a stretch band) that improve rounded shoulders and back by strengthening and supporting muscles.

Weight-loading exercises for the arms and shoulders include push-ups (full body and modified), twisting stationary objects like door-knobs with each arm for five seconds and then reversing directions, or sitting push-ups where you place your hands on the seat of a chair and use your arms to raise your body off the chair one-half inch.

Resistance exercises for the arms and shoulders include holding a resistance stretch band with elbows pressed against the waist and then gradually opening the forearms outward, or holding the stretch band at chest height with arms fully extended and then slowly opening the arms wide without locking the elbows or flinging the arms apart.

For more information about osteoporosis, refer to *The Bodywise Woman* or consult Melpomene's Research Center (see chapter 8) which offers over three thousand articles on health-related topics.

WEIGHT MANAGEMENT

Dr. P. J. Palumbo of the Mayo Clinic in Rochester, Minnesota, is director of Clinical Nutrition, director of the Nutrition Clinic and the Lipid Clinic, and editor of the *Mayo Clinic Proceedings*, a general scientific journal.

"People come from short and long distances to the Mayo Clinic for weight problems and eating disorders," Dr. Palumbo stated, "and we also provide nutritional support to people who are in the hospital and can't eat, or who come to us with a cholesterol or triglyceride problem. There are no easy, quick solutions to weight management. It takes years to gain weight, and it takes years for people to successfully change their eating and exercise habits. Behavior is the most important factor in a weight problem.

"There are two components of successful weight management," he advised, "a moderate intake of food based on dietary requirements, and a regular exercise program. We measure a person's basal metabolism and base their caloric intake on that measurement. It's done through a breathing test. You take in a certain amount of oxygen and then you put out carbon dioxide, and we measure each amount and calculate indirectly the energy expenditure of the individual at rest. The test is available at medical centers, particularly those that have the patient volume to support the specially trained technicians.

"Our weight-loss program, the only authentic Mayo Clinic Diet, has a basic menu of 1,400 calories—55 percent from carbohydrates, 20 to 25 percent from protein, and less than 30 percent from fat," he stated. "But first people have to calculate how many calories they can safely consume and still lose a pound a week. It varies with each individual. We rarely advise dropping below 1,400 calories per day. We may increase a person's level of exercise, but we tend to maintain 1,400 calories because otherwise the diet will be missing important nutrients.

"A typical 1,400 Basic Menu includes seven servings of starch (one serving = one slice of bread), five protein servings (one serving = one ounce of lean meat, poultry or fish), three milk servings (one serving = one cup of skim milk), three fruit servings (serving sizes vary), two or more vegetable servings (one serving = one-half cup cooked vegetables) and two fat servings (one serving = one teaspoon of margarine), and eight eight-ounce glasses of water.

"Walking is the main component and the easiest component of weight management," Dr. Palumo continued. "It's an exercise that doesn't require any training or equipment. It comes naturally to people and it can be done anywhere." Dr. Palumbo recommends:

• Walk at least 2 miles, thirty minutes a day (that's at a brisk pace of a fifteen-minute mile or faster). Walk longer periods of time to burn more calories, but you only need to walk 2 miles, thirty minutes a day to maintain your weight.

• Walk at least three times a week, and every day if possible.

• If you need to lose weight, decrease your calories (but not below 1,400 per day) or increase the distance of your walk.

• Walk whenever it's convenient and safe to walk. "The important thing," Dr. Palumbo advised, "is to get out and walk. We would prefer that people walk before the evening meal or an hour after the evening meal because that's when the metabolic rate is dropping. By maintaining an activity late in the day, you can burn calories that wouldn't be expended by your body."

• Eat your main meals at breakfast and lunch and eat a light evening meal. "Calories consumed in the evening," he added, "may be more readily stored as fat."

• Drink eight glasses of water a day to keep adequately hydrated. "We recommend water, skim milk, or fruit juices. We do not advise the consumption of alcohol when you are trying to lose or manage weight. Large quantities of caffeinated drinks, such as coffee, may cause indigestion or produce jitteriness or palpitations."

• Wear walking shoes. "Do not wear high heels or other inappropriate shoes," he added, "because you'll develop orthopedic problems. If you develop any foot or leg pain, see your doctor."

• If you have orthopedic problems or are extremely overweight, walking may aggravate bone injuries. Water aerobics provides the same beneficial effects as other aerobic activities without stressing the joints.

"Walking is neutral in terms of appetite," Dr. Palumbo continued. "Some people report that walking before a meal tends to decrease their appetite. We haven't any data that prove walking increases or decreases appetite.

"Fitness starts at birth," he stated. "Exercise should be an important part of everyday activities, just like brushing teeth, or eating three meals a day. You eat, and you exercise. It should be that simple. It has to begin in preschool and continue all the way through elementary, junior high, and high school. Unless we change our approach and emphasize prevention, we will continue to see an increase in childhood and adult obesity."

HEALTH RISKS

Dr. Elizabeth A. Arendt, assistant professor in the Department of Orthopaedic Surgery at the University of Minnesota Medical School and director of the Sports Medicine Institute at the University of Minnesota Hospital and Clinic, is a specialist in over-use sports injuries.

"Walking is a relatively benign activity from an orthopedic viewpoint," Dr. Arendt stated, "but it's still an upright activitity that causes your foot, ankle, leg, knee, and hip to undergo repetitive activity. Whenever you walk, a force of three times your body weight is moving through your joints. When you run, you can pass seven to twelve times your body weight through the joints. Walking implies that you have two feet on the ground, in what we call the 'double stance' phase, so there is less stress on each foot than there is when you run. Runners are more prone to over-use kinds of injuries, but you can still get over-use injuries with walking because it is a repetitive activity. Injuries can occur anywhere from the great toe all the way up to the spine. Racewalkers are more prone to over-use injuries than other walkers because the movements are repeated at a greater pace, but they still have far fewer injuries than runners."

Some of the more typical walking problems, according to Dr. Arendt, are:

Bunions. "People usually have a family history of bunions. Bunions are aggravated by tight-fitting shoes. Make sure your shoes have plenty of width," she advised, "and put a good arch in your shoe. Bunions may eventually require specially constructed shoes or surgical correction."

Hallux Rigidis (arthritis of the great toe) is usually related to trauma in some way. This can be prevented by wearing stiffer-soled shoes and walking on level rather than inclined surfaces.

Plantar Fasciitis (similar to a heel spur) usually is indicated when you have pain in the medial (inside) part of your heel and is frequently associated with walking on cement surfaces, or walking with high heels on cement surfaces, and usually occurs in a flat and/or pronated (turned in) foot. Use a medial arch support and keep stress off the heel.

Achilles Tendonitis (a soreness in the tendon that connects the back of the heel with the calf muscle) is sometimes a problem with walkers. Warm-up exercises can reduce the strain on the tendon. "You have to have a supple Achilles tendon that can accommodate a twenty degree flexion to be a good walker," she explained, "and it's even more important in racewalking where you need at least a thirty degree flexion of the foot. When you don't have a supple tendon, the other parts of the foot take the brunt of the activity and can cause problems."

Shin Splints (pain at the mid-length of the bone in the calf of the leg). "You can alleviate strain on the leg by walking on level surfaces. Choose your surfaces wisely. Cement is harder on the legs than softer surfaces. Be sure to wear a good shoe with an arch."

Knee Injuries. "Injuries to the kneecap or the tendons surrounding the kneecap can occur, especially in racewalkers. Good support shoes can keep the foot in position and prevent injuries to the knee."

Back Problems. Although walking is rarely the cause of back problems, repeated walking can aggravate a preexisting back injury or back arthritis. Walk on softer surfaces, wear good support shoes, and walk on flat surfaces rather than hills.

Osteoarthritis and osteoporosis. Walking is the recommended exercise for people with these conditions, but if the condition is advanced, then even walking is too strenuous; the person may have to change to a non-weight-bearing sport like water walking or swimming.

"We do encourage walking and feel that it's good for muscle strengthening and burning calories," Arendt stated. "The usual guideline is that you need to exercise at your target heart rate for twenty minutes at least three times a week. Unconditioned people should get their heart rate to 60 percent of their target heart rate, and conditioned people should work up to 80 percent level. A good indicator that you're not working over your limit is that you should have enough breath left when you exercise to talk or sing when you walk."

• You can increase your heart rate by involving the arms (racewalking form), increasing the load you're carrying (a weight belt around the pelvis is better than wrist or ankle weights), lengthening your stride, or increasing the angle of the terrain (walking up hills). Using weights on an extremity makes you more susceptible to an over-use injury.

• Get a good walking shoe. "Invest in an all-terrain shoe if you engage in many different sports," she continued. "Even the best of feet will have problems if you don't have a good support shoe. Don't wear canvas, wedged shoes, or sandals when you walk. Adults and children walkers need a walking shoe with a cushioned sole and a good arch."

• If you have a foot position that is not functional, it can cause problems farther up the leg. Feet are neglected until they hurt you. You may need to change the alignment of the foot through corrective shoes. An injured or damaged foot can severely change the quality of your lifestyle.

• Be considerate when you're walking with children. Children have less muscle mass, and they take many more strides than adults. One adult stride is usually three to four children's strides, so their legs are working harder to walk the same distance.

• Think about your extremities during cold weather. "Many people can tolerate more coldness on their legs than the legs can feel," she stated. "Walkers often assume if their torso is warm that their legs are fine, when in fact the cold is straining the muscle-skeletal system, especially wherever there has been a previous muscle strain or a ligament sprain. The muscle-skeletal system can be likened to oil in a car—it works better when it's warmed up. Layered clothing is helpful. Endogenously derived heat (heat that radiates from the body outward) is the best. Therefore, start walking slowly, keep your extremities covered and take off clothes only as needed."

• During the winter, don't walk on snow or ice. Snow's uneven surface is much more difficult to walk on than a smooth surface and it places great demands on your foot or ankle. Walking on snow can cause problems for an unconditioned foot.

• See a doctor if you have pain or swelling that persists until the day after the activity, or pain that recurs or increases whenever you do the same activity. Pain and swelling are warning signals that need to be looked at by a doctor.

MOSQUITOES AND TICKS

Insects are part of the environment. They may be bothersome, but they serve a purpose in the ecological chain of life. You need to know about the harm some insects can cause, take the necessary precautions, and then get out in the woods and enjoy yourself. Just remember to:

• Wear light-colored cotton clothing (long pants, long-sleeved shirt).

• Protect children from insects by having them wear protective clothing and repellent.

• Tuck the cuffs of your pants into your socks and tuck in your shirt.

• Apply strong mosquito repellent on your clothes and exposed areas of skin. Be sure to read and follow label directions.

• Wear a headnet when insects are bothersome. Mosquitoes and ticks are part of the Minnesota experience. Don't panic if you get bitten. Remove the insect, and keep on walking.

Mosquitoes. Mosquitoes can be particularly bothersome in swampy and wooded areas. There are more than fifty mosquito species in Minnesota. The only mosquito that walkers should know about is the Tree Hole Mosquito, which can carry LaCrosse Encephalitis to children up to eighteen years of age.

Dave Neitzel, the LaCrosse/Lyme program leader of the Metropolitan Mosquito Control District stated, "LaCrosse Encephalitis is a *very rare* disease. Only one or two cases are reported per year in the seven-county metro area, and five to ten cases statewide. Tree Hole Mosquitoes breed in water-holding tree holes and artificial containers (old tires, buckets) that are less than seven feet off the ground. The Metropolitan Mosquito Control District works with neighborhoods and park systems to identify and eliminate these breeding sights." For a free brochure on the Tree Hole Mosquito, call 612/645-9149 and ask for information about the LaCrosse Encephalitis Prevention Program.

Ticks. There are two species of tick that you may commonly encounter in the woods: the wood tick and the deer tick. Wood ticks are in the woods from June through August, and deer ticks are active from late April through October. Ticks cling to vegetation—they don't drop out of trees or fly overhead. When you brush against vegetation as you walk, they may cling to your clothes or your skin. When you walk through the woods, periodically look for ticks. Most can be removed by brushing your clothes with an ID card. Ask your walking partner to check your back. To remove an attached tick use a tweezers. Apply steady, even pressure on the point of contact between the tick and your skin. Don't squeeze the tick's body because it may inject fluid into you. If you think it's a deer tick, save it and have your doctor take a look at it. Wash the bite area when you get home and apply antiseptic.

Wood ticks. Wood ticks are flat, have brown and white markings, have curved arms and legs, and are about the size of this capital letter O (see enlarged illustration). Wood ticks also attach themselves to pets. Wood ticks are annoying, but in Minnesota they are harmless. **Deer ticks.** Deer ticks are much smaller than wood ticks—about the size of a small black freckle. They have no white markings. Deer ticks can carry Lyme disease, a slow progressive disease that can lead to arthritis, nerve problems, and heart problems. This is an uncommon disease, with only ninety cases reported in Minnesota per year. The Minnesota Department of Health and the Metropolitan Mosquito Control District are working together to identify where the ticks are and what percentage are infected with the disease. For a free brochure about Lyme disease, call the Minnesota Department of Health at 612/623-5414.

Wood Tick

Deer Tick

PERSONAL SAFETY

Just as you protect yourself from the sun, the heat, injuries, and insects, you should protect yourself from physical danger. When you're thinking about what to wear and what to carry, you should also think about how to have a safe walk. Some basic safety practices will significantly decrease your chances of ever being the victim of a crime when you walk.

• Stay alert. Don't wear earphones when you walk.
• Find a walking partner and schedule walks together.

• When walking solo, avoid verbal or eye contact with people. Do not answer questions or engage in conversations. You're not being rude, you're being safe.

• Develop a personal safety plan for each walk. Decide where potential problems might be, or where you would go for help. Become familiar with businesses that are open when you walk.

• If you need to walk alone early in the morning or late at night, walk indoors in a mall.

• Walk with confidence. Assume a positive, aggressive carriage. Keep your head up and keep moving with purpose.

• If you are new to an area, or traveling in a new city, call the local crime prevention program and ask when and where it is safe to walk.

• Whenever you feel uneasy, go to a place where there are other people.

• Do not wear gold jewelry or expensive watches.

• Carry ID and a minimum amount of money in a hip pack, not a purse.

According to John Baumann, associate director of Special Programs for the Minneapolis Community Crime Prevention/SAFE Department, walkers need to put crime into perspective. "Of course you want to be careful," he stated, "but people have a distorted sense of who commits crimes and where they occur."

"Most violent crimes involve people who know each other," he explained. "Stranger-to-stranger crimes are not very frequent, and yet those are the crimes that are carried by the media. People sometimes have an exaggerated sense of danger. Stranger-to-stranger rapes and assaults do occur, but date and acquaintance rapes are much more prevalent.

"People also have an inaccurate sense of how crimes occur," Baumann continued. "People expect to be approached by a stranger lurking behind a bush, or a door. Again, there are situations when this occurs, but people are more apt to be approached by someone asking for the time or directions. Criminals often use a casual conversation to break down the defenses of the other person, to check the person out to determine if he or she will resist or pose a threat, and then to manipulate the person into an increasingly danger-ous situation.

"Before you walk," Baumann advised, "you should do some planning. That's when you begin to take control of your own safety. Before children walk to school or to the store, parents should walk with them and develop a personal safety plan. Talk about where it's safe and not safe to walk. Identify places where they can get help if they need it, such as fire stations or McGruff houses."

Some people are afraid to walk in urban areas where they live or work because of crime. In 1987, the City of Minneapolis developed the SAFE program, which has become a forerunner in urban crime prevention. It is the only program in the nation that uses a two-person team—a civilian organizer and a police officer—to resolve neighborhood crime and noncrime issues. The goal of the program is to make neighborhoods safer and more livable (and ultimately, more walkable) and reduce opportunities for crime. The program empowers residents to solve issues when they can without involving the police, and to work with the police in solving neighborhood crimes.

"We divide the city into districts, and each district has a SAFE team assigned to it," Baumann explained. "Their presence in the neighborhoods, along with strong community involvement, sends a very clear message to the criminals that the streets belong to the people. We want people to be able to live and walk in every part of the city, but in order to do that, they have to feel safe.

"The teams have closed down crack houses," Baumann added, "but they also go after other problems that might effect the livability and walkability of the block such as boarded up houses, mattresses piled in a yard, broken glass in an alley, overgrown yards. No one would want to live in or walk through a neighborhood that looks like that, so the neighbors work together to solve the problem. They've cleaned up the yards, planted flowers, and they're reclaiming their sidewalks."

Community crime prevention programs, such as the one established in Minneapolis, benefit walkers in a number of ways:

• Personal safety workshops are available free to all residents. The workshops focus on basic self-defense, weapons, police reporting, services for victims, and ways to avoid and de-escalate confrontations. Walkers of all ages can benefit from the information presented at these types of sessions.

• The Neighborhood Crime Data program gives walkers information about crime occurrences in various parts of town.

• Neighborhood Watchforce programs teach neighbors to watch out for each other. This block club program provides walkers with added security as they stroll through neighborhoods, knowing that the people in the houses are concerned about their safety and ready to help if necessary. Walkers have an opportunity to organize pedestrian patrols that give neighbors a chance to visit and fight crime while they stroll the neighborhoods.

• McGruff Houses, clearly identified with a window decal, are safe havens for children who are lost, being followed, or being harrassed by neighborhood bullies. Children feel safer walking to the store or school knowing that help is just down the street.

• Crime alert bulletins keep residents (and walkers) informed of specific crime patterns.

• National Night Out provides neighborhoods with an opportunity to celebrate citizen involvement in crime prevention. In 1990, over six hundred blocks in Minneapolis participated in this national event that honors the longevity and success of the program.

Even though citizen participation in crime prevention programs has decreased in some cities over the years, it continues to increase in Minneapolis.

Through the SAFE program in Minneapolis and other community-based crime prevention programs, residents are working together to reclaim their precious pavement.

Jack-in-the-pulpit

CHAPTER 4

Walking and Creativity

Something wonderful happens when the mind and body start working in unison. Ideas settle somewhere in the back of the brain, and when the legs and arms start moving and the heart starts pumping, they pop, one after the other, into the conscious mind. Gnarled thoughts or feelings disengage and become more manageable. Out of nowhere come solutions to problems that seem so simple, so obvious, and yet, without a walk, would remain beyond reach. And every so often come the fireworks—thoughts that explode with possibility, whirl down to the legs, and end in a leap of joy.

Researchers and artists are just beginning to understand and describe the simple yet complex relationship between physical movement and creativity.

RESEARCH ON EXERCISE AND CREATIVITY

Joan C. Gondola, associate professor of Physical Education at Baruch College in New York, has been studying the relationship between aerobic exercise and creativity since 1985 and has published over thirty articles on exercise and mood enhancement. She's an avid skier, runner, tennis player, and swimmer as well as a musician, composer, and artist. "Since the fitness boom of the 70s," she stated, "there has been a growing trend to document the benefits of exercise, but only recently has the focus shifted to the impact of exercise on creativity.

"We've discovered that even moderate exercise such as pleasure walking enhances creativity," Gondola stated. "R.W. Diensthier in *Exercise, catecholamine and personality* (1980) provides a model of great importance in establishing a connection between exercise and altered perceptions. He suggests that adrenaline crosses the blood brain barrier during aerobic exercise and that feelings of well-being and euphoria follow, in addition to an increase in the attentional process." She added, "Reduced anxiety and energy arousal are in evidence in post-exercise, which are both important to the concentration and perceptual process. With a greater sense of relaxation and dissipation of inhibition, our ability to overcome interferences increases.

"Using this as a theoretical model," she continued, "the connection between exercise and creativity becomes clearer. Not only are we more sensually acute, but we experience our environment in more challenging, less stressful ways, and are more willing to drop inhibitions which interfere in our creative process."

Gondola believes the link between exercise and creativity has tremendous implications for the entire spectrum of education, from preschool through college and beyond. "Both exercise and creativity are ignored or bypassed in school systems. Programs of art, music, and physical education are considered frivolous, nonacademic, and money wasting. These findings are especially important because severe cutbacks have been made in nonacademic curriculum."

She explained further about her concern regarding the systematic elimination of art and exercise courses from school curricula. "Creativity is the focal point of our perceptual framework. How we see, move, hear, and organize our world is based on our creative energy. There are definite links between our creative and motor learning abilities.

"First, there are mediation periods in both, during which learning takes place between the introduction and solution of a problem. Fatigue dissipates during this time frame and new associations are made. Secondly, both creativity and motor learning involve kinesthetics and images, not reproduction. Muscle imaging and muscle memory are the basis of both tasks. Sensory awareness, in particular, is advanced through the movement processes. Thirdly, both appear tapped into right-brain processes, which are based on exploratory and original responses, not systematically logical sequences.

"Looking carefully at these results and those of studies which involve mood enhancement through exercise," she concluded, "it appears that positive gains in psychological areas can no longer be ignored. They are not frills, but should be central to our learning and educational processes."

Gondola's research establishes a definite link between aerobic exercise and creativity. Although all forms of aerobic exercise may improve creativity, walking, according to Minnesota artists, is one of the most effective ways to nourish and sustain creativity.

INTERVIEWS WITH ARTISTS

Mary Keilty, Painter, Sculptor, Spinner

You won't find her works hanging in galleries, but you will find them in her own home and in the homes of Minnesotans who have purchased her work at an annual December sale held with a handful of other well-known Minnesota potters, weavers, and artisans. Art is, and always has been, not a career, but an extension of Keilty's being that must be expressed. At a very young age, Keilty realized that she had a different learning style. Fortunately, she had teachers who were able to accept and direct her differences into productive and rewarding classroom experiences.

"When I was young, there weren't any Barbie dolls or commercial toys forcing me into one train of thought, so I used to draw pictures and faces, and I'd draw people, with kind of abstract legs and arms and bodies, and then they'd became real people in my imagination," she laughed. "My mom bought me tablets of paper, and then I started making paper dolls and clothes, and then I made them for all my friends so they could play with me. That's how we played. We made our own toys.

"When I was five years old I went into first grade, and I didn't want to be there because I didn't know how to relate my play to school, or what I should do in school. So I cried a lot. I felt out of place and I couldn't figure out how to *want* to learn letters and numbers. They weren't figures or people, they were things. Luckily, the teacher eased me into school by allowing me to draw on dittos so the class could color my drawings, and this built my self-esteem. I was very lucky to have her. Today, people are starting to pay more attention to developmental learning, and I'm glad, because everyone learns differently.

"I eventually learned to write my name, but I had trouble learning to read because they didn't teach phonics back then, and I had a terrible time with math," Keilty stated. "I've always thought in color and form, and it took me a long while to realize other people don't think that way. To learn numbers, I assigned colors to numbers. Even today, when I see 123, I think white, yellow, and orange. Five is red, seven is brown, six is green, and nine is purple, and they possess personalities as well. Once I was able to apply my system to what was being taught, I was able to get straight As. I think a lot of kids have made it through school by creating their own systems for learning."

Keilty started taking long walks when she was a child. "I've always walked. I used to walk after supper by myself. It was just something I used to do to finish the day, to feel complete. Now that I'm older, I realize that walking is, and always has been, a tool that I use to do my work.

"I really started using it as a tool about ten years ago when I was hired to do over three hundred drawings," she continued. "I took long walks to think through the problems related to the project and I noticed that whenever I walked, I could focus on one thing at a time, and think very clearly. I could think very clearly, even in living color, about what I needed to do. I could think through what I wanted to do, and what the project director wanted me to do, and come up with solutions that were comfortable for both of us. Walking is a very effective tool for problem solving. It's like fine tuning or massaging my brain. It's left, right, solar, lunar — it creates a very important body/mind wholeness.

"The more I walk, the more things I produce," she added. "A few years ago I had back surgery and had to walk for recuperation. I walked 10 miles a day and painted more than ever in my life. I was *so* elated!" Now, when time allows, she walks, runs, and practices yoga. "Walking and running are very different experiences, even though they involve almost the same physical movements," she explained. "I feel almost invincible when I run, and much more physically vulnerable when I walk. I'm very aware of my personal safety at a slower pace.

"Running feels good, but I think running is too fast paced for creative thinking. In fact, I notice that even when I start walking too fast, something shuts off the thoughts — it's like a door closes. I think it has something to do with the breathing pattern. So I walk at a steady pace, but not too fast. I can always tell when I'm going to have a 'perceptive' walk because I'll have all kinds of ideas in my head that will be struggling to get out. So I'll grab a notebook and pencil, and write down all the ideas that surface as I walk. I find walking is also a form of spirituality, a way to go within yourself and meditate."

Recycling is an integral part of Keilty's art. "I hate to waste anything so I use up every bit of material, thread or paint. I'll take cloth from an old shirt, cut it in stripes and then crochet it together with other cloth and make a basket or some other weaving. Most recently, I've been making triptychs (wooden paintings with doors that open) like they used to make for ancient Rome altar pieces. I haven't been spoiled with a lot of formal art training, so I'm freer to move through different media. I'm not real disciplined, but I'm always working on something. I just love to make things and I just can't wait to see what I'm going to come up with next because I never know."

Keilty extends her love of walking into family life and the classroom. She and her husband and four sons operate a summer camp for teenagers in northern Minnesota that offers extensive hiking trips through the Boundary Waters Canoe Area, as well as other noncompetitive activities such as canoeing and climbing. As an occasional guest artist in classrooms, she focuses on a body/mind approach to education. "When I go into the schools, I incorporate walking into what they're doing—whether they're writing poetry, or doing yoga, or focusing on careers. We take deep breaths and then focus on what we'll do, and I tell them if they ever get muddled, about anything, they should take a walk and bring it to living color. It's very simple and it always works."

R. D. Zimmerman, Writer

With five published novels and a number of successful commercial endeavors (mystery puzzles and teen sleuth books) to his credit, R.D. Zimmerman is gaining an international following for his work. In 1990, as a member of the International Association of Crime Writers, he was one of eight Americans selected to participate in the week-long Black Week festival in Spain, a country-wide celebration that honors mystery writers from around the world with parades, picnics, and guest readings. On his own production schedule of writing one novel per year, Zimmerman uses a number of techniques, including walking, to tap into his creative thoughts.

"I bike a lot during the summer and try to work out regularly at a club. That fluctuates, of course. Sometimes I have a deadline that gets in the way, sometimes my travel schedule throws everything off, and sometimes I just don't feel like it. The one constant form of exercise I get, though, is walking," he explained. "I walk at least thirty minutes to an hour every day, even if it's just to walk to Uptown to mail a letter or get a cup of coffee. I try to give my walking a destination and purpose. I used to walk a lot more with my dog, and when she died, I noticed I put on a few pounds. Having a dog is a great incentive to walk because there's always something by your side saying 'let's get out of here and go for a walk.'

"Someone once told me that the conscious decides the dance and the subconscious decides the steps," Zimmerman stated, "and it's hard to get the two to link up. Boring, repetitive motion, like walking, does that for me. If I have a creative problem to solve, I walk out the door and just go on automatic, and somehow, that boring, repetitive motion lets me escape the unimportant and gives me the momentum to get to the important stuff.

"Walking is very successful for me. So is taking a long ride in a car or an airplane, because when things are going by that I don't have to think about, my mind can take flight. It's like there's this layer of rock keeping you away from the creative good stuff, and you can try to sledgehammer your way through it, or you can relax and slip through the cracks in the rock to this core of good ideas.

"I use walking and self-hypnosis to get to my creative reservoir. If I'm really nervous, waiting for a review, walking calms me down and lets me escape into a better place. Often when I start walking I just blank out," he laughed. "In fact, just this morning, I walked down the stairs and out of the house and the next thing I knew I was three blocks away. I wondered if I locked the door. It can be very similar to the same state you reach in hypnosis.

"I think it's important if you work at home that you take a break at lunch time and at the end of the day," he advised. "Some people like to walk early in the morning because it gets them in the mood to work, so I think it's different for each person, but it's important to get up and move around, especially if you have a sedentary job like writing.

"I don't believe in inspiration," he continued. "When an idea hits, you have to nudge it, nurse it, hammer it, and slip through to that problem-solving state or idea. I'll push something as far as I can when I'm sitting at the computer, but when I can't move it any further, I'll get up and start moving physically. When I walk, I let go and move from a work place to a creative problem-solving place. When I walk, it's like letting a chariot or carriage run away with an idea, letting it run and bolt as far as it will go."

Zimmerman walks through all seasons, in all kinds of weather, at all hours of the day. "I don't mind walking when it's very cold out, but I don't enjoy walking in the extremely high heat because there's no way to escape it. I walk almost exclusively in urban areas, particularly around the lakes in Minneapolis because the lakes have a start point and a stop point and you can go on automatic pilot from one point to the other.

"When I'm on a problem-solving walk, I'll ask 'what if?' What if this happened? What if so-and-so was an agent of such and such a country? What if he died? What if she died? What if they both died? You can work through those kind of problems when you're walking."

Wild Bergamot

Zimmerman keeps track of his thoughts and each novel's problems and solutions in a writing journal. "Writing it down helps you get away from the distractions, calm down, and get a good look at the problem. Sometimes I'll walk fifteen or twenty minutes to a cafe, get a cup of coffee, work on my journal, then walk some more, write a little bit more, and walk again."

When he's in the research phase of a novel, he walks to gather data. While working on *Deadfall In Berlin*, he spent a week in Germany walking the streets and observing neighborhoods. "I'd leave the hotel by nine in the morning, come back at 5 P.M. to change shoes and grab something to eat, and then I'd be out walking until 10 P.M. or later. It got kind of compulsive. I took photographs and made notes in my journal and just kept walking, trying to get a better feel for the place.

"I pushed myself too hard, but sometimes you have to do that. I had a limited amount of time, and a number of things I had to see. I can only write about something that I can see in my mind's eye. Walking through a city is a slow enough process to absorb the impressions and sensations. In that way, it's a very active process.

"When I'm by myself, I walk a lot more than when I'm with somebody," Zimmerman observed. "Walking by yourself is really a wonderful form of entertainment. You get to see things that you wouldn't see otherwise, you look like you've got a purpose, and it's just like opening one package after another — it's very stimulating."

Libby Larsen, Composer

Her works have been performed throughout the United States and Europe, and the *Los Angeles Times* referred to her as one of today's "most active and sought-after young American composers." Her most recent work, *Frankenstein, The Modern Prometheus*, was performed in the summer of 1990 by the Minnesota Opera.

Over the years, she's learned not only how to compose intricate, innovative scores of music, but she's learned how to nourish and use her creativity. "In school, I was presented with the myth of a composer sitting for hours and hours, with only the brain in motion. In my case, it's the exact opposite," she stated. "Although I can concentrate for days on end without interruption (when left alone to do that) I cannot enter the creative process in a sedentary fashion. I need a great deal of physical release, or physical partnering to my brain. I found that my creative process is much clearer and truer if I respect my need to physicalize the creative process."

Now that she's written over forty commissioned pieces of music, Larsen is very aware of what it takes to move a musical piece from thought into reality. "The creative process happens for me in three areas," she explained. "First, I need to get very peaceful and I let an idea enter my head. Second, I spend time working out the music. The third phase is rehearsal and performing.

"I use walking in all three of those areas, but mostly in the first part, when I'm trying to conceive a piece. I use walking as a way to gentle myself, to slow my energy down so that I can get hold of my thoughts and move them into the very critical part of the creative process, which is working them out on paper," she added. "Walking is an unconscious, robotic activity for me. There's so much energy there because the part of the brain that generates ideas is so loose, so fluid. All the ideas are bright and shiny and want to find their footing. I feel like I could fly outside my body, just fly away. A great deal of composing happens in a nonlinear fashion, and much faster than any computer—it's like seven computers all coming together at once. The conceptualizing doesn't take very long, but writing it all out is very tedious.

"I do a lot of short destination walks around Lake of the Isles when I'm gathering thoughts, or sometimes I'll walk to the corner store and back, but I always have a specific destination in mind because when I'm using a walk as a way to go to a creative place, I need to be sure that I can get back, literally. So if I have a destination in mind, then I know I can return 'home.' That's how it works for me. I'll get to that creative spot and stay there. I'm usually zoned out so that I don't consciously hear airplanes or urban noise. I walk to absorb nature. I let nature surround and observe me rather than attempting to control my observations of it."

Larsen continued, "During the writing phase, I walk to hear music and I'll keep walking until it sounds instinctively right. Later, I'll walk again to re-hear it. For instance, if I need to know if a flute part should be played in a soft or loud dynamic, all I have to do is go back and listen to that segment in my head. It's not the full piece that I'm hearing but the building blocks of the piece. I want to make very sure all those blocks are conceptualized. I used to walk until the piece was worked out, but now that I'm composing longer pieces, I can't do that or I'd be walking for weeks," she laughed.

"When I'm writing music," she stated, "I become very critical and I use the walks to step aside from the work and ask, Is it really right? Is it good enough? I also find that walking helps me release the parts that aren't good enough so that I can sleep at night. I use walking to identify and solve artistic problems and to release energy to make my life more well.

"During the rehearsal and performance phase, I use walking to remain true to the piece. As soon as the personalities involved in a musical performance begin to sing or play one note, they begin to own the piece. The question for me at that point is, how do I detach myself from the piece, yet remain true to it and guide it through this period of its life so that by the premier it's as close to the way it should be? That's difficult, because I don't even know what that should be since I'm in not in the performing/owning part, so it's very complicated. It's a tough psychological process, and during this phase, I walk to sort out all the emotions.

"I am a deeply competitive person and that causes problems in my life because it creates unneeded stress, and yet it keeps me sharp in my work. I've learned to handle my competitiveness by competing against myself when I run marathons, and I compete against myself and nature when I'm sailing. But I can't reach the creative side of me when I'm running or sailing. Sailing requires conscious attention to detail and when I run, I think about my body all the time, and I'm very conscious of my breathing. Running is a very egocentric activity for me.

"Walking brings out my noncompetitive, creative side. It's a vehicle for energy and thought process. I find that if I overexert then my heart rate gets too fast and the interior monitor in me switches, and I start thinking about my body. When I walk at the right pace, I can focus entirely on what my brain is doing.

"I've had the gift of being able to get out and walk since I was four years old. I walked eight blocks to Fulton School and then back again. When I went to Southwest High School, I walked around Lake Harriet and then down 46th Street and back again. I learned early to use that walking time to gather my thoughts about the day, and to think about the day's activities. Taking a walk has always been a ritual, and I always walk with something in my hand—a letter, a piece of grass. Even one minute of walking is quieting—it's like meditation or yoga."

Larsen finds it difficult to protect the privacy that is so integral to the creative process. "Our culture doesn't value creativity," she stated. "Even though the creative process, at the end, is a very public thing, in the beginning it's a very private thing. Our society has become so intrusive that it's difficult to facilitate a smooth flow of work because there are so many details to handle, so many interuptions."

She finds as her notoriety increases, her privacy decreases. "People are beginning to recognize me when I'm walking and it's very disruptive. It's *more* than disruptive. People stop and talk to me and it takes me a while to come back to the surface and see a face there, I get that lost. And then it's hard to get back to where I was. When I'm interrupted, I feel as though I should return a graceful greeting, but I'd really rather not. For many people, walking is a social activity, but for me, it's a very private activity because I'm away from my phone, my office, and all the systems of my life. When I'm on a private walk, I don't maintain eye contact. The closest thing I can compare it to is gardening, where you actually have your head down in the dirt, and you're in a very private space. There's nothing really quite like it," she smiled, "because it lets you *feel* the andante, the allegro tempos of movement in your life."

Philip Larson, Sculptor, Art Historian, Professor

Along a walkway in the Minneapolis Sculpture Garden is *Six Crystals* by Philip Larson — an extended granite bench supported by six earth-toned "crystals," each with its own unique pattern. Larson's sculptures are cast-iron forms in ensembles. They are intended to suggest ruins, remains, fragments of something lost or something faintly remembered, like an archeological site or collected curious pieces. His work represents "a kind of mystical union of architecture with nature, a theme in many cultures, in many centuries, but one that invites revival today," he explained. In 1990, he also designed a walkway and benches for the grounds of General Mills's international headquarters to give employees access to gardens and outdoor sculptures.

His fascination with ruins and fragments began in childhood as he searched the prairie near Marshall, Minnesota, for something interesting to look at. "There were very few things that stood more than a few feet off the ground," he recalled. "Farmers hate stone piles because they take up valuable land and attract badgers and skunks, but as a kid, I found the piles inspiring. I would sit and look at the stones, walk around them, hold them, throw them. I also enjoyed looking at piles of machinery and scrap heaps because of their mystery and involvement."

Today, he continues to walk through his environment, always in search of evocative, mysterious forms. "To me, buildings are just as romantic and just as involving as nature," he explained, "especially in an older residential area. I love to walk in my neighborhood. I walk down alleys because I like to look at the backs of houses and backyards. Looking at a backyard is like looking into someone's life — and as families change, their backyards change from swingsets and sandboxes to gardens and patios. Walking, for me, is a way to have a sense of communion with my neighborhood."

Larson walks through his neighborhood at least once a day, usually at night. "I'm more interested in the houses than the people because the housing mix in this country is more extreme and varied than almost anywhere on earth. In the houses, you can see individuality as opposed to conformity. Even in tract houses, people have put on a different color of brick, have flipped the plan around, or have surrounded the house with their own lawn ornaments. Some of the more recent townhomes built by corporations take on a kind of European conformity, but the single family house is still an American ideal; it's still affordable. There aren't many places in the world where that's possible. You can walk through a neighborhood and see everything — decay, revival, desecration, historic preservation.

"I cannot sit in my studio for eight hours a day and be productive—it's too limiting," he stated. "When I'm in a production schedule, I find my work getting narrower and narrower when I'm physically inactive. We are built to stand, built to squat, and built to walk. A chair puts us in a position somewhere between standing and walking. There weren't many chairs until the eighteenth century, so the chair is a relatively modern invention. I find if I sit too much I get sleepy, so I stand when I draw, and I walk around the studio. If I get stuck, rather than sitting there sharpening pencils, I'll get up, walk around outside for twenty minutes, then I'm ready to go again.

"My real seminal ideas, the doodles in my mind, occur at two times: when I'm walking (and then I have to go back to the studio and draw them up) or when I have a sketch pad and I'm sitting by the kids as they watch television. I have certain expectations of walking: it won't tire me out, it will enliven me, and it will make associations start to flow, because that's what my art is about, the associative power of geometric and architectural entities with more functional qualities.

"Walking frees what is already within, associations and images that are there all along," he continued. "I have plenty of ideas, about six lifetimes of art in my head. Walking provides the proper kind of relaxation/stimulus to bring ideas out. Sometimes images I saw several years ago will emerge. I get an initial idea, a point of departure, then I have to go back to the studio and work extremely hard to make something out of it."

Walking is a family tradition in the Larson household. Philip, his wife Miriam, and two daughters have walked the trails of Lake Louise at Banff in Alberta, Canada, and Glacier National Park in Colorado. "We're also a great fan of the state park system in Minnesota," he stated, "and we explore a new park every year." In the fall, when Larson's daughters have a break from school, the family makes an annual pilgrimage to the North Shore and, Larson added, "we hike the trails down to *our* ocean—Lake Superior."

"Walking, for me, is a gift," he stated. "When I was five years old, I had a very severe injury, was almost killed. My left ankle was shattered, became seriously arthritic, very painful every day of my life. But I still walked, even though I knew I would be up at night, trying to sleep in spite of the pain. After taking cortisone injections in the ankle for over a year, I knew I had to have radical surgery on my left foot. There were definite risks involved—I didn't know if I'd ever be able to walk again without some irritating plastic device.

"Before surgery, Miriam and I decided to take a trip, decided to walk somewhere we'd never been before. We flew to the ancient quarter of Rome and rented a room two hundred feet from the great portico of the Pantheon. It's one of the most famous and historic places in the world, near the Piazza Navona, with three fountains along what used to be a Roman race track. We walked all day, walked late into the night along Rome's narrow, jagged streets. I've always loved Renaissance and Baroque architecture, and I figured if this was going to be my last walk, it was going to be a memorable one. The surgery was a success, but to this day, I still feel very fortunate to have the use of both of my legs. I continue to walk whenever I can with family or friends. A walk, for me, is an exchange of information, affection, and companionship. I *never* take the act of walking for granted."

CHAPTER 5

Worksite Walking Programs

A briefcase, a healthy bag lunch, and a comfortable pair of sneakers have become standard business accessories. More and more employees, in an effort to fit some form of exercise into their workday, are walking to, from, or during work.

A number of worksites throughout the state support the fitness goals of their employees by sponsoring lunch-hour walking programs during the summer, indoor walking programs in the winter, and special walking events throughout the year. Worksites in Minnesota vary from corner bakeries that employ a handful of people to large multinational firms that employ thousands of people. Regardless of size, location, or budget, all worksites can offer inexpensive walking programs designed to improve employee health and morale.

Employers are discovering that offering a worksite walking program is *the* most economical way to provide a year-round wellness program. No special equipment or facilities are needed; it takes very little time to organize and maintain a walking program; and the cost of providing a worksite walking program (including promotions and incentives) rarely exceeds $500 per year.

Employees are finding that a walk during the lunch hour improves their mental awareness and productivity, reduces on-the-job stress, and often helps generate creative solutions to problems. A midday walk also provides an opportunity for employees to socialize as they support each other in their fitness goals.

The term "high noon," once associated with the two-martini business lunch, now refers to the energy and exhilaration that comes from a brisk midday walk. Walking is a natural, simple, healthy, and economical way to keep the mind, body, and spirit refreshed throughout the workday.

This chapter contains tips on how to start and maintain a successful worksite walking program. First, create a solid foundation for your program that promotes awareness and provides health education. Second, based on the experiences of other successful worksite programs, design a "behavior change" program that will meet the needs of your particular employees.

THE FOUNDATION—A WELLNESS PROGRAM

One of the best ways to ensure the success of a walking program is to first, develop a wellness program that promotes health awareness and education, such as the American Heart Association's Heart At Work program.

Although health issues are addressed continually in newspapers and magazines, worksites can go one step further to provide employees with the information and resources they need to develop a healthier lifestyle. Fitness seminars, routine health screenings, low-fat menu selections in the cafeteria, and newsletter articles can make it more convenient for employees to actively manage their health (and long-term health care costs) on a day-to-day basis.

Health awareness and education programs are the cornerstones of a successful walking program.

Heart At Work, sponsored by the American Heart Association (4701 West 77th Street, Minneapolis, MN 55435, 612/835-3300)

"We provide an entree to worksites into the areas of health promotion and education. We help them set up a program, figure out how to get employees involved in the planning, select a wellness coordinator, and develop a flexible, inexpensive program. We encourage worksites to develop walking programs because walking is a safe exercise that doesn't need any elaborate equipment or facilities." Teri Woodhull, program specialist for Worksite and Community Programs, Minnesota Affiliate of the American Heart Association.

In 1984, the national headquarters for the American Heart Association, located in Dallas, Texas, developed and pilot-tested an easy-to-implement wellness program for worksites that addressed employee health in five areas: 1) high blood pressure; 2) smoking cessation; 3) exercise; 4) nutrition and weight control; and 5) signals and actions for survival (for heart attacks and strokes).

In 1985 and 1986, the Minnesota affiliate, located in Minneapolis, decided to pilot-test the program at nine worksites located in Duluth and Alexandria. Thanks to a successful pilot test and significant program expansion, the Heart at Work program is now in place at over 250 worksites throughout Minnesota.

The Heart At Work program establishes a worksite wellness program on three levels: awareness (through paycheck stuffers and posters), education (seminars, classes, videos), and behavior change (ongoing worksite activities that support employees' commitment to lead a healthier lifestyle). The program concentrates on the first two levels — awareness and education. It provides ideas for behavior change activities (such as walking programs), but each worksite must develop its own activities in conjunction with existing community resources.

The program is flexible so that it can be used in small, nonprofit agencies or large corporations, and the program is positioned to complement and promote, rather than compete with, other health education programs. Once a worksite starts a wellness program, there is usually a need to move beyond the simple awareness level. Other organizations in each community provide worksites with services ranging from ongoing health screenings to designing an elaborate fitness center.

Common Milkweed

Walking programs have proven to be a very cost-effective way for worksites to offer a behavior change activity. A lunch-hour walking challenge can be implemented with a small amount of preparation which includes the development of promotional materials (available through the Heart At Work program), a recommended walking map, and incentives for participation. A number of Heart At Work walking programs are highlighted in this chapter.

The American Heart Association is able to offer the Heart At Work program for minimal cost thanks to a corps of dedicated, well-trained community volunteers who provide all the marketing and training services. If you would like more information about the Heart At Work program, or would be interested in learning about volunteer opportunities, call your local chapter of the American Heart Association.

WALKING PROGRAMS

Awareness and education programs document how nutrition, stress, and exercise can affect an individual's health, fitness, and longevity. Successful behavior change programs provide the support and incentives people need to adopt a healthier lifestyle.

Some worksites offer short-term walking programs that help employees develop their own walking programs at work or at home. Other worksites offer year-round walking opportunities that enable employees to get their required twenty- to thirty-minute workout three to four times a week during their lunch hour or before or after work. Factors such as the number of employees, the size of the worksite, and the safety and convenience of walking paths around the worksite will affect the design of any walking program.

Here is a sampling of some of the walking programs available at worksites in Minnesota.

Walk Your Socks Off, Good Shepherd Community (1115 Fourth Avenue North, Sauk Rapids, MN 56379, 612/252-6525)

"Everyone participates—supervisors, line staff, men and women, full-time and part-time employees. It's a no-budget program that our employees really enjoy. Walkers have a support person at work or at home verify their walks and interesting things happen during the process—supervisors take time to give a word of encouragement during the day, neighbors wave from their windows. It's a great way for employees to let other people know they're making a change in their lives. We give away walking socks as incentives. They love the socks and complete the bonus phase of the program to get another pair." Diane Schellinger, human resource director, Heart At Work program coordinator.

The Good Shepherd Community consists of two senior apartment complexes and a nursing home on a thirty-acre campus just outside St. Cloud, Minnesota. Over 220 employees work one of three eight-hour shifts. The challenge facing The Good Shepherd Community was to design a behavior change activity that would enable all employees to participate in their wellness program.

The Good Shepherd Community developed a flexible walking program that would encourage people to participate at home or on the job. The Walk Your Socks Off program is offered in the fall. It's a six-week program that usually runs from September through October, followed by a five-week bonus phase that lasts through Thanksgiving. To participate in the program, employees have to walk briskly three times a week for 1 mile or twenty minutes, whichever occurs first. They keep track of their mileage, and have someone (a neighbor, family member, or supervisor) verify each walk. At the end of the six weeks, they turn in their completed self-check chart and receive a pair of walking socks. If they continue for another five weeks, they receive another pair of socks.

To promote walking during the lunch hour, Good Shepherd provides a map of a 1-mile walking route around the grounds. The walking program is promoted through Good Shepherd's newsletter and paycheck stuffers, and every year approximately fifty employees participate. Walking socks for the program are donated by a local sporting goods store. Employees who complete either phase of the program are honored in the employee newsletter.

Having someone verify each walk is an integral part of the program. It builds support for the effort and is a collaborative effort between the employee and a support person.

What has Good Shepherd learned about developing a walking program? Make sure the employees are informed well ahead of time about the program and that they understand the criteria and how to complete the charts. Word of mouth is important. If you get the supervisors involved, the program has a better chance of succeeding. Offer great incentives and make the program fun!

Walk Into Wellness, Foldcraft Company (615 Centennial Drive, Kenyon, MN 55946, 507/789-5111)

"With more than 53 percent of today's health risks being life-style related, the opportunity for members of a group to impact the number and severity of the collective risks is substantial. The HELP (Healthy Employee Lifestyle Premium) program rewards those employees who participate in the pursuit (or maintenance) of healthy, reduced-risk lifestyles. Foldcraft is taking an innovative approach to health coverage because the company is committed to the health of its employees. Our assumption is that a healthy employee is a productive community citizen, and a productive employee. A healthy workforce will eventually reduce the amount the company spends on health coverage, but that's down the road. Our goal is to provide our employees with the information and resources they need to improve their health on a day-to-day basis." Steve Sheppard, chief executive officer.

Foldcraft, a manufacturer of Plymold booths used in restaurants, provides employees with financial discounts on their health insurance premiums for taking control of their health and accomplishing health goals.

The HELP program is divided into three phases. The Assessment and Screening Phase includes on-site employee testing in six controllable risk areas: tobacco usage, body fat composition, blood pressure, heart recovery/oxygen uptake, cholesterol, and flexibility. All tests are conducted at company expense during working hours. Employees receive a confidential, personal booklet with their results. They don't have to share the information with the company. Just for participating in the Assessment and Screening phase, employees receive a $20 monthly discount on their health insurance premium. Spousal participation is required for the discount because two-thirds of the company's incurred health claims are generated by spouses and children, and because spousal involvement moves the responsibility for health maintenance into the home.

The second phase of the HELP program is the Incentive Phase. If employees choose to share their results with the company they are eligible to receive further discounts. Each of the above-mentioned six risk factors is assigned a weight and a set of norms so that participants can compare themselves to the general population tested. Participants receive one of the following ratings for each of the six categories: very low risk, low risk, moderate risk, high risk, very high risk. Depending on their composite rating, they receive additional monthly discounts that range from $40 for those in the very low risk category to $5 for those in the very high risk category. Following their assessment, employees are encouraged to improve their risk status.

The third phase of the HELP program is the Maintenance Phase in which participants elect to be re-screened in hopes of improving their risk status and further lowering their insurance premiums.

Foldcraft is committed to providing opportunities for their employees to improve their health. For instance, Foldcraft offers a Walk Into Wellness program that encourages people to walk over the lunch hour. The company has mapped out various 1- and 2-mile routes near the factory, as well as a route through the building that people use during bad weather. Two loops around the indoor path equals 1 mile.

To promote the Walk Into Wellness program, Foldcraft sponsors Wellwalk, a simulated trip to a distant city. Employees accumulate miles on an honor system that equal the mileage to another location in Minnesota. During the *Wellwalk to Red Wing*, employees had to walk 39 miles within a six-week period, and their names were put into a drawing for a dinner for two at the St. James Hotel in Red Wing. During the *Wellwalk to Stillwater*, employees had to walk 89 miles to be eligible for a drawing for dinner for two at the Lowell Inn in Stillwater. The program has been very successful—approximately thirty-five to fifty employees out of a workforce of 275 participated in these events.

What advice would Foldcraft give to a company interested in starting a similar program? Companies have to focus on the long-term benefits of the program to employees and to the company because all the health assessments and premium discounts will significantly increase the cost of a company's health program.

Saturday Walk/Run Group. Bemidji School District #31 (201 15th St. N.W., Bemidji, MN 56601, 218/759-3285)

"Exercise is for everybody. Walking is a great way to get your exercise in and have fun at the same time. Exercise has to be fun or people won't participate. It's important to have friends who encourage and support you in whatever activity you choose. We're starting to help build the support groups that are necessary to prevent exercise lows and maintain regular fitness routines." Robert Wagner, director of community education, Heart At Work Program Coordinator.

As director of community education, Robert Wagner coordinates health and wellness programs for school district employees as well as the thirteen thousand households within the Bemidji School District. "Our activities are designed to reach everyone in the school district," he explained, "so we sponsor a number of walking programs that bring our employees and the community together."

Every Saturday morning throughout the year, employees of the Bemidji School District meet at a local track and walk or run together. About twenty people show up every week, and after their workout, they usually go out to breakfast together.

The school district also sponsors an annual Volkslauf Walk/Run that is held on the first Sunday in May. *Volkslauf* is a German word that means "people's event," and over the years it truly has become a people's event. The school district sponsors an eight-kilometer (5-mile) cross-country walk/run and a four-kilometer (2.5-mile) walk within the beautiful forest of Lake Bemidji State Park. Grandparents, parents, teenagers, children, people of all ages come together to participate in this event.

Everyone who registers gets an incentive such as a free cap or water bottle. There are fourteen different age classes, and ribbons are provided to the top five finishers in each category so just about everyone gets an award. Registration fees are minimal to encourage family participation. There are special discounts for families with three or more members.

Also, Bemidji community education sponsors fitness walking and water walking classes. Scholarships are available for residents on fixed incomes.

Other school districts that are thinking about implementing a walking program should keep in mind three things: 1) keep entrance fees to competitive events reasonable for everyone so that families are able to participate; 2) involve the community businesses, and offer lots of rewards and incentives; and 3) provide some sort of social gathering at all events that gives people a chance to mingle.

Stepping Out For Health, Flour City Packaging (500 Stinson Boulevard, Minneapolis, MN 55413, 612/378-2100)

"I recommend that companies offer a wellness program that encourages all forms of exercise, and offer a walking program as part of that program. People enjoy all kinds of aerobic activities like biking, running, and basketball and they should be encouraged to participate in any activity that they enjoy. I would like to see businesses in the area form an association to develop walking paths for employees. A nice 1- or 2-mile stretch of landscaped walking path through some of these industrial sections would be an incentive for people to work in this area. It would make a daily walk more pleasant and enjoyable, and improve employee health at the same time." Steve Law, health and safety consultant.

Flour City Packaging was started at the turn of the century when Minneapolis was known as the "Flour City" instead of the "City of Lakes." Designing and manufacturing folding cartons and boxes continues to be their forte.

The company, with 160 employees, has its headquarters in northeastern Minnesota and a plant in Isanti, Minnesota. Most of the employees work in the factory headquarters in Minneapolis that operates around the clock in three eight-hour work shifts.

Steve Law, a health and safety consultant for printing and packaging companies, has implemented a number of wellness programs for Flour City Packaging including a smoke-free work environment and a wellness information program that includes supervisor training and a self-help medical guide for all employees.

In 1987, Law worked with St. John's Hospital to implement a lunch-hour walking program called Stepping Out For Health. Employees received a brochure with walking tips and a map of a 1-mile indoor walking route through the factory. A large wall map near an employee entrance also identified 1-, 2-, and 3-mile walking routes through the neighborhood.

Mileage cards were distributed to all employees and their family members. All participants were eligible to win a free pair of walking shoes, and those who walked 100 miles received Stepping Out For Health t-shirts.

The walking program worked well during the first few years. It was eventually incorporated into a larger wellness challenge that includes other forms of aerobic activities.

Noonwalk, General Mills (Number One General Mills Boulevard, Golden Valley, MN 55426, 612/540-2182)

"A walking program is one of the best ways to encourage employee fitness. We wanted get away from the jock image of exercise that leaves the impression that you have to run a marathon to be healthy. We also wanted an ongoing, low-cost, easy-to-maintain exercise program for all of our employees. We have a very nice campus, and decided that a walking program would be a great way to get people to exercise during the day and take in some of the art work and landscaping on the General Mills grounds." Andy Wood, R.P.T., supervisor of Health Promotion and Fitness, Health and Human Services Department.

General Mills is one of the nation's leading providers and marketers of consumer foods and a leader in the full-service dinnerhouse restaurant segment. Best known for its cereals (Total, Wheaties, Cheerios), Betty Crocker desserts, and family restaurants (Red Lobster and The Olive Garden), General Mills has over ninety-seven thousand employees throughout the world.

In the Minneapolis area, twenty-eight hundred employees located at three different worksites enjoy a comprehensive health and wellness program that includes seminars, on-site medical specialists, and diagnostic screenings.

The company's walking program began as a celebration of National Employee Health Day in May 1987, and again in 1988, when General Mills challenged employees to walk or bike to work. Awards were provided to employees who earned the most mileage in each category. The walking program expanded in 1989 when Andy Wood, supervisor of Health Promotion and Fitness and the Riders and Striders Club, developed the Noonwalk program.

In the Noonwalk program, mileage is accumulated during the lunch hour. When employees reach walking milestones of 50 or 100 miles they submit their mileage to an Employee Club representative and receive an award. During the first year of the program, employees received a "General Mills Noonwalk" t-shirt for walking 50 miles and a pedometer for walking 100 miles. Different incentives are offered each year.

General Mills maintains the major portion of a 1-mile walking course that extends to public paths maintained by the City of Golden Valley. Another mile of brick walking paths, designed by sculptor Philip Larson, was added to the grounds in 1990. A map has also been developed for an interior walking route that is used by employees during the winter months.

The Noonwalk program is promoted and revitalized annually in May during National Employee Health Week with a grand 1-mile walk. The company rents a large time clock and several executives lead the event. Employees in the department with the most participants receive a department-designed t-shirt honoring their achievement. The walking program reaches about six hundred employees per year through the promotions, the kick-off event, and the incentive program.

The Noonwalk program costs less than $500 per year including incentives, promotions, and information materials. The company used the Rockport Walk Leader Program (617/485-2090) to start the program. Other recommendations for starting a quality, low-cost walking program include inviting a celebrity to attend your kick-off event, and asking a local shoe store to provide discounts for employees.

Nature Walks, MSI Insurance (Two Pine Tree Drive, Arden Hills, MN 55112, 612/631-7327)

"Worksites are placing more emphasis on exercise, weight control, handling stress, and learning about the environment. If you have any open space, get people out walking. And if they can learn something about what they're seeing, all the better." Peggy Wedell, R.N., Medical Services, Heart At Work coordinator.

"We meander and mosey so that we can observe the exciting things that are unfolding before us. We explore insects, birds, wildflowers, trees, prairies, ponds, even weather. Once, shortly before a storm, the birds and other animals were very agitated, and then immediately before the storm, they quieted down. It's not often that you get a chance to demonstrate that to a group. It was one of those lucky days. We focus on phenomenology so that employees can understand the chain of events that impacts their immediate surroundings." Chase Davies, naturalist.

MSI is a multiple-line insurance company licensed to sell products in forty-three states and the District of Columbia. MSI has over twenty-five hundred agents, brokers, and sales representatives. Approximately seven hundred people are employed at MSI's headquarters in Arden Hills.

A paved, 1-mile walkway on the campus is maintained year-round by MSI. The path leads through secluded woods and semi-restored prairie. An employee suggested the Nature Walk program, and the company contacted Chase Davies, an outdoor education specialist and naturalist, to provide educational nature walks for employees. Walkers meet on Tuesdays during the lunch hour. The walks last anywhere from thirty to forty-five minutes and are offered once in March, every other week in April, every week in May when there are dramatic changes in the environment, and then once a month through the summer and fall until the end of September.

The Nature Walk program is promoted through the company's monthly newsletter. The program can comfortably accommodate fifteen employees per walk. Throughout the year, approximately fifty employees participate in one or more nature walks.

The goal of program is to help employees become more aware of the environment in which they walk. Employees report they enjoy the program even more the second year when they begin to recognize things on their own and ask questions with more depth and understanding.

In addition to the Nature Walk program, MSI employees use the company's walking paths during their lunch hour and at break times. The company also sponsors a "Slim Down For Summer" program that involves teams of four employees competing against other teams of employees in categories such as "most pounds lost by a team," "most pounds lost by an individual," and "best team name." Team walks during the lunch hour provide the support and motivation necessary to achieve personal and team fitness goals.

Medtronic Mile, Medtronic Corporate Center (7000 Central Avenue Northeast, Minneapolis, MN 55432, 612/574-3405)

"We have a tradition and culture at Medtronic of being a health-oriented company, so we continually offer a variety of health programs. We use our health program as one of our recruiting tools. We find that when all else is equal, a person will usually choose Medtronic because we provide a number of opportunities for our employees to exercise before, during, or after work." Jerry Kolb, Full Life and technical education manager

Medtronic celebrated its fortieth anniversary in 1990 and employs over seven thousand people. The company's corporate headquarters is located in Minneapolis, but it has manufacturing plants throughout the world. Medtronic, which started in a garage in northeast Minneapolis, is now recognized as a leader in biomedical products such as heart pacemakers, artificial valves, transcutaneous electrical nerve stimulators, rehabilitative products, and instrumentation.

Medtronic sponsors a number of walking events throughout the year. The company's annual Medtronic Mile, which started fifteen years ago as a running event, is now a run/walk competition that involves more than four hundred employees, family members, and friends. The event begins at corporate headquarters, and then moves to a nearby outdoor track where walking and running events are held throughout the afternoon. Winners in the various age categories (and special categories such as "Best Costume") receive t-shirts and other incentives. A contest is held among employees to design the Medtronic Mile t-shirt, and the winning designer gets a free membership to Medtronic's fitness center. Following the competitive events, Medtronic hosts a picnic for all participants that includes door prizes and other carnival activities.

Medtronic's fitness center sponsors Action Teams that consist of four or more employees who participate in a common activity, such as a walking group. Team members recruit other members, and if the team needs financial assistance to continue its activity (such as pedometers, or racewalking judges for a competitive event) the company will assume 50 to 100 percent of the cost, depending on the item. Action Teams meet one or more times per month.

Medtronic also sponsors an Incentive Program that encourages employees to participate in a variety of social, recreation, and aerobic activities. A brochure outlines how many points will be awarded for different types of activities. For instance, a person walking at a fitness level receives more points per minute of activity than a person walking at a social level. Employees keep track of their activity points on a computerized scanner in the fitness center that automatically tallies their points and indicates when they have earned enough points for a reward. Employees receive t-shirts, towels, and other equipment as they reach different activity milestones, and their names are placed on a wall in the fitness center.

Medtronic also promotes walking through its "Sneakers and Sweats Day" held every summer. Employees wear comfortable clothing to work so that they can take a brisk walk or run along a pre-marked course during the lunch hour. Healthy snacks (carrot sticks, fruit juices) are provided to all participants. About two hundred to three hundred employees join in the activities.

In addition to the formal walking programs offered through the company, employees have formed an informal walking club that meets throughout the year during the lunch hour. Up to fifteen people gather and take a brisk walk along the company's paths near Rice Creek, or if the weather is bad, the group walks the halls of the office complex.

Take a Hike, Minneapolis Health Department (250 South Fourth Street, Minneapolis, MN 55415, 612/673-2304)

"Take a Hike is designed to encourage City of Minneapolis employees to use the streets and skyway routes to reach their personal walking goals for fitness." Karen Kiemele, program coordinator.

The City of Minneapolis Health Department makes it as easy as possible for city employees to walk during their workday. For an annual fee of five dollars, employees receive a walking guide with indoor and outdoor walking routes of the downtown area, a personal walking log to keep track of progress, quarterly lunch-hour seminars on walking and health, a quarterly newsletter, and a walking pin.

Shape-Up Challenge, City of Bloomington (2215 West Old Shakopee Road, Bloomington, MN 55431-3096, 612/887-9601)

"Previously sedentary employees find the Challenge a non-threatening and supportive opportunity to begin exercising regularly." Carolyn Larson, Shape-Up Challenge coordinator.

The annual Shape-Up Challenge is a worksite fitness program that involves friendly competition among Bloomington worksites. All employees, part-time and full-time, with and without disabilities, are encouraged to participate. There are two divisions: Division I (less than one hundred employees) and Division II (more than one hundred employees). Worksites pay a minimal "cost recovery" registration fee based on the number of their employees participating in the program.

The Challenge awards points to employees for doing aerobic activities such as walking, swimming, wheelchair basketball, or skating. At the end of the six-week Challenge, awards and grand prizes are given to winning worksites.

Participating worksites receive an activity guide for each employee, promotional posters, six weekly newsletters with weekly standings, training for all worksite coordinators, trophies and plaques for winning worksites, and player packets for employees.

The Challenge was developed by the University of Minnesota in 1985 and is now sponsored by the City of Bloomington Parks and Recreation Division with assistance from the Bloomington Heart and Health Program. The program is extremely successful: Over seventy worksites participate, and the employee participation rate is greater than 50 percent.

Additional Worksite Resources

Another resource for Minnesota employers is The Minnesota Worksite Wellness Resource (106 Union Plaza, 333 North Washington Avenue, Minneapolis, MN 55401, 612/349-2716), a nonprofit organization committed to the healthy well-being of businesses, schools, and public agencies. The organization offers information resources, a quarterly newsletter, training and development, and a membership network for successful worksite wellness programs. MWWR can assist employers by making referrals and providing behavior change program ideas through seminars and networking forums for wellness coordinators.

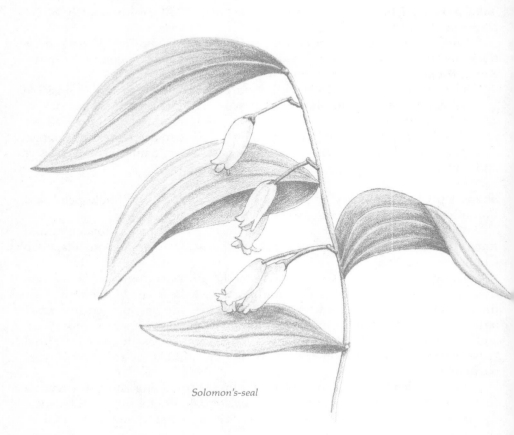

Solomon's-seal

CHAPTER 6

Walking Tours

If you want to really learn about a city, school, neighborhood, country, or culture, take a walking tour! More and more walking tours are being offered by chambers of commerce, civic groups, historical societies, businesses, and environmental groups to 1) promote fitness; 2) increase neighborhood, city, or worksite pride; and 3) provide information about local ecology, history, architecture, art, and culture.

Before taking a walking tour or developing one for your community, it may be helpful to consider the thoughts of Minnesotans who have invested a considerable amount of time and effort in exploring the ins and outs of the walking tour business.

Here is a look at walking tours from the perspective of the tourist and the tour developer.

TYPES OF WALKING TOURS

Walking tours come in a number of different formats: 1) self-guided tours that convey information through books, booklets, or brochures; 2) self-guided tours that provide information through audiocassettes or video cassettes; and 3) guided tours that provide a group leader to identify highlights and answer questions. Self-guided walking tours are usually free or available for a minimal fee. Guided tours vary in cost depending on the size of the group, length of the tour, and the type of amenities (food and transportation) provided. Walking tours vary in length from thirty minutes to fourteen days.

HOW TO LOCATE WALKING TOURS

What's the best way to find out about walking tours? Contact the local visitor's center, chamber of commerce, historical society (city and county), and city park or recreation department. They usually know about walking tours that are available in an area. You also may want to visit the local library and look up "walking tours." A number of walking tours have been developed in conjunction with community celebrations; following the event, the walking tour pamphlet or booklet is donated to the city or county library. However, if the tour hasn't been offered recently, be prepared for some route or site changes. Other good resources for walking tours are bookstores, map stores, newspapers (travel section), and walking or outdoor magazines.

WALKING TOUR VACATIONS

Walking tour vacations vary from short, self-guided walks to very elaborate (and in some cases, expensive) tours with guides, transportation, and meals. Walking tours are available in just about every part of the world and are gaining in popularity. What should you look for in a quality walking tour vacation?

Helen Liu, Walking Tour Enthusiast

"Something happened to me on the Lake District tour in England. I assumed their Lake District would be similar to our lakes in Minnesota, but many of their lakes are up in the mountains so you have to climb up to a lake, and then down and up again to another lake. The first day we climbed 1,100 feet just for a warm up. The second day we climbed 2,500 feet in two hours! We walked on the top of the mountain ridge and it was exhilarating. I thought about my family and friends and how wonderful the experience really was. I never felt that kind of a 'high' before. And I realized that just a few years ago I never would have been able to make it up the hill. I could feel how far I had come in those few years." Helen Liu

Helen Liu has explored Wales and England (the Cotswolds area and the Lake District) on foot. Liu became an avid walker during a year she spent in Taiwan with her dying father. She credits walking with keeping her spirit intact during that very difficult and painful year of her life. Since then, walking has become an important part of her life, whether she's at home or traveling abroad. Here are some of Liu's tips for having a successful walking tour vacation.

Determine why you are taking the tour. Every walker joins a walking tour for a different reason. Some may be looking for, and occasionally find, romance. Others may be celebrating an anniversary or retirement. Some may be seeking solace or inspiration. Others may be improving their health. Whatever the reason, walkers won't be disappointed if their goal is to meet interesting people and learn new things about the region they're exploring.

Select a tour that's right for you. Decide how much you want to spend, where you want to go, when you are able to travel, and how much walking you want to do. Expensive tours offer a lot of pampering and fairly easy walking. Mid-priced tours offer lots of walking, good lodging, and meals.

Most walking tours fall into one of three categories: beginner (even, level trails, walking shoes are sufficient, one to three hours of walking per day); intermediate (a few hills, sturdy hiking boots are recommended, four to six hours of walking per day); advanced (steep climbs and descents, sturdy hiking boots required, five to seven hours of walking per day).

The walking tour season in the United States and Europe is from May through October. Winter walking tours are available in Hawaii, Australia, South America, Africa, and Asia.

Get in shape for your walking tour. Training for a walking tour should begin at least six weeks in advance. Training programs that include walking, climbing stairs, and lifting weights can prevent some of the common walking tour aches and pains such as a stiff neck, sore legs, or a sore back. Build up your stamina by walking up and down hills. Coming down takes half as much time but twice as much effort. When you walk downhill, lace your boots very tight for more ankle control. It's almost like adjusting the brakes on your bike as you pedal downhill. You need the extra support as you descend, and then you loosen them up again for the rest of the trip.

Minnesota offers excellent training areas for those interested in international walking tours. County parks have long, flat stretches of paved trails to build up speed and endurance. State parks offer miles of varied terrain and challenging hills that provide a day or more of walking adventures. The

Superior Hiking Trail in northeastern Minnesota, like the Appalachian Trail on the East Coast, attracts walkers and hikers from all over the world. If you're thinking about a one-week or longer walking tour, you may want to break in your body and your boots right here in Minnesota!

Bring adequate clothing. When you sign up for a tour, you will probably receive a list of things to bring. Typical gear includes: one pair of walking shoes, one pair of hiking boots, rain gear (usually a waterproof hooded jacket), a windbreaker, a hat or visor, sunglasses, sunscreen, insect repellent, bandages, small backpack or large waist pack, cotton clothes, hand gloves (for cool days and evenings), plastic bags (for storing muddy shoes and boots), and several pairs of extra thick cotton or wool socks.

One of the best way to break in your gear before the trip is to wear your shoes and socks and around the neighborhood when you take your daily strolls. Also, you may want to experiment with taping your feet to prevent blisters. Apply moleskin (a foot tape product sold in most drugstores) to all the areas where your foot comes in contact with your boot or shoe (see illustration).

Carry only what you need during the day. Although walkers tend to carry as much as possible on the first day, eventually they learn it's much easier to carry only basic essentials such as a passport; travelers checks, money, or credit cards; water or cartons of juice; hard candy (for instant energy); essential personal care items; and an extra pair of socks (your feet might get wet by midmorning from dew). Some walkers carry guidebooks about flowers, birds, and insects; others bring along binoculars and cameras.

Become familiar with the tour agenda. Walking tour companies usually arrange for lodging in quality hotels and manors with dining facilities. For an extra fee you may request a private bedroom or bath. Tours usually begin with an evening meal where walkers get acquainted, meet the tour guides, and review the itinerary for each day. A hearty breakfast is provided the following morning and the walking begins about one hour afterward.

Walking tours typically include ten to fifteen people including the leaders. Leaders are responsible for walking with the group, moving luggage from lodge to lodge, arranging for meals, and transporting tired walkers when necessary.

Three groups of walkers usually emerge during a tour—the slow walkers, the intermediate walkers, and the fast walkers. Sometimes guides will keep the fast walkers in line by not telling them where the group is going, forcing them to backtrack or wait for the group at junctions. Eventually everyone arrives at the same point.

Be prepared for changes in weather and terrain. If it rains, you walk. If it's hot and sunny, you walk. European walking tours go through forests, medieval towns, marshes, moors, up hills, down rocky slopes, and through farmlands. In England, where the general public has the right of way through private farmlands, walkers have to climb over or through wooden gates called "stiles."

"At the end of one very wet and muddy walk, I was climbing over the stiles with increasing ease until my fellow walkers noticed that I had actually added two extra inches in height because of the mud under my boots." Helen Liu

Learn as much as you can. The groups are a blend of couples and singles. People range in age from twenties to seventies. Some groups are formed according to age, others are formed according to walking ability. During the course of the tour you will probably get a chance to walk side by side more than once with everyone in the group including the guides. Walkers rarely discuss jobs or families—most conversation pertains to the landscape, the history of the country, and local traditions.

"In the Lake District of England they refer to hills as 'fells'. The shepherds participate in a sport called fell running and some of the competitions last for twenty-four hours—they run up and down the hills in the dark! As we were struggling up 2,500 feet, these people would run right past us. They run so fast that their feet would barely touch the loose stones and they would never trip over them. It was amazing!" Helen Liu

Celebrate your accomplishments. Tours usually end with a festive meal, photographs, and an exchange of names and addresses. Most walkers find that a week is just about the right length of time for a walking tour. By the end of the week you're reluctant but ready to leave the group and get back to your own life.

DEVELOPING YOUR OWN WALKING TOUR

A great walking tour is unforgettable because you "feel" the information with all your senses—the sights, sounds, smells, tastes, textures (and facts) are deeply impressed in your memory.

If you are proud of a geographic area or a historic building and want others to share your enthusiasm, take them on a walking tour! How do you develop a walking tour? Where do you begin? How do you move people from one point to another? How much information should you include about points of interest? How long should a tour last? There are a number of elements that work together to provide a quality walking experience at home or abroad.

In any walking tour, you should expect: 1) easy access to the tour information. Self-guided tour information should be available in a convenient public place so that people can take the tour at their convenience (days, evenings, weekdays, weekends, holidays, different seasons); 2) a clear, readable map; 3) *current*, accurate information; 4) concise, to-the-point description of highlights; 5) a multicultural, inclusive view of history, architecture, and art; 6) a route that is accessible for people using wheelchairs, strollers, or walkers.

Four Minnesotans have earned the respect and gratitude of walkers by designing interesting, informative, and fun walking tours. Even though Ruth Humleker, Angela Anderson, Bob Ripsin, and Dot Lilja have developed walking tours for different locations and audiences, their approaches are remarkably similar. If there are any standards for quality walking tours, they have discovered them the hard way—through trial and error. They know what works and what doesn't.

Ruth Humleker, Author of Self-guided Walking Tour Books

"If you walk in any structured way you begin to see what's really around you. You begin to use your eyes, your ears, and all your senses come alive. One time I was in the Botanical Gardens in Washington, D.C. with a friend and he said, 'Aren't those the most beautiful flowers you ever saw?' I looked to my right, to my left, in front of me, and behind me and finally asked, 'Where?' He pointed. I looked up and saw the most incredible orchids hanging down everywhere. I would have walked through there and never seen them if it wasn't for him. So I've learned to look up. About 50 percent of the most interesting things in the world are up over your head. People might think they know an area, but they really don't because they've been looking at it from the ground level. When you look up, you discover all kinds of interesting things." Ruth Humleker

Humleker is the author of two walking tour books, *New York for the Independent Traveler* and *London for the Independent Traveler*. As the former public relations director for the City of Minneapolis Park and Recreation Board, she also developed a number of walking tours through Minneapolis neighborhoods. Here is her advice for developing an interesting walking tour.

Ask questions. A wonderful walking tour evolves from questions, and questions are prodded by exploring uncharted territory. Don't include obvious information. Help walkers discover new things about what they're seeing and feeling. The more you pay attention to details, the more questions you have. You begin to wonder. Who was the architect? How did that sculpture get here? If there are tulips planted in the summer, what's planted in the fall? Every time you see something simple, like a flower or a tree, if you begin to really look at it, you'll begin to have questions, and from those questions, you can learn all kinds of things—history, art, botany. The more you look, the more questions you have, the more you see, and the more curious you become.

Visit local libraries and historical societies. You can usually answer your own questions with a trip to the local library or historical society. Let the librarians or historians know what you're trying to accomplish with your walking tour and they can lead you to other resources.

Talk with people who live in the area. Talk to people in cafes and stores. Ask people about their history; get them to tell you about their lives, their past, their dreams. When you talk with people in the neighborhoods you find things you never knew existed. Talk to the owners of small businesses. You usually only have to ask one or two questions, and then people start opening up. People have such wonderful stories. Once you win a person's trust, they'll hand you to someone else with another interesting story and they will say, "Tell her Grace said to call." Once people know you're there to learn, not to inspect or exploit, it's easy. You'll simply be handed from one person to another and then the information you need will take care of itself. Let the walking tour unfold organically.

Record your information. Always carry a small notebook to write down the names of places, interesting bits of information, whatever you think will be useful. You may also want to carry a tape recorder to capture the sounds of busy city streets, interesting bells, or bird calls. It's easier to write about a sound when you have it right with you. Some people become intimidated during interviews when you introduce a tape recorder. Taking notes during an interview is less intrusive, but it interrupts the flow of conversation. Sometimes it's best to listen, then write from memory.

Keep them wanting more. The mind works like a camera, and you only have so much film. People don't want a lot of information. If they want to know more, they can find out for themselves. There's a fine line between giving way too much information and not giving them enough. Provide walkers with an informational appetizer that will make them want to learn more.

Use existing maps and use numbers to mark points of interest. There are all kinds of wonderful existing maps, so don't try to draw your own. Mark your start and finish points and use numbers to identify points of interest. Make the maps as easy to read as possible.

Try not to retrace your steps. When possible, design a walking tour that makes a complete circle. People usually travel by car, so they need to return to the area where they parked.

Carry your interests with you. If you're designing a walking tour for a particular group of people, lead them through areas that reflect their interests and hobbies. For instance, if you are designing a walking tour for sailors, your walking tour would include marine museums, harbors, anything that has to do with boats. If the walking tour is for children, you would want to include playgrounds, toy stores, pet stores.

Know when to stop. The longer you work on a tour the more you find out. It's almost like painting a picture—it's hard to know when to stop. Almost without exception, an area will give you more information than you ever expected, so the challenge is trying to refine and contain the information.

Angela Anderson, Landscape Architect

"A good walking tour will challenge people to think about the interdependence of our urban and natural environments. Some people only want to see the most pleasant side of a city, but a good walking tour will also pass through the buffer zones that move people from a downtown area, along highways (especially the strip development along highways, because it's unpleasant to move through that environment slowly), to a residential area and then into natural areas because that's how you really get a sense that many of our built environments disregard the human scale. When you walk next to a skyscraper or a freeway it's almost unbearable. You can't see or hear anything. Planners and developers rarely consider what people need spiritually to survive. Stark, mechanical environments are upsetting, and walking through these areas makes you more aware of how important it is to consider human proportion and scale. It's been said before, a walkable city is a livable city." Angela Anderson

Anderson works in the trail programs section of the Minnesota Department of Natural Resources. As the editor and program coordinator for *Trail*

Explorer, a publication for walkers and hikers, Anderson traveled throughout the state and developed walking tours that offered a blend of natural and rural experiences. Born and raised in Bavaria, West Germany, Anderson's tours included a number of European elements that added depth and character to the walking experience. Here are some of her ideas regarding the elements of a quality walking tour.

Give your walking tour a purpose. Walking is a form of exercise, but it's also a form of travel, a way to move from one point to another. Walking is not a goal, but a process. Walking tours should connect people with an area and move them to feel, or think, or act.

Begin the tour in an accessible, common area. In Europe, people used to gather and exchange products and ideas in an area of town known as "the commons." Walking tours should begin where people naturally gather, not at some distant, remote point. The starting point should have historic or cultural interest and should be convenient for the people who live and work in the area. Today, in the United States, parks can be perceived as commons, and so can population centers. In addition to being good starting points, parks are also good destinations.

Connect people with services. Walking tours should make it easy and convenient for people to walk and shop (rather than drive). Involve walkers in the day-to-day activities of an area. If they participate in local celebrations and festivals, they'll remember the area fondly because they were connected with the people in a very specific way.

Focus on an area's unique features. Connect walkers with what they're experiencing and give them a sense of belonging to the area. Let the people who live there help you with that. Ask them, Why do you live here? What gives this area its integrity? How is it different today? Residents can provide the inside information that will bring out the best of an area.

Design walking tours to help people slow down. You can't really experience much from a bus or a car because you're moving too fast to see things in detail. Walking helps you slow down and become aware of your micro-environment. It is very difficult to design a good walking tour. You have to provide a larger vision, yet capture the essence of a specific environment and highlight it with great care so that people can gain an appreciation for it.

Use quad maps for natural areas. Quad maps (U.S. Geological Survey quadrant maps) provide geological details such as altitude, forests, and lakes. Quad maps guide people by natural reference points, and this is especially important in remote areas void of human habitation. It helps to know where you're going, especially when no one is around.

Write a travel log. In your walking tour, you may want to include a comprehensive geological and cultural history of the area, a seasonal events calendar, an overview of local highlights, and lodging and transportation options.

Take pictures as you go. Include photographs of the different points of interest in your walking tour to support and illustrate the written word.

Bob Ripsin, Author of a Self-guided, Illustrated, Walking Tour Booklet

"I'm not an artist or a writer. I just started putting down what was there. I took photographs and then went home and started drawing some of the landmarks. I went through a lot of paper. Your mind's eye will tell you when it's right, when it's in proportion. I think illustrations are better than photographs because if there's a tree in the way, you can take it out of an illustration. You have a freedom with illustration that you don't have with photography. I also drew the maps and proportioned them with a ruler. I really enjoyed being down there by the river, sitting on one of those big metal utility boxes, drawing." Bob Ripsin

Bob Ripsin's curiosity has led him on a number of interesting and productive adventures throughout his life. He has pursued tap dancing, candle making, sewing (he made his daughter's prom dress), and working on model railroad dioramas (three-dimensional scenes). His project for the winter of 1989 was developing an illustrated walking tour of the St. Anthony Falls area. "I just happened to be walking down there one day," he explained, "and I became very curious. I saw all these old buildings with faded signs such as Pillsbury's Best and Gold Medal Flour and I wanted to know more about the companies that started here. I figured other people would feel the same way." Here is some of what Ripsin learned while writing *Your Guide To St. Anthony Falls Historic Sites and Parkways. (See Chapter 8.)*

Walking tours are good winter projects. If you're looking for something to do during the winter months, create a walking tour. It's a good time to do all the research because you work indoors at the library.

Be prepared to invest a lot of time. Tour developers spend anywhere from one to six months working part-time to complete the different phases of the project. You have to decide at the start if you want to invest that much time because it's a lot more work than you think.

Write about something that you care about. It's important to write about something that means something to you, that fascinates you in some way so that the tour is fascinating to other people. If you love the riverfront, write about it.

Be aware of copyright restrictions. If you want to use material in your walking tour that has already been published elsewhere, you may need to obtain permission from the publisher or author before reprinting the information. Be sure to comply with current fair use and copyright laws.

Hire out the work you can't do yourself. You don't have to own a lot of fancy equipment to finish a project like this. If you have a home computer, you can develop most of the walking tour on your equipment. Otherwise, you may have to hire someone to enter the text on a wordprocessing or typesetting machine. Local printers can print, fold, and staple your materials but you may want to do some of those tasks yourself to save money.

Be prepared to get different responses from people. Some people really value information in a walking tour—it's like giving them a thousand dollars. Others could care less about the area or the walking tour. It just doesn't interest them. You can't take it personally. You can't expect other people to share your interest in the history of an area.

Don't develop a walking tour to make money—do it to have fun. If you develop a walking tour to learn about something that interests you, then you won't be disappointed. Most people expect to pay a minimal fee for a walking tour booklet or brochure to cover production costs, but it's hard to make a profit on them. Encourage people to recycle the information after they've used it by passing it on to someone else.

Dot Lilja, Former Tour Guide, Audiocassette Tour Developer

"I particularly enjoyed a bus tour of Gettysburg because while we were looking at gravestones and monuments, we were listening to audiocassetes that featured story after story, with professional voices and sound effects. It was beautifully done. That's when I got the idea to do Tape Tours." Dot Lilja

Dot Lilja started *Tape Tours*, an enterprise that produced two self-guided audiocassette tours of downtown Minneapolis—an outdoor version along Nicollet Mall and an indoor version through the skyway system. At one time she also conducted custom-designed walking tours of Minneapolis for large and small groups of all ages, including school children. "Walking tours for children have to take place within a limited distance and time, and they have to take into consideration their ages and interests," she explained, "but those are some of the most interesting tours because children see things from a totally different perspective. Once a child noticed a hotel's customized imprint in a sand ashtray. I enjoy working with children because I always come away from a tour with a new viewpoint." In this section, Lilja shares what she learned about the walking tour business.

Take classes and learn about your subject. Informal community education classes in architecture and art history, and tours sponsored by your local downtown council or historical society will give you enough information to get you started. The classes will give you a foundation in the various disciplines, and then it's up to you to fill in the details through extensive research.

Talk with other tour directors. Participate in tours in different cities and observe how they've made the information interesting. Also, talk with your local tour managers association—people from local businesses and organizations who give tours. Find out what's already available, and collaborate when possible on tour promotions.

Consider audiocassette tours. It is easier for people to listen to (rather than read) something when they walk. Also, audiocassettes are great for nonreaders and for people with disabilities who are using their hands to move wheelchairs or push walkers. Although the younger generation is very comfortable with headsets, some older people feel very conspicuous with them, so you may have to also provide printed text. Audiocassettes should only be used in safe, secure areas since personal safety becomes an issue when people are listening to headphones and not to the sounds in their immediate environment.

Another issue for audiocassette tour developers to consider is that technology continues to change. Changes in the design of tape recorders, cassette tapes, or batteries may make your initial equipment obsolete.

Figure out a marketing and distribution system for your tour. Centralized information centers for visitors are usually willing to carry free walking tour brochures or booklets but resist projects that require cash transactions or equipment rentals. Prominent information displays or kiosks in convention or shopping centers will promote your walking tour, but if equipment rental is involved, you may have to consider the additional expense of hiring an employee. It is important to develop a reliable, cost effective distribution system during the planning stage, before you've invested a significant amount of time or money.

Base the length of the tour on the audience. Tours for children typically last from thirty to forty-five minutes at the most. Tours for adults last one or two hours, depending on their interests. An hour seems to be just about the right length of time for most people.

Make tours accessible to everyone. Some of the newer buildings are accessible, but the older ones aren't. Some of the skyways are not accessible to people in wheelchairs because there are doors and stairs that are impossible to negotiate. It's helpful to plan a route with points of interest and accessibility in mind.

Field test your tour with friends. Ask your friends to take your tour and give you comments. People interpret directions very differently. You don't realize the misunderstandings that can occur in written or verbal directions. Some people have trouble telling left from right, and other people simply don't listen to directions. Field testing your product will help you give more explicit directions.

Be prepared to revise your tour. Tours of historical places such as Gettysburg or Independence Mall in Philadelphia aren't likely to change significantly over the years, but if you do a walking tour of a downtown area, things are likely to change before you even get the tour on the market. Identify points on the tour by unchangeable landmarks such as parks or monuments. Make sure your landmarks are close together—people need to be assured every so often that they are where they should be.

Be aware of tour bias. A tour developed by hotel operators usually includes architectural points of interest at different hotels, and at hotel shops and restaurants. A tour sponsored by a downtown business association or a historical society will present information from a particular point of view. Define your bias so that people know what they will be seeing and why.

Trillium

CHAPTER 7

Looking Ahead

With over 4,000 miles of walking trails throughout the state, Minnesota is well positioned to become one of the most popular walking spots in the world. The effort that began in the late 1800s to create and maintain public walkways is alive and well today. However, a number of cultural changes must occur if we are to successfully integrate walking back into the daily routine of life.

Rather than looking to someone else to make these changes, walkers, like the turn-of-the-century public land advocates, have to direct some of their time, talent, and financial resources to the work ahead, or it won't get done.

What can you personally do to make your community more walkable? Here are some of the issues that have been raised by people who were interviewed for this book. Some of the issues are questions posed for solution. Others are solutions in need of action.

GREENWAY DEVELOPMENT

As stated in the introduction, a greenway is a path that connects residential areas with business, retail, education, cultural, and recreation centers. Years ago, only a handful of avid backpackers, bird watchers, and bikers were concerned about greenway and trail development. Today, a growing number of walkers and hikers in just about every community have joined the effort to promote greenway development. More greenways are needed, especially in densely populated areas.

Walkers have an opportunity to influence greenway and trail development by 1) using trails throughout the entire state; 2) participating in community planning; 3) directing financial donations to trail development; and 4) lobbying, in collaboration with other trails users (bikers, cross-country skiers), for trail improvements.

Although trail improvement proposals are typically followed by polite discussion, trail *development* proposals usually generate heated, emotional debate. As the greenway movement gains momentum, trail advocates and opponents throughout the United States are asking the same questions: Is trail usage by walkers and other groups a short-lived fad, or will it continue to be an important form of outdoor recreation? To what extent should trails be maintained and improved? Should more greenways and trails be developed? Should abandoned railway lines be used for pedestrian and bike traffic or light-rail transit? Should trail surfaces remain grass or dirt, be covered with wood-chips, or be paved? What impact will trail development and usage have on the environment? On neighborhoods? On property values? On trail users?

Arne Stefferud, park planner for the Metropolitan Council, a government coordinating body for the seven-county metro area, sees an increase in the number of city councils and resident task forces that are 1) developing a coordinated community trail plan that links schools, parks, libraries, and shopping centers; 2) coordinating their trail-development plans with those of other communities so that people can walk or bike from city to city; and 3) requiring developers to include extensive trail sytems in all their residential and business developments.

"When some of the older subdivisions were built, sidewalks weren't installed because planners assumed that people would drive their cars to get from one point to another," Stefferud stated. "But things have changed. People prefer to walk or bike two or three blocks to do their errands. We're seeing an increase in the number of people who take walks or ride their bikes after work and on weekends, and we're also seeing a 7 percent annual increase in the number of people who use the regional parks."

Newer, rapidly growing communities have the luxury of developing trails through residential and business districts without much opposition. In recent years, there has been persistent opposition to trail development in older, more settled communities because residents fear 1) a decrease in property values if trails are built near or through their property; 2) an increase in crime; 3) an increase in the number of trail users, which could result in overcongestion; 4) an increase in the number of accidents due to mixed usage (walkers, bikers, skaters, pets); and 5) an increase in the amount of litter and natural waste products in the area.

The conclusions of a report titled *The Burke-Gilman Trail's Effect on Property Values and Crime*, developed by the Seattle Engineering Department in 1987, did not support the fears typically expressed by trail opponents. The value of residential and commercial properties along trailways *increased*. Crime along the trailways continued to reflect the rate of crime in the surrounding neighborhoods.

Stefferud added, "Yes, there will be more people using the trails, but the people will be your family, friends, and neighbors. Trails give people a chance to say hello to each other, a chance to get to know other people in the community. Trails are getting neighborhoods back together again."

Bob Hill, Loop Trail coordinator for the city of Minnetonka, observed, "The trails are wide enough to accommodate bikers and hikers. Motorized vehicles are not allowed on the trails (except those used by people with physical disabilities). In addition, Minnetonka's trail system, which is maintained year-round, is regularly patrolled by police and maintenance staff. Trail users of all ages, for the most part, are very courteous, considerate people. If there is a problem, we'll get on it right away, but people seem to appreciate the trails, and they're glad other people are using them. We have had few if any problems, not even with litter. People who use the trails seem to care about keeping them clean.

"In recent years, trail access has been used as a selling point for residential homes. Now, some people won't even consider buying a home that doesn't have trail access within a block of where they live, and we are starting to get petitions from neighborhoods who want immediate access to the trail system."

Long before greenways had a name or a following, the Minnesota Department of Natural Resources had the foresight to secure abandoned railroad beds and begin a number of "rail-to-trail" conversions throughout the state. Paul Swenson, former director of Trails and Waterways stated, "We've started segments of trails throughout the state and have plans to acquire more land and eventually link these trail systems."

Swenson identified a number of factors that influence trail development. "The roles of the various governments involved is a major factor," he explained. "At the state level, we've interpreted our role to mean that we provide the long distance linear corridors throughout the state, while the county and city units of governments provide the loops that connect these trails. That's the theory. It doesn't always work that way. Some of the counties and cities simply don't have the tax base or staff to develop trails," he said. "And then you have larger, more established counties with a solid tax base, plenty of staff, and the capability to develop all kinds of trails.

"Another reality is that the history of trail development in Minnesota is one of special interest groups," he added. "The groups who have been very organized, like snowmobilers, have done very well. There are 12,500 miles of snowmobile trails in this state. We know walking is more popular, but we don't see any major thrust in Minnesota outside the Superior Hiking Trail because walkers are not organized. Snowmobilers, and now horseback riders, are very well organized financially and socially, but for some reason, bikers, walkers, and cross-country skiers are not as adamant about their needs.

"Special interest groups have had a tremendous influence on what we do," he continued, "but we need to focus on the larger picture. There is only so much land and so much money. It's impossible to develop separate trails for different users, so the trail users are going to have to get along with each other and share the trails. Simple rules of ettiquette go a long way.

"Minnesota has been, and will continue to be, more forward-looking than other states," he concluded. "I think it's very encouraging to see so much interest in the environment and outdoor recreation. There are a lot of trail segments in this state, but to finish what we've started we'll need continued interest in trail development, more people using the trails, more funding from the state legislature, government agency collaboration on all levels, and more volunteers."

PUBLIC AND PRIVATE PARTNERSHIPS

A number of park systems, faced with decreasing tax dollars to maintain and expand their programs, are seeking alternate sources of funding. Private donations, memorials, and volunteers are keeping the parks and trails open, but to improve or expand upon existing facilities is going to require a comprehensive effort that involves the entire community.

There are at least two private-public partnership development models. In the first model, the public owns the land and leases the land to a private enterprise. In the second model, the private enterprise owns the land and leases the land to the public.

One example of the second arrangement is the Opus 2 development in Minnetonka. Ann Perry, Minnetonka planning director, explained: "The Opus 2 project was originally conceived back in 1974 as a true mixed-use development that would include residential, office, and retail areas so that people would be able to more or less function within their community. A secondary road and trail system was developed to provide golf cart or small vehicle access to the different sites. The separation of the secondary road from the main road was achieved through the construction of bridges for cars and underpasses for pedestrians.

"Over the years, the land use has changed," she added. "There isn't a retail component, some of the residential areas were converted to office and industrial areas, and the secondary road system has become more of a pedestrian and bicycle trail."

The Opus Corporation and the city of Minnetonka are partners in the development and maintenance of the trail system. Opus owns the lands under the trails, paid for the construction of the trails, and is responsible for additional trail improvements such as lighting. Minnetonka has an easement or right to use the trails (so the trails are public trails) and the city is responsible for trail promotion and maintenance.

"The city benefited from this partnership in a number of ways," Perry stated. "Our residents have access to some large natural and development areas that you can only get to by walking. It was one of the first trail systems in our city, and it gave our trail development efforts a real boost. The Opus trail system has become a backup for our own trail system, because eventually we're going to link these trails with other trails in the community."

What are the benefits of such an arrangement to the private or corporate partner? Bob Worthington, executive director of Governmental Affairs of the Opus Corporation, was involved in the original design and construction of the Opus project. "Of course the immediate benefit of the project," he stated, "is that people who live or work at Opus have access to the trails, but beyond that, investing in trail development is a way for developers to give something back to the community. The trails also provide tremendous visibility for the companies in the development.

"Up until about ten years ago the government provided incentives for developers to invest in the community," Worthington explained. "The cities were able to sell bonds or make grants available to developers for improvements such as trails. Over time, the developer was able to pay the city back and retire the bonds, but those incentives are no longer available. In today's economy, there's a tremendous amount of risk involved in putting together a five hundred acre development, and some developers are finding it very difficult to commit large sums to things like trails, ponds, or related types of amenities. Some cities are willing to pick up the expense of road and other public improvements surrounding a development and share in the financial risk of a large project, but not to the extent that they did in the past. Developers are more willing to pursue public and private partnerships in the larger cities and suburbs because there's less risk in those areas and some incentives are still available.

"In some of the smaller communities, there is a trend toward the 'privatization' of public facilities," he added. "These are usually one-shot public works or recreation types of projects that don't involve developers. Small cities usually can't afford to build large facilities like sports arenas or community centers without raising taxes, so the private sector steps in, builds the facility, and then leases the facility to the public for its use. The public sector rents and is responsible for operating the facility, but you have a public facility built with private rather than public dollars."

Ann Perry added, "If you're a community that's trying to create a good deal for the developer and a good deal for the city, then you're much more willing to negotiate. If you're a community that's willing to take development at any cost, then you probably won't get anything in return. We now require the dedication of trail and sidewalk easements as part of any development. We've had disagreements with developers over where the trails should be located, but developers expect to provide trails and don't mind doing so, because they know they will benefit their business.

"Cities have a right to ask for trail development, but to ask for one that doesn't go anywhere, or isn't part of a larger trail development plan doesn't make any sense," she continued. "Trails should link people with community facilities and services. Once the trails are constructed, it is the responsibility of the city to maintain them. Cities need to be aware of what those costs are because you don't want a deteriorating trail system that promotes a negative attitude toward trail development. It takes the commitment of the entire community to implement and maintain a successful trail development project. The Opus model, which has been very successful, was used to develop a trail system for the new Carlson Center that will eventually join other trails in the Minnetonka Trail Corridor System."

"We hear from people all the time," Perry stated, "who will call and report that they saw a deer, an egret, or other wildlife while walking the Opus trails. People from all over the metro area use the trails, and they walk away with a good feeling about the city."

PEDESTRIAN PLANNING

The development of more greenways through public bonds or public and private partnerships will provide safer and more interesting walking opportunities for people of all ages and abilities, but what about the streets and sidewalks that already exist?

Jay Walljasper, editor of *Utne Reader*, a Minnesota magazine that provides summaries of the "best of the alternative press," stated, "I think more people would walk if it was safer to walk, but every time you cross the street you risk your life. Pedestrians are viewed as a nuisance, as a barrier to the free flow of traffic. I don't think walking is ever taken into account in city planning. There isn't enough time to cross the street—you get about four steps off the curb and the 'don't walk' light starts flashing. I can rush across the street, but older people, parents pushing strollers, and young children must find it a terrifying experience. With the addition of the 'right on red' ordinance, it's just about impossible to walk across the street because traffic is moving all the time. People in city departments of transportation and engineering could give us a break by making walking a safer, more pleasureable activity.

"Once you're in a car behind the wheel," Walljasper continued, "it's easy to view pedestrians as something from another planet or another era. The roads are constructed so that you can get up to 35 miles an hour in the city, and when a pedestrian starts crossing the street, you think 'get out of my way.'

Sometimes even people who walk quite a bit get into that way of thinking. When you're in a car, you want to get where you're going as fast as you can, and you don't want anything to get in your way. When you're in a car, you don't think like a pedestrian."

Four cities—Boston, Philadelphia, Ottawa, and Tucson—have taken the lead in making it safer to walk in urban areas. Groups of pedestrians (people who regularly walk in motorized traffic) and walkers (people who regularly walk in malls, trails, and greenways) have joined forces to identify and improve hazardous intersections and increase the number of pedestrian walkways and bridges in these cities. Some communities are in the process of establishing a "pedestrian advocate," an employee in the city planning department who represents the needs of pedestrians in all city issues that may affect them.

"Sidewalks are the basic building block of human civilization because they allow you to walk and engage your sense of wonder and imagination," Walljasper continued. "When you live in a neighborhood where people walk, you meet people on a face-to-face basis, and you can talk or smile. When you're in a car, the best you can do is beep your horn. I don't think you can have any type of relationship with nature at all through a windshield.

"We should focus on meeting our own needs for energy conservation. How difficult can it be to build more bike paths and walkways or add mass transportation systems along existing highways?"

YOUNG WALKERS

Angela Anderson, landscape architect with the Minnesota Department of Natural Resources and mother of two children, is concerned about the barriers created for both children and adults in "car-oriented" societies. Born and raised in Bavaria, West Germany, Anderson respects the way Europeans encourage independent mobility of people of all ages through the development and maintenance of walkways and trails in conjunction with good public transportation systems.

"Being a child, a teenager, a car-less adult, or a senior citizen in America is very difficult," she explained. "We are a car-oriented society, and if you don't have a car, you're disconnected from many things. You're dependent on friends or family to take you to and from your destination and who wants to be so inadequate?

"In Germany," she stated, "you see groups of teenagers walking and biking together. On Sundays, families and friends go for walks through urban environments to parks or well-managed rural landscapes that have been there hundreds of years. But here, things are so far apart. Even in the urban areas, it's incredible how spread out things are. It's difficult and often unpleasant to walk from place to place."

Even though Minnesota's trails are cited as one of the best systems in the nation, Anderson views the trails as "fragmented." "If you don't know any different," she stated, "you don't see it that way, but to have to drive your car to a trail, walk it, and then drive home doesn't make any sense. You should be able to step out your front door and walk in a pleasant environment. You should be able to walk or have mass transit available to go to the grocery store, or to the library, to government offices, or to the theatre."

Anderson believes that greenway development should be based on a hierarchy of needs. "Most of all," she explained, "greenways are needed where people live, and where people will use them for everyday trips and entertainment. Then, greenways should be developed to parks and trails in outlying areas, in natural settings, that are easy to reach and close to home. Finally, greenways should link urban areas with state parks and remote areas.

"I understand why kids and teenagers are always talking on the phone," she added. "They can't transport themselves and they are stuck. They have to ask to be driven somewhere. Imagine if we adults had to depend on someone else to get us to work, to the store, and to social events. Children and young adults need to be able to safely transport themselves, need to have some independence."

There are a number of ways that adults can encourage people under sixteen years of age to become avid walkers: 1) support the development of more greenways to vital places like schools, playgrounds, and libraries; 2) offer fitness walking classes as part of physical education programs; 3) take regular walks with young people through nature centers, urban areas, and forests; 4) take low-cost walking vacations with children and young adults in Minnesota; and 5) incorporate walking in major celebrations (a birthday walk at a child's favorite park, a "coming of age" graduation hike along the Superior Hiking Trail).

"In this day and age," Anderson continued, "it should be mandatory for community development plans to include alternative forms of transportation to the private automobile, and allow for walking, biking, or public transportation. In order to get children into walking, one has to start at an early age with short, exploratory walks, leading to longer walks as they get older.

"Children need time to build their observation skills and interest," she continued, "and learn that their legs are meant to transport them. They have to feel proud of their accomplishments and most of all, they have to see their parents walking. I was very proud of my eight-year-old when she suggested to her babysitter to walk to downtown Stillwater and later take the bus back, as we often do. She proudly reported to me later that she had to show the babysitter how to use the bus. Children have to learn and experience that there are enjoyable alternatives to the private automobile."

FITNESS WALKING IN THE SCHOOLS

In May 1990, the fourth-grade students at Groveland Park Elementary School in Saint Paul participated in a fitness and racewalking clinic provided by volunteers from Walk Sport America, Inc., and the TC Walkers. During a one-week period, students in Sue Sajevic's physical education classes participated in racewalking skill training and drills. The high point of the week

Pasque

occurred on the last day of the clinic when all of the students participated in a .75-mile racewalk around the school grounds and were judged on correct race-walking form. The pilot program also offered Saturday morning racewalk clinics throughout the summer to all the family members of the students in the class so that 1) the students could practice and refine their racewalking skills; 2) parents and children could develop a shared interest in walking; and 3) more parents and children would participate in community-sponsored walking events. The pilot program is now being implemented throughout the Saint Paul School District.

Sara Struve, president of Walk Sport America, Inc., explained: "School-based racewalking programs don't require any equipment except a comfortable pair of walking shoes. You don't need large athletic complexes or protective equipment. All you need is a long level segment of a sidewalk or dirt trail.

"By getting children involved at a young age," she stated, "we hope to start them on a lifelong fitness path, thereby offsetting the effects of TV viewing and other sedentary pastimes.

"Racewalking is a lifetime sport," Struve added, "that can provide the necessary vigorous cardiovascular workout that tones the heart and all of the other muscles. A handful of students may go on to become competitive racewalkers, but the majority of the students will be learning the correct fitness walking form—their ticket to a lifetime of healthy pleasures."

EDUCATING THE SENSES

Philip Larson, sculptor, educator, and father, believes the development of more greenways should not be based on the "fad" of walking for exercise, but deeply rooted in a greater and ever-enlarging appreciation of nature. He believes all high school students in Minnesota should be required to take a natural science course that includes using the five senses.

"I'm astounded at the number of college-level students who don't know anything about their environment," he commented. "They don't know the difference between a red oak and a white oak. They can't name one species of moth. They can't name one species of butterfly other than Monarch.

"They may know something about the human spleen," he added, "but they don't know about the human face. They don't understand or appreciate the small, magnificent details that make each face a work of art or qualities that distinguish Japanese from Chinese.

"We need to look at science in an entirely new way," he recommended, "and blend physiology with astronomy, geology, biology, and anthropology. We need to educate the senses so that we can see, hear, touch, smell, and taste with knowledge and passion! We need to move classrooms outdoors so that students are learning about real trees, right in their own neighborhood.

"There is a commonly held belief that art comes from art," he added. "However, even in our century, art comes from nature. Art comes from *observable* nature, like looking at a stone when it's wet and when it's dry, or at a red pine that's over 120 feet tall, or at all the heaving stones on Lake Superior that were arranged by the glaciers. The only way to experience some of these things is by walking to them, around them, over them, through them. Greenways will be the classrooms of the future."

INCLUSIVE WALKING PARTNERSHIPS AND CLUBS

In recent years, people with physical or developmental disabilities have finally gained access to parks and trails, and many have become avid trail users. Mo Fahnestock, adaptive recreation supervisor of the City of Bloomington, observed, "It's easy to build accessible ramps, trails, and restrooms, but that's only part of the issue. The marketing, recruitment, and registration strategies of a walking club control participation. Most people who are typically excluded from programs don't make it through this beginning phase because there are so many physical and emotional barriers to their participation.

"It's important for walking programs and clubs to have a mission," Fahnestock stated, "and to define their goals and objectives. Who are you going to serve? What services are you going to provide? That's when you begin to include or exclude people from your membership."

TRAIL MANAGEMENT

Larry Killien and Martha Reger, Region VI area trails and waterways supervisors for the Department of Natural Resources, manage the Gateway Segment of the Willard Munger Trail and the Luce Line Trail. Over the years, they've had some interesting and, at times, frustrating experiences with trail management issues. Here are some of their recommendations:

Become a trail ranger. Martha Reger explained, "We routinely survey the trail, but we can't be out there every day. We depend on people who use the trails to call us if something is wrong. Please call and report injured or dead animals, trees or branches that have fallen, or people who misuse the trail. If you see a motorcycle on a nonmotorized trail, get as much information as you can (license number, description of the vehicle) and report the incident to the agency that operates the park, your conservation officer, sheriff, or the local police."

Educate your community about how to dispose of tires and household refuse. "Last year people dumped over twenty-two hundred tires and four dumptruck loads of refuse on the trails," said Larry Killien. "Trails are occasional dumping grounds for yard waste, remodeling materials, appliances, just about anything you can imagine. People who don't use the trails think they are large open landfills. If you see someone dumping, please take down their license number and call us. Litter is not as much of a problem because most people are very concerned about keeping the environment free of refuse. It's really only a handful of people who think they have a right to get rid of their larger items on public land."

Respect the rights of other people who are using the trails. "Because tax dollars are used to build the trails," Killien continued, "users think 'this belongs to me' when in fact the trails belong to all users. Be considerate of other users. If someone is moving faster than you, step aside so they can get by. As you turn corners, you may want to cough or say something out loud like 'walker on your left' to warn the people you might be approaching or overtaking."

Report all trespassing violations. "Some people who live near the trails mistakenly believe they have a right to cut down trail vegetation, or use the land around the trail to plant a garden or build a horseshoe pit," Killien added. "Usually there is a one hundred-foot trail corridor along each trail that is reserved for public, not private use. Please report any trespassing violations to us."

Reger added, "Once a person called and reported seeing thistle on the trail, which is considered a noxious weed in some cities and needs to be destroyed. We went out and were spraying the weed when another trail user approached and was appalled that we were using chemicals to destroy a plant that birds use as feed. So please understand that at times we get caught in the middle. Some people don't understand that we let natural vegetation grow along the corridor to attract wildlife. Some people have taken it upon themselves to landscape the corridors because they don't want to see or hear wildlife from their home. People have very different ideas about how the trails should be used and managed."

Teach young people to respect trail facilities. "Last year we had to replace numerous trail signs that were stolen, smashed, or used for target practice," Killien reported. "All the money that is spent on replacing and repairing damaged equipment could be used to develop and maintain more trails. If you are a parent or teacher, talk with young children and teenagers about the importance of trail facilities and the cost to maintain them. Please report any vandalism you see along the trail. Remember, the tax dollars you save may be your own."

In addition to the previous issues identified by people during interviews for this book, here are a number of issues identified by the authors.

PERSONAL SAFETY DEVICES

Walking in remote, isolated areas does wonders for the spirit, but it can jeopardize the physical safety of walkers. Why has so much attention been placed on developing alarms for houses and cars, but not for people?

Minnesota is known for its advanced technology. One of the greatest contributions that could be made before the end of the decade is the development of an affordable, reliable, personal safety device that could alert people in the immediate area that someone needed help and send a distress signal from anywhere in the state to a transfer station, where it would then be confirmed and forwarded to the nearest 911 emergency station.

Walkers who were lost, injured, or in danger would be able to signal for help; on a much larger scale, such a device would make it difficult for a number of crimes to occur.

PARK TRANSPORTATION

Mass transit and light-rail systems are designed to move people to and from metro and suburban areas so they can work or go to school without using the automobile. When designing mass transportation systems, little thought is given to moving people to and from parks. Most of the walking sites identified in this book are not available by greenway or bus, and are therefore only available to people who own cars.

A park transportation system should be developed, either as part of a larger mass transportation plan, or as an independent bus or van line. A park transportation system would not only reduce the amount of air pollution caused by car emissions, it would enable non-car owners (and visitors without private transportation) to access state, county, and city parks, nature centers, and trails. Ideally, a park transporation system would be able to transport people and bikes, strollers, wheelchairs, and cross-country skis.

TRAIL IMPROVEMENTS

In the past, trails through forests and prairies were primarily used by hikers who carried water, food, and a compass. A number of features should be added to the trails to make them more usable by walkers.

Provide updated trail maps. Trail maps range from elaborate quad maps that contain geological details and altitudes to hand-drawn maps that are not drawn to scale. Trail maps should face north, not east, west, or south. Most maps are outdated and do not include the most recently added trails. As a result, walkers may arrive at a five-trail junction that is marked as a two-trail junction and have to select a trail without knowing how long the trail is or where it leads. Getting lost in a forest on a hot, sultry day without water or a compass can turn a two-hour afternoon walk into a six-hour nightmare.

Map development and revision is typically a very low budget priority for most park and recreation departments and nature centers. There are a number of solutions to this problem: 1) park and recreation boards could make map revision a higher priority; 2) walkers who are surveyors, cartographers, typesetters, or printers could assist with map development; and 3) walkers could direct their financial donations to a map revision fund.

Make updated trail maps available at all hours of the day. Most trail maps are available through a visitor center or park office. People who walk before or after office hours are unable to obtain the information they need to fully enjoy self-guided tours or walking trails. One solution is to build outdoor, water-proof map boxes. Some parks use rural mailboxes on a post with a simple sign that says "trail maps." Keeping outdoor map boxes well stocked would make it easy for people to walk the trails early in the morning or late in the day.

Develop standards for trail signs. Very few trail junctions along state, county, or city trails are marked. If they are marked, the symbol or informa-tion offered is usually not helpful because it's outdated or doesn't provide enough information to guide the walker.

There are a number of trail junction sign systems in use throughout the state. "You are here" information posts include a map of the entire trail system and a colored dot marking your current position. Numbered trail junctions are designed to be used with a trail map. Trail names ("Oak Trail," "Marsh Trail") are usually posted along the trail route and at major trail junctions. Trail letters (A, B, C) are often posted along the trail route or at major trail junctions.

Most park personnel believe their trails are "very well marked." However, park personnel are usually so familiar with the trails they can walk them in the dark. They can easily distinguish a main path from a side path, a maintenance road from a dirt path, a cross-country ski trail from a hiking trail, but a walker who has never been on the trail before sees five trails at a junction, not two. A considerable amount of valuable time can be wasted following a trail that leads to a remote maintenance shed. Every trail at every junction should be marked. If it's an unused maintenance trail, it should be marked as such. If it's a trail used by cross-country skiers in the winter, it should be marked. To the average walker, they all look the same.

Minnesota has led the way in trail and greenway development for over a century. Developing standards for trail junction signs would make it much easier and far more enjoyable for everyone to use the trails. Road and street signs have to meet certain standards. Why not trail signs?

Developing trail sign standards will not be an easy task, because walkers who will be reading the signs include visitors from other countries, nonreaders, people who have trouble reading maps, and people who are visually impaired. Alternatives such as color-coding the trails should be considered.

Add more level, wide, paved paths. Dirt, grass, wood-chip, and sand trails are not accessible to people who use strollers or wheelchairs. Accessible trails should be at least six feet wide, paved with asphalt, and have a low grade. Young children, older adults, and people of all ages with physical disabilities need accessible trails.

Add more accessible water pumps and restrooms along the trails. Unlike bikers who can cover a significant distance in an hour, walkers typically cover 2 to 3 miles per hour. Water pumps and restrooms along the trails are either nonexistent or too far apart. Ideally, portable or stationery accessible restrooms should be available every 2 to 5 miles along the trail.

Provide more environmental interpretation. The best way to learn about a park is to take a guided tour with a naturalist. Some parks provide brief videos that describe the park's wildlife, vegetation, and topography. Information posts along the trail offer people a chance to learn as they walk. Too many information posts would detract from the experience of being in the woods, but having a rest station or information post area every couple of miles would refresh the mind and body.

GIVING BACK

Most of the previously mentioned issues must be addressed by communities, but there is also a need for individuals to personally and directly support park and trail development. There are many ways to become involved.

Become a park volunteer. Work in a nature center, or help coordinate a Volksmarch. Organize a walk patrol to ensure the safety and well-being of people on the trails. Donate your time to help clear, maintain, or beautify the trails. Offer your personal talents and skills to improve the parks and trails.

Become familiar with Minnesota wildlife. Take free courses offered through the parks and nature centers. Learn about the environmental issues facing native plants and animals. Let park personnel know if you find injured animals or damaged vegetation along a trail. Volunteers are needed to assist with bird recovery and prairie restoration programs.

Direct annual donations to your favorite park or trail system. Parks and nature centers typically have long-range development plans, and private donations are used to fund one or more of the projects that are on the drawing board. Some park systems direct private donations into one general fund, and other parks have "wish lists" that enable donors to direct their funds to specific projects. Donors with a particular project in mind might have to contact a number of parks to see if they have any similar project in the planning stages.

If you own any land, consider donating it in your will to your favorite park system. The land can be converted into a natural area, or it can be traded for another piece of property along a trail line. (For specific information about volunteer and donation opportunities, refer to the "Giving Back" section of each walking site in chapter 9.)

CHAPTER 8

Resources for Walkers

One of the best ways to learn about resources for walkers is to explore the indoor and outdoor walking sites in chapter 9. Many of the sites identified in this book offer walking programs, clubs, seminars, or tours. Talk with other walkers to find out where they walk, shop, and travel. Another way to keep in touch with what's happening is to read articles that pertain to walking in the sports section of the newspaper and in local and national magazines.

How can you locate resources for walkers when you travel? First, call the city's Visitor's Center or Chamber of Commerce to find out if they know of any organized walking clubs or groups. You may also want to call the following resources because they are usually aware of community services and programs.

- Nature centers and outdoor education programs
- Sporting goods stores that sell walking clothes and equipment
- Park and recreation departments (city, county)
- State department of natural resources
- Shopping malls
- Local hospitals
- Private health clubs, YMCA, YWCA
- Bookstores or travel stores that sell walking books, maps, and equipment
- Public school district or community education programs
- Local colleges and universities—departments of physical education

Here is a sampler of the resources available to walkers in Minnesota. Again, this is not a comprehensive list. New resources are being developed all the time, so you'll have to do a little sleuthing to find out what's currently available in an area. This chapter is divided into three categories of resources:

- Basic reference materials
- Walking clubs, organizations, programs, and publications
- Walking sticks

BASIC REFERENCE MATERIALS

If you're visiting Minnesota, or if you're a resident about to explore another area of the state, you may want to obtain the following publications. These booklets and maps will provide you with a comprehensive visual and narrative overview of walking opportunities in the metro area and throughout the state. All of these publications are free and are excellent reference guides.

Minnesota Office of Tourism: 375 Jackson Street, 250 Skyway Level, St. Paul, MN 55101. Phone: 800/657-3700 (Phone is answered M-F 8 A.M. to 5 P.M.).

The Minnesota Office of Tourism's Travel Information Center offers a variety of guides to restaurants, resorts, hotels and motels, campgrounds, inns, and special events. It also offers regional guides for activities such as fishing and cross-country skiing.

Official Minnesota Highway Map—This is one of the most important resources for finding your way around Minnesota. This map identifies state parks, wayside parks, and historic sites as well as mass transportation options into each city. This map is revised at least every other year, so be sure to get the most recent edition.

Explore Minnesota Canoeing, Hiking, and Backpacking—This publication offers a range of walking experiences, from short interpretive trails, to day hikes, to wilderness backpacking treks. This guide offers a sampler of fifty great trails throughout Minnesota's state parks and forests, Chippewa and Superior national forests, Voyageurs National Park, and Isle Royale National Park.

Explore Minnesota Accessibility—This is a comprehensive guide to Minnesota's accessible parks, camps, sports programs, transportation, and special events for people with physical and/or developmental disabilities. This twelve-page booklet designates a letter code for the facilities available at each site, such as paved or hard-packed trails, ramped entryways, wheelchair-accessible restrooms, handicap parking, doors that are at least thirty-one inches wide, large print on signs, interpreters for visitors with hearing impairments, tape cassettes for visitors with visual impairments, drinking fountains that are thirty-three inches from the floor, and wheelchair-accessible campgrounds, picnic areas, showers, and visitor centers. It's also a great primer for learning about accessibility issues.

Minnesota Department of Natural Resources (DNR): Information Center, 500 Lafayette Road, St. Paul, MN 55155-4040. Twin Cities: 612/296-4776; Toll-free in Minnesota: 800/652-9747; TDD: 612/296-5484.

Minnesota State Parks—Naturally—This free twenty-four-page handy booklet contains a brief description of each state park and a statewide map, color coded by regions, and is the best visual guide to the state park system. The back of the booklet contains the address, phone number, and facilities description for each state park. Comprehensive trail maps are available at each state park, or you can order them directly (up to ten at a time) through the DNR Information Center.

Trails and Waterways—This map-size brochure identifies all the hiking trails in Minnesota with a brief description of trail facilities and mileages. It provides an important, easy-to-read visual overview of the state's trail system.

Minnesota Trail Explorer—The Trail Explorer provides self-guided weekend hiking tours of the various regions in Minnesota, including a geological and cultural history of each area, seasonal events, state park and state trail highlights, and lodging and transportation options. Back issues of this publication are available at no charge. There is a charge, however, for ordering ten issues

Arrowhead

or more. (Special rates for classrooms are available.)

Open the Outdoors: A Guide to Recreation Opportunities and Their Accessibility — This booklet provides information about accessible state parks, state trails, state forests, fishing and hunting opportunities, and other organizations in the state that provide outdoor experiences for people with physical and developmental disabilities. This is an important resource for people who use walking aides such as wheelchairs, strollers, or walkers.

CLUBS, ORGANIZATIONS, PROGRAMS, AND PUBLICATIONS

If you enjoy walking, then you may enjoy learning about orienteering, a compass-guided sport. Or, you may want to take a long walk at midnight and learn about the environment. Here are some Minnesota resources that may help you maintain and expand your interest in walking.

Autumn Hiking Adventures: Hennepin Parks, 12615 County Road 9, Box 47320, Plymouth, MN 55447-0320. Phone: 612/559-9000.

The Autumn Hiking Adventures program runs from September through October. Walkers can pick up a "Hiking Verification Card" at any of the parks and join the program. Special wood-chip or turf trails are marked at the different parks. When walkers complete a trail, they mark their card with a special trail stamp (stampers are located along the designated trails). After completing any four of the eleven designated trails, walkers present their card to any nature center or outdoor recreation center. Completed cards entitle walkers to special discounts on a walking staff and an annual Autumn Hiking Adventures medallion. Walkers who complete a card are also eligible for a drawing for different walking-related prizes every year.

Bicentennial Bicycling/Hiking/Tour Maps: City of Bloomington, Department of Community Services Park and Recreation Division, 2215 West Old Shakopee Road, Bloomington, MN 55431. Phone: 612/881-5811.

A series of five walking tour pamphlets were developed to commemorate the city's bicentennial. The tours are (A) Old Shakopee Trail, (B) Lyndale-Oxboro, (C) Old Bloomington, (D) Bloomington Ferry, and (E) Hyland-Bush Lake. The free pamphlets contain maps with historic narration and point-to-point mileage. The tours vary in length from 5 to 12 miles and can be walked in segments.

Dayton's Bluff — Take A Hike: Dayton's Bluff District 4 Community Council, 678 East Seventh Street, St. Paul, MN 55106. Phone: 612/722-2075.

This informal walking group gets together on the first Saturday of every month at Mounds Park (at the corner of Earl and Mounds Boulevard). Hikers, cross-country skiers, and recreational trail supporters are invited to join the group as they explore trails in the Dayton's Bluff area.

Downtown Guide and Atlas: Saint Paul: Saint Paul Downtown Council, 600 North Central Tower, St. Paul, MN 55101.

This general guide to downtown Saint Paul includes three walking tours (public art tour, historic buildings tour, and Lowertown tour). The book is available through the Downtown Council and local bookstores. Price varies.

Fitness In Style: 643 Seventh Avenue South, Hopkins, MN 55343. Phone: 612/935-0486.

Fitness In Style publishes the *Walk Connection* three times a year, a newsletter for racewalkers that includes a schedule of upcoming races and other events of interest to walkers. The annual subscription rate is $3. Fitness In Style also offers fitness consulting, aerobics classes, racewalk clinics, racewalk analysis and training programs (video tape analysis is available), and fitness classes for children and adults who are overweight.

Lakewood Community College Walking Club: 3401 Century Avenue, White Bear Lake, MN 55110. Phone: 612/779-3358.

The Lakewood Community College Walking Club promotes walking as a lifetime fitness activity and enhances participation opportunities available through the college's recreational sports program. The walking club is open to all members of the community, not just the students and faculty. Club members walk at the Maplewood Mall and at a number of outdoor trails. There is no membership fee. Members receive an identification card, log books, and a monthly newsletter. The club sponsors walking and social events and provides an incentive awards program. A membership application form is available.

Leisure Connections: Arc of Hennepin County, Diamond Hill Center, Suite 140, 4301 Highway 7, Minneapolis, MN 55416-5810. Phone: 612/920-0855.

The Leisure Connections program matches the needs and interests of people with developmental disabilities with those of a volunteer friend in the community. Walking is a very popular shared interest. Program participants are matched according to gender, age, interests, residence proximity, and time availability. For more information about the program call Arc of Hennepin County or any of the fifty local Arc chapters throughout Minnesota that provide support and advocacy services to people with developmental disabilities and their families. Many of the chapters offer similar recreation programs.

Mayo Foundation for Medical Education and Research: 200 First Street Southwest, Rochester, MN 55905. Phone: 800/888-3968.

The *Mayo Clinic Health Letter* provides reliable information about health issues, nutrition, fitness, and how decisions on these matters affect health. Newsletter articles focus on the nutritional value of foods, walking exercise tips, and research findings. The annual subscription rate is $24.

Melpomene Institute: 1010 University Avenue, St. Paul, MN 55104. Phone: 612/642-1951.

The Melpomene Institute is a center for research and public education on the health concerns of physically active women and the effects of exercise on girls and women at all stages of life. The Institute develops and sells educational materials such as brochures, informational packets, a video on osteoporosis, and the *Melpomene Journal*, published three times a year. Many of the articles in the *Melpomene Journal* focus on current research being conducted in the areas of exercise and infertility, exercise and women with disabilities, the role of exercise in women's recovery from chemical dependency, exercise for larger women, and fitness for high school girls. The annual membership fee of $25 includes a subscription to the Journal and discounts on materials from the resource center. (See WALKS, this chapter.)

Minnesota Distance Running Association (MDRA): 5701 Normandale Boulevard, Edina, MN 55424. Phone: 612/927-0983. Raceline: 612/925-4749.

Although the MDRA is a statewide organization for runners, some of the information the group publishes pertains to walkers. Annual memberships are available for $15. The MDRA publishes *Running Minnesota,* a handbook that contains a schedule for all running races (and running/walking races) in the state of Minnesota. It includes tips for warm-up exercizes and a personal training log. The handbook is available to nonmembers for $10.95 through the MDRA. The MDRA also publishes *Minnesota Runner,* a quarterly newsletter and magazine that features upcoming races and statewide news. The MDRA also sponsors a running/walking program during the winter at the Metrodome. (For more information about the walking program in the Metrodome see chapter 9, Metro-A.)

Minneapolis Municipal Hiking Club: City of Minneapolis Park and Recreation Board, 310 Fourth Avenue South, Minneapolis, MN 55415. Phone: 612/348-2226.

Started in 1925, this walking club, sponsored by the Minneapolis Park and Recreation Board, has over three hundred members. An annual membership fee of $7 entitles you to an annual membership directory and a monthly newsletter filled with weekly events. The group sponsors at least three events per week, including walking tours of local parks and historic places, theatre evenings, and "picture night" get-togethers where friends exchange photos from walking vacations. The group also provides group travel opportunities to Europe and Asia. A sample monthly newsletter is available.

Minnesota Orienteering Club (MNOC): Box 730, Minneapolis, MN 55458.

Orienteering, a year-round recreational activity and competitive sport for people of all ages and abilities, is becoming an increasingly popular sport among walkers. The object of the sport is to use a map and compass to locate control markers placed at designated land features as fast as you can. The navigation and route choice is left entirely up to the individual. Orienteering can be described as a cross-country run, jog, or walk through woods and open country with a map and compass, that challenges both the mind and body. Most, if not all, orienteering events have four to six courses ranging from shorter, easier courses for beginners to longer, more difficult courses for the experts. You may participate at any level you wish. This is an international sport, with national trials and world cup championships, and is a recognized Olympic sport. The purpose of the Minnesota Orienteering Club is to host orienteering events (including an annual state championship) during the spring, fall, and winter seasons, to be a community resource for information and education on orienteering and navigational techniques, and to provide social activities for members. The following annual memberships are available: $5 student (under 21); $6 individual; $8 family. Membership includes instruction on orienteering, bi-monthly newsletter, and events throughout the year. A brochure is available.

Minnesota Rovers Outing Club: Box 14133, Minneapolis, MN 55414. Phone: 612/522-2461.

The Minnesota Rovers Outing Club is a diverse group of people who hike, bike, ski, canoe, climb, snowshoe, camp, sightsee, and take an active role in the preservation of the wilderness. If you're an interested beginner hiker, seasoned Rovers will help you develop the outdoor skills you need for climbing a sheer cliff or backwoods trail. Weekly meetings feature slide programs on past trips, demonstrations of techniques and equipment, and talks on outing opportunities and wilderness preservation. All you need to join is suitable outdoor clothing and enthusiasm for the outdoors. The club's extensive inventory of "loan gear" includes backpacks, skis, bicycle panniers, sleeping bags, and hundreds of other items. Memberships available are: $15 individual, $10 student, and $2 per day for nonmembers or visitors who want to join a trip. Trip expenses are shared to keep the price of trips in the low to moderate range. A brochure is available.

Minnesota Volkssport Association (MVA): 221 26th Avenue North, St. Cloud, MN 56303. Phone: 612/253-4762.

The purpose of MVA is to promote the health, physical fitness, and well-being of Minnesotans by organizing, promoting, and conducting noncompetitive, family-oriented, lifetime sports including but not limited to walking, jogging, running, bicycling, swimming, and cross-country skiing as sanctioned by the International Federation of Popular Sports (IVV) and the American Volkssport Association (AVA). There is a $15 membership fee. Volksmarches ("people walks") are held throughout the year. A number of chapters offer Volksmarches that can be completed by individuals on any day of the year. Club members receive a yearly calendar of events, discounts on walking products, and credit toward pins and international awards. There are a number of MVA affiliates within the state, including:

> Hawley Volkssport Associates, Hawley, MN.
> Hennepin Parks, Plymouth, MN.
> Iron Trail Convention & Visitor's Bureau, Eveleth, MN.
> Judi's Walk, Eveleth, MN.
> Minnesota State Parks Volkssport Club, Department of Natural Resources, St. Paul, MN.
> New Ulm Park and Recreation Assocation, New Ulm, MN.
> Northern Lights Volksmarchers, Osseo, MN.
> Riverbend Striders, North Mankato, MN.
> River Bend Nature Center Volkssport Club, Faribault, MN.
> Springbrook Nature Center Volkssport Club, Fridley, MN.
> Syttende Mai Komiteens Folkemarsj Stiftelse, Spring Grove, MN.
> Twin Cities Volksmarchers, Mendota Heights, MN.

Volksmarches are held throughout the world, so if you're traveling from state to state or country to country, you may want to obtain a list of walking events. For current information about Volkssport affiliates and a yearly schedule of activities, contact the Minnesota Volkssport Association.

North Country Trail Association: Chippewa National Forest, HCR 73, Box 15, Walker, MN 56484. Phone: 218/547-1044.

or

Roderick MacRae, NCTA Coordinator, 1210 West 22nd Street, Minneapolis, MN 55405. Phone: 612/377-0130.

The North Country Trail Association promotes the development of the trail as a nonmotorized route crossing sections of New York, Pennsylvania, Ohio, Michigan, Wisconsin, Minnesota, and North Dakota, and fosters and promotes cooperation and coordination between individuals, clubs, and related groups throughout the country who believe in and/or use the trail. The NCTA promotes the improvement of the trail by active volunteer participation in construction, repair, cleanup, and maintenance activities. Annual individual memberships begin at $10. Members receive a quarterly newsletter.

Plymouth Pedestrians: City of Plymouth, 3400 Plymouth Boulevard, Plymouth, MN 55447. Phone: 612/550-5130.

This city-sponsored walking club is open to residents and nonresidents of all ages. Individual membership fees are $5 per year. Incentives are provided as walkers reach successive milestones. The club sponsors an annual Volksmarch in October. A Volksmarch brochure is available from the Park and Recreation office starting in mid-August.

Pocket Architecture—Minneapolis/Saint Paul: by Bernard Jacob and Carol Morphew, Minnesota Society American Institute of Architects, 275 Market Street Suite 54, Minneapolis, MN 55405.

This pocket-size guidebook takes you on walking tours of downtown Minneapolis and downtown Saint Paul with wonderful details about architecture, history, and art. This book is available in most bookstores.

Special Olympics Minnesota: 625 Fourth Avenue South, Suite 1430, Minneapolis, MN 55415. Phone: 612/333-0999.

Founded in 1968 by the Joseph P. Kennedy Jr. Foundation, Special Olympics is the largest program of year-round sports training and athletic competition for children and adults with developmental disabilities, age eight and older. Special Olympics Minnesota offers four walking events: a 50-meter walk, a 400-meter walk, an 800-meter walk, and a 2K walk. In addition, international competition includes five long-distance racewalking events: 1,500 meters, 3,000 meters, 5,000 meters, 10,000 meters, and 15,000 meters. For information about sports training, competitions, and volunteer opportunities, contact the Special Olympics Minnesota office.

Star of the North State Games: 1700 105th Avenue Northeast, Box 34144, Blaine, MN 55343. Phone: 612/785-5678.

The Star of the North State Games is an Olympic-style, multisport festival open to all Minnesotans regardless of age or skill level. This annual competition will be held June 14–23 in the Twin Cities communities of Blaine and Coon Rapids during 1991. The Star of the North Games conducts a 3.5K

(2 mile) fitness walk event which includes a special gift item, entertainment, and free admission to opening ceremonies. The track and field competition will feature racewalk events (400 meter, 3,000 meter, and 5,000 meter) for both men and women along with a division for special athletes. Preregistration is required for the racewalk events and on-site registration is permitted for the fitness walk. For more information, call the Star of the North State Games Office.

Superior Hiking Trail Association: Box 4, Two Harbors, MN 55616-0004. Phone: 218/834-4436.

The Superior Hiking Trail Association was incorporated in December 1986 to build, promote, and maintain a continuous footpath along the ridgeline overlooking the North Shore of Lake Superior. Currently, 150 miles of the proposed 250-mile trail are open to backpackers and day hikers. The Association is a nonprofit volunteer organization dependent upon members and volunteer hours to administer and maintain the trail. Members receive *The Ridgeline*, a bimonthly publication containing trail information and articles of interest to hikers.

Take a Hike: Washington County Parks Division, Lake Elmo Park Reserve, 1515 Keats Avenue North, Lake Elmo, MN 55042. Phone: 612/731-3861.

To join the Take a Hike program, pick up a walking log at the Lake Elmo park office. When you walk 30 miles in Washington County Parks, turn in your walking log at Lake Elmo and you will receive a certificate. Individuals under ten years or over sixty years can complete 15 miles to receive a certificate. Commemorative walking pins can be purchased for $3 to mark your achievement.

TC Walkers: c/o Fern Anderson, 3152 Kentucky Avenue South, St. Louis Park, MN 55426. Phone: 612/926-3514.

The mission of TC WALKERS is to promote competitive and noncompetitive walking, to provide walking instruction, and to encourage the health and well-being of walkers of all ages and abilities through a personal walking program. The group meets every Saturday at 9 A.M. throughout the year at the Linden Hills Community Center in south Minneapolis at 43rd and Xerxes Avenue South for a walk around the lakes. Members meet throughout the metro area during the week (call for specific information regarding days and times). Annual membership is $10 per individual and includes a t-shirt and free access to all club-sponsored events. A club brochure is available.

The Athletic Congress (TAC): 1939 Bayard Avenue, St. Paul, MN 55116. Phone: 612/698-4100.

The Athletic Congress publishes *TAC Times Minnesota*, a quarterly newsletter that includes all track and field events (including racewalking events) in the central region of the United States and Minnesota. The annual membership fee of $9 includes a subscription to the *TAC Times* newsletter.

Twin Cities Society for Children and Adults with Autism, Inc. (TCSAC): 253 East Fourth Street, St. Paul, MN 55101. Phone: 612/228-9074.

TCSAC sponsors an annual Racewalk Classic for Autism, a judged event that includes a 5K (3.1-mile) Racewalk and Fun Walk and a 1-mile Junior Racewalk Competition for those twelve and under. The event takes place in September at Lake Harriet. Awards are given for first-, second-, and third-place male and female winners in over sixteen different categories. For information about the race or volunteer opportunities call TCSAC.

WALKS: Melpomene Institute, 1010 University Avenue, St. Paul, MN 55104. Phone: 612/642-1951.

WALKS is sponsored by the Melpomene Institute. For an annual fee of $10, members receive a comprehensive guidebook, a special walking calendar, a quarterly newsletter, the opportunity to find either a group or walking partner, access to walking clinics, and discount coupons for use at area retailers. Although the group is primarily for seniors, it is open to people of all ages. The club sponsors walking events and clinics throughout the year, conducts research on the health benefits of walking, and offers a medical referral program for patients who need help in establishing a healthier lifestyle. A club brochure is available.

Walk Sport America, Inc.: 817 Osceola Avenue, St. Paul, MN 55105. Phone: 612/291-7138.

Walk Sport America is a health and fitness firm dedicated to designing and implementing successful, diversified walking and fitness programs for the public and for health and wellness programs. Services include training clinics in racewalking and fitness walking, seminars, instructor workshops, individual coaching, fitness evaluations, health fair demonstrations, and walking clubs. In 1990, the firm developed a pilot racewalking program for the Saint Paul School District and a pilot racewalking program to use in integrated settings for people with developmental disabilities.

Walk When the Moon Is Full: Hennepin Parks, 12615 County Road 9, Box 47320, Plymouth, MN 55447-0320. Phone: 612/559-9000.

The Walk When the Moon Is Full program invites walkers to discover the mysteries of nature after dark through special interpretive programs on the night of the full moon. Each month's session includes a moonlit hike and a related nature topic. This program is offered throughout the year. After completing four moon walks, participants may purchase a commemorative pin. The program is held at various Hennepin Parks locations throughout the metro area. Reservations at all sites will be taken no sooner than seven days prior to the program. This is a very popular program, so call ahead for reservations.

Wasie Therapeutic Swimming Pool: Abbott Northwestern Hospital—Sister Kenny Institute, 800 East 28th Street, Minneapolis, MN 55407. Phone: 612/863-5238.

Water walking classes are available in the winter months for people with disabilities. Classes are led by a qualified lifeguard instructor. The pool has an accessible ramp and staircase and accessible showers and locker rooms. The water in the pool is maintained at a comfortable ninety-two degrees. Swimming ability is not required.

Wilderness Inquiry: 1313 Fifth Street Southeast, Box 84, Minneapolis, MN 55414. Phone: 612/379-3858.

The purpose of Wilderness Inquiry is to integrate people with disabilities with able-bodied people on wilderness trips throughout North America and the world. If you are interested in information about upcoming walking or hiking adventures, call the Wilderness Inquiry office.

Winged Walkers: Blaisdell YMCA, 3335 Blaisdell Avenue, Minneapolis, MN 55404. Phone: 612/827-5401.

Winged Walkers, co-sponsored by Melpomene WALKS, is for walkers of all ages. The group meets at various times throughout the week and takes jaunts to metro walking sites, both indoor and outdoor. The annual membership fee is $10.

Your Guide to St. Anthony Falls Historic Sites and Parkways: Bob Ripsin, 2923 Logan Avenue North, Minneapolis, MN 55411.

This twenty-page illustrated booklet contains a brief history of the City of Minneapolis and the St. Anthony Falls area, a narrative guide to historic sites and landmarks of St. Anthony Falls, an illustrated map of the area, a walking tour, and a list of prominent names that can be found on area streets and landmarks. This booklet sells for $1 (plus postage) and is available through the author.

WALKING STICKS AND STAFFS

Walking sticks come in just about every shape, size, and length. If you walk only on sidewalks and paved trails, you might want to invest in a fashionable, antique walking stick or cane. Antique and collectible stores usually have a few on hand. If you have a particular wood or style in mind, let the dealers know so they can search for walking sticks at estate sales and auctions.

Otherwise, you will probably want to invest in a more durable stick or staff that can be used, especially in the spring and fall, when the ground is icy, muddy, and wet. Make sure your stick is sealed to withstand water damage.

In Minnesota, diamond willow walking sticks are very popular. Holace Nelson, an artisan, explained why. "When I was a kid during the Depression I remember seeing all kinds of things like hat trees and lamps that were made out of this interesting wood called 'diamond willow.' Forty years later I was on a canoe trip with a friend and asked him if he knew what a diamond willow looked like, and to my delight, he pointed to a nearby tree. Subsequent research revealed that diamond willow isn't the name of a tree—it's the manifestation of a disease that attacks the cambium layer of a tree and forms diamond-shaped patterns. The Peach Leaf Willow and the Pussy Willow are most susceptible to the disease, but not the traditional narrow-leafed willows that you picture when you think of a willow tree. The branches and stems that are affected make excellent walking sticks because the twisting of the cells makes the wood stronger but still light in weight."

The following walking sticks and staffs are all made in Minnesota. A walking stick varies in length from 36 to 48 inches, and a walking staff is 48 to 84 inches.

Alexander G. Kovach: Rural Route 2, Box 183-C, Akeley, MN 55433. Phone: 218/652-2952.

If you want to talk with Alexander Kovach, you have to call him before 7 A.M. Central Time, because during the day throughout most of the year he's outside working his farm. In his spare time he makes walking sticks and walking staffs from red oak, one of Minnesota's best hardwoods. His sticks are works of art, with intricately carved figures at the top such as squirrels, loons, beavers, and birds. Each stick takes ten to twelve hours of carving and finishing. Many of his sticks are custom-designed. His sticks are sold at the following stores: Wind Song in Nisswa, Roxie's in Emily, and Feather O'Dam in Leech Lake.

Bending Branches: 1101 Northeast Stinson Boulevard, Minneapolis, MN 55413. Phone: 612/378-1825.

Bending Branches, a manufacturing firm that develops multiseasonal products such as hockey sticks and canoe paddles, also offers three styles of walking sticks: the Wader (with notched markings on the bottom to test the depth when you are wading in water), the Walker, and the Mountain Staff. The sticks are sold at Midwest Mountaineering, Hoiggards, and other fine sporting goods stores. The development of the Mountain Staff was inspired by Dale Kicker, president, who walked across the United States from Mexico to Canada along the Pacific Crest Trail in 1977 when he was only nineteen years old.

Leonard Caouette: 8679 Goodhue Street Northeast, Minneapolis, MN 55434. Phone: 612/784-5235.

Leonard Caouette finds great pleasure in stalking the woods for just the right-shaped diamond willow branch that will make a great walking stick or staff. He sells them from his home and at craft shows throughout Minnesota. His sticks come in all different lengths and are tipped at the bottom to withstand all types of weather. Many of his customers display them on fireplace mantels as works of art.

Holly Industries: Holace Nelson, Box 65341, St. Paul, MN 55165. Phone: 612/455-1839.

Holace Nelson makes and sells diamond willow sticks, staffs, pool cues, and letter openers at the Minnesota State Fair (during the last week of August every year) and at his niece's bookstore, the Bookshelf, located at Thomas Lake Center, 1565 Cliff Road, Eagan, MN (phone: 612/452-8344). He also sells ready-to-finish sticks and staffs that are cut and ready to be sanded, sealed, and tipped. He demonstrates cane making and sells his products at the annual Festival of Nations held in Saint Paul in the spring.

Tamarack

CHAPTER 9

Places to walk in Minnesota

During an interview for this book, one fellow asked, "How in the world are you going to identify places to walk in Minnesota? The whole state is great for walking!" No doubt about it! With over 4,000 miles of walking trails and many more indoor walking opportunities, Minnesota is a walker's paradise.

With so many walking opportunities available, where do Minnesotans and visitors walk? A report issued by the Minnesota State Planning Agency in February 1990 analyzed the outdoor recreation habits of state residents and visitors. Here are some of the report's findings that directly pertain to walkers:

• Recreation time spent on walking and hiking occurs almost exclusively (90 percent) within one-half hour of home.

• Minnesotans stay within thirty minutes from home for almost three-fourths of their total outdoor recreation time but are willing to travel an hour or more 22 percent of the time. Fifteen percent of outdoor recreation occurs more than two hours away from home.

• Walking was the most popular recreation activity for Minnesota residents, accounting for 18 percent of time spent in outdoor recreation activities.

• By the year 2000, planners predict, walking will increase in popularity and will account for 29.1 percent of time spent in outdoor recreation activities.

In summary, walkers tend to use the same paths over and over again. Why? Convenience is a major factor. Exercise has to be easy, affordable, and time efficient. The purpose of this book is to make it easy for residents and visitors to explore walking sites within a half-hour range of their home (or hotel) and then to move beyond that range to explore walking sites throughout the entire state.

This chapter includes over 150 walking sites, outdoor and indoor, throughout Minnesota. All include narrative information. Most include maps. You'll probably have to use both the first time you walk a new site.

Please keep in mind that this is only a sampler of Minnesota's walking sites, not a comprehensive guide. The sites highlighted in this book are no better or worse than any other walking sites. They were randomly selected without any theme or plan in mind.

The trails are not rated. So many factors influence a walking experience that it serves no purpose to identify the "must-see" sites. The weather, the season, the plants, the animals, and the mood of the walker all come together to create a quality experience—not a four-star rating.

These are walking sites, not walking tours. The narrative that accompanies each map includes a limited amount of information about the unique aspects of the trail such as vegetation, wildlife, or the historical significance. The narrative is simply designed to help you walk from one point to another.

The walking sites included in this book have been arranged into metro and outstate locations. The term "metro" refers to a heavily populated region around the cities of Minneapolis and Saint Paul that includes the following counties: Hennepin, Ramsey, Dakota, Anoka, Washington, Carver, and Scott. According to 1988 population estimates, approximately 50 percent of the state's population lives within the seven-county metro area. In the metro area, eighty outdoor walking sites (1–80) and eighteen indoor walking sites (A–R) are featured.

The term "outstate" refers to all the counties in Minnesota excluding the metro area. In the outstate section, forty-six outdoor walking sites (81–126) and eight indoor walking sites (S–Z) are highlighted.

OUTDOOR WALKING SITES

There is quite an array of outdoor walking sites in this book. Trails lead through city, county, and state parks, residential areas, cemeteries, industrial parks, fairgrounds, and gardens.

Each walking site has its own beauty and offers something new to learn and experience. The walking sites vary in their level of development. Some of the parks have comprehensive programs and facilities; others are just getting their first roads and water fountains. Some cities have newly paved trail systems; others use existing sidewalks, roads, and dirt paths to guide you from one point to another. Minnesota offers dramatic and intriguing walking experiences at almost every turn.

INDOOR WALKING SITES

"Southdale is climate controlled, so people who have hayfever or asthma are able to walk and breathe without any problems. Our goal is to provide a safe, comfortable walking environment for everyone. We've kept our hours flexible so that people can walk early in the morning, during their lunch hour, or after dinner." —Laurel Muedeking, Marketing, Southdale Center

Another great resource in Minnesota is the number of shopping centers and malls that open their doors early and welcome walkers by the hundreds into their climate-controlled environments. Whether the temperature is hovering at a sweltering one hundred degrees or a frigid minus thirty degrees, you can always walk in comfort in a shopping mall.

On any given morning, in any region of the state, you can find quite a blend of walkers at the malls: young parents pushing strollers; children, teenagers, and adults with asthma or hayfever; people recuperating from heart attacks, strokes, or accidents; avid outdoor walkers seeking shelter from bad weather; groups of friends gathering for an early morning walk followed by breakfast (some restaurants open early for walkers).

In addition to providing weather-proof walking sites, shopping malls also offer on-site security, barrier-free walking routes, walking clubs, special parking privileges, seminars, and periodic blood pressure and cholesterol screenings.

Mall walking is a great way to meet other walkers!

Indoor walking sites are identified on the overview maps with letters A–Z. Indoor walking site information is at the very end of the book.

HOW TO USE THIS CHAPTER

• At the beginning of this chapter there are **two overview maps**—a metro overview map and an outstate overview map.

• Outdoor walking sites are identified with numbers. Indoor walking sites are identified by letters of the alphabet.

• Outdoor walking sites are highlighted at the beginning of the chapter while indoor sites are listed at the end. To locate a particular site, match the number or letter on the map with the boxed number or letter on each page. (Do not refer to page numbers.)

• Larger maps for most of the walking sites in Minnesota are available free of charge from the agency responsible for operating the site.

• Two pages are devoted to each outdoor walking site—a map page and an information page. The map page includes a drawing of the walking site, a recommended walking route highlighted in green, and then an overview of essential facilities (restrooms, water, and phones).

• Maps are not drawn to the same scale. Regardless of the length of the trail, the maps were sized to fit the page. Trail systems vary in length from approximately 1 mile to over 150 miles. To get a sense of the size of each trail system, you'll have to read the text. The following symbols are used on the map page:

Ⓟ	= parking area
✶	= start point
———	= recommended walking route
- - - -	= other walking trails
➤	= direction to follow

• The information page includes directions on how to get there (via car or bus), where you can obtain additional information about the walking site, and points of interest. A special "Tips for Walkers" section includes important things you'll need to know before you walk the trail. The recommended route is usually a small segment of a larger trail system. The recommended route will help you decide whether or not you want to explore more of the trail system. The "giving back" section makes it easy to become a trail or park volunteer or direct your financial donation to your favorite trail system.

• The information in this section of the book was designed to be accurate through 1993. However, keep in mind that trail systems continually change. Obtain an updated trail map when possible.

• Before you walk a trail, make sure you have your essential equipment.

• Always be conscious of your personal safety.

• Enjoy the splendors of Minnesota!

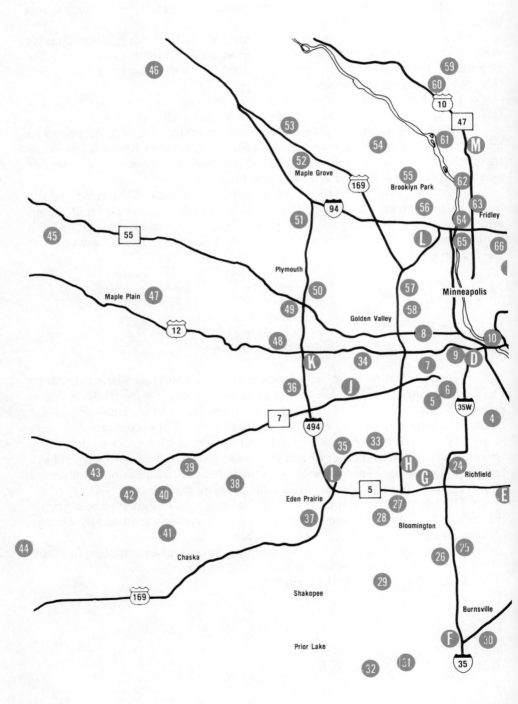

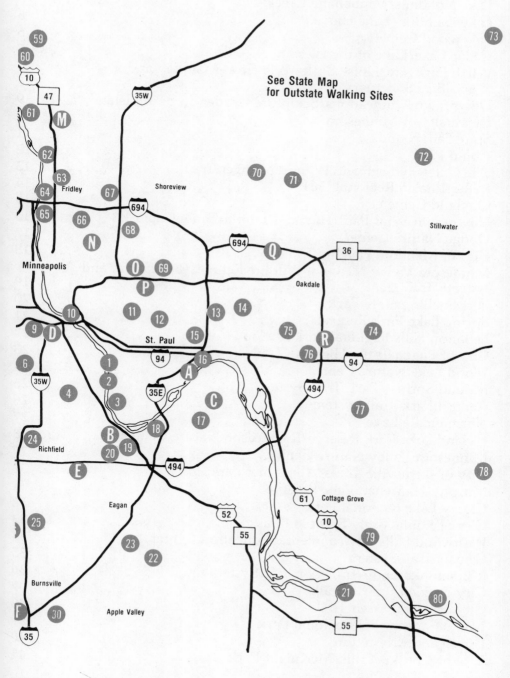

See State Map
for Outstate Walking Sites

Outstate Walking Sites—Overview

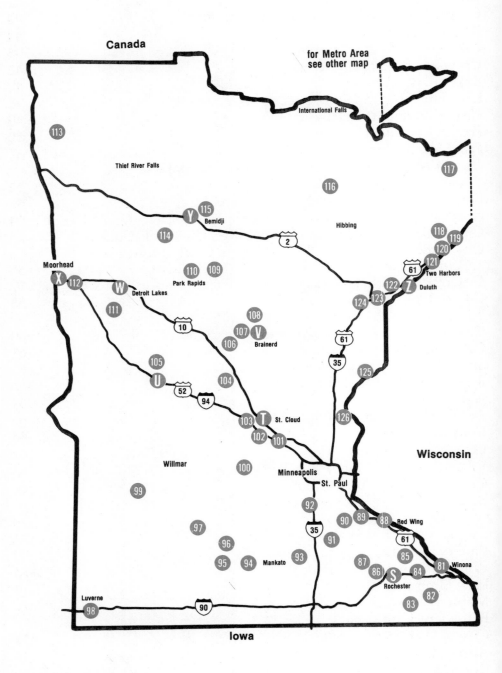

Canada

for Metro Area
see other map

International Falls

Thief River Falls

113

116

Hibbing

Y 115 Bemidji

114

2

118
119
120
Two Harbors
61
121
Duluth

Moorhead
X 112

W Detroit Lakes

110 109
Park Rapids

111

10

108

107 V
106 Brainerd

122
Z
123
124
125

61

35

105
U

52

104

94

103 T St. Cloud
102
101

100

Minneapolis
St. Paul

Willmar

99

92

90 89
88 Red Wing

97

91

61

96

95 94 Mankato

93

85

87

86 S
83

81 Winona

84

82

Rochester

Wisconsin

126

Luverne

98

90

83

Iowa

METRO WALKING SITES—INDOOR

OUTSTATE WALKING SITES—OUTDOOR

OUTSTATE WALKING SITES—INDOOR

PUBLIC TRANSPORTATION

There are a number of public transportation options throughout Minnesota that make it possible to arrive at some of the walking sites via a metropolitan bus line or a dial-a-ride van, saving money, oil and gas. If you own a car and you're going to a walking site that cannot be reached by public transportation, it makes sense to call a few walking partners and car pool.

Dial-a-ride systems are different from traditional bus lines in a number of ways:

- You call to schedule a van that will pick you up, take you to a walking site, then pick you up at an arranged time. Most dial-a-ride systems prefer that you call a day ahead of time. Some systems will accept same-day orders, but will increase the fare.
- Most dial-a-ride systems honor transfers (but not bus passes) from metropolitan bus lines. A one-way ride on the van costs anywhere from fifty cents to two dollars, depending on your age. Rates for seniors and young children are reduced.
- Most dial-a-ride systems require that parents bring car seats for children under four years of age. Some van lines are equipped with wheelchair lifts. You can carry on only luggage (backpacks) that you can hold in your lap; there is a limit of two grocery bags. Only animals in cages are allowed on the vans. Smoking is prohibited.

The best way to locate bus and dial-a-ride systems is to call the local chamber of commerce. Dialing Information is not helpful since you have to know the exact name of a company before the operator will give out a number. Here are a few of the public transportation options in Minnesota.

City to city transportation:
Amtrak: 800/USA-RAIL; Greyhound/Jefferson Lines: Call your local bus station. In the metro area call 612/371-3311.

Metro bus lines:
Minneapolis and Saint Paul: Metropolitan Transit Commission at 612/645-6060 category RIDE (7433); North Suburban Line (St. Paul, Roseville, Little Canada, Vadnais Heights, Circle Pines, Lino Lakes, Blaine) at 612/784-7196; Roseville Area Circulator (Roseville) at 612/631-8826.

Metro dial-a-ride systems:
Anoka County Traveler (most of the cities in Anoka County): 612/464-8883; Northeast Suburban Transit (NEST) (Maplewood, Oakdale, Saint Paul): 612/227-6378; White Bear Lake Area Transit: 612/464-8876; Shakopee Dial-A-Ride: 612/445-9040; Southwest Metro Dial-A-Ride (Eden Prairie, Chaska, Chanhassen): 612/944-7126; Plymouth Dial-A-Ride: 612/559-5057.

Outstate bus lines and dial-a-ride systems:
Duluth: Duluth Transit Authority at 218/722-7283; Saint Cloud: Saint Cloud Metro Transit Commission at 612/253-2420; Rochester: Rochester City Lines at 507/288-4353; Brainerd Dial-A-Ride: 218/829-7077.

Minneapolis/Saint Paul Greenways

Operated by the Minneapolis Park and Recreation Board and the Saint Paul Division of Parks and Recreation

"By delving back into the history of one's own community, an understanding is gained as to how these matters of common interest and value came about; a proper appreciation is drawn of what our ancestors have attained for us; and some idea is obtained as to why and how we can and should further our community's interests for coming generations."
— Theodore Wirth, Superintendent of Minneapolis Parks, 1906–1935.

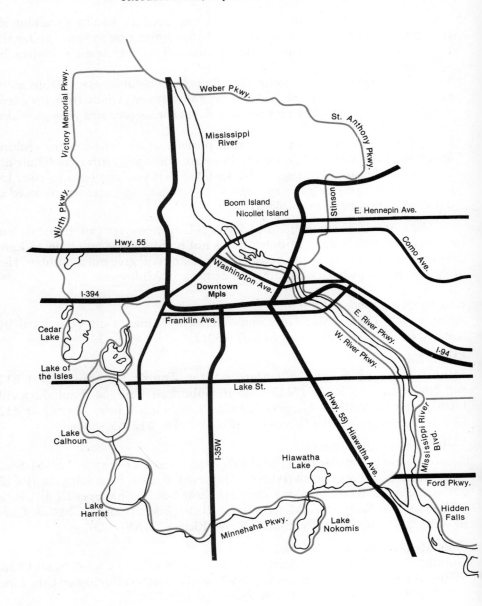

GREENWAY MILEAGES (Pedestrian*):

St. Anthony Pkwy: 4 miles
Weber Pkwy: 4 miles
Victory Memorial Pkwy: 2.84 miles
Wirth Pkwy: 3.54 miles
Cedar Lake Pkwy: 1.68 miles
Lake of the Isles Pkwy: 2.6 miles
Dean Pkwy
  (between Isles/Calhoun): .59 miles
Lake Calhoun Pkwy: 3.1 miles
Wm. Berry Pkwy
  (between Calhoun/Harriet): .56 miles
Lake Harriet Pkwy: 2.75 miles
Minnehaha Pkwy: 4.93 miles
Lake Nokomis Pkwy: 2.7 miles

East River Pkwy
  (Ford Bridge to Lake St.): 2.25 miles;
  (Ford Bridge to Washington
  Ave. Bridge): 5.5 miles
Mississippi River Blvd.
  (Summit to Crosby Farm): 4.5 miles
Hidden Falls Park: 3.3 miles
Crosby Farm Park: 3.6 miles
Summit Avenue: 5 miles
Lake Como: 1.8 miles
Wheelock Pkwy: 4 miles
Lake Phalen: 2.9 miles
Johnson Pkwy: 2.5 miles

*Mileages do not include bike paths that are walkable in winter, or other connecting segments.

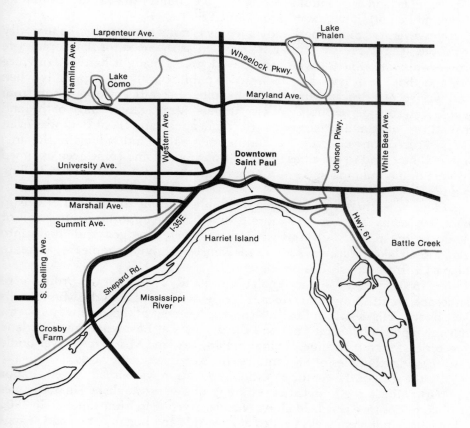

MINNEAPOLIS/SAINT PAUL GREENWAYS

There are 93 miles of paved, accessible walkways within the city limits of Minneapolis and Saint Paul, making the Twin Cities system one of the largest urban greenway systems in the United States. There are 6,385 acres of parks operated by the Minneapolis Park Board, and another 3,500 acres operated by Saint Paul Parks and Recreation. When you add those to the 3,300 acres in Fort Snelling State Park that are operated by the Minnesota Department of Natural Resources, that brings the total to over 13,000 acres of parkland within the Twin Cities!

Park development in the Twin Cities started in 1849 when Henry Rice, John R. Irvine, C.S. Whitney, and Robert Smith donated three tracts of land to the City of Saint Paul that eventually became known as Rice, Irvine, and Smith parks. Rice Park became the first "public square" located in downtown Saint Paul and soon became a favorite site for circuses, celebrations, and concerts.

In 1857, Edward Murphy donated two blocks of land to the City of Minneapolis in a downtown area now known as Murphy Square. It too became a natural gathering place for people doing business in the city. That same year, land was acquired for Central Park in New York City. These and other similar land acquisitions throughout the country marked the beginning of the public park movement in the United States.

However, the public park movement was not supported by the majority of people. Other pressing urban issues such as the need for developing fire protection, water lines, sewers, and paved streets made it hard to convince residents that it was necessary to set aside public parklands, especially when land was so plentiful in Minnesota. In spite of significant opposition from people who considered public parks a "useless extravagance," most of the land around the lakes and streams in both Minneapolis and Saint Paul was eventually secured for public use. A number of wealthy individuals in the area donated their land to the cities for public parklands, and some even assumed the cost of maintaining and improving the parks until the cities were willing to do so.

Over time, there was a shift in the public attitude toward park development, especially as more and more people had an opportunity to stroll or picnic in the parks. Overgrown swamps were dredged and made into recreational lakes. Pathways and roads were built, giving people free access to the parks. Trees and shrubs were planted.

In 1883, Horace William Shaler Cleveland, a well-known professor of landscape architecture from Chicago, presented his ideas to the Minneapolis Park Board. His designs influenced the development of the greenway systems in Minneapolis and Saint Paul and the grounds at Lakewood and Oakland cemeteries. Summit Avenue, Lexington Parkway, and Mississippi River Boulevard provide examples of his fondness for tree-lined boulevards.

By the turn of the century, outdoor recreation was already a very important part of life in the Twin Cities. Hiking clubs were established in both cities. In 1905, a foot race was held along Nicollet Avenue in Minneapolis. In 1906, gymnastics equipment was installed at Riverside and Logan parks, and swings merry-go-rounds, and sandboxes were added to neighborhood parks. During the Roaring Twenties, it was fashionable to sport a walking stick and cap and spend the afternoon walking along the Mississippi or St. Croix rivers.

Although land acquisition for public parks came to a standstill during the Great Depression, park improvements, including the construction of bridges and walkways, were able to continue, thanks to the work of the Civilian Conservation Corps.

The next surge in park development took place in the post-war era of the 1950s when thoughts returned to recreation, and communities worked together to build softball diamonds, picnic shelters, and bandstands. As the urban population increased, land acquisition once again became an important issue. Minneapolis eventually achieved its goal of having a park within six blocks of every home, and today it boasts 770 square feet of parkland for every resident, more than any other city in the United States! In 1989, the City of Minneapolis Park and Recreation Board won the prestigious Gold Medal Award from the National Park and Recreation Congress. The "grand rounds" greenway system in Minneapolis was also featured in the June 1990 issue of *National Geographic*.

No matter where you are in the Twin Cities, you are close to miles and miles of paved, accessible walkways along lakes, streams, and rivers. A number of gardens are also along the route—the Sculpture Garden near downtown Minneapolis, the Rock Garden at Lake Harriet, the Eloise Butler Wildflower Garden along Theodore Wirth Parkway, and the Como Conservatory and the Ordway Memorial Japanese Garden at Como Park in Saint Paul.

For those who enjoy the bustle of an urban park, there is plenty of activity at Lake of the Isles, Lake Calhoun, Lake Harriet, Lake Nokomis, Lake Como, and Lake Phalen. For those who enjoy the tranquility of the woods, there is plenty of solitude at Hidden Falls Park, Crosby Farm, and Cedar Lake.

If you walked an average of three miles per day, it would take you thirty-one days to walk the greenways in the Twin Cities. Whether you have a month, a day, or even a few hours to spend in the Twin Cities, be sure to bring your walking shoes and explore Minneapolis and Saint Paul, one step at a time. And don't be surprised if you cross paths with ducks, deer, or Canadian geese—wildlife is plentiful in Minnesota, even in very populated areas.

Just think. One hundred fifty years ago, public parkland was limited to a two-block area in downtown Saint Paul. Imagine what life would be like today if we all had to share those few blades of grass.

If you would like to know more about the history of park development in the metro area, you may want to read *Minneapolis Park System, 1883–1944* by Theodore Wirth, former superintendent of Minneapolis Parks (available in the Minneapolis Public Library), "Minneapolis Parks and Recreation: A History of the Park and Recreation Board Since World War II," a historical study written by C. Ben Wright (available at the Hennepin County Historical Society) and "The Political History of Establishing a Regional Park System in the Twin Cities Metropolitan Area," a thesis written by John Walter Christian (available at the University of Minnesota, Wilson Library).

Mississippi River Boulevard

Operated by the Saint Paul Division of Parks and Recreation and the Minneapolis Park and Recreation Board

"We enjoy walking along the river because there's always something new to discover. Even though this trail is in the heart of the metro area, you feel like you're walking in the country because of all the woods." —Mike and Maureen McTeague, Saint Paul residents.

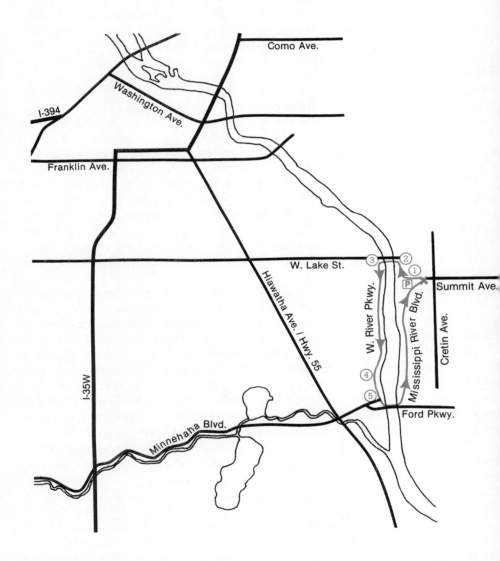

FACILITIES

 ✓ **Restrooms** are not available along the recommended route.
 ✓ **Water** is available at fountains at various points along the trail.
 ✓ **Public telephones** are not available along the route.

DIRECTIONS: The Mississippi River Boulevard trail is located along the borders of Minneapolis and Saint Paul. **Public transportation** is available on MTC Routes # 21A (to Otis and Marshall), 14 (to Highland Center), 3 (to St. Thomas College), 9A (to Cleveland), or 9B (to Shepard and Gannon). **From Interstate 94:** Exit on Cretin/Vandalia and proceed south on Cretin, west on Summit Avenue to the Mississippi River. **Park** in the lot by the monument.

INFORMATION: Call Saint Paul Parks and Recreation at 612/292-7400 or Minneapolis Park and Recreation Board at 612/348-2243. *A Bike, Hike and Jog brochure is available through Saint Paul Parks and Recreation. A Grand Rounds Parkway System brochure is available through the Minneapolis Park and Recreation Board.* There is no admission fee.

HIGHLIGHTS: • 5.5 miles of trails through wooded areas • Beautiful views of the Mississippi River • Ford Lock and Dam.

TIPS FOR WALKERS: • Carry water because there is a considerable distance between water fountains. • Street clothes are recommended. • You may want to carry a camera.

RECOMMENDED ROUTE: 8.8 K (5.5 miles)
PAVED/DIRT SURFACE. LEVEL/STEPS. SHADED/UNSHADED.
Start to the right of the World War I monument. A drinking fountain marks the beginning of the trail. Follow the trail to the ① **stone wall** donated to the City of Saint Paul by the Kettle River Company. Continue on the trail as it curves along the road. You will eventually reach the ② **steps to the Lake Street Bridge.** Cross the bridge. A gas station is available on the corner for water and snacks. Turn left and follow the path along the other side of the river. The path ③ **splits into exclusive walking and biking paths.** Continue to follow the path (down the steps) as it winds along the river. The path along this stretch is well shaded. Follow the path until you get to the ④ **stone steps** that go back up toward the street. Continue to follow the street path until you get to the Upper Mississippi River lock and dam sign. Go left to explore the dam or cross the street and go to the left to the ⑤ **dirt path** that takes you to the Ford Parkway Bridge. Follow the bridge across the river and take the path back to the parking lot, enjoying the scenic overlooks along the way.

GIVING BACK: To volunteer call 612/292-7400. Direct financial donations to the Saint Paul Division of Parks and Recreation, 300 City Hall Annex, 25 West Fourth Street, St. Paul, MN 55102, or the Minneapolis Park and Recreation Board, 310 Fourth Avenue South, Minneapolis, MN 55415, or call 612/348-2243.

Hidden Falls/
Crosby Farm Regional Park

Operated by the Saint Paul Division of Parks and Recreation

"I usually walk in Minneapolis, but I ventured over here and found another nice place to walk with my dogs."
                                                                —Julie Doffing, Minneapolis resident.

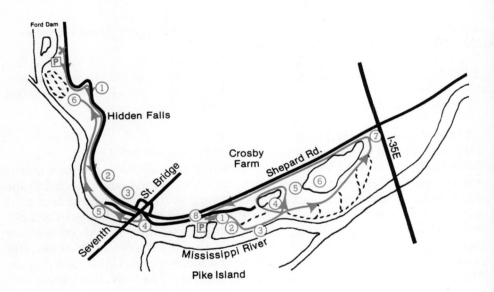

3

DIRECTIONS: Hidden Falls/Crosby Farm parks are located along the east bank of the Mississippi River. **Public transportation** is available on MTC Routes #9A, 9B, 10, 14, and 20. **From Interstate 494:** Proceed south on Snelling Avenue, west on Ford Parkway, and just before you reach the bridge, turn south onto Mississippi River Boulevard. **Hidden Falls:** Just a short distance from the bridge on the right side of the road is the Hidden Falls Scenic Overlook and a small parking lot. **Park** in the lot. **Crosby Farm:** Continue along Mississippi River Boulevard (quite a distance) past both entrance gates to Hidden Falls Park. At the stop light at Gannon Road, turn right into Crosby Farm Park. Follow the entrance road to the picnic shelter. **Park** by the shelter.

INFORMATION: Call 612/292-7400. The park is open from sunrise to 10 P.M. There is no admittance fee.

HIGHLIGHTS: • 8.4 miles of walking trails • Natural floodplain.

TIPS FOR WALKERS: • Trail clothes are recommended.

RECOMMENDED ROUTE (HIDDEN FALLS): 5.3 K (3.3 miles)
PAVED. SEVERAL STEEP HILLS. MOSTLY SHADED.
Proceed to the scenic overlook and take the trail to the left. You will come to another overlook on the right. The steps to the far right lead down to a waterfall. Take the trail to the left to view the waterfall from above. Then, continue walking along Mississippi River Boulevard. You will pass the ① **north gate entrance.** Continue walking along the river. Across the river you can catch glimpses of ② **historic Fort Snelling.** When you reach the ③ **south gate entrance** enter the park and go down a huge hill. At the bottom, proceed to the ④ **walking path.** Soon you will reach a ⑤ **picnic area** on your right. Continue past the boat launch and another picnic area until you reach a ⑥ **picnic pavilion.** Follow the steep hill to the top and proceed left on the trail back to the start point.

RECOMMENDED ROUTE (CROSBY FARM): 5.8 K (3.6 miles)
PAVED. LEVEL/ONE STEEP HILL. MOSTLY SHADED.
From the ① **picnic shelter** follow the trail to the left. At the first ② **trail junction,** turn right onto the Canopy Trail. As you walk along the river you will see a ③ **large orange sign** warning boaters of a large tree. At the next ④ **four-way trail junction,** go straight onto the Wetland Trail. You will soon reach the ⑤ **floating boardwalk.** Follow the path around and stay to the left at all trail junctions. When you get back to the same four-way junction, proceed straight ahead onto the Canopy Trail. Follow the trail past ⑥ **Crosby Lake** to the top of the hill to ⑦ **Shepard Road.** Turn left, follow Shepard Road back to the park entrance, down the hills past the ⑧ **marina** to the start point.

GIVING BACK: To volunteer call 612/292-7400. Direct financial donations to Saint Paul Division of Parks and Recreation, 300 City Hall Annex, 25 West Fourth Street, St. Paul, MN 55102.

Lake Nokomis/Minnehaha Creek ____

Operated by the Minneapolis Park and Recreation Board

"Although many people considered parks as frills that cost too much for their perceived value, the historical reason for parks persisted based on five basic arguments, most of which are still valid today: public health, morality, the development of the Romantic movement, economics and education." —Ruth Humleker, People for Parks News, October 1989.

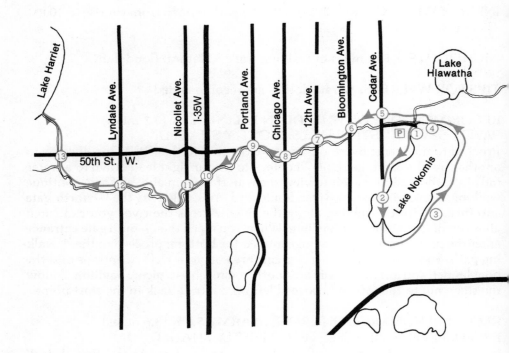

4

DIRECTIONS: Lake Nokomis is located in south Minneapolis. **Public transportation** is available on MTC Routes #19 and 35. **From Interstate 494:** Proceed north on Cedar Avenue, turn east (right) onto East Lake Nokomis Parkway. **Park** near the public beach.

INFORMATION: Call 612/348-2243. The Minneapolis Park and Recreation Board has three brochures available—*Park Highlights, The Grand Rounds Parkway System*, and *A Walk Along the Mississippi Mile*. There is no admission fee.

HIGHLIGHTS: • 7 miles of hiking trails • Minnehaha Creek • Wooded walkways • Picnic area • Beach • Fishing • Exercise course • Concession stand.

TIPS FOR WALKERS: • There are parking areas along both sides of the creek. • At bridges and street crossings, paths are shared with bikers. • You may want to bring a camera. • Trail mileage: Lake Nokomis pedestrian (2.7), and bike (2.78); Minnehaha Creek (4.93). • *During the winter, the biking trails at Lake Nokomis are open to walkers.*

RECOMMENDED ROUTE: 20 K (12.5 miles)
PAVED SURFACE. LEVEL (ONE STEEP HILL). SHADED/UNSHADED.
From the parking lot, proceed to the ① **paved pedestrian path** in front of the beach house and turn right. You'll pass a sailboat harbor as the trail winds around to the ② **Cedar Avenue bridge.** You'll walk along the south shore of the lake (on sidewalk); along the eastern shoreline watch for ③ **scenic views of the downtown skyline.** Steps lead down to the shore at one point. After you cross a footbridge over a creek, ④ **turn right, cross the street,** and walk along the paved trail to the left (it's shared with bikers). You'll cross a footbridge, then turn left along East Minnehaha Parkway, and cross ⑤ **Cedar Avenue.** The trail continues along the creek. After you cross ⑥ **Bloomington Avenue,** you will cross over the creek. There are other path junctions, but keep to the main path. You will cross ⑦ **12th Avenue South** and then turn left over the street bridge. Turn right onto the walkway and you will now be walking on the left side of the creek. The trail continues to ⑧ **Chicago Avenue** as you walk under a bridge. You'll see a water pump along the trail. Continue across ⑨ **Portland Avenue** and keep going straight. Proceed right over the bridge, then left. Then you will walk under ⑩ **Interstate 35W** (a huge bridge). You will cross ⑪ **Nicollet,** turn left, then right again. Continue ahead under the ⑫ **Lyndale Bridge,** and you will eventually turn left and cross another bridge, then turn right. Cross ⑬ **West 50th Street** and you'll see Lynnhurst Park on the left. Continue to Lake Harriet. Retrace your steps to the start point.

GIVING BACK: For information about volunteer and donation opportunities, contact the Minneapolis Park and Recreation Board at 310 Fourth Avenue South, Minneapolis, MN 55415, or call 612/348-2243.

Lake Calhoun/Lake Harriet

Operated by the Minneapolis Park and Recreation Board

"On the west shore of Lake Calhoun in 1898...the 130-acre tract was known as Menage's Lake Side Park and the Lake Side Park Hotel. On the high elevation a tall, wooden observatory, eighty feet high, was maintained, from which a splended view could be obtained over the city."

—Theodore Wirth, *Minneapolis Park System, 1883–1944.*

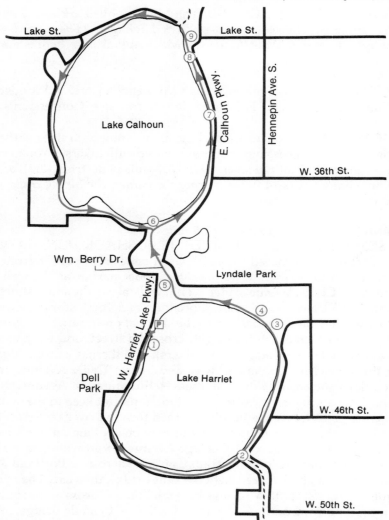

FACILITIES

- ✓ **Restrooms** (accessible) are located at the Lake Calhoun boathouse and in a building near the Lake Harriet bandshell.
- ✓ **Water** is available at hand pumps at the south shore of Lake Calhoun and the north shore of Lake Harriet.
- ✓ **Public telephones** are available at the Lake Calhoun boathouse and the Lake Harriet bandshell.

5

DIRECTIONS: Lake Calhoun and Lake Harriet are located in south Minneapolis. **Public transportation** is available on MTC Routes #28 and 6. **From Interstate 94:** Proceed south on Hennepin Avenue, right on 36th Street, left onto East Calhoun Parkway, and left at the light to William Berry Drive. Follow the entrance road up a hill, and turn right at West Lake Harriet Parkway. **Park** in the lot near the bandshell.

INFORMATION: Call 612/348-2243. The Minneapolis Park and Recreation Board has three brochures—*Park Highlights,The Grand Rounds Parkway System,* and *A Walk Along the Mississippi Mile.* There is no admission fee.

HIGHLIGHTS (Lake Harriet) • Trolley rides • Pontoon boat cruise • Concerts • Playground • Concession stand • Picnic area • Beach • Thomas Sadler Roberts Bird Sanctuary • Lyndale Park Rose and Rock Gardens **(Lake Calhoun)** • Canoe rental • Playground • Beach • Picnic area • Concession stand • Under-bridge passageway to Lake of the Isles.

TIPS FOR WALKERS: • You may want to bring a picnic basket. • Street clothes are recommended. • Walkers use the inner trail; bikers, skaters use the outer trail. Trail mileage: Lake Harriet pedestrian (2.75) and bike (2.99). Lake Calhoun pedestrian (3.10) and bike (3.19). William Berry Drive (.56). *The outer bike paths are cleared for walkers in the winter.*

RECOMMENDED ROUTE: 11.2 K (7 miles)
PAVED. ROLLING HILLS. SHADED/UNSHADED.
From the parking lot, proceed to the ① **Lake Harriet Music Facility** (bandshell). Take the pedestrian walkway south (right). Proceed around the south shore of the lake. Note the ② **trail to Minnehaha Parkway** that leads to Lake Nokomis. Continue around Lake Harriet. Turn right at ③ **Rose Way Road,** and follow the path to the Bird Sanctuary and Rock Garden. After a self-guided tour of the rock garden, walk through the turnstile to the ④ **Bird Sanctuary.** Follow this quarter-mile linear path to the end and you will exit at a parking lot. Continue on the trail to the right along ⑤ **William Berry Drive.** Cross ⑥ **East Calhoun Parkway** and proceed to the pedestrian trail that leads north (to the right). Note the ⑦ **historical marker.** Continue around the shoreline, passing the ⑧ **Lake Calhoun boathouse.** You may proceed on the trail that goes under the bridge to Lake of the Isles or ⑨ **continue on the trail over the bridge, along Lake Street.** Caution: Bikers and walkers share this path. Follow the path past the beach and playground area. Continue along the west shore of Lake Calhoun. Take William Berry Drive back to your start point.

GIVING BACK: For information about volunteer and donation opportunities, contact the Minneapolis Park and Recreation Board, 310 Fourth Avenue South, Minneapolis, MN 55415, or call 612/348-2243.

Lakewood Cemetery

Operated by the Lakewood Cemetery Association

"A walk through Lakewood Cemetery is a walk through history. From the magnificent mosaic chapel built in 1910 to the memorials that honor famous Minnesotans, at almost every turn there is something new to see and learn."
—Ron Gjerde, Manager.

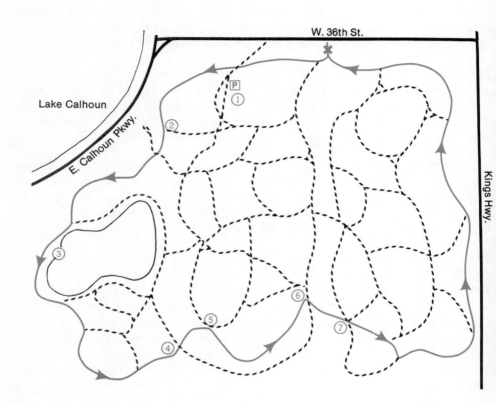

FACILITIES

✓ **Restrooms** (accessible) are available in the office and mausoleum during regular hours (see information).

✓ **Water** is available in the mausoleum during regular hours.

✓ **A public phone** is available in the office during business hours.

6

DIRECTIONS: Lakewood Cemetery is located south of downtown Minneapolis. **Public transportation** is available on MTC Routes #6, 52L and 28. **From Interstate 94:** Proceed south on Hennepin Avenue approximately six blocks past Lake Street. Hennepin ends at the gates of Lakewood Cemetery. Follow the entrance road to the office and **park** on the road near the office.

INFORMATION: Call 612/822-2171. Gates to the cemetery open at 8 A.M. every morning and they close at the following hours during the year: April 1 until the beginning of Daylight Savings (6 P.M.); Daylight Savings until Labor Day (8 P.M.); Labor Day until the end of Daylight Savings (7 P.M.); end of Daylight Savings until April 1 (5 P.M.). The office is open Monday through Friday from 8 A.M. to 5 P.M. and on Saturday from 8 A.M. to noon. *Stop in at the office and pick up a map called* A Tour Through History *that will provide you with a self-guided tour of the cemetery.* There is no admission fee.

HIGHLIGHTS: • Lake • Beautiful grounds • Historical monuments • Solitude • Lakewood Chapel contains one of the largest true mosaics in the western world • 250 acres of gentle hills between Lake Calhoun and Lake Harriet • Designed by H.W.S. Cleveland.

TIPS FOR WALKERS: • Street clothes are recommended. • There are many unmarked, circular roads—you may get lost without the map. • You may want to bring a notebook and pen. The peacefulness of the cemetery and the quiet lake are sure to bring up reflections you may wish to record.

RECOMMENDED ROUTE: 4.1 K (2.6 miles)
PAVED (ROAD). LEVEL. MOSTLY SHADED.
Start just inside the main gates and head west (to the right). On your left you'll pass the ① **mausoleum** with its fountains and pool in front. As you continue on, you'll catch glimpses of Lake Calhoun through the screen of trees at the cemetery's boundary. As the path curves to the south, look for the ② **grave of Maggie Menzel,** the first person buried at Lakewood Cemetery. After a short distance you'll reach a ③ **small lake** and follow the road along the shoreline. Keep to the right through the next three intersections. At the ④ **next intersection** you'll see a "no thru traffic sign" to the right. Curve to the left, then to the right. At the next ⑤ **four-way junction,** take a right. At the next ⑥ **intersection,** you will take not a far right, but the second to the far right turn past the Section 12 sign. At the ⑦ **five-way intersection,** take the second to the far right turn. Follow the road back to your start point, keeping to the right at every intersection.

GIVING BACK: Donations can be directed to Lakewood Cemetery's General Care Fund, 3600 Hennepin Avenue, Minneapolis, MN 55408. Lakewood Cemetery is a non-sectarian, non-profit perpetual care cemetery.

Cedar Lake/Lake of the Isles

Operated by the Minneapolis Park and Recreation Board

"There were originally four islands in Lake of the Isles—two near the south shore and the two (north islands) that now remain. The two north islands . . . were to become residential sites made accessible by means of a roadway over an inter-island bridge and a fill to the mainland, which would have made the furthermost island a peninsula. With the acquistion of the lake properties by the Board, these plans luckily became naught."

—Theodore Wirth, *Minneapolis Park System, 1883–1944.*

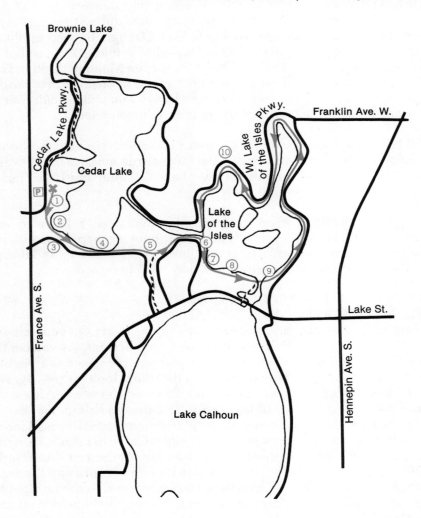

7

DIRECTIONS: Cedar Lake and Lake of the Isles are located southwest of downtown Minneapolis. **Public transportation** is available on MTC Route #1. **From State Highway 100:** Proceed east on Glenwood Avenue, south (right) on Theodore Wirth Parkway. You'll cross over I-394/12 and then over another bridge where you'll come to a stoplight intersection. Veer left onto Cedar Lake Parkway. **Park** in one of the lots on the left. Note: Parking is also available along Lake of the Isles Parkway.

INFORMATION: Call 612/348-2243. The Minneapolis Park and Recreation Board has three brochures—*Park Highlights, The Grand Rounds Parkway System,* and *A Walk Along the Mississippi Mile.* There is no admission fee.

HIGHLIGHTS: • Wildlife bird refuge on the islands in Lake of the Isles • Canada geese • Scenic views of downtown Minneapolis • Cedar Lake beach

TIPS FOR WALKERS: • You may want to bring a camera. • Street clothes are recommended. • At bridges and intersections bikers, skaters, and walkers share the same path, so be careful. • **Trail mileage:** Cedar Lake Parkway pedestrian (1.68 miles); Dean Parkway (.59 miles); Lake of the Isles pedestrian (2.6 miles) and bike (2.97); Lake Calhoun pedestrian (3.1) and bike (3.19). *The outer bike paths are cleared for walkers in the winter.*

RECOMMENDED ROUTE: 9 K (5.6 miles)
PAVED. LEVEL. SHADED/UNSHADED.
From the parking lot, proceed to the ① **paved trail** that loops around the south end of the lake. You will pass through a wooded area, with Cedar Lake to your left. Note the ② **fishing dock.** Note the ③ **hill** across the street, the former site of the Oak Grove House, an octagon-shaped hotel built in the 1870s. Proceed past ④ **Cedar Lake Beach** on the sidewalk, across the railroad tracks, past Benton Boulevard, down the hill. Turn left on ⑤ **Dean Parkway.** Continue walking past houses and along the channel that connects the two lakes. When you come to the ⑥ **first bridge,** cross the street. You may want to stop and take pictures of the Minneapolis skyline. Proceed to the ⑦ **walking path down the hill** (it's just to the right of the bridge as you're looking at downtown). Follow the path past the ⑧ **hand pump** to the ⑨ **second bridge.** If you want to go to Lake Calhoun, cross the street and follow the walker's path to the right that winds under two bridges to Lake Calhoun. Otherwise, continue walking around Lake of the Isles. Note ⑩ **Peavey Fountain** at Kenwood Parkway, a former watering site for horses. Continue around the lake, and when you return to the bridge, take a right across the street and proceed back to your start point.

GIVING BACK: For information about volunteer and donation opportunities, contact the Minneapolis Park and Recreation Board, 310 Fourth Avenue South, Minneapolis, MN 55415, or call 612/348-2243.

Wirth Parkway/

Eloise Butler Wildflower Garden and Bird Sanctuary

Operated by the Minneapolis Park and Recreation Board

"For years the undulating wooded land of the original Saratoga Springs acquisition of 1889 had been a Mecca for teachers and students of nature study because of its heavy timber, luxuriant wild undergrowth and bird-life; a section of that tract was set aside and fenced during 1907. . . . In 1911, Miss Eloise Butler, a retired botany teacher, became its first official curator. . . . During her tenure as curator, Miss Butler served most loyally and efficiently for the preservation and enlargement of the collection of native plant material."

—Theodore Wirth, *Minneapolis Park System, 1883–1944.*

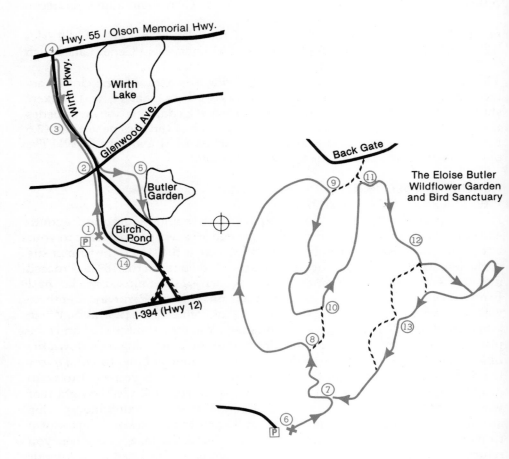

FACILITIES

 ✓**Restrooms** are located inside the entrance to the garden.
 ✓**Water** is available at fountains inside the entrance to the garden.
 ✓**Public telephones** are not available, but the shelter phone is available for emergency use during regular hours.

8

DIRECTIONS: Theodore Wirth Parkway is located west of downtown Minneapolis. **Public transportation** is available on MTC Routes #55, 20, and 9. **From State Highway 55:** Proceed south on Wirth Parkway. Just beyond Glenwood Avenue you will be turning right into a small parking area with an information post/kiosk. **Park** in this horseshoe lot.

INFORMATION: Call 612/348-2243 or the Eloise Butler Garden at 612/348-5702. The Butler Garden is open daily from April 1 through October 31 from 7:30 A.M. to dusk. The shelter just inside the gate provides an excellent self-guided tour booklet titled *Eloise Butler Wildflower Garden and Bird Sanctuary*—an excellent guide to Minnesota wildflowers. There is no admission fee.

HIGHLIGHTS: • Abundance of wildflowers, vines, shrubs, trees • Birds, small mammals • Rich scents • Benches • Some trees and plants have name plaques • Shelter offers nature tours, night hikes, classes, birding opportunities.

TIPS FOR WALKERS: • Trail clothes are recommended. • Bring a camera. • On Wirth Parkway, you'll be sharing the trail with walkers and joggers, so keep to one side. • *Wirth Parkway trails are cleared in the winter for walkers.*

RECOMMENDED ROUTE: 3.2 K (2 miles)
PAVED/WOODCHIP SURFACE. HILLY. MOSTLY SHADED.
From the parking lot kiosk, proceed north on the ① **paved trail along Wirth Parkway.** Cross ② **Glenwood Avenue** and continue walking north past the ③ **Loring Cascade bronze tablet.** Proceed north to ④ **Highway 55,** cross Wirth Parkway, and head south again. When you cross Glenwood Avenue, the trail resumes. Take the side path to the left through the parking lot to the ⑤ **natural spring.** Follow the trail to the Butler Garden parking lot. Proceed ⑥ **down the steps** and to the left through the entrance gate. ⑦ **Turn left** at the shelter and water fountain. When you come to a circle of benches and another water fountain, ⑧ **turn left again.** You will eventually cross a bridge, and follow the ⑨ **arrow to the right** that leads to a series of footbridges over a bog. When you come to the next ⑩ **trail junction,** turn left. After climbing a hill, follow an ⑪ **arrow to the right.** Near ⑫ **marker #36,** turn left, make a loop, and then come back out and follow the trail to the left. At the next two trail junctions, continue left toward marker #45 and you will walk along ⑬ **shoulder-high flowers.** Continue back to the garden entrance. At the garden parking lot, turn left (south) back down the hill to Wirth Parkway. Cross the road and walk north along the parkway, past ⑭ **Birch Pond** to the parking lot.

GIVING BACK: For information about membership, volunteer, or donation opportunities, contact the Friends of the Wildflower Garden, Inc., 3800 Bryant Avenue South, Minneapolis, MN 55409.

Downtown Minneapolis/

Sculpture Garden to Boom Island Park

Operated by the Minneapolis Park and Recreation Board

"At one time, Boom Island was not really an island, but a log boom. It is thought that continual silting from the logs and eventual filling from a variety of sources created the island which was separated from the mainland by a narrow water course."

—Boom Island Dedication pamphlet, June 27, 1987.

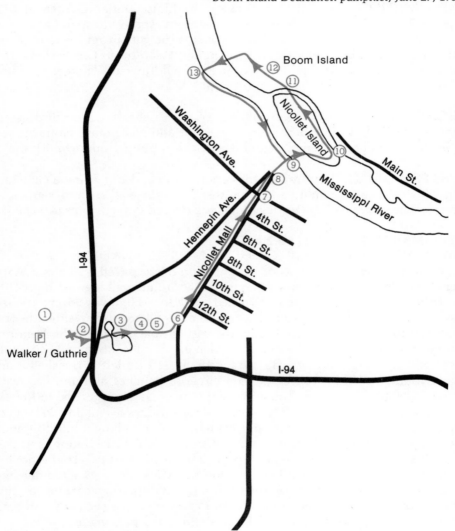

FACILITIES

✓ **Restrooms** (accessible) are available along the route.
✓ **Water** is available along the route.
✓ **Public telephones** are available along the route.

9

DIRECTIONS: Downtown Minneapolis is along the west shore of the Mississippi River. **Public transportation** is available on MTC Routes #1, 4, 6, 12, 28, and 51. **From Interstate 94:** Proceed to Hennepin Avenue. If you're heading west on 94 toward downtown Minneapolis, take the Hennepin/Lyndale exit, then the Hennepin (north) exit. Get in the left lane as soon as possible, and turn left to Vineland Place. If you're heading east on 94 toward downtown, take the Hennepin/Lyndale exit and stay in the right lane. Turn right at Vineland Place. Follow the entrance road past the Walker Art Center/Guthrie Theatre on the left and the Sculpture Garden on the right. **Park** in the large public lot near the Sculpture Garden.

INFORMATION: Call the Riverfront Coordinator at 612/348-2226. *The Park Board publishes* A Walk Along the Mississippi Mile, *four walking tours along the city's historic riverfront. A detailed guide to the Sculpture Garden is available in the Cowles Conservatory and the Walker Art Center.* The buildings are open Tuesday–Saturday, 10 A.M. to 8 P.M., Sunday 11 A.M. to 5 P.M., and closed on Monday. There is no admission fee to the garden. There is a parking fee.

HIGHLIGHTS: • Sculpture Garden • Irene Hixon Whitney Bridge • Loring Park • Downtown Minneapolis • Gateway Park • Nicollet Island • Boom Island Park • West River Parkway.

TIPS FOR WALKERS: • You may want to plan on spending the day in downtown Minneapolis. • Street clothes are recommended.

RECOMMENDED ROUTE: 7.2 K (4. 5 miles)
PAVED/DIRT SURFACE. LEVEL (SOME STAIRS). MOSTLY UNSHADED.
From the parking lot proceed to the ① **Minneapolis Sculpture Garden.** After a self-guided tour of the garden, cross the ② **Whitney Bridge** to ③ **Loring Park.** Proceed to the footbridge and follow the path to the left around the lake, heading for the spherical ④ **Berger Fountain.** Cross the street and take the steps up to ⑤ **Loring Greenway** to Nicollet Mall. Turn left at ⑥ **Nicollet Mall.** Walk to the north end of the mall and cross ⑦ **Washington Avenue** and walk up a few stairs under the arches to ⑧ **Gateway Park.** Proceed north on ⑨ **Hennepin Avenue,** and from the bridge, turn right on ⑩ **Wilder Street onto Nicollet Island.** Walk along Wilder Street past the Nicollet Island Inn and turn left onto Island Avenue (just before the bridge to St. Anthony Main). On Island Avenue, follow the sidewalk and then the street along the north side of the island. At the end of the island, follow the stairs to the right that lead to a ⑪ **footbridge** to ⑫ **Boom Island.** Walk across Boom Island, then take the stairs up and walk across the bridge to ⑬ **West River Parkway.** Follow the pedestrian trail to the dirt hiking trail along the shoreline, and follow the trail back to the Hennepin Avenue Bridge. Take the stairs up to the bridge, turn right, proceed south on Hennepin, left on Washington Avenue, and right on Nicollet Mall back to your start point.

GIVING BACK: For information about volunteer and financial donation opportunities, call the Minneapolis Park and Recreation Board at 612/348-2234.

University of Minnesota

Operated by the State of Minnesota

"We have a walking program for students, faculty and staff that is beginning to catch on. The program works because walkers know we'll be there to provide support, supervision and motivation. We also offer all kinds of incentives to walkers who accumulate points. Participants report they are seeing some major changes in their lives because they're finally getting exercise on a regular basis."

—Kim Lillie, Walking Program Coordinator and Lynda Johnson, Fitness Program Coordinator.

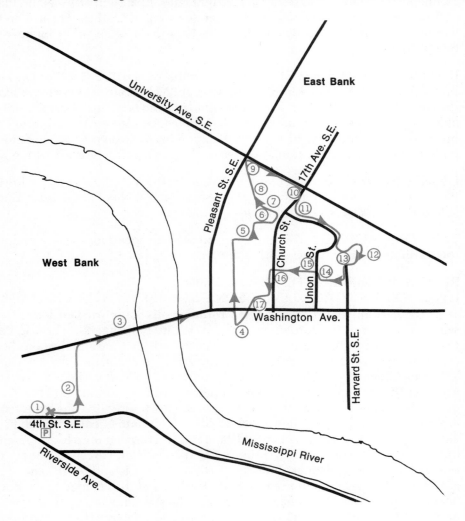

10

DIRECTIONS: The University of Minnesota is located due east of downtown Minneapolis. It has an East Bank and a West Bank campus. **Public transportation** is available on MTC Routes #2, 7, 16, 19, 20, 73, and 52. **From Interstate 35W:** Take the U of M exit and follow the signs for the West Bank Campus. Proceed east on Washington Avenue, south on 19th Avenue South, and east (left) on Fourth Street Southeast. **Park** in the West Bank Ramp across from the Wilson Library.

INFORMATION: Faculty, students, and staff are eligible for the "Walking Into Fitness" program. Call Recreational Sports at 612/625-6800. However, anyone may walk the recommended route through the campus.

HIGHLIGHTS: • Campus designed by Cass Gilbert • Pillsbury Hall built in 1889 • Northrop Auditorium • Aquatic Center.

TIPS FOR WALKERS: • Street clothes are recommended. • Walking paths are cleared all year-round. • You may want to stop for lunch along the way.

RECOMMENDED ROUTE: 4 K (2.5 miles)
PAVED SURFACE. LEVEL. SHADED/UNSHADED.
From the parking lot, proceed across ① **Fourth Street Southeast,** then walk toward the Wilson Library. When you get to ② **the courtyard,** follow the bike lines on the ground and they will lead you to ③ **the Washington Avenue Bridge.** Cross the bridge, and then proceed to the ④ **Coffman Union** on the right where you can obtain a campus map. Then, walk over the bridge to the steps of the ⑤ **Northrop Auditorium.** Turn right, take a few steps down, then turn left and walk toward ⑥ **Pillsbury Hall** (the older building with the checkered brick). Walk between Pillsbury Hall and ⑦ **Nolte Center** to Williamson Hall and the ⑧ **Minnesota Book Center.** Continue to Folwell Hall where you will ⑨ **turn right on the corner of Pleasant Street Southeast and University Avenue Southeast.** Follow University, then turn right at 17th Avenue Southeast (Church Street) past the ⑩ **Bell Museum of Natural History.** Cross the street and walk around the ⑪ **Armory,** past the Field House and turn left at the pedestrian crossing to the ⑫ **Aquatic Center.** Turn ⑬ **south onto Harvard Street** and turn right and walk along the road past the Harvard Street Ramp. Turn right on ⑭ **Union Street Southeast,** then ⑮ **turn left** and walk along the Electrical Engineering building. Turn left on Church Street and walk past ⑯ **Lind Hall.** Just beyond the round cement barriers, turn right and walk along ⑰ **Ford Hall.** When you get to the mall, turn left and take the steps up and over the bridge to Coffman Union. You may proceed to the left if you want to explore University of Minnesota hospitals, or right, to retrace your steps to your start point.

GIVING BACK: Direct financial donations to the University of Minnesota Foundation, 120 Morrill Hall, 100 Church Street Southeast, Minneapolis, MN 55455.

State Fairgrounds

Operated by the Minnesota State Fairgrounds

"People walk here every day, either on the roads or in the Coliseum. Some people have commented that walking around the grounds brings back memories of the State Fair, and that can be the added boost that people need to exercise on a cold winter day." —Susan Ritt, State Fairgrounds.

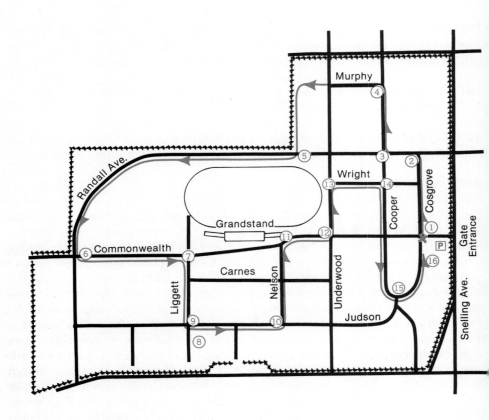

FACILITIES

✓ **Restrooms** (accessible) are available at the Service Building (near the entrance gate) and the Coliseum.

✓ **Water** is available at the Service Building and Coliseum.

✓ **Public telephones** are available along Commonwealth Avenue.

11

DIRECTIONS: The State Fairgrounds is located north of I-94 on Snelling Avenue. **Public transportation** is available on MTC Routes #4 and 5. **From Interstate 94:** Proceed north on Snelling Avenue. The entrance to the State Fairgrounds is on the left. **Park** along Cosgrove Street, the first street to the right just inside the entrance.

INFORMATION: Call the State Fairgrounds office at 612/642-2200 or 642-2204. The State Fairgrounds is open from 6 A.M. to 11 P.M. daily except the week preceding, during, and following the State Fair in August. The indoor Coliseum is open to walkers from early November to early March, Monday through Friday from 11:30 A.M. to 1 P.M. There is no admission charge for walking the grounds, but the fee for walking in the Coliseum is $2 for adults (17 and older) and $1 for youth (16 and under).

HIGHLIGHTS: • Over 5 miles of paved roadways • Interesting buildings and sculptures • Adjacent to the University of Minnesota agricultural grounds • Security patrols • Streets are well lighted for evening walking.

TIPS FOR WALKERS: • Street clothes are recommended. • Watch out for occasional bikers, skaters. • *Roads are cleared in the winter for walkers.*

RECOMMENDED ROUTE: 4.3 K (2.7 miles)
PAVED SURFACE. LEVEL. SHADED/UNSHADED.
From the entrance gate, proceed north on ① **Cosgrove** to Randall Avenue. Turn left on ② **Randall Avenue,** then right on ③ **Cooper Street.** Turn left at ④ **Murphy Avenue** past the Farm Tech Plaza, into the Tiger and Owl parking lots. Note the land to the right owned by the University of Minnesota. You may see or hear some horses or sheep. Take a right on ⑤ **Randall Avenue** and follow this road as it curves west and south. As you pass the Giraffe parking lot, look for horses in the field to your right. Turn left on ⑥ **Commonwealth** and then right on ⑦ **Liggett Street** to the ⑧ **Coliseum.** Turn left at ⑨ **Judson** and left on ⑩ **Nelson.** Turn right on ⑪ **Commonwealth** again. Turn left at ⑫ **Underwood Street,** right on ⑬ **Wright Avenue,** and right on ⑭ **Cooper.** Follow the road as it curves around the ⑮ **Space Needle,** past the ⑯ **International Women's Year Sculpture** on the right. Proceed back to the start point.

GIVING BACK: The State Fairgrounds does not recruit volunteers or solicit donations.

Como Park

Operated by the Saint Paul Division of Parks and Recreation

"I enjoy walking because it's a way to meet new friends." —Jeff Eikens, Saint Paul resident.

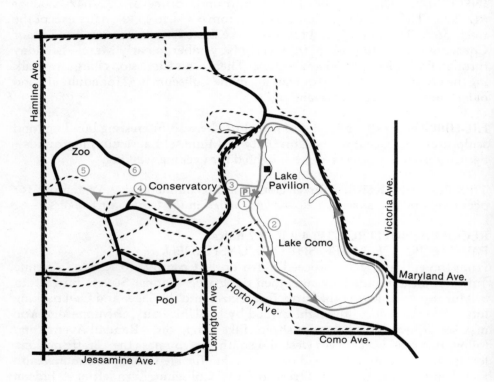

12

DIRECTIONS: Como Park is located in northwest Saint Paul. **Public transportation** is available on MTC Routes #4, 5, and 12. **From Interstate 94:** Proceed north on Lexington Parkway for about two miles to the park entrance. Continue on the entrance road until you come to the Como Lake Pavilion. **Park** near the large pavilion.

INFORMATION: Call Como Park at 612/488-7291, the zoo at 612/489-5571, or the conservatory and the Japanese garden at 612/489-1740. Como Park is open from sunrise to 10 P.M. year-round. The zoo is open from 8 A.M. to 8 P.M. during the summer and 8 A.M. to 5 P.M. during the winter. The zoo buildings open at 10 A.M. The conservatory opens at 10 A.M. and is open until 6 P.M. during the summer and 4 P.M. during the winter. The Japanese garden is open during limited hours from May through the summer. There is no admission fee.

HIGHLIGHTS: • 3.5 miles of walking trails • Como Zoo • Amusement rides for children in the summer • Como Conservatory offers year-round greenery and flowers • Como Pool and Golf Course is open to the public • Ordway Memorial Japanese Garden • Refreshments • Souvenir stores • Concerts, plays • Fishing

TIPS FOR WALKERS: • Street clothes are recommended. • You may want to bring a camera.

RECOMMENDED ROUTE: 5.6 K (3.5 miles)
PAVED. LEVEL. SHADED/UNSHADED.
From the parking lot, proceed to the ① **paved path,** then follow the path around ② **Lake Como.** When you return to the parking lot, proceed to the path near the ③ **flowered "Gates Ajar."** Cross the street at the pedestrian crossing. Follow the path into the woods, across a bridge to a street. Turn right and walk along the street to the ④ **Como Conservatory.** A paved path begins just beyond Nora Place. After you walk through the conservatory, proceed back to the entrance. Proceed to the right and enter the ⑤ **Como Zoo.** Walk through the zoo, keeping to the right at most junctions. There are a number of exhibits including Large Cats, Aquatic Animals, Primates, and Wolf Woods. When you finish touring the zoo, return to the conservatory and tour the ⑥ **Japanese Garden.** Retrace your steps back to the start point.

GIVING BACK: To volunteer at the zoo call 612/488-4041 and at the Conservatory call 612/489-1740. Direct financial donations to the Saint Paul Division of Parks and Recreation, 300 City Hall Annex, 25 West Fourth Street, St. Paul, MN 55102.

The Gateway Segment
Willard Munger Trail

Operated by the Minnesota Department of Natural Resources

"The Gateway Segment begins just north of downtown Saint Paul and within the next few years it will extend for 17 miles up to Pine Point Park in Washington County. Eventually, it will be possible to walk, bike, ski or ride horses on this trail from the Twin Cities to Duluth."
— Larry Killien, Area Trails and Waterways Supervisor Region VI.

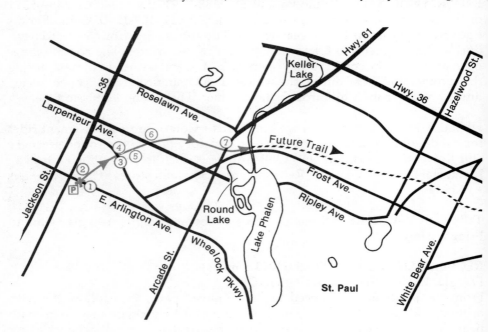

DIRECTIONS: The Gateway Segment of the Willard Munger Trail is north of downtown Saint Paul. **Public transportation** is available on MTC Routes #2 and 8. **From Interstate 35E:** Take the Maryland Avenue exit. Proceed east on Maryland one block, then north on Westminister. Turn left on Arlington for one block. The parking lot is on the left (south) side of the road next to I-35. **Park** in this lot.

INFORMATION: Call the Region VI Trails and Waterways Division at 612/772-7935. Trail maps are available through the Minnesota Department of Natural Resources. There is no admission fee.

HIGHLIGHTS: • Currently, 1.7 of the 17 miles are paved and accessible. The trail is under development at the present time. • The trail winds through residential areas and parks • Keller-Phalen Regional Park.

TIPS FOR WALKERS: • Street clothes are recommended. • Carry water. • The trail is shared with other users, so keep to the right. • Excellent trail for aerobic walking because it is level and paved.

13

FACILITIES

✓ **Restrooms** (portable units) are available at the parking lot.
✓ **Water** is not available.
✓ **Public telephones** are not available.

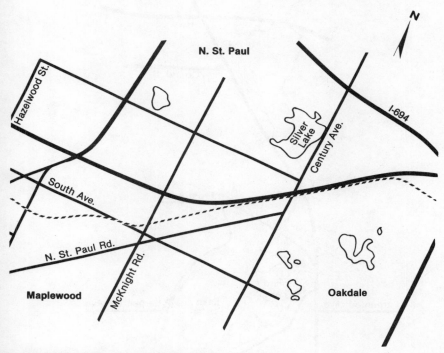

RECOMMENDED ROUTE: 4.8 K (3 miles)

PAVED SURFACE. LEVEL. SHADED/UNSHADED.

From the parking lot proceed across Arlington Avenue to the ① **beginning of the trail.** Continue walking and you will cross a ② **bridge** and then another ③ **bridge.** You will pass ④ **Forest Lawn Cemetery** on your left and the public ⑤ **Hillcrest Golf Club** on your right. You will walk under the ⑥ **Larpenteur Avenue Bridge** and then another ⑦ **bridge under Highway 61/Arcade Avenue.** Proceed to the Keller Lake/Lake Phalen junction. At this point you may return to your start point or proceed to the Keller Lake picnic area (to your left) or Lake Phalen (under the bridge to your right).

GIVING BACK: For volunteer opportunities, call the Trails and Waterways office. Volunteers are needed to assist with trail plantings, information posts, and trash pick-up. Direct financial donations to Minnesota Parks and Trails Council, E-1311 First National Bank Building, St. Paul, MN 55101, or call 612/291-0715 or 800/289-1930, or contact the MNDNR Trails and Waterways Division, 500 Lafayette Road, St. Paul, MN 55155, or call 612/296-1151.

Keller-Phalen Regional Park

Keller Park is operated by Ramsey County Parks and Recreation
Phalen Park is operated by the Saint Paul Division of Parks and Recreation

"I like being outside a lot. I enjoy walking around with people and getting my exercise."
—Virjean Toensing, Saint Paul resident.

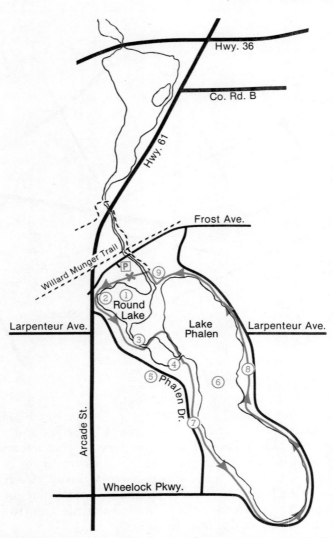

FACILITIES

✓ **Restrooms** (accessible) are available at the Lakeside Activities Center, Picnic Pavilion, and the beach.

✓ **Water** is available at the Lakeside Activities Center, Picnic Pavilion, and the beach.

✓ **Public telephones** are available at the Lakeside Activities Center, Picnic Pavilion, and the beach.

14

DIRECTIONS: Keller Park is located in Maplewood and Phalen Park is located in Saint Paul. **Public transportation** is available on MTC Routes #14, 10, 11E, 15. **From Interstate 35E:** Proceed east on State Highway 36, south on U.S. Highway 61 for about .75 mile (ignore all the signs you see for Keller Regional Park along Highway 61), east on Frost Avenue (less than .75 mile). The entrance to Keller Regional Park—Round Lake Picnic Area is on the right. **Park** in the lot near Round Lake.

INFORMATION: Call Ramsey County Parks and Recreation at 612/777-1707 or the Saint Paul Division of Parks and Recreation at 612/292-7400. The trails are open from sunrise to 9 P.M. A trail map is available through the Saint Paul Division of Parks and Recreation. There is no admission fee.

HIGHLIGHTS: • Paved, accessible trails • Swimming • Golf course • Amphitheater • Centennial Ice Palace Memorial • Civilian Conservation Corps Memorial • Picnic area •Willard Munger Trail segment • Boating • Fishing.

TIPS FOR WALKERS: • Street clothes are recommended. • Paths are cleared for walkers in the winter. • Paths are lit for walking/skiing at night.

RECOMMENDED ROUTE: 5.6 K (3.5 miles)
PAVED SURFACE. LEVEL/ONE HILL. SHADED/UNSHADED.
From the parking lot, proceed to the path to the right around ① **Round Lake,** to a ② **flagstone overlook** that gives you a glimpse of the park. Continue on the walking path (stay to the far right) over two ③ **footbridges.** Just past the second footbridge you might want to take a detour to the right and pass in front of the ④ **brick amphitheater** to see the ⑤ **St. Paul Winter Carnival Ice Palace Memorial,** "a labor of love." Then, follow the path between the amphitheater and the pavilion to ⑥ **Lake Phalen.** Just before you reach the Lakeside Activities Center, you may want to observe the memorial dedicated to the ⑦ **Civilian Conservation Corps** of 1937. The path winds past a beach house on the southern end of the lake. On the east shore, you'll proceed up a ⑧ **steep incline** that provides a wonderful view of the area. At the end of the trail along the north shore, follow the ⑨ **Keller Picnic Area** path that leads north. You have a choice of returning to the parking lot via the footbridge or walking under the stone bridge to explore more of Keller Park.

GIVING BACK: For information about volunteer or donation opportunities, call Ramsey County Parks and Recreation at 612/777-1707 or the Saint Paul Division of Parks and Recreation at 612/292-7400.

Oakland Cemetery

Operated by the Oakland Cemetery Association

"Oakland's Board of Trustees engaged H.W.S. Cleveland to landscape the cemetery's grounds at a cost of five dollars per acre. He was empowered to superintend the work in accordance with his plans which have continued today to be the basic beautification plans of the cemetery."

—Robert Orr Baker, from *A Safe and Permanent Resting Place.*

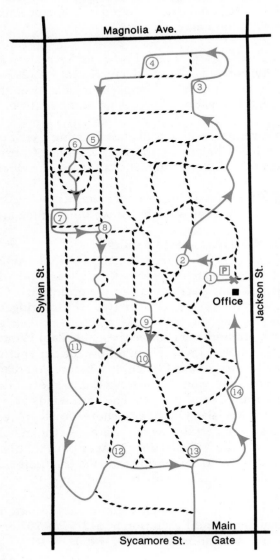

15

DIRECTIONS: Oakland Cemetery is north of downtown Saint Paul. **Public transportation** is available on MTC Routes #8 or 2. **From Interstate 35E:** Proceed west on Maryland, south on Jackson. Turn right at the Jackson Street entrance. **Park** near the office.

INFORMATION: Call the office at 612/224-2366. The cemetery is open from 8 A.M. to 8 P.M. during the summer and 8 A.M. to 4:30 P.M. during the winter. The office is open Monday through Friday from 8:30 A.M. to 4:30 P.M. *A free detailed walking tour guide*, An Oakland Tour, *is available at the office.* Also, a historical booklet with a centerfold map is available for $3. There is no admission fee.

HIGHLIGHTS: • All types of memorial art including Grecian head stones, Renaissance stones crowned with classic pediments, curved and molded Colonial forms, Celtic crosses (Irish and Iona), obelisks, shafts, and Athenian temples • Stone chapel built in 1924 • Gravesites of early settlers and famous Minnesotans.

TIPS FOR WALKERS: • Street clothes are recommended. • The roads are unmarked.

RECOMMENDED ROUTE: 3.2 K (2 miles)
PAVED/DIRT SURFACE. LEVEL. MOSTLY SHADED.
From the office, proceed west on the entrance road. At the ① **first junction** turn right, and then left. At the ② **next junction** turn right, turn right again, and then continue straight ahead on this road through another junction along the edge of the cemetery until you reach ③ **Zion Cemetery,** incorporated into Oakland in 1904. Continue around the outer road, passing the ④ **Russian graves.** Follow the road along the edge of the cemetery, then ⑤ **turn right** and then turn left and follow the ⑥ **dirt road** through the circular pathways, turn right, and look for the grave of ⑦ **Alexander Ramsey,** first territorial governor of Minnesota. Turn left, then ⑧ **turn right** and proceed past the I.O.O.F. monument. Turn left and then proceed past the ⑨ **Webb bird bath,** one of four public memorials within the cemetery. Proceed straight ahead, and then ⑩ **turn right** at the next junction. Follow the road past the first intersection. At the ⑪ **second intersection,** turn left and follow the road (Sylvan Street is to your right). Stay to the right at the first intersection, then take a left at the second intersection. Turn right as you walk by the ⑫ **chapel.** Cross the main entrance road, then ⑬ **follow the road** that curves to the left and runs parallel with Jackson Street until you come to a ⑭ **dirt road** that leads back to the office.

GIVING BACK: For information about volunteer or donation opportunities, contact the Oakland Cemetery Association at 927 Jackson Street, St. Paul, MN 55117, or call the office at 612/224-2366 during regular business hours.

Downtown Saint Paul/
Harriet Island to State Capitol

Operated by the Saint Paul Division of Parks and Recreation

"We have over 40 miles of beautiful parkways and trails throughout Saint Paul. There's something for everyone—downtown parks for people who live and work in the city; extensive walkways along the Mississippi River for people who want to get back to nature; and Como Park and Lake Phalen for people who seek a variety of recreational activities."

—John Wirka, Saint Paul Parks and Recreation.

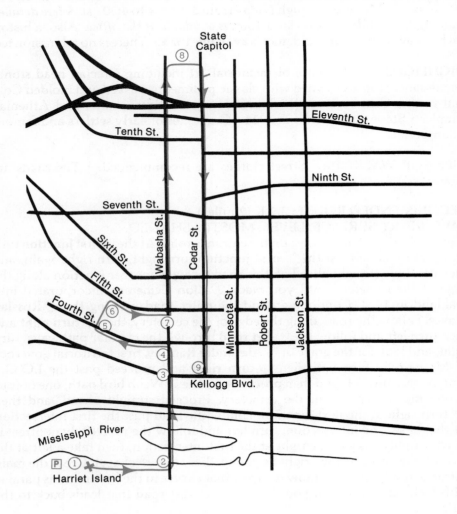

FACILITIES
- ✓**Restrooms** (accessible) are available along the route.
- ✓**Water** is available along the route.
- ✓**Public telephones** are available along the route.

16

DIRECTIONS: Saint Paul is located on the east side of the Mississippi River south of Interstate 94. **Public transportation** to Harriet Island is available on MTC Routes #5, 7, 8, 11, and 29. **From Interstate 94:** Proceed to Harriet Island. If you're heading east on I-94 to downtown Saint Paul, take the Fifth Street exit, turn right on St. Peter Street, left on Kellogg, and right onto the Wabasha Bridge. If you're heading west on I-94 to downtown Saint Paul, take the Sixth Street exit, turn left at Jackson, right on Kellogg, and left onto the Wabasha Bridge. At the end of the bridge make a sharp right onto Yacht Club Road. Follow the main road to the beige brick building. **Park** in the lot by the building along the river.

INFORMATION: Call Saint Paul Parks and Recreation at 612/292-7400. *A Bike, Hike and Jog brochure is available as well as a* Historic Lowertown Walking Tour *brochure.* Saint Paul parks are open from sunrise to 10 P.M. year-round. There is no admission fee.

HIGHLIGHTS: • Harriet Island • Rice Park • Downtown Saint Paul • State Capitol • Mississippi River • Free "on the hour" tours of the Capitol on Mondays through Fridays 9 A.M. to 4 P.M., Saturdays 10 A.M. to 3 P.M., Sundays 1 P.M. to 3 P.M. Call 612/296-2881 for more information. The tours last 45 minutes.

TIPS FOR WALKERS: • Street clothes are recommended. • You may want to spend the day in downtown Saint Paul.

RECOMMENDED ROUTE: 4.8 K (3 miles)
PAVED SURFACE. LEVEL. UNSHADED.
From the parking lot, ① **proceed east on the path along the river,** then walk along the entrance road past the excursion boats and harbor. When you get to Walter Drive, follow the paved walk to the ② **Wabasha Bridge.** Proceed across the bridge, noting the Minnesota Boat Club below. Proceed straight ahead, crossing ③ **Kellogg Boulevard.** Continue straight ahead, then ④ **turn left at Fourth Street.** You may want to take a look at the "Indian God of Peace" just inside the entrance to the Ramsey County Courthouse on the left. Cross St. Peter Street and continue straight ahead to ⑤ **Rice Park** at the corner of Fourth Street and Market. Points of interest around the park include the **James J. Hill Library,** the **Saint Paul Public Library,** the **Ordway Music Theater,** and the **Landmark Center.** Proceed across the park plaza and ⑥ **turn right on Fifth Street.** Proceed east (right) along Fifth Street, then ⑦ **turn left onto Wabasha Street** and follow Wabasha past the World Trade Center all the way to the ⑧ **Minnesota State Capitol.** From the Capitol, follow Cedar Street all the way across Kellogg Boulevard to the ⑨ **Kellogg Mall Park.** Turn right to return to the Wabasha Bridge and your start point.

GIVING BACK: For information about volunteer or financial donation opportunities contact the Saint Paul Division of Parks and Recreation, 300 City Hall Annex, 25 West Fourth Street, St. Paul, MN 55102.

Dodge Nature Center

Operated by the Thomas Irvine Dodge Foundation

"In addition to the numerous school programs conducted during the week, we offer year-round programs for families and adults on evenings and weekends. Birds, Night Hikes, Wild Edible Foods, Astronomy, Snowshoeing, Spring Arrivals Festival and Prairie Day are just a few examples of these public programs."
—Al Singer, Senior Naturalist.

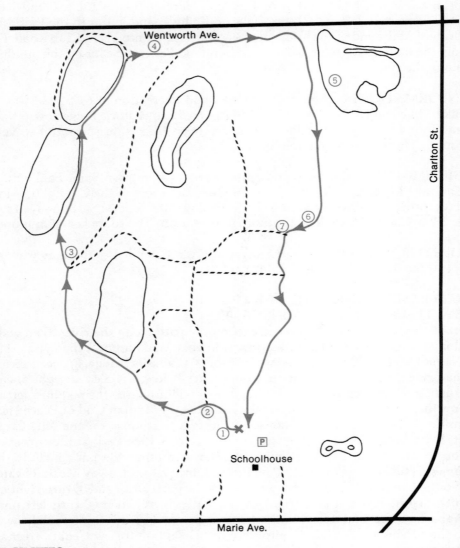

FACILITIES

- ✓ **Restrooms** are available in the Red School House.
- ✓ **Water** is available in the Red School House.
- ✓ **Public telephones** are not available. An office phone is available for emergency use only.

17

DIRECTIONS: The Dodge Nature Center is located about 3 miles southwest of Saint Paul in West Saint Paul. **Public transportation** is available on MTC Routes #5 and 7. **From Interstate 35E:** Proceed east on Highway 110, then north (left) on Charlton Street. The main entrance gate is on the left, just beyond Marie Avenue. Follow the entrance road to the Red Schoolhouse. **Park** near the schoolhouse.

INFORMATION: Call the Nature Center at 612/455-4531. The trails on the main property are open on the first Thursday evening and the third Sunday of the month from noon to 5 P.M. Naturalist staff is available at the Red School-house to provide trail maps and information. There is no admission fee.

HIGHLIGHTS: • Red Schoolhouse • Converted farmhouse • Model farm • Apiary with demonstration shed • Nature Center Sales Shop (located on Charlton Street north of the main entrance).

TIPS FOR WALKERS: • Trail clothes are recommended. • You may want to bring binoculars. • Bicycles and pets are not allowed on nature center trails. • More trails and a new Visitor Center are being developed at another location in Mendota Heights. Ask the staff for details.

RECOMMENDED ROUTE: 1.6 K (1 mile)
DIRT/GRASS SURFACE. LEVEL. SHADED/UNSHADED.
The following text was provided by the Dodge Nature Center:
From the Schoolhouse, follow the paved driveway down the hill past the gardens and the office and ① **turn right on the gravel road.** Follow the road around to the left past the large rhubarb patch and ② **proceed up the small hill** instead of following the gravel road to the right. Continue following the trail past the service road on the left and enjoy the restored grass prairie on either side of the trail. The trail leads downhill and over a dike, which converted a marsh into the pond you see to the north. Follow this trail around the western portion of the pond until you come to a ③ **gravel road.** Cross the road and follow the wood-chip Nature Trail along the eastern edge of two ponds. Turn right at the second junction and follow this through a ④ **small arboretum.** The grass trail leads past ⑤ **another pond** to the ⑥ **Model Farm.** Follow the gravel road between the sheds and the garage and ⑦ **turn left just before the corn crib.** The boardwalk begins here and winds through a cattail marsh. Some portions of this boardwalk are loose and uneven, so be careful. Eventually you'll come to a wood-chip trail that leads you past the compost bins and weather station. Once you reach the paved driveway, turn left and walk back to the start point.

GIVING BACK: For information about membership, volunteer, and donation opportunities, contact the Dodge Nature Center, 1795 Charlton Street, West St. Paul, MN 55118, or call 612/455-4531.

City of Mendota Heights Trails

Operated by the City of Mendota Heights

"The Mendota Heights trail system has been designed in response to a resident's review committee that was created to develop a trail system. Our goal is to connect all the parks and neighborhoods through walking trails so residents can walk, shop, and exercise."

—Guy Kullander, Engineering Technician, Mendota Heights.

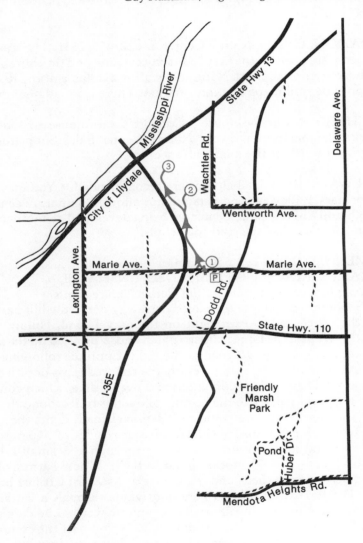

FACILITIES

✓ **Restrooms** (portable units) are located at the beginning of the trail.
✓ **Water** is not available along the trail.
✓ **Public telephones** are not available.

18

DIRECTIONS: Valley Park is located south of downtown Saint Paul in Mendota Heights. **Public transportation** is not available. **From Interstate 35E:** Proceed east on State Highway 110, north on Dodd Road, west (left) on Marie Avenue. The park is unmarked, so watch for children's playground equipment on the north side of the road. **Park** in the lot just off Marie Avenue.

INFORMATION: Call the City of Mendota Heights at 612/452-1850. The trails are open from 6 A.M. to 10 P.M. There is no admission fee.

HIGHLIGHTS: • Alternate wooded and open prairie environment • Picnic area • Children's playground • Tennis courts • Trails link local neighborhoods • Provides an interesting mix of urban and wildlife sounds.

TIPS FOR WALKERS: • Carry water. • Street clothes are recommended.

RECOMMENDED ROUTE: 3.2 K (2 miles)
PAVED SURFACE. LEVEL. MOSTLY UNSHADED.
From the parking lot, follow the trail across the ① **wooden walking bridge.** A picnic shelter is located just on the other side of the bridge. You will pass tennis courts to the left. Go past the shelter and follow the trail into the woods. As you come out of the wooded area, notice all the power lines and towers that run along the highway. Soon you will cross another wooden bridge. The trail then becomes heavily wooded for about a block and then opens again into a prairie environment. When you reach the fork in the trail you have two options. The ② **trail to the right** leads up a steep hill that dead-ends in a residential area. The ③ **trail to the left** will take you to Highway 13. Plans are underway to link this trail with the Lilydale Park System trails. When you reach the end of either trail, retrace your steps back to Valley Park.

GIVING BACK: For information about donation opportunities, call the Mendota Heights Parks and Trail system at 612/452-1850.

Minnesota Valley/

National Wildlife Refuge, Recreation Area, and State Trail

**Operated by U.S. Fish and Wildlife Service
and the Minnesota Department of Natural Resources**

"I have a special feeling when on the refuge—a realization and understanding of the need to preserve natural systems. I think this feeling comes from being able to experience this remarkable naturalness within a developed urban area. The refuge is an incomparable setting to reflect upon one's values." —John Schomaker, Outdoor Recreation Planner.

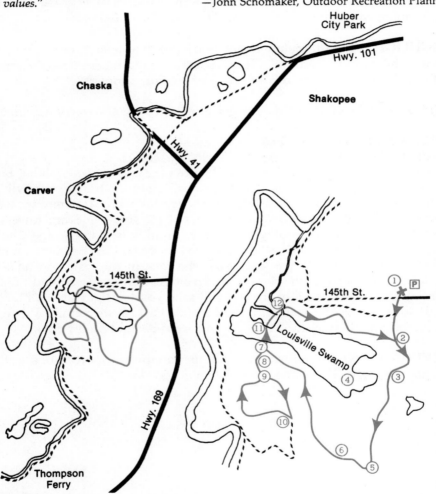

FACILITIES

✓**Restrooms** (accessible) are available at the Visitor Center. Pit toilets are available in the parking area of the Louisville Swamp. Restrooms are available in the cities of Carver, Chaska, and Shakopee.

✓**Water** is available at the Visitor Center and in the cities along the trail.

✓**Public telephones** are available at the Visitor Center and at Carver, Chaska, and Shakopee.

19

DIRECTIONS: The Visitor Center is located near the airport along Interstate 494. The Louisville Swamp is located southwest of the metro area south of Carver. **Public transportation** is available to the airport via MTC Routes #7 or 15. You will need to take a cab from the airport to the Center. Public transportation to the Louisville Swamp is not available. **From Interstate 494:** Proceed south on 34th Avenue South, turn left (east) on 80th Street. Follow the signs to the Minnesota Valley Visitor Center. Park in the main lot. After a tour of the Visitor Center, proceed west on Interstate 494, south on Interstate 35W, west on State Highway 13 (which turns into Highway 101, then 169). Turn right on 145th Street and follow it to the parking lot for the Louisville Swamp. **Park** in the lot.

INFORMATION: Call the Visitor Center at 612/854-5900. Call the State Trail Manager at 612/492-6400. The Visitor Center is open from 9 A.M. to 9 P.M. year-round. The Louisville Swamp is open during daylight hours year-round. *A trail map is available at the Visitor Center.* Admission to both facilities is free.

HIGHLIGHTS: • Visitor Center has wonderful "see and learn" stations that make it easy and fun to learn about the environment • Eventually the Refuge, Recreation Area, and State Trail will include 24,000 acres and extend for 72 miles between Fort Snelling and LeSueur • The Louisville Swamp has sections of prairie, swamp, and forest • Jabs Farm.

TIPS FOR WALKERS: • Trail clothes are recommended. • You may want to bring binoculars. • At the Visitor Center you can take a .5-mile self-guided tour with information provided via a portable cassette.

RECOMMENDED ROUTE LOUISVILLE SWAMP: 9.6 K (6 miles)
DIRT SURFACE. LEVEL. UNSHADED.
From the parking lot, walk to the ① **Information Board** at the south end of the lot and proceed straight ahead on the trail. At the junction, take the trail to the left. At the next junction take a left onto the ② **Mazomani Trail.** After you pass the ③ **Ehmiller Homestead,** and the ④ **Louisville Swamp,** walk along a ⑤ **dirt road** and then back onto a ⑥ **grass trail** where you will see a large glacial boulder. You will then come to the historic ⑦ **Jabs Farm.** At the farm, you will proceed south onto the ⑧ **Johnson Slough Trail.** At the ⑨ **next trail junction,** keep to the left. At the ⑩ **next junction,** take a right through a beautiful prairie area, which loops around back to Jabs Farm. Proceed north on the ⑪ **Mazomani Trail,** passing over a creek on a rock walkway and then up a hill into a wooded area. At the next ⑫ **trail junction,** turn right. At the next junction, take a left back to the parking lot.

GIVING BACK: For information about volunteer and donation opportunities, contact the Friends of the Minnesota Valley, Box 20244, Bloomington, MN 55420, or call the Visitor Center at 612/854-5900.

Fort Snelling State Park

Operated by the Minnesota Department of Natural Resources

"At Fort Snelling we attempt to preserve and interpret the social and cultural history associated with this land, as well as provide an opportunity for people to do whatever form of recreation they enjoy, whether it's walking, biking, swimming, or roller blading."

—Wallace Bartel, Park Manager.

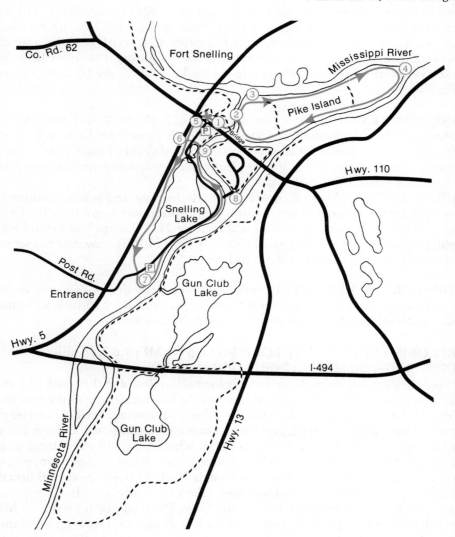

FACILITIES

✓ **Restrooms** (accessible) are located at the park office, Interpretive Center, and at the beach area.
✓ **Water** is available at the park office, Interpretive Center, and beach area.
✓ **Public telephones** are available outside the park office.

20

DIRECTIONS: Fort Snelling State Park is located in the metro area across from the Minneapolis/Saint Paul International Airport. **Public transportation** is available to the Fort Snelling Federal Building via MTC Routes #7, 15, 9B. Walk to the historic site and then to the state park following the signs. **From Interstate 494:** Proceed north on State Highway 5 to the Post Road Exit to the park entrance. Proceed to the main office, and then continue along the entrance road. **Park** in the lot under the Mendota Bridge.

INFORMATION: Call the park at 612/725-2390. The park is open year-round from 8 A.M. to 10 P.M. Park office hours vary with the season. Pick up the *Junior Park Naturalist* brochure at the Interpretive Center to help you identify plants and wildlife. *Trail maps are available at the park office.* A yearly motor vehicle pass or a daily pass is required.

HIGHLIGHTS: • 18 miles of hiking trails • 5 miles of accessible paved trails • Swimming beach on Snelling Lake • Picnic and recreation areas • Interpretive Center • Fort Snelling historic site • Sibley House historic site • Junction of the Mississippi and Minnesota rivers • Wildlife • Site of University of Minnesota Raptor Release program.

TIPS FOR WALKERS: • Street clothes are recommended. • You may want to bring a camera or binoculars. • Travelers: *If your plane is delayed or if you have a layover, you may want to rent a car or take a cab to this state park located just across the highway from the airport.* • Trails are closed to walkers in the winter.

RECOMMENDED ROUTE: 10.2 K (6.4 miles)
PAVED/DIRT SURFACE. LEVEL. MOSTLY SHADED.
From the parking lot, proceed east and you will see a ① **trail sign** directing you into a wooded area. Cross the ② **bridge** and turn left and walk about one-third of a mile to the ③ **Pike Island Interpretive Center.** After you browse around and explore the exhibits, walk around the back of the building and take the trail to the left along the Mississippi River. Continue walking to the end of island where the ④ **Mississippi River meets the Minnesota River.** You will walk back along the Minnesota River shoreline. Cross the bridge again, and follow the trail to the left that leads back to the parking lot. Proceed to the paved trail at the other end of the parking lot. If you want to visit the historic site, follow the trail to the right. Otherwise, ⑤ **follow the trail to the left** and proceed south. At the trail junction, take the trail to the right along the west shore of ⑥ **Snelling Lake.** Go around the ⑦ **park office** and follow the trail along the Minnesota River. At the next ⑧ **trail junction,** stay to the left. At the next junction, ⑨ **turn left** and follow the trail back to the parking lot.

GIVING BACK: For volunteer opportunities, call the park office at 612/725-2390. Contact the park manager for a copy of the Fort Snelling "Wish List" that identifies park priorities and opportunities for memorials and financial donations.

Spring Lake Park Reserve

Operated by Dakota County Parks Department

"You get exercise, you can hear birds, see nature, and walk in dirt and mud."
— Nicole, Amanda, and Billy Nathe and Maria and Ben Gaebel.

"These kids are my neighbors. We're here for a family reunion, and we all decided to take a walk in the woods and explore real life, true life. It's so beautiful, so peaceful."
— Dorine VonWahlde, a park visitor from Freeport, Minnesota.

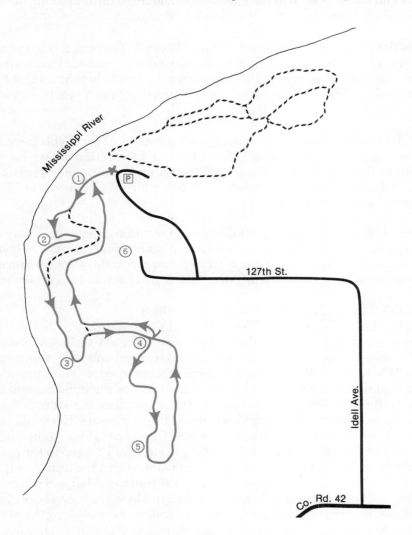

FACILITIES

✓ **Restrooms** are located in the picnic area.
✓ **Water** is available in the restrooms.
✓ **Public telephones** are not available. An office phone is available for emergency use only during office hours (8 A.M. to 4:30 P.M. Monday through Friday).

21

DIRECTIONS: Spring Lake Park is located southeast of the metro area in Hastings. **Public transportation** is not available. **From Interstate 494:** Proceed south on State Highway 56, east on State Highway 55. Ignore the first County Road 42 sign, continue on the road, and eventually veer left on County Road 42. Turn left on Idell Avenue and left on 127th Street to the entrance marked "Shaar's Bluff." **Park** in the lot near the picnic area.

INFORMATION: Call the Dakota County Parks Department at 612/437-6608. Spring Lake Park is open from 8 A.M. to 11 P.M. *Trail maps are available through Dakota County Parks.* There is no admission fee.

HIGHLIGHTS: • 3 miles of hiking trails • Great views of the Mississippi River and Spring Lake • Picnic areas • The office of the Dakota County Park system is located in the house along the west trail.

TIPS FOR WALKERS: • Trail clothes are recommended. • A walking stick may be helpful on the hills. • Most trail junctions are well marked. • The walking trails are available *exclusively* for walkers during the spring, summer, and fall (trails are closed to walkers in the winter). • Carry water. • You may want to bring a camera to capture some of the views.

RECOMMENDED ROUTE: 3.2 K (2 miles)
DIRT SURFACE, ROLLING HILLS. SHADED/UNSHADED.
From the parking lot (facing the Mississippi River) turn left and follow the ① **wood-chip trail** into the woods. You'll walk along the shoreline. (Caution: There are no fences along the bluff.) You'll walk along both sides of a U-shaped bluff. As you walk along the shoreline again, you may want to take the short trail to the right to the ② **scenic overlook.** Continue on the main path. Keep to the right at the trail junction and eventually you will walk up a steep hill. You will arrive at a ③ **picnic shelter.** The trail continues to the left of the shelter. Turn right at the next trail junction. Notice the field study site in the fenced area. ④ **Turn right** at the next trail junction. Continue walking and you will pass through an ⑤ **avenue of pines.** At the next trail junction, take a right. Just a few feet away the trail forks again; take the left trail. Continue walking past the ⑥ **offices of the Dakota County Parks.** Follow the trail (always stay to the right) back through a field to the parking lot.

GIVING BACK: Direct financial donations to the Dakota County Parks Department at 8500 127th Street East, Hastings, MN 55033.

Lebanon Hills Regional Park

Operated by Dakota County Parks Department

"Dakota County has a wide diversity of natural terrain including lakes, rivers, wooded hillsides and grasslands. It is the goal of the Dakota County Park System to preserve and protect this wealth of natural amenities, to develop and manage these resources, and to provide the public with a wide variety of outdoor recreational and educational opportunities and facilities."

—Sue Chapman, Special Services Coordinator.

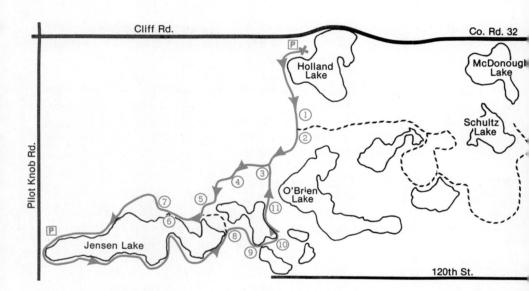

FACILITIES

✓ **Restrooms** are available during the summer at the Jensen Lake entrance. Portable units are available at the Holland Lake Entrance.

✓ **Water** is available (summer only) in the restrooms near the Jensen Lake entrance; Holland Lake, and Shulz Lake.

✓ **Public telephones** are available (summer only) at the Shulz Lake beach house.

22

DIRECTIONS: Lebanon Hills Regional Park (East Section) is located near the Minnesota Zoological Garden. **From Interstate 35E:** Proceed east on Cliff Road, past Pilot Knob Road, to the Holland Lake entrance (on the right). **Park** in the lot.

INFORMATION: Call the Dakota County Parks Department at 612/437-6608. The trails are open from 8 A.M. to 11 P.M. *Trail maps are available through Dakota County Parks.* There is no admission fee.

HIGHLIGHTS: • 6 miles of wood-chip and dirt trails • Picnic rest areas.

TIPS FOR WALKERS: • Trail clothes are recommended. • You may want to carry a walking stick. • Carry water. • Walking paths intersect with horse trails. • *The recommended route is available to walkers in the winter.*

RECOMMENDED ROUTE: 7.2 K (4.5 miles)
DIRT/WOOD-CHIP SURFACE. ROLLING HILLS. SHADED/UNSHADED.
From the parking lot follow the cement stairs, turn left, and follow the path into the woods. Follow the steps down to the lake, turn right, and follow the trail through the woods to an open area. Take the trail to your left. Follow it down, then up into a clearing to a ① **trail junction.** Proceed straight ahead to the next ② **trail junction.** Continue straight ahead into a wooded, swampy area. At the ③ **table (A-frame) shelter,** take the path to the right. At the next ④ **table shelter,** go straight ahead. The trail will split again; take the path past the third table shelter down to the lake and take a right over the ⑤ **footbridge.** Continue walking around ⑥ **Jensen Lake.** You'll pass through ⑦ **privately owned land.** Cross the street, follow the trail a bit, cross the street again, and continue around the lake until you reach a ⑧ **trail junction.** Take the trail to the right and cross the ⑨ **bridge** into the woods. At the ⑩ **table shelter,** take the trail to the left, then take a quick right up a short hill into an open field and follow the wide path that leads away from the lake. At the next ⑪ **trail junction,** take the main path (it will be straight ahead of you but it veers to the right). Keep walking until you come to a four-way junction. Take the path that leads down into the open area again. Take the first trail to the right into a clearing and follow the trail back to the Holland Lake entrance.

GIVING BACK: Direct financial donations to the Dakota County Parks Department at 8500 127th Street East, Hastings, MN 55033.

City of Eagan Trails/
Highline Trail

Operated by the City of Eagan

"We enjoy using the trails as frequently as possible. How far we walk depends on the children, the mosquitoes, and the weather." —Anna and Leary Gates, Eagan residents.

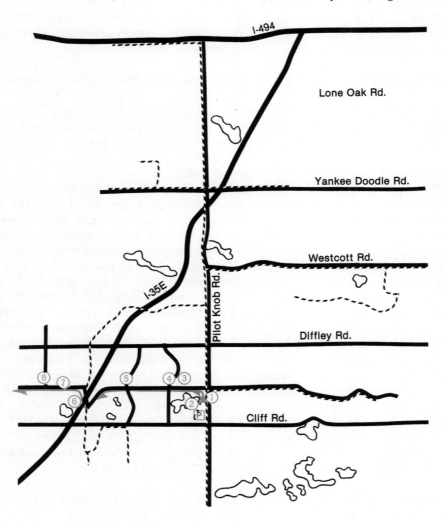

23

DIRECTIONS: The City of Eagan is south of downtown Saint Paul. **Public transportation** is not available. **From Interstate 35E:** Proceed east on Diffley Road, south on Pilot Knob Road. Watch for Wilderness Road on the left because the entrance to Thomas Lake Park is just a few feet away on the right side of the road. **Park** in the main lot.

INFORMATION: Call Eagan Parks and Recreation Department at 612/454-8100. The trails are available from sunrise to sunset. There are a number of trail publications available to walkers. *Trails—Discover Us!* provides an overview of the city's trail system. *Passport to Good Health, An Adventure in Walking* identifies nine different walking sites and includes a walking log and health tips. Also, the city publishes a large *Discover Us!* map of all the parks with a complete list of facilities. There is no admission fee for the parks or trails.

HIGHLIGHTS: • Wildflowers • Forests • Marsh areas • Animal life.

TIPS FOR WALKERS: • Trail clothes are recommended. • The trail is shared with bikers.

RECOMMENDED ROUTE: 7.2 K (4.5 miles)
PAVED SURFACE. HILLY. SHADED/UNSHADED
From the parking lot, proceed to the ① **asphalt trail** to the north that runs parallel with Pilot Knob Road. You will pass a small picnic shelter, and then the trail curves to the left past a pond and the ② **Thomas Lake Native Prairie.** At all trail junctions, continue straight ahead. You will pass the ③ **Thomas Lake Elementary School** on your right. You will pass more ponds as you walk through a wooded area. Cross ④ **Thomas Lake Road;** the trail continues across the street. Proceed up the hill; you will be walking under large power lines. The trail winds through woods, past a pond (that can flood the path after a hard rain), and in one mile you will cross ⑤ **Johnny Cake Ridge Road.** The trail resumes across the street through a residential area, toward the freeway. You will walk parallel to the freeway, then ⑥ **cross the freeway bridge** on Blackhawk Road and turn left onto the path on the other side of the road. The trail continues its westward route near the fire hydrant. Proceed through another residential area, past ⑦ **Meadowland Park** on the right. Continue until you cross ⑧ **Rahn Road** and enter Rahn Park with picnic areas and a playground. There is a large shopping center to the south on Cliff Road with restrooms, beverages, and food. Retrace your steps back to the start point.

GIVING BACK: For information about volunteer or donation opportunities, call the City of Eagan Parks and Recreation Department at 612/454-8100.

Wood Lake Nature Center

Operated by the City of Richfield

"An early morning walk is a blessing for the whole day."
—On a memorial bench in honor of William M. Peters from his wife, Mildred.

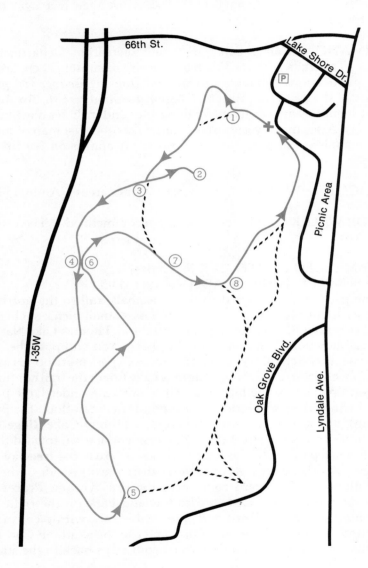

24

DIRECTIONS: Wood Lake Nature Center is located in Richfield, south of Minneapolis. **Public transportation** is available on MTC Routes #15 and 47. **From Interstate 35W:** Proceed east on 66th Street, turn south (right) on Lake Shore Drive. The entrance is on the right. **Park** in the main lot near the entrance.

INFORMATION: Call the Nature Center at 612/861-9365. The trails are open from sunrise to sunset daily. The Nature Center is open Monday through Saturday from 8:30 A.M. to 5 P.M. and on Sundays from 1 P.M. to 5 P.M. Call for seasonal events. *A trail map and a bird list are available at the Nature Center.* There is no admission fee.

HIGHLIGHTS: • 120 acres of cattail marsh • 10 acres of renovated prairie • More than 200 different species of birds and 30 species of mammals • Eighty-seat auditorium for group presentations • Equipment rental • Classes for children and adults • Touch-and-see museum • Floating boardwalk.

TIPS FOR WALKERS: • You may want to bring binoculars. • Street clothes are recommended. • Watch your footing on the floating boardwalks—they move as you walk. • *The trails are open in the winter for walkers and skiers.*

RECOMMENDED ROUTE: 4.8 K (3 miles)
LIMESTONE/BOARDWALK SURFACE. LEVEL. SHADED/UNSHADED.
Proceed from the parking lot through the gate to the right. The trail begins just past the Nature Center. At the ① **first junction,** take the trail to the right for a short loop around the woods. When you've finished the loop, turn right onto the main trail. Proceed to the next junction and follow the trail to the far left to the ② **overlook.** Proceed back to the ③ **main trail.** At the next ④ **trail junction,** keep to the right. At the next ⑤ **trail junction,** take a left and you will walk through woods and then into a marsh via boardwalks and dirt trails. At the next ⑥ **trail junction,** take a right and then another right to the loop that will take you to another ⑦ **boardwalk** through a marsh. At the ⑧ **next junction,** turn left and follow the path back to the Nature Center. Note the observation blinds on the side path just before you reach the Nature Center.

GIVING BACK: There are summer volunteer opportunities for a limited number of youth (4th through 6th grades). There is also an adult naturalist internship program that trains volunteers to provide seminars and classes for school groups. Financial donations may be directed to Wood Lake Nature Center. Financial donations are used to fund the center's current projects. Past donations were used to develop the memorial benches, overlooks, and numerous plantings.

*Mound Springs Park Trail System*___

Operated by the City of Bloomington

*"This trail takes you right back to nature, and it's only fifteen minutes out your back door. It's
undisturbed, very beautiful, and we look forward to walking it in the fall."*

—Sharon and Pat Vandenabeele, park visitors from Saint Paul.

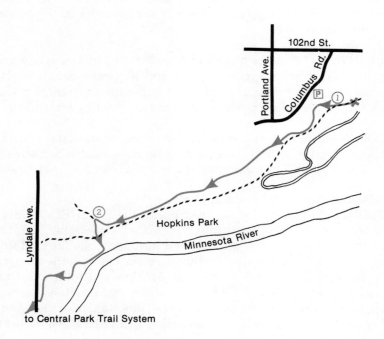

FACILITIES ─────────────────────────────────────

✓**Restrooms** are not available.
✓**Water** is not available.
✓**Public telephones** are not available.

25

DIRECTIONS: Mound Springs Park Trail System is located south of the metro area in Bloomington. **Public transportation** is available on MTC Route #18. **From Interstate 35W:** Proceed east on 98th Street, south on Portland Avenue, east on 102nd Street. Watch for the "Columbus Road" sign—the sign is on the left side of the road, but you'll be turning right on Columbus Road. The road curves around to the right a bit. Watch for the park sign on the left. **Park** on the street.

INFORMATION: Call Bloomington Park and Recreation Division at 612/ 887-9601 (or TDD 887-9677) for updated trail information. The trail is open from sunrise to 10 P.M. daily throughout the year. *Trail maps are available through the City of Bloomington.* There is no admission fee.

HIGHLIGHTS: • 3.3 miles of unspoiled, natural trails • Isolated, remote forest areas, open grasslands • Occasional views of the Minnesota River.

TIPS FOR WALKERS: • Trail clothes are recommended. • This isolated trail is shared with bikers, so listen for approaching walkers or bikers, particularly around curves. • You may want to bring a walking stick for the hills. • Trail junctions are not marked.

RECOMMENDED ROUTE: 5.6 K (3.5 miles)
WOOD-CHIP/DIRT SURFACE. SOME STEEP HILLS. MOSTLY SHADED.
The trailhead begins to the left of the parking area (facing the Minnesota River). At the ① **trailhead junction,** take the narrow footpath to the right ("To Lyndale"). Stay on the main trail. At the first trail junction, keep to the right. You will walk quite a distance, and when you begin to hear traffic, you will come to a ② **trail junction** where you will turn left onto the stone trail. At the end of the trail, you will have a magnificent view of the Minnesota River. You will pass over a creek, then a pond, and eventually the road will widen to a six-foot dirt road. You will be able to see the I-35W bridge above. Walk through the open field to the end of the trail at Lyndale Avenue. Turn around and retrace your steps back to the start point.

GIVING BACK: For information about volunteer and donation opportunities, call the Bloomington Park and Recreation Division at 612/887-9601.

Central Park Trail System

Operated by the City of Bloomington

"The City of Bloomington has approximately 8,000 acres in its park system and there are walking trails in just about every part of the City that loop around area lakes and natural areas."
— Gene Kelly, Manager, Bloomington Park and Recreation Division.

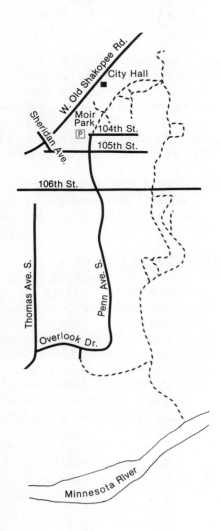

FACILITIES

- ✓ **Restrooms** are not available.
- ✓ **Water** is not available.
- ✓ **Public telephones** are not available.

26

DIRECTIONS: The Central Park Trail System is south of the metro area in Bloomington. **Public transportation** is available on MTC Route #47. **From Interstate 35W:** Proceed west on 98th Street, then veer left onto Old Shakopee Road. You will pass City Hall. Beyond the bridge, turn left onto Sheridan Avenue, left on 105th Street, left on Penn Avenue, right on 104th Street to the entrance to Moir Park (on the left). **Park** in the lot.

INFORMATION: Call Bloomington Park and Recreation Division at 612/887-9601 (or TDD 887-9677) for updated trail information. The trail is open from sunrise to 10 P.M. daily throughout the year. *Trail maps are available through the City of Bloomington.* There is no admission fee.

HIGHLIGHTS: • 5 miles of unspoiled, natural trails along Nine Mile Creek • Environmentally sensitive area • Wetland • Picnic tables • An alternative Upper Bluff Trail (with steep hills, more challenging hiking experience).

TIPS FOR WALKERS: • Trail clothes are recommended. • This isolated, wild trail in the heart of the metro area offers a reflective getaway. • This trail is shared with bikers, so listen for approaching walkers or bikers, particularly around curves. • You may want to bring binoculars for observing wildlife in the wetlands. • Trail junctions are not marked. • *If you want to walk only a segment of this trail, walk the portion from Moir Park to 106th Street (3.6 miles roundtrip) or 106th Street to the lake bed (5.3 miles round trip).*

RECOMMENDED ROUTE: 14.4 K (9 miles)
At the time this book went to print, we were unable to walk the entire length of trail because a Lower Valley Bank Stabilization and Restoration and major Trail Improvement Project is underway in the Nine Mile Creek Lower Valley from Moir Park to the Minnesota River, funded by the Nine Mile Creek Watershed District and the City of Bloomington.

Accessible trail improvements will include bituminous surface from Moir Park to 106th St. and crushed rock firm surface from 106th Street to the river. The improvements will be completed by the summer of 1991. The improvement includes the replacement of several bridges that were washed away in the flood of 1987. Please contact the Bloomington Park and Recreation Division (887-9601) for updates on the status of the improvement project. Approximately 2.7 miles of trail improvements are proposed. The total length of the Central Park Trail is 4.47 miles.

GIVING BACK: For information about volunteer and donation opportunities, call the Bloomington Park and Recreation Division at 612/887-9601.

Normandale Lake

Operated by the City of Bloomington

"Normandale Lake has accessible parking, paved trails, and a Vita Health course with two sets of exercises at each station—one for able-bodied people and another for people who use wheelchairs. The park is a wonderful example of how careful planning can preserve the natural integrity of an area and yet make it accessible to everyone in the community."

—Cynthia Blomgren, Accessibility Specialist, City of Bloomington.

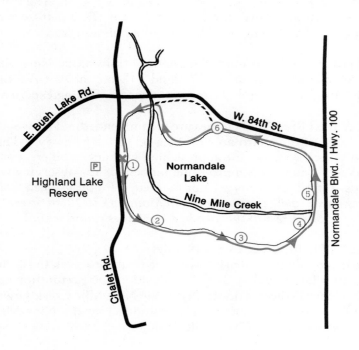

FACILITIES

- ✓**Restrooms** (accessible) are available at the A-frame facility in the parking lot.
- ✓**Water** is available at the A-frame facility in the parking lot.
- ✓**Public telephones** are available near the A-frame facility in the parking lot.

27

DIRECTIONS: Normandale Lake is located southwest of Minneapolis in Bloomington. **Public transportation** is not available. **From Interstate 494:** Proceed south on Highway 100/Normandale Boulevard, west (right) on 84th Street, south (left) at Chalet Road (the first stop light) to the parking area on the right. **Park** near the A-frame shelter at the far end of the lot.

INFORMATION: Call Bloomington Park and Recreation Division at 612/ 887-9601 (or TDD 887-9677). The park is open from sunrise to 10 P.M. daily throughout the year. *A trail map is available through the City of Bloomington.* There is no admission fee.

HIGHLIGHTS: • 3.9 miles of paved trails • Oak savanna • Prairie • Wildflowers • Wetland flood control project • Vita Health stations • Wildlife • Adjacent to Hyland Regional Park, the Richardson Nature Center, and Bush Lake Park.

TIPS FOR WALKERS: • Bring wildflower books to help identify flowers along the trail. • Although this park is located in an urban area, it has many of the sights, sounds, and herbal smells of a more rustic experience. *The paths are cleared in the winter for walkers.* Note: If you use the bicycle trail in the winter, one lap around the lake is 2 miles.

RECOMMENDED ROUTE: 3.04 K (1.9 miles)
PAVED. LEVEL/ROLLING HILLS. SHADED/UNSHADED.
From the parking lot, proceed to the ① **pedestrian crossing** near the phone booth. Cross the street and take the paved trail to the right that winds through the woods. Note the Vita Exercise stations along the route. You may want to stop at the ② **viewing benches and garden area.** Continue along the path and you will come to another ③ **viewing area.** Note the ④ **information post** that describes the history of the park and its facilities. You will walk over a footbridge across Nine Mile Creek. The trail winds through an ⑤ **open prairie** area with prairie grasses to your left and wildflowers to your right. Continue along the path, keeping to the left along the shoreline, and you will walk by a ⑥ **wide variety of wildflowers** on your left. Continue following the path back to the start point.

GIVING BACK: For information about volunteer and donation opportunities, call the Bloomington Park and Recreation Division at 612/887-9601.

Hyland Lake Park Reserve/
Richardson Nature Center

Operated by Hennepin Parks

"I think I get back more than I give when I volunteer. I enjoy the activities at Hennepin Parks. I learn new skills and sharpen old ones. I'm promoting environmental consciousness, and I just love to see people enjoying all the activities." —Barbara Arveson, Hennepin Parks volunteer.

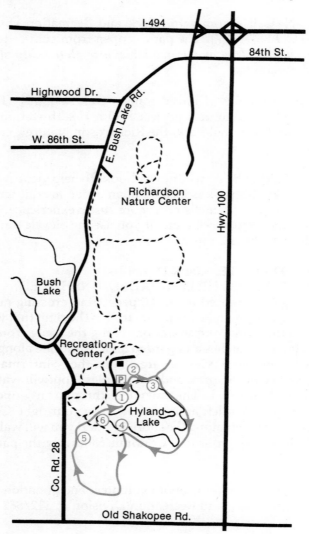

FACILITIES

✓ **Restrooms** (accessible) are available at the Recreation Center and the Richardson Nature Center.

✓ **Water** is available at the Recreation Center and Richardson Nature Center.

✓ **Public telephones** are available outside the Recreation Center.

154

28

DIRECTIONS: Hyland Lake Park Reserve is located southwest of Minneapolis in Bloomington. **Public transportation** is not available. **From Interstate 494:** Proceed south on Highway 100 (Normandale Boulevard), and then west (right) on 84th Street (which turns into East Bush Lake Road). Proceed south on East Bush Lake Road. You will pass park signs to the ski area and to the Richardson Nature Center. Turn left at the sign for the Hyland Outdoor Recreation Center. **Park** near the Recreation Center.

INFORMATION: Call the Recreation Center at 612/941-4362 or the Richardson Nature Center at 612/941-7993 for seasonal hours and events. The park and trails are open from 5 A.M. to sunset. *Trail maps are available at the Recreation Center.* The parking fee is $16 annually, or $3.25 daily. Hennepin Parks has reciprocal parking agreements with Anoka, Carver, and Washington counties.

HIGHLIGHTS: • 5 miles of paved, accessible trails; 2 miles of wood-chip hiking trails • Accessible creative play area, boat launch, fishing area, nature center, and picnic grounds • Richardson Nature Center • Group picnic site can accommodate up to one hundred people for a walking event • Group campsite • Equipment rental • Recreation Center with food concession • Within walking distance of Normandale Lake trails and Bush Lake Park trails • Deer, songbirds.

TIPS FOR WALKERS: • "You are here" maps are posted at most trail junctions. • Trail clothes are recommended. • You may want to bring a tape recorder to capture bird sounds. • Paved trails are shared with bikers. • *Most trails are closed to walkers in the winter but the Richardson Nature Center trails are open year-round.*

RECOMMENDED ROUTE: 5.8 K (3.6 miles)
WOOD-CHIP/PAVED SURFACE. LEVEL. SHADED/UNSHADED.
Go around the back of the Recreation Center to the boat launch area. The trail begins to the left of the ① **boat rental building.** Follow the narrow dirt trail along the shoreline, across a picnic area to the ② **wide, wood-chip trailhead.** At the ③ **first trail junction,** take a right (the left trail is a maintenance road). Stay on the wood-chip trail. Do not enter any of the side foot trails. Watch for white egrets as you walk along Hyland Lake. You will come to ④ **a point where a paved trail runs parallel with the wood-chip trail.** Cross over about 3 feet of grass and and turn left onto the paved trail. Stay on the right side of the trail. At the next ⑤ **trail junction,** stay on main paved path past Hyland Lake. ⑥ **Cross over from the paved path to the grassy path** along the shoreline and follow it into a picnic area and back to the Recreation Center.

GIVING BACK: To volunteer, call 612/559-9000. Direct your financial donation to the Hennepin Parks Foundation, 12615 County Road 9, Box 47320, Plymouth, MN, 55447-0320.

Minnesota Valley Nature Center

Operated by the Minneapolis Chapter of the Izaak Walton League

"One can take a circle tour of this thirty-acre wonderland, hiking down the hill, along the stream to the Minnesota River, and then back to the Nature Center which is used for club meetings, educational films, lectures, discussions, and a beginning wildlife museum."

—Delia Setzel, President.

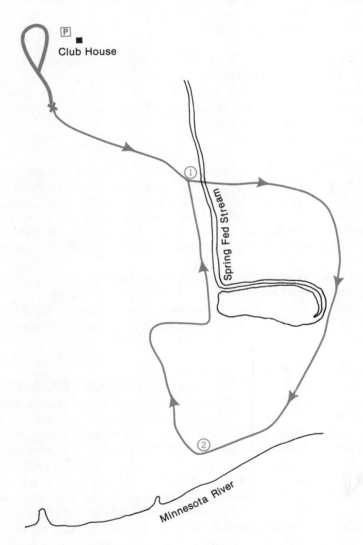

P

Club House

Spring Fed Stream

①

②

Minnesota River

FACILITIES

- ✓ **Restrooms** are available in the Nature Center, which is open by appointment only.
- ✓ **Water** is available in the Nature Center, which is open by appointment only.
- ✓ **Public telephones** are not available.

29

DIRECTIONS: The Minnesota Valley Nature Center is located about 8 miles southwest of Minneapolis in Bloomington. **Public transportation** is available on MTC Route #47. **From Interstate 35W:** Proceed west on 98th Street, and curve left to Old Shakopee Road, turn left on Normandale Boulevard (which becomes Auto Club Road). As the road bends, you will pass the Masonic Home on your left. Just over the bridge you will be taking a left into the very first driveway in the woods (you cannot see the sign from the road). It's very easy to miss. It's just a few feet from the last bridge railing. Proceed down the entrance road to the large house/nature center. **Park** along the side of the road or in the loop, allowing for other vehicles.

INFORMATION: Call the Izaak Walton League at 612/944-1423. There is a wooden trail map posted near the trailhead. There is no admission fee. Membership to the Nature Center is available for $15 per year and to the Izaak Walton League for $25 per year.

HIGHLIGHTS: • Close-up views of the Minnesota River • Wild, uncut trees and vegetation • Quiet, serene, contemplative trail • Huge cottonwoods (seventeen feet in circumference) • Wildflowers • Wildlife.

TIPS FOR WALKERS: • Trail clothes are recommended. • You may want to bring a tape recorder to capture wildlife sounds. • Wear shoes or boots with ankle supports because of the hills and narrow trails. • Bikers are not allowed on nature center trails. • This trail takes less than 1/2 hour to walk, so you may want to dawdle and enjoy the small, specific parts of this preserve. *This trail is open in the winter to walkers (be careful of snow and ice on steep hills).*

RECOMMENDED ROUTE: 1.2 K (.75 miles)
DIRT/GRASS SURFACE. HILLY. SHADED.

From the parking area, proceed just beyond the wooden map to the opening in the woods. (Do not proceed to the white archway that used to be the trailhead.) Follow the steep slope down into the woods. At the ① **first junction,** turn left at the "start here" sign. You will pass over a brook. Follow the trail (which is sometimes just a narrow dirt path through low forest plants) and eventually you will walk along the shoreline of the ② **Minnesota River.** This portion of the shorelines ends at a bluff, and the trail continues to the right. Continue walking until you come to the main trail junction; turn left and walk back up the hill to the entrance point.

GIVING BACK: For information about volunteer and donation opportunities, contact the Izaak Walton League, 6601 Auto Club Road, Minneapolis, MN 55431, or call 612/944-1423.

City of Burnsville Trails/
Alimagnet Park

Operated by the City of Burnsville

"Burnsville has over sixty-nine parks totalling 1,600 acres, and over half the acreage is woodlands, ponds, and wetlands. People use the park trails throughout the year for hiking and cross-country skiing."
—Randy Oppelt, Director of Parks and Recreation.

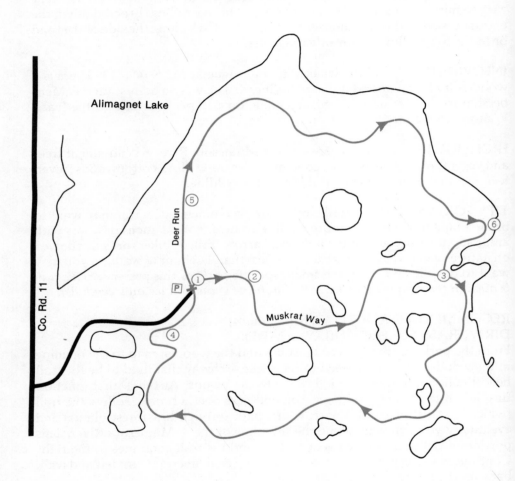

FACILITIES

✓ **Restrooms** (portable units) are available near the parking lots and baseball diamonds during the summer months.
✓ **Water** is not available.
✓ **Public telephones** are available.

30

DIRECTIONS: Alimagnet Park is located south of the metro area in Burnsville. **Public transportation** is not available. **From Interstate 35W/35E:** Proceed east on County Road 42, and then north (left) on Lac Lavon Drive/County Road 11. The park is just up the road to the right. Drive past the Art Center. **Park** in the lot near the baseball fields.

INFORMATION: Call the Burnsville Parks and Recreation Department at 612/895-4500. *A ski trails brochure that identifies hiking trails is available.* The city also publishes a large city parks map. There is no admission fee.

HIGHLIGHTS: • Hardwood forests • Wildlife • Marshes and wetlands • Views of Lake Alimagnet.

TIPS FOR WALKERS: • Bring a compass. • Trail clothes are recommended. • There are also walking trails at Terrace Oaks Park. Refer to the ski maps for details.

RECOMMENDED ROUTE: 4.8 K (3 miles)
GRASS/DIRT SURFACE. HILLY. SHADED.
From the parking lot, proceed ① **east along the road,** past the baseball diamond to your right. Across from the public telephone, you'll see a trail sign along the fence. Turn right and follow the ② **wide path along the fenceline** until you come to the beginning of Muskrat Way to the left. Follow the wide trail into the woods. At the ③ **first trail junction, turn right.** You will encounter other trail junctions along the way, but keep to the right. At another junction by a marshy area, keep to the right. Go up a hill, cross a road, and go down a hill. You'll end up at the ④ **baseball diamonds** again. Walk past the parking lot and proceed to the ⑤ **Deer Run,** which starts out as paved, but turns into a grass/dirt trail by the swing sets. This trail follows the curves of ⑥ **Lake Alimagnet,** and at one point you can leave the trail and walk down to the lake. At the next junction, take a right and then a left back to Muskrat Way (into the forest, away from the meadow). You'll end up at the now-familiar baseball diamonds.

GIVING BACK: For information about volunteer and donation opportunities, contact the Burnsville Parks and Recreation Department at 100 Civic Center Parkway, Burnsville, MN 55337, or call 612/895-4500.

Murphy-Hanrehan Park Reserve

Operated by Hennepin Parks

"Murphy-Hanrehan is a breathtaking, unpolished gem of wilderness. There is so much wildlife activity that it's like seeing a new park when the seasons change."

—Karin Rorem, Park Operations Coordinator.

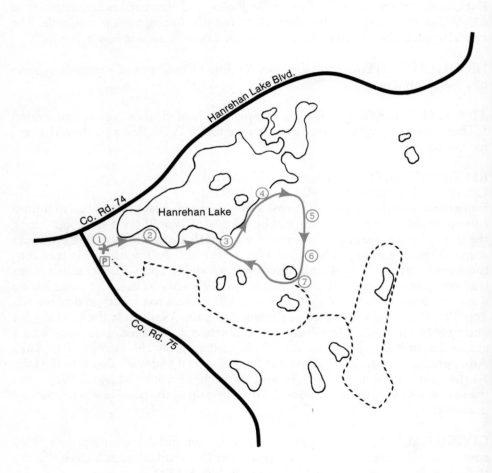

31

DIRECTIONS: Murphy-Hanrehan is located south of the metro area in Savage. **Public transportation** is not available. **From Interstate 35W:** Proceed west on County Road 42, south on County Road 27, east on County Road 74, south on County Road 75. **Park** at the entrance.

INFORMATION: Call Cleary Lake Recreation Center at 612/447-2171 for trail conditions and seasonal events. The park and trails are open from 5 A.M. to sunset. *Trail maps are available in the map box near the buildings.* The parking fee is $16 annually, or $3.25 daily. Hennepin Parks has reciprocal parking agreements with Anoka, Carver, and Washington counties.

HIGHLIGHTS: • 1.5 miles of turf hiking trails • Hilly terrain.

TIPS FOR WALKERS: • This is more of a hiking experience than a walking experience, so trail clothes are recommended. • Some portions of the trail may be flooded after a significant rainfall. • The designated hiking trails at this park change each season, so be sure and check the route before you walk. • You may want to bring a walking stick. • Trails are closed to walkers in the winter.

RECOMMENDED ROUTE: 2.4 K (1.5 miles)
TURF SURFACE. STEEP HILLS. SHADED.
Proceed from the① **trail map mailbox** to the wide grassy trail that leads into the woods. A hiker sign is posted at the entrance. Walk along the② **slightly hilly shoreline.** At the first③ **trail junction,** take a left (proceed through the open gate). Once you walk up a④ **steep hill,** you will have a great view of the lake. You will pass over a⑤ **footbridge** that takes you right through a swamp. At the next⑥ **trail junction,** keep to the right, following the hiker sign. Notice the hollow tree! At the next⑦ **trail junction,** take a right, again following the hiker sign. When you get back to the first trail junction, take a left and follow the trail back to your start point.

GIVING BACK: To volunteer, call 612/559-9000. Direct your financial donation to the Hennepin Parks Foundation, 12615 County Road 9, Box 47320, Plymouth, MN 55447-0320.

Cleary Lake Regional Park _____

Operated jointly by Scott County and Hennepin County

"As a Hennepin Parks volunteer, I have the satisfaction of doing something I like to do while I'm also doing something for someone else." — Bob Scott, Hennepin Parks volunteer.

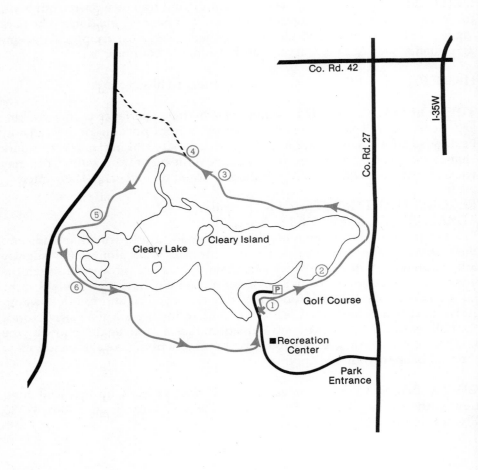

FACILITIES _____

- ✓ **Restrooms** are available in the Outdoor Recreation Center. Accessible restrooms are located in the beach house.
- ✓ **Water** is available in the beach house and Outdoor Recreation Center.
- ✓ **Public telephones** are available outside the beach house.

32

DIRECTIONS: Cleary Lake is located south of the metro area near Prior Lake. **Public transportation** is not available. **From Interstate 35W:** Proceed west on County Road 42, south on County Road 27. Go past the first sign (Golf Maintenance Shop) to the park entrance. **Park** in the lot near the beach.

INFORMATION: Call the Recreation Center at 612/447-2171 for seasonal hours and events. The park and trails are open from 5 A.M. to sunset. *Trail maps are available at the Recreation Center.* The parking fee is $16 annually, or $3.25 daily. Hennepin Parks has reciprocal parking agreements with Anoka, Carver, and Washington counties.

HIGHLIGHTS: • 3.5 miles of paved, accessible walking trails • 1.3 miles of wood-chip hiking trails • Accessible beach area, picnic area, golf course, and boat launch • Creative play area • Campsites • Equipment rental • Fitness course • Large pavilion can hold up to 175 people for a walking event (by reservation only).

TIPS FOR WALKERS: • Paved trails are shared with bikers and skaters, so stay to the right. • Street clothes are recommended. • The trail is circular without any distractions—great place for a "think" walk. • *Trails are closed to walkers in the winter.*

RECOMMENDED ROUTE: 5.6 K (3.5 miles)
PAVED. LEVEL. UNSHADED.
From the parking lot, proceed to the ① **trailhead** on the golf course side of the road. You'll pass a ② **large boulder** on the left side of the path. Continue on the path and you'll eventually cross over a ③ **footbridge.** At the ④ **trail junction,** keep to the left. There is a ⑤ **water pump** located just to the side of the trail. As you walk, you may want to try some of the ⑥ **fitness center** challenges at each of the stations to test your endurance. Return to the start point.

GIVING BACK: To volunteer, call 612/559-9000. Direct your financial donation to the Hennepin Parks Foundation, 12615 County Road 9, Box 47320, Plymouth, MN 55447-0320.

City of Edina Trails/
Bredeson Park

Operated by the City of Edina

"There are two main areas to walk in the city. You can walk across Edina from 50th and France to the Braemer Golf Course, or you can explore the forests, prairies and marshes of Bredeson Park."
— Bob Kojetin, Director of Parks and Recreation.

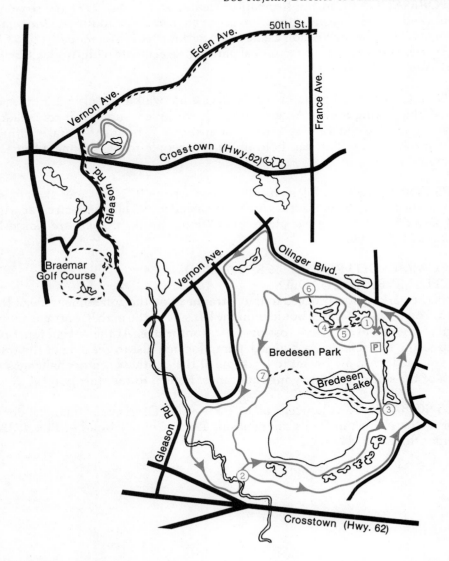

FACILITIES

- ✓ **Restrooms** are located at Bredeson Park.
- ✓ **Water** is available at Bredeson Park.
- ✓ **Public telephones** are available at the entrance.

33

DIRECTIONS: Bredeson Park is located southwest of the metro area in Edina. **Public transportation** is available on MTC Route #4N. **From State Highway 62 (Crosstown):** Proceed north on Gleason Road, then bear right on Vernon Avenue, and turn right on Olinger Boulevard to the park entrance. **Park** in the lot near the comfort station.

INFORMATION: Call the Edina Parks and Recreation Department at 612/ 927-8861. *A Bredeson Park brochure with a trail map is available.* The city also publishes a city park and events calendar. There is no admission fee.

HIGHLIGHTS: • 4 miles of walking trails • Wildflowers • Songbirds • Hardwood forest • Wildlife.

TIPS FOR WALKERS: • Street clothes are recommended. • There are separate paths for bikers. • You may want to bring a camera or tape recorder. • *The paths are open year-round for walkers.*

RECOMMENDED ROUTE: 5.6 K (3.5 miles)
PAVED/DIRT/CRUSHED ROCK SURFACE. HILLY. MOSTLY SHADED.
From the parking lot, proceed to the right past the comfort station ① **north on the paved walking path.** You'll walk through a hardwood forest, marshes, and fields of wildflowers. Keep to the left at the junctions. You'll cross over some footbridges over Nine Mile Creek, and eventually you will come to a ② **turnstile that leads to the natural area.** Once inside, turn to the right and follow the trail past a marsh. At the ③ **trail junction, keep right** and continue past Bredeson Lake and the parking area. At the next ④ **trail junction, turn right** at the "you are here" map and then just a few feet away ⑤ **turn left** at the next junction; this will lead around a marsh. Keep to the right at the next two ⑥,⑦ **trail junctions.** When you exit at the turnstile, turn left and proceed back to the parking lot.

GIVING BACK: For information about volunteer and donation opportunities, contact the Edina Parks and Recreation Department at 4801 West 50th Street, Edina, MN 55424, or call 612/927-8861.

Westwood Hills

Environmental Education Center

Operated by the City of St. Louis Park

"There are so many changes in three weeks that it seems like a different park. It's a great place to observe wildlife because the animals are very visible. It's a great place to walk and think."

—Nancy Henry-Socha, Naturalist Intern.

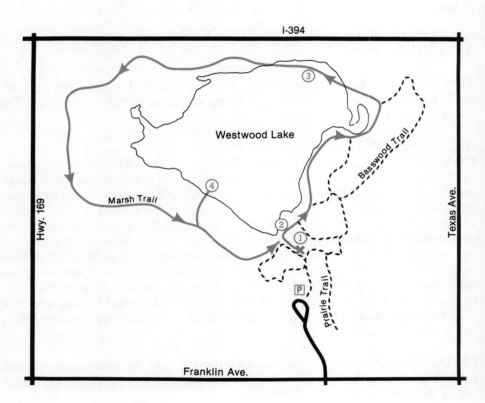

34

DIRECTIONS: Westwood Hills Environmental Education Center is located in St. Louis Park, just west of downtown Minneapolis. **Public transportation** is available to Cedar Lake Road on MTC #9 and to I-394 and Penn on MTC #51 (any 51 bus except 51C). Cross I-394 at Penn, then walk four blocks east to Texas, then turn right on Franklin Avenue. **From State Highway 100:** Proceed west on Cedar Lake Road about .7 mile, north (right) on Texas about .5 mile, left on Franklin Avenue about .3 mile. The entrance is on the right. **From State Highway 169:** Proceed east on Cedar Lake Road for 1 mile, north (left) on Texas, left on Franklin Avenue to the park entrance on the right. **Park** in the main lot.

INFORMATION: Call the Education Center at 612/924-2544. The trails are open throughout the year from dawn until dusk. Education Center hours are Monday through Friday from 8 A.M. to 4:30 P.M. and weekends from noon to 5 P.M. *Trail maps and program brochures are available at the Education Center.* There is no admission fee.

HIGHLIGHTS: • Marsh/prairie/forest walks • Education Center displays and classes • .75-mile accessible trail with observation deck and wildflower gardens • Lake trail with .25-mile floating boardwalk • Small picnic area.

TIPS FOR WALKERS: • Trail clothes are recommended. • You may want to bring binoculars. • Boardwalks and floating docks move, so watch your footing. • *Trails are open to walkers in the winter.*

RECOMMENDED ROUTE: 4.8 K (3 miles)
WOOD-CHIP/BOARDWALK SURFACE. LEVEL. SHADED/UNSHADED.
From the parking lot, follow the paved trail to the Education Center. Proceed to the wood-chip trail that begins in front of the ① **Education Center.** At the first junction take a right to see the ② **floating "Y" dock.** Then take the Marsh Trail around Westwood Lake (keep to the left at every trail junction). There are benches along the way where you can stop and observe birds and other wildlife. First, the trail winds through a wooded area, then opens into a marsh and leads to the ③ **floating boardwalk.** You will walk through grasslands and prairie, and then back into a wonderfully secluded section of forest. As you near the end of the trail be sure and walk out on the ④ **floating "T" dock.** If you want to extend your walk, try the Basswood Trail (.75 miles) or the Prairie Trail (.2 miles).

GIVING BACK: Information about volunteer and donation opportunities is available through the Westwood Hills Environmental Education Center, 8300 West Franklin Avenue, St. Louis Park, MN 55426, or call 612/924-2544.

Opus 2 Trail System

Operated by the City of Minnetonka

"I walk at Opus because it's quiet, nice, and there's no traffic."

—Joellen Gustafson, resident of Hopkins.

35

DIRECTIONS: Opus is located southwest of Minneapolis. **Public transportation** is available on MTC Routes #4 and 12. **From County Road 62 (Crosstown):** Proceed north on Shady Oak Road a very short distance—you will be making a quick right turn into the Opus 2 complex just beyond the intersections of Crosstown and Shady Oak Road. Turn left immediately into a restaurant parking area. **Park** in either lot.

INFORMATION: Call the Minnetonka Loop Trail Corridor Information Number at 612/93-TRAIL. The trails are open from dawn to 10 P.M. *A detailed trail map is available through the Opus Corporation, 936-4444.* There is no admission fee.

HIGHLIGHTS: • Very wide, accessible trails • Well landscaped • 550-acre office, industrial, commercial, and residential park linked with greenways • Marshes, woods, wildlife • Healthbeat exercise course along the trails.

TIPS FOR WALKERS: • Street clothes are recommended. • Trails are shared with bikers. • Trails are not marked. • *Trails are not plowed in the winter.*

RECOMMENDED ROUTE: 4.8 K (3 miles)
PAVED SURFACE. LEVEL. SHADED/UNSHADED.
From the parking lot, proceed to the paved path that runs parallel with the road and turn left. You will pass under two bridges as the trail winds through a business park. At the ① **first junction,** take a right. You will walk through a section of woods past a ② **small pond with two islands.** After you pass under a bridge, take the ③ **trail to the left.** At the next ④ **trail junction,** stay on the path to the left (don't cross the road). You will pass under a very well-landscaped bridge. At the next ⑤ **trail junction,** take a right up a slight hill. At the next ⑥ **trail junction,** take a left under a bridge. You'll pass a willowed pond with picnic tables and resting benches. At the next ⑦ **trail junction,** take a right into the residential portion of the trails. You will walk past ⑧ **tennis courts and a pool.** Do not take the path under the bridge—go straight ahead. Turn ⑨ **left** under a bridge and you will walk past some townhomes. You will cross a small access road—the trail continues on the other side. At the next ⑩ **trail junction,** keep on the main trail (do not take the trail to the right). At the next fork in the road, continue straight ahead. At the next major ⑪ **trail junction,** keep to the right. At the next ⑫ **trail junction,** you may want to take a detour (about 1 mile round trip) that leads to the Margaret E. Feltl Memorial. Otherwise, keep to the left and follow the trail under the Bren Road bridge. At the next ⑬ **junction,** keep on the same path. At the next ⑭ **junction,** take a right. Take another right and proceed back to the start point.

GIVING BACK: If you are interested in volunteering or making a financial donation, call 612/93-TRAIL.

Minnetonka Loop

Trail Corridor System

Operated by the City of Minnetonka

"The trails here are excellent. We have seen deer and pheasant. We wish there were many more of these wonderful, interesting places to walk."

—Steve and Carroll Anne Jesberg, residents of Minnetonka.

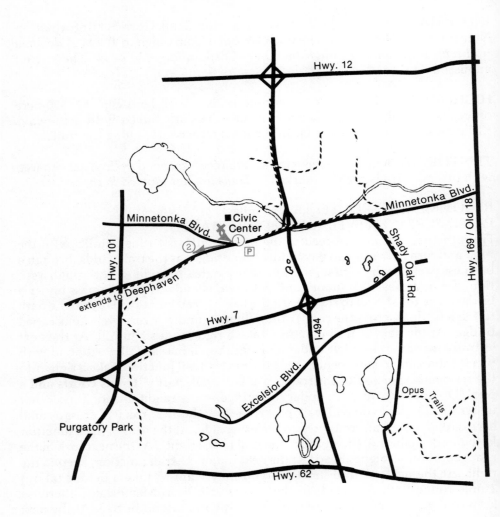

FACILITIES

✓ **Restrooms** (accessible) are available in the Civic Center during regular hours.
✓ **Water** is available in the Civic Center during regular hours.
✓ **Public telephones** are available in the Civic Center during regular hours.

36

DIRECTIONS: The Minnetonka Loop Trail Corridor System is west of the metro area. **Public transportation** is available on MTC Route #67. **From Interstate 494:** Proceed west on Minnetonka Boulevard (County Road 5), north on Williston Road (the Civic Center is on the corner of Williston and Minnetonka Boulevard). **Park** near the Civic Center.

INFORMATION: Call Minnetonka Loop Trail Corridor Information Number at 612/93-TRAIL. The trails are open from dawn to 10 P.M. *Trail maps are available at City Hall (next to the Civic Center) or through the mail by calling the 93-TRAIL line.* There is no admission fee.

HIGHLIGHTS: • 14 miles of wide, *accessible* trails • The Minnetonka Loop Trail Corridor System links with trails in Deephaven, Greenwood, Excelsior, and Victoria, with additional links to other communities planned.

TIPS FOR WALKERS: • Street clothes are recommended. • Trails are shared with bikers, so keep to one side. • You may want to carry water. • It's also an excellent trail for anyone beginning a walking program, especially children. • *Trails are plowed in the winter for walkers.* • The trail system is expanding. If you are interested in walking more trails, obtain an updated map through the city.

RECOMMENDED ROUTE: 3.2 K (2 miles)
LIMESTONE (PACKED DIRT) SURFACE. LEVEL. SHADED/UNSHADED.
From the Civic Center parking lot, proceed south on the paved trail to the intersection. Cross ① **Minnetonka Boulevard** and turn right onto the trail. Continue walking for a mile. You'll pass through wooded areas, a small business area and neighborhoods. You will come to an intersection and a small blue sign that says ② **Tonkawood Road.** You may continue if you want to increase your mileage or retrace your steps back to the Civic Center. **Note:** If you start at the Civic Center and turn left (east) onto the trail, the loop to Shady Oak Road and back again is three miles.

GIVING BACK: If you are interested in volunteering or making a financial donation, call 612/93-TRAIL.

City of Eden Prairie Trails

Operated by the City of Eden Prairie

"Eden Prairie is an interesting town in which to walk. It's definitely designed with the self-propelled traveler in mind." —Roderick MacRae, Coordinator, Staring Lake Outdoor Center.

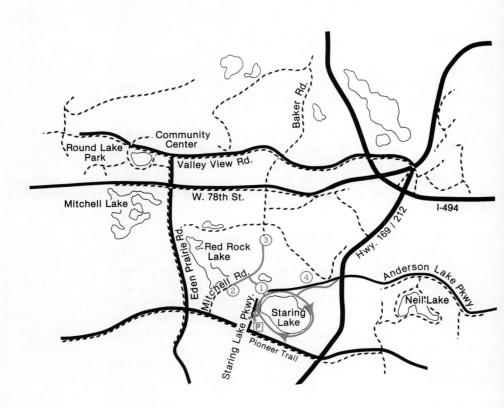

FACILITIES

✓ **Restrooms** (portable units) are available during the spring, summer and fall along the trail.

✓ **Water** is not available.

✓ **Public telephones** are not available but emergency calls may be made at the Outdoor Center during regular hours.

37

DIRECTIONS: Staring Lake is located in Eden Prairie. **Public transportation** information is available through Southwest Metro Dial-A-Ride at 612/944-7126. **From Interstate 494:** Proceed south on U.S. Highway 169/212 for 2.5 miles to Pioneer Trail/County Road 1. Turn right and follow Pioneer Trail west for 1 mile to the park entrance. **Park** in the lot near the shelter building and informational kiosk.

INFORMATION: Call the Eden Prairie Parks and Recreation Department at 612/937-2262 for information or the Staring Lake Outdoor Center at 941-8336 Monday through Thursday from 1 P.M. to 5 P.M. *A map of the city's trail system is available through the Parks and Recreation Department.* There is no admission fee.

HIGHLIGHTS: • The City of Eden Prairie has 45 miles of paved (eight-foot-wide) trails • Staring Lake highlights include a park shelter, an Outdoor Center, an amphitheater, benches, bridges, shaded trails, and a variety of bird and animal life.

TIPS FOR WALKERS: • Trails are shared with bikers, so keep to the right side. • Eden Prairie offers walkers a chance to experience a completed trail system that makes it easy (and enjoyable) to walk through residential, business, commercial, industrial, and wildlife areas.

RECOMMENDED ROUTE: 4.2 K (2.6 miles)
PAVED. LEVEL. SHADED/UNSHADED.
Starting in front of the park shelter building, follow the pathway on the east side of the building down the hill passing the play area and amphitheater until the trail intersects with the loop trail around the lake. The path around Staring Lake is circular, so keep to your left at all intersections and you will return to your start point for a 2.6-mile walk. However, you may want to venture off and explore more of the trails that lead to local schools or parks. On the northwest side of the lake you can cross Staring Lake Parkway and continue on a ① **trail along Twin Lakes Crossing** that leads to Mitchell Road. Turning left you can follow a trail that leads to ② **Redrock Lake Park** or, turning right, follow a trail that leads to ③ **Pheasant Woods Park.** On the northeast side of the lake you can venture off on a trail adjacent to Staring Lake Parkway that leads to ④ **Oak Point School.**

GIVING BACK: For information about volunteer opportunities or donations, contact Eden Prairie Parks and Recreation at 612/937-2262.

City of Chanhassan Trails

Operated by the City of Chanhassan

"I like to walk here because we've seen snakes, ducks, baby geese, beaver. It's a nice trail; they keep it mowed and we enjoy walking around the pond."

—Doris Giese and her grandson Steven Freseth, a Chanhassan resident.

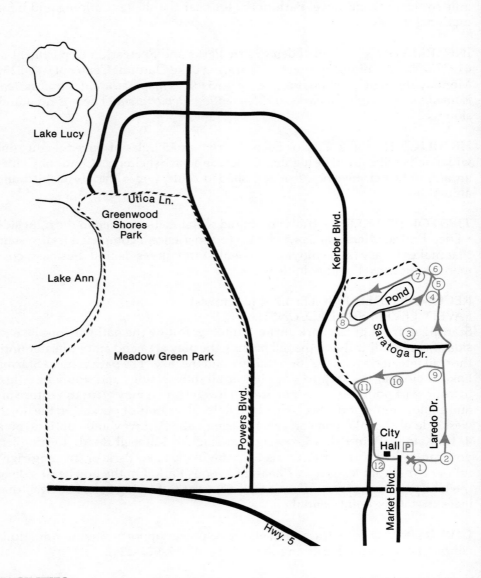

38

DIRECTIONS: Chanhassen is southwest of the metro area. **Public transportation** information is available through Southwest Metro Dial-A-Ride at 612/944-7126. **From Interstate 494:** Proceed west on State Highway 5, north (right) on Market Boulevard to the very end of the road. **Park** in the lot to the left near the Chanhassen City Hall Administration Offices.

INFORMATION: Call the City of Chanhassen at 612/937-1900. *A trail map is not available.* The parks and trails are open from 6 A.M. to 10 P.M. There is no admission fee.

HIGHLIGHTS: • Chanhassen Pond • Wildlife • City Center Park.

TIPS FOR WALKERS: • Check trail condition. • Trail clothes are recommended.

RECOMMENDED ROUTE: 2.4 K (1.5 miles)
PAVED/DIRT SURFACE. HILLY/STEPS. MOSTLY SHADED.
From the parking lot, proceed east across① **Market Boulevard** and follow the sidewalk to ② **Laredo Drive.** Turn left, walking past a fire station, an elementary school, and through a residential area. Cross③ **Saratoga Drive,** then turn left at the entrance to ④ **Chanhassen Pond Park.** The paved path leads through a residential area, and then it turns into a dirt/gravel path. There is an ⑤ **observation deck** to your left. Follow the ⑥ **steps** or the trail down to the pond. You will walk through a shaded, wooded area and over a⑦ **footbridge.** The trail continues around the pond, past wildflowers and bird houses. You will cross another⑧ **bridge** and continue around the south shore of the pond. At the next junction, take the trail to the right and continue to Laredo Drive. As you return on Laredo Drive, take a right just before the elementary school on the⑨ **paved path by the fence.** You will walk past a playground and tennis courts and then through a field along a stand of pine trees. At the next junction, take a left and follow the trail through an open space in ⑩ **City Center Park** to ⑪ **Kerber Boulevard.** Turn left on Kerber, and proceed toward City Hall. Turn left on ⑫ **Coulter Drive** and follow the sidewalk back to the parking lot.

GIVING BACK: For information about volunteer or donation opportunities, call the City of Chanhassen at 612/937-1900.

Lake Minnewashta Regional Park ___

Operated by Carver County Parks

"Lake Minnewashta is a natural preserve as well as a developing recreational park with walking trails, picnic areas, a beach, and boat launches. We are replanting hardwoods such as basswood, maple, ash, and oak over an open area of approximately forty-five acres in order to recreate the pre-settlement "Big Woods." —Mike Liddicoat, Park Director.

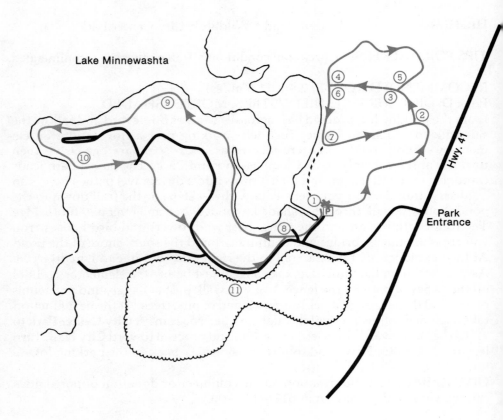

FACILITIES
✓**Restrooms** (vault latrines) are available in picnic areas and accessible restrooms are available at the beach and ski shack.
✓**Water** is available on the Marsh Trail, at the picnic areas, and at the beach.
✓**Public telephones** are available at the beach house.

39

DIRECTIONS: Lake Minnewashta Regional Park is located southwest of the metro area. **Public transportation** is not available. **From Interstate Highway 494:** Proceed west on Highway 7, south on State Highway 41 for about a mile to the entrance gate on the west side of the highway. **Park** in the first lot to the right off the entrance road.

INFORMATION: Call Carver County Parks at 800/642-7275. The park is open daily from 8 A.M. to 9 P.M. or one hour after sunset, whichever is later. Admission is $12 for an annual vehicle permit, or $2.25 for daily parking. *A Carver County Parks brochure that includes walking trails is available from the county. Trail maps are also available at the park.* Carver County has a reciprocal parking agreement with Hennepin Parks.

HIGHLIGHTS: • 5 miles of walking paths • Boat access to Lake Minnewashta • Beautiful beach area and picnic grounds • Reforestation project • Ski shack.

TIPS FOR WALKERS: • Trail clothes are recommended. • Check trail condition after it rains.

RECOMMENDED ROUTE: 8 K (5 Miles)
GRASS/GRAVEL SURFACE. SLIGHT HILLS. SHADED/UNSHADED.
The first part of this walk will take you on a figure-eight loop of the nature trails. From the parking lot, proceed onto the cut grass area going east until you see the ① **open pathway.** Take the path to the right and you will walk through an open prairie area. At the trail junction take the ② **Vista/Marsh Trail** to the right. At the next junction, take the ③ **Vista/Marsh Trail** to the left. Proceed to the next junction and take the ④ **Marsh Trail** to the right. Walk around the marsh until you come to the next junction and take the ⑤ **Vista Trail** to the right. Proceed to the next junction and take the ⑥ **Vista/Prairie Trail** to the left. Turn left again at the ⑦ **Prairie Trail.** Keep to the right until you return to your start point. Walk over to the boat launch area and proceed on the ⑧ **path to the west of the boat launch.** Lake Minnewashta will be to your right, and a wooded area will be to your left. Follow the trail to the ⑨ **picnic areas** and then around the bay to the ⑩ **beach area.** Follow the road back to your start point. On your way back you will pass thousands of small trees that are part of the ⑪ **Reforestation Project.**

GIVING BACK: To volunteer, call 800/642-7275. Direct your financial donations to Carver County Parks, 10775 County Road 33, Young America, MN 55397, or call 612/467-3145.

Landscape Arboretum

Operated by the University of Minnesota

"We encourage everyone to walk through all the collections and native areas in the Arboretum because wildlife and microclimatic things really can't be experienced from cars or trams."

—Peter Olin, Director

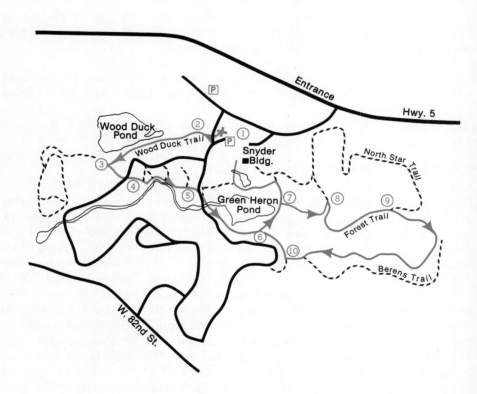

40

DIRECTIONS: The Arboretum is southwest of the metro area in Chanhassen. **Public transportation** information is available through Southwest Metro Dial-A-Ride at 612/944-7126. **From State Highway 7:** Proceed south on State Highway 41, west on Highway 5. The entrance to the Arboretum is on the left. **Park** in the main lot.

INFORMATION: Call 612/443-2460. Grounds are open from 8 A.M. to sunset every day of the year. The Snyder Building is open Monday through Saturday from 8 A.M. to 4:30 P.M. and Sundays and holidays from 11 A.M. to 4:30 P.M. Admission is $3 per person (16 years and older). Special senior rates are available. *A trail map is available at the entrance gate and the Snyder Building.*

HIGHLIGHTS: • 5 miles of walking trails, 3 miles of paved road • Walking tours (spring through fall) at 10 A.M. every Tuesday, Wednesday, and the first Saturday of the month • Information center with a library • Tram tours • Cafeteria.

TIPS FOR WALKERS: • Trail clothes are recommended. • *Main roads and walking paths are open to walkers in the winter.* • A tour of the gardens and collections is recommended before or after the walk.

RECOMMENDED ROUTE: 4.8 K (3 miles)
DIRT/PAVED SURFACE. LEVEL. SHADED/UNSHADED.
From the ① **main parking lot** proceed to the ② **Evaporator House** (on the west side of the parking lot—you can barely see the roof). Directly behind the second building the Wood Duck Trail begins. After you pass a pond to your right, you will come to a ③ **trail junction.** Turn left up the slope and cross the road in the direction of the ④ **Wildflower Garden.** Continue past the sign that says "Woodland Garden" and take a left at the "T" path. At the steps, turn right, walking on the main wood-chip path. Cut across the parking lot to the ⑤ **Ordway Shelter** and find the beginning of the **Bog Trail** (to the right of the shelter). Proceed through a tunnel of trees to a ⑥ **trail junction,** where you'll turn left to follow the wooden path across the bog. Turn right on the boardwalk to the ⑦ **Green Heron Trail.** The dirt trail resumes. Turn left at the junction. At the ⑧ **trail junction,** turn right up the hill onto the Forest Trail. At the next junction, take a left, following the Forest Trail signs. At the ⑨ **next junction,** take a right onto Forest Trail and walk through a grassy area. Bear right at the next three junctions (ignore the Forest Trail sign that points left into the woods). At the next major junction (the sign says Forest, Berens, Green Heron trails), take a left. You will pass a pond on your left. Follow the ⑩ **Forest/Green Heron** trail to the right (across a grassy area), back to the Ordway Shelter. Follow the brick-lined path back to the Snyder Building.

GIVING BACK: For volunteer opportunities, call the Arboretum. Direct financial donations to Minnesota Landscape Arboretum Foundation, 3675 Arboretum Drive, Box 39, Chanhassen, MN 55317.

City of Chaska Trails/
McKnight Park

Operated by the City of Chaska

"We live in Jonathan and we've been walking the trails ever since we moved here twelve years ago. In fact, one of the reasons we moved here was because of the trails. From our backyard we can walk for miles and miles. We walk all year-round because we enjoy watching the seasonal changes."

—Helen and Bob Cleveland, Chaska residents.

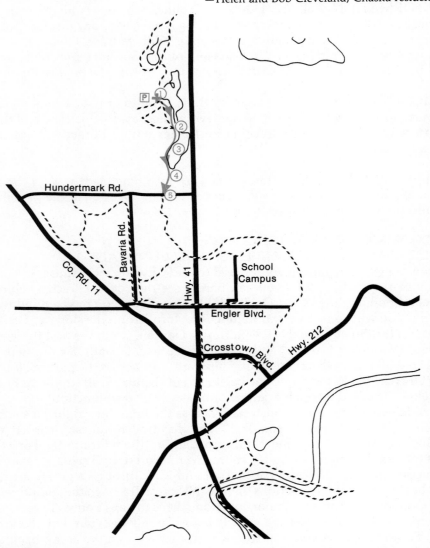

FACILITIES

✓ **Restrooms** are not available.
✓ **Water** is not available.
✓ **Public telephones** are not available.

41

DIRECTIONS: Chaska is southwest of the metro area. **Public transportation** information is available through Southwest Metro Dial-A-Ride at 612/ 944-7126. **From Interstate 494:** Proceed west on State Highway 5, south on State Highway 41, west (right) on South Jonathan Boulevard, right at Terrace Road to McKnight Park. Follow the entrance road to the parking area. **Park** in the lot (open area) to the right.

INFORMATION: Call the Chaska Parks, Recreation, and Arts Department at 612/448-5633. Chaska parks and trails are open from dawn to dusk every day of the year. *A trail map of the city's trail system is available through Chaska Park, Recreation, and Arts.* There is no admission fee.

HIGHLIGHTS: • McKnight Park • Covered boardwalks • Lake Grace • 6 miles of walking trails • Beach area • Playground.

TIPS FOR WALKERS: • Street clothes are recommended. • Trails are shared with bikers.

RECOMMENDED ROUTE: 3.2 K (2 miles)
PAVED/DIRT. HILLY. MOSTLY SHADED.
From the parking lot, proceed down to the playground and then ① **turn right on the paved path** along the lakeshore. The trail winds along the lake with a hill to your right. You will pass through a ② **covered bridge** over to ③ **Lake Grace.** Follow the trail along the west shore of the lake to the ④ **beach and picnic area.** Continue south into the woods until you reach ⑤ **Hundertmark Road.** At this point you may turn around and retrace your steps back to the start point. An unmarked trail continues on the other side of the road. The trail follows the creek for a while, and leads through more covered bridges, over footbridges, and up into a residential area. The trails are not marked so be sure to take note of natural landmarks.

GIVING BACK: For information about volunteer and donation opportunities, contact Chaska Parks, Recreation, and Arts at 1661 Parkridge Drive, Chaska, MN 55318, or call 612/448-5633.

City of Victoria Trails

Operated by the City of Victoria

"Located only thirty-five minutes from downtown Minneapolis, the City of Victoria offers a semirural setting within easy reach of the Twin Cities. Its proximity to Carver Park Reserve and area lakes within the city make it a most desirable place for hiking and skiing."

—Miriam Porter, City Administrator.

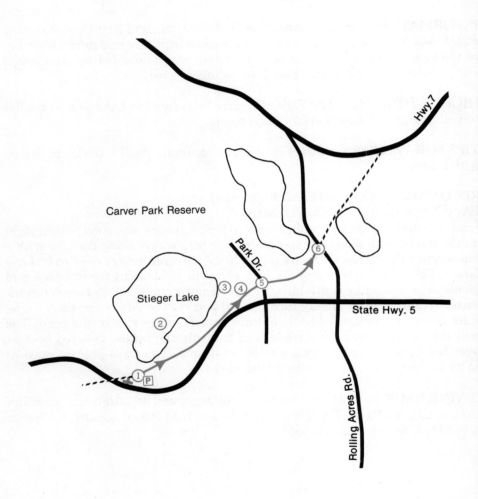

FACILITIES

✓**Restrooms** are not available.
✓**Water** is not available.
✓**Public telephones** are not available.

42

DIRECTIONS: Victoria is southwest of the metro area. **Public transportation** is not available. **From Interstate 494:** Proceed west on State Highway 5 (Arboretum Boulevard) into the town of Victoria. Turn right (north) on Victoria Drive (the street sign is on the left side of the road only). A lumber company is on the right side of the road. Curve right on Stieger Lake Lane, left on 79th Street, and make a quick right to the parking area by the trailhead. **Park** by the old railroad building.

INFORMATION: Call the City of Victoria at 612/443-2363. The trail is open from dawn to dusk. There is no admission fee.

HIGHLIGHTS: • Rail-to-trail line • Views of Carver Park • Woods, wildlife.

TIPS FOR WALKERS: • Carry water. • Trail clothes are recommended. • Wear shoes with ankle support because there are portions of the trail with large stones. • This is an excellent "thinking" trail because it's linear, you can't get lost, and it's relatively flat walking.

RECOMMENDED ROUTE: 4 K (2.5 miles)
STONE/GRAVEL SURFACE. LEVEL. MOSTLY SHADED.
From the parking lot, proceed to the ① **wide, limestone trail that heads east.** You will pass ② **Stieger Lake** and sections of ③ **Carver Park Reserve.** The trail offers scenic views of the lake and woods. At the ④ **first trail junction,** go straight ahead (don't turn left). You will cross a ⑤ **dirt road.** The trail turns to dirt and gravel as you walk through the woods. Eventually, you will reach ⑥ **Rolling Acres Road.** Turn around and retrace your steps back to the start point, or you may continue walking—the trail continues all the way to the City of Minnetonka.

GIVING BACK: For information about volunteer and donation opportunities, contact the City of Victoria at 612/443-2363, or write to the city at 7951 Rose, Box 36, Victoria, MN 55386.

Carver Park Reserve/
Lowry Nature Center

Operated by Hennepin Parks

"I've walked this park for twenty-three years and I'm still fascinated by all the activity. It's one of the best birding parks in the state, and we also have plenty of foxes, deer, and raccoons. During the summer we have hunting ospreys that stay until they migrate in September. During the winter, you can walk and see all kinds of animal tracks. The trails go in and out of forest, marsh, and meadow, and sometimes walkers can see the wildlife that tends to concentrate in the changeover areas."
— Kathy Heidel, Naturalist.

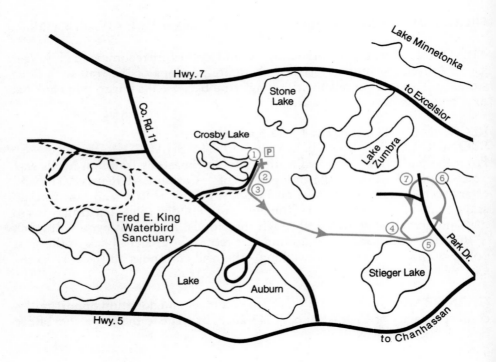

43

DIRECTIONS: Carver Park Reserve is located southwest of the metro area near Victoria. **Public transportation** is not available. **From State Highway 7:** Proceed south on County Road 11. The park entrance will be on the left. Follow the entrance road to the Lowry Nature Center. **Park** in the Nature Center lot.

INFORMATION: Call the Lowry Nature Center at 612/472-4911 for hours and seasonal events. The park and trails are open from 5 A.M. to sunset. *Trail maps are available in the Nature Center.* The parking fee is $16 annually, or $3.25 daily. Hennepin Parks has reciprocal parking argeements with Anoka, Carver, and Washington counties.

HIGHLIGHTS: • 8.5 miles of paved, accessible walking trails • 6.5 miles of wood-chip hiking trails. • Accessible fishing, camping, and boating areas • Lowry Nature Center • Trumpeter swan refuge • Fred E. King Waterbird Sanctuary with a waterfowl viewing blind (access by car only along County Road 11) • Brief (fifteen minutes) wildlife videos are available for viewing in the Nature Center • Gift shop with books, bug kits, etc.

TIPS FOR WALKERS: • Street clothes are recommended. • Paved trails are shared with bikers. • *Trails are closed to walkers in the winter.*

RECOMMENDED ROUTE: 8.5 K (5.3 miles)
PAVED SURFACE. HILLY. SHADED/UNSHADED.
Stop in the ① **Lowry Nature Center.** Just inside the door you'll find a large "What's Happening" bulletin board that describes what you may observe as you walk. From the Nature Center, walk on the left side of the entrance road (on the wide, grassy shoulder). You will pass a pond that may have ② **trumpeter swans.** Proceed down the road until you cross a small bridge where the ③ **paved trail begins.** Follow the paved trail through an open prairie. As you walk along the trail, you'll find brown information posts that describe park history and wildlife. Take a ④ **right at the first trail junction.** Follow the path and eventually you will cross a ⑤ **dirt road.** Continue on the trail and watch for ⑥ **Schutz Lake** on your right. You will pass the campgrounds and then ⑦ **cross the dirt road again.** Continue back to the main trail junction and then turn right and proceed back to your start point.

GIVING BACK: Volunteers and donations are needed. To become a Hennepin Parks volunteer, call 612/559-9000. Direct your financial donation to the Hennepin Parks Foundation, 12615 County Road 9, Box 47320, Plymouth, MN 55447-0320.

Baylor Regional Park

Operated by Carver County Parks

"We're gathering financial support for an observatory in Baylor Regional Park that will include telescopes for public viewing. This would be the first observatory of its kind in Minnesota, with regularly scheduled programs. Baylor is excellent for star gazing because it's close enough to the cities to be convenient, and yet far away from all the lights to have very dark skies."

—Max Radloff, Minnesota Astronomical Society.

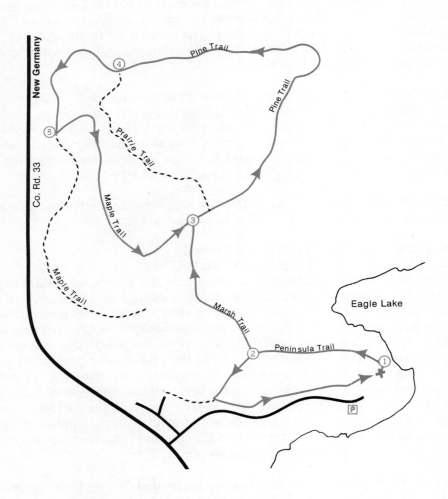

FACILITIES

✓ **Restrooms** (portable units and pit toilets) are available along the walking trail. Accessible restrooms are available at the park headquarters and beach area.

✓ **Water** is available in the beach area.

✓ **Public telephones** are available at the park headquarters year-round and at the beach house during the summer.

44

DIRECTIONS: Baylor Regional Park is located near Young America. **Public transportation** is not available. **From Interstate 494:** Proceed southwest on State Highway 212, north 2.5 miles on County Road 33. You will enter the park on the right side of the highway. Keep to the right and **park** in the lot near the playground and beach areas.

INFORMATION: Call Carver County Parks at 800/487-7275. The park is open daily from 8 A.M. to 9 P.M. or one hour after sunset, whichever is later. Admission is $12 for an annual vehicle permit, or $2.25 for daily parking. *A Carver County Parks brochure that includes walking trails is available from the county. Trail maps are also available at the park.* Carver County has a reciprocal parking agreement with Hennepin Parks.

HIGHLIGHTS: • 5 miles of accessible walking paths • Beach area • Recreation area • Picnic areas with shelters • Natural prairie grasses restored • Floating boardwalk across the marsh • Assortment of wildlife and plants • Future plans call for an Astronomical Observatory to be built in the park • Maple syrup production in March.

TIPS FOR WALKERS: • Trail clothes are recommended. • The boardwalk moves as you walk, so watch your footing. • You may want to bring your tape recorder. This is an excellent park to record bird and nature sounds. • *Trails are available for walking in the winter.*

RECOMMENDED ROUTE: 4.8 K (3 miles)
GRAVEL/BOARDWALK SURFACE. LEVEL. MOSTLY SHADED.
From the parking lot, proceed northeast to get on the trail by the playground area and head east toward the ① **bathhouse.** At the first trail junction take a right to the ② **floating boardwalk** across the marsh. You may want to record the sounds of the marsh. At the end of the boardwalk, turn right onto the ③ **Pine Trail** and continue along through the prairie grasses and into the wooded area. At the next trail junction, take the ④ **Prairie Trail** to the right. (It doesn't seem like prairie since you're still in the woods.) At the next trail junction, take a left onto the ⑤ **Maple Trail.** Follow the trail back to the floating boardwalk. At the end of the boardwalk take a right and circle the picnic area back to the parking lot.

GIVING BACK: To volunteer, call 800/642-7275. Direct your financial donations to Carver County Parks, 10775 County Road 33, Young America, MN 55397, or call 612/467-3145. Donations are also being accepted to build the Astronomical Observatory. Write the Minnesota Astronomical Society, c/o The Science Museum of Minnesota, 30 East 10th Street, St. Paul, MN 55101, or call the information hotline at 612/643-4092.

Lake Rebecca Park Reserve

Operated by Hennepin Parks

"My favorite time to use the trails in some of the parks is in the winter moonlight. We lead groups of cross-country skiers and it's very quiet, clear, and cold."

—David Tigges, Hennepin Parks volunteer.

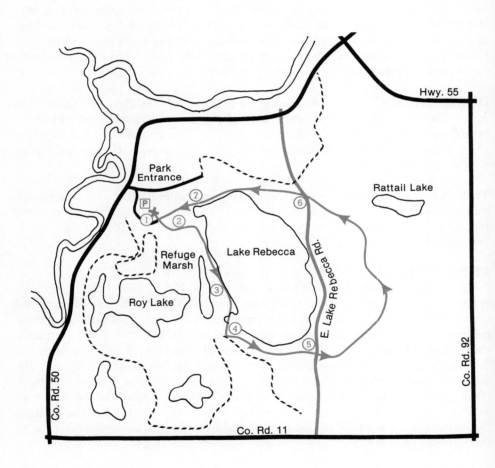

FACILITIES

✓**Restrooms** (vault toilets) are located in the parking lot and picnic areas.
✓**Water** is located in the picnic areas during the summer.
✓**Public telephones** are available at the trailhead building.

45

DIRECTIONS: Lake Rebecca Park Reserve is west of the metro area near Rockford. **Public transportation** is not available. **From State Highway 55:** Proceed south on County Road 50 to the park entrance. Drive past the entrance gate and turn left. Drive past the "Chestnut Area" and proceed to the "Boat Launch/Rentals" area. **Park** near the boat launch.

INFORMATION: Call Hennepin Parks at 612/476-4666 for seasonal events. The park and trails are open from 5 A.M. to sunset. *Trail maps are available through Hennepin Parks.* The parking fee is $16 annually, or $3.25 daily. Hennepin Parks has reciprocal parking agreements with Anoka, Carver, and Washington counties.

HIGHLIGHTS: • 6.5 miles of paved, accessible walking trails • 8 miles of turf hiking trails • Accessible picnic area, beach, fishing piers, campgrounds, boat launch, and equipment rentals • Trumpeter swan refuge • Large picnic area can accommodate up to 2,500 people.

TIPS FOR WALKERS: • Trail clothes are recommended. • You may want to bring binoculars to observe trumpeter swans. • Paved paths are shared with bikers, so keep to the right. • There are information posts along the trail. • *Trails are closed to walkers in the winter.*

RECOMMENDED ROUTE: 5 K (3.1 miles)
DIRT/PAVED SURFACE. STEPS/HILLY. MOSTLY UNSHADED.
As you face the lake from the boat launch, proceed on the ① **grassy trail** to the right along the shoreline of Lake Rebecca. At the ② **first trail junction,** take the trail to the far left along the lakeshore. You will walk a short distance. At the "Lake Trail 3.1 Mile" sign, proceed up the wooden railroad tie steps up into the woods. Stay on the wide, grassy path. You will walk along the shoreline of the ③ **trumpeter swan refuge** (to your right). Proceed ahead to the observation benches and information post. The trail resumes beyond the observation area. Continue to follow the wide, grassy path up a hill where you can catch another glimpse of the swans. At the ④ **paved path junction,** follow the path to the left. You will eventually cross ⑤ **Lake Rebecca Road** and then the trail continues through meadows and woods. When you cross Lake Rebecca Road again, follow the ⑥ **dirt road** (not the paved path) that leads to the beach and picnic area. When you get to the picnic area, proceed along the shoreline. The trail resumes to the left of the restroom near the ⑦ **large slide.** Proceed back to your start point.

GIVING BACK: Volunteers and donations are needed. To become a Hennepin Parks volunteer, call 612/559-9000. Direct your financial donation to the Hennepin Parks Foundation, 12615 County Road 9, Box 47320, Plymouth, MN 55447-0320.

Crow-Hassan Park Reserve

Operated by Hennepin Parks

"It's fun to work with the other volunteers. I think the reason we work so well together is that we're all in it for the same reason — we want to give back some of what we've experienced in the parks."
— Larry Martin, Hennepin Parks volunteer.

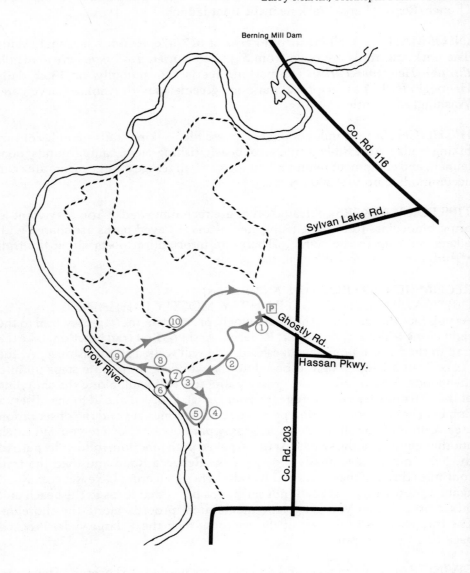

FACILITIES

- ✓**Restrooms** (pit toilets) are available at the entrance.
- ✓**Water** is available at the entrance.
- ✓**Public telephones** are available at the entrance.

46

DIRECTIONS: Crow-Hassan is located northwest of the metro area west of Rogers. **Public transportation** is not available. **From Interstate 94:** Take the Rogers exit and proceed south 1.2 miles on County Road 150, turn right and proceed on County Road 116 for 3 miles, turn left on County Road 203 and proceed 1.4 miles to the park entrance. **Park** near the trailhead building at the entrance.

INFORMATION: Call Hennepin Parks at 612/424-5511 for park information and seasonal events. The park and trails are open from 5 A.M. to sunset. *Trail maps are available in the trail map box near the building.* The parking fee is $16 annually, or $3.25 daily. Hennepin Parks has reciprocal parking agreements with Anoka, Carver, and Washington counties.

HIGHLIGHTS: • 11.7 miles of turf trails • Group campsites • Fishing along the Crow River • Canoe access and canoe campground.

TIPS FOR WALKERS: • Trail clothes are recommended. • Most trail junctions are marked with "you are here" maps. • There are abandoned dirt roadways, horseback riding trails, and snowmobile trails available for walking. • You may want to bring a walking stick. • Some portions of the trail may be flooded after a significant rainfall. • *Trails are closed to walkers in the winter.*

RECOMMENDED ROUTE: 4.6 K (2.9 miles)
DIRT SURFACE. HILLY. SHADED/UNSHADED.
From the parking lot, proceed to the ① **trail map mail box.** The trailhead begins just a few feet away. The gate may be closed with a chain to keep out motorized vehicles, so just walk around the chain. Follow the wide, grassy path into the woods. At the first ② **trail junction,** take the path to the left for a scenic view of the area. Proceed down a hill. When you get to the next ③ **trail junction,** continue on the path to the left. (The path to the right leads back to where you started.) At the next ④ **trail junction,** take a left. You will proceed through an open area and then into some woods. At the next ⑤ **trail junction,** take a right through the woods. At the next juncture with a map post, take the trail to the right up the ⑥ **steep hill bypass.** A few yards away you'll come to ⑦ **another junction** and take a left down a stony dirt road that eventually leads to open prairie. At the ⑧ **next junction,** continue on the main trail (not the trail to the left). Eventually you will walk up a hill. At the ⑨ **next junction,** take the trail to the right. You will walk through open prairie. At the ⑩ **next junction,** take the trail to the right. Cross a dirt road and continue on the trail along the treeline. Watch for a wooden directional sign that says "to trailhead" and follow that trail through an open field back to the parking lot.

GIVING BACK: To volunteer, call 612/559-9000. Direct your financial donation to the Hennepin Parks Foundation, 12615 County Road 9, Box 47320, Plymouth, MN 55447-0320.

Baker Park Reserve

Operated by Hennepin Parks

"Baker is a reserve which means that no less than 80 percent of the land will remain in its natural state. We have a six-mile paved path that winds through part of the reserve with marshes and woodlands providing a natural habitat for a wide variety of wildlife."

—Bob Gove, Northern Division Manager, Hennepin Parks.

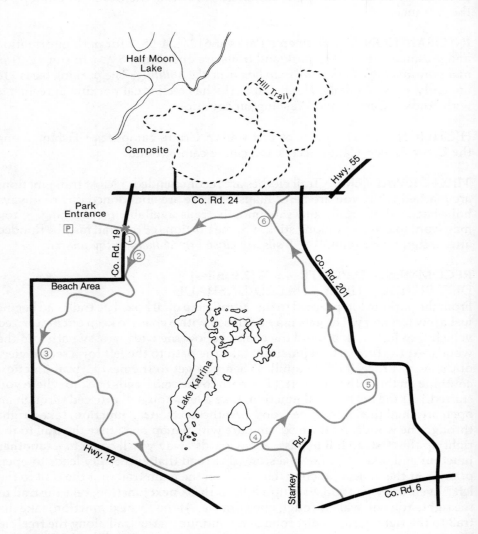

47

DIRECTIONS: Morris T. Baker Park Reserve is located west of the metro area near Maple Plain. **Public transportation** is not available. **From State Highway 55:** Follow County Road 24 (Dunkirk Lane) west for 7.3 miles (past the Golf Driving Range sign) to County Road 19, turn south, and follow 19 to the main entrance on the right. **Park** in the first lot just beyond the entrance gate.

INFORMATION: Call the office at 612/476-4666 or the gate at 612/479-2258 for seasonal hours and events. The park and trails are open from 5 A.M. to sunset. *Trail maps are available at the entrance gate.* The parking fee is $16 annually, or $3.25 daily. Hennepin Parks has reciprocal parking agreements with Anoka, Carver, and Washington counties.

HIGHLIGHTS: 6.2 miles of paved, accessible walking trails • 2.5 miles of turf trail • Accessible picnic grounds, beach area, golf course, camp grounds, and boat launch • Equipment rental • Creative play area • Hardwood forest.

TIPS FOR WALKERS: • If you walk a fifteen-minute mile, you can walk Baker in about one hundred minutes. • Street clothes are recommended. • This is an excellent trail for a long-distance fitness walk because it's smooth and flat. It's also a great place for a "think" walk because the trail is circular and you don't have to watch where you're going. • Walking trails are shared with bikers and skaters, so stay to the right. • Wooden signs identify most side trails. • *Trails are closed to walkers in the winter.*

RECOMMENDED ROUTE: 10 K (6.2 miles)
PAVED SURFACE. LEVEL. MOSTLY UNSHADED.
From the parking lot, proceed to the entrance road, walk past the entrance gate, and cross County Road 19. The ① **trailhead** begins on the other side of the road. Follow the path to the first ② **trail junction** and turn right. Continue on the paved path. You will eventually come to a rest area with restrooms. At the next ③ **trail junction,** continue on the main trail. Eventually, you will arrive at the ④ **Starkey Road Exit.** Continue on the main path, crossing a dirt road marked "group camp." You'll cross another ⑤ **dirt access road** and then enter a short stretch of woods. Just a bit down the path, you'll enter a larger stretch of woods and cross another dirt road. At the next ⑥ **trail junction,** keep on the main path. You'll cross another dirt road and a trail junction marked "Lake Independence Facility." When you get to the County 19 junction, take a right and proceed back to your start point.

GIVING BACK: To volunteer, call 612/559-9000. Direct your financial donation to the Hennepin Parks Foundation, 12615 County Road 9, Box 47320, Plymouth, MN 55447-0320.

Luce Line Trail

Operated by the Minnesota Department of Natural Resources

"The trail segment that begins in Plymouth provides a countrylike setting within an urban area. As the trail proceeds westward, it offers a very rural walking experience through rolling farmlands and prairie remnants." —Dick Schmidt, Trail Manager.

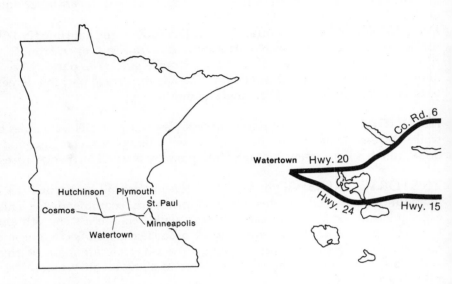

DIRECTIONS: The Luce Line trailhead begins in Plymouth, northwest of the metro area. **Public transportation** information is available through Plymouth Dial-A-Ride at 612/559-5057. **Plymouth entrance from State Highway 55:** Proceed south on Vicksburg Lane, just past County Road 6. Look for "Luce Line Trail" sign on the right. Turn right just beyond 10th Avenue North. Follow the entrance road to the parking area. **Stubbs Bay Road entrance from State Highway 12/394:** Proceed south on Stubbs Bay Road just beyond Bederwood Park. Watch for "Luce Line Trail" signs. Turn right. **Park** in lot.

INFORMATION: Call the Minnesota DNR at 612/296-6699 for information. *A trail map/brochure with a Travel Log is available through the Department of Natural Resources.* There is no admission fee.

HIGHLIGHTS: • 65 miles of converted railway trails that stretch from Plymouth to Cosmos • Hardpacked limestone surface makes portions of the trail accessible • The trail map distinguishes paved surfaces from natural surfaces.

TIPS FOR WALKERS: • Carry water, food. • Trails are shared with bikers. • Check trail conditions after a rain. • Trail clothes are recommended. • Carry a watch or pedometer to measure your time or distance. (Mileages are available on the trail map.)

48

FACILITIES

✓**Restrooms** are available at the Vicksburg Lane trailhead.
✓**Water** is not available along the trail.
✓**Public telephones** are not available along the trail.

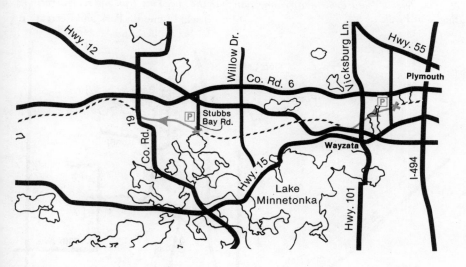

RECOMMENDED ROUTES:
LIMESTONE SURFACE. LEVEL. SHADED/UNSHADED.
Because the Luce Line is a linear trail, you'll need to set a time or distance goal and then retrace your steps back to the start point. You may sample the Luce Line from two different access points in the metro area or from any point west.

Route #1 Plymouth entrance 3.2 K (2 miles): From the parking lot, turn right (west) on the trail and you will walk over a wooden bridge across Gleason Lake. Viewing benches are available. You will pass through a residential area. The Wayzata water tower will come into view. When you reach Highway 101 (the only paved road) turn around and retrace your steps back to the start point.

Route #2 Stubbs Bay entrance: 6.4 K (4 miles): From the parking lot, turn right (west) onto the trail. This segment of the trail offers more of a remote, isolated walking experience through open fields, woods, and farmlands. When you reach County Road 19, turn around and retrace your steps back to the start point.

GIVING BACK: Direct financial donations to the Minnesota Parks and Trails Council, E-1311 First National Bank Building, St. Paul, MN 55101, or call 612/291-0715 or 800/289-1930. Or contact the MNDNR Trails and Waterways Division, 500 Lafayette Road, St. Paul, MN 55155, or call 612/296-1151.

City of Plymouth Trails/

Parker's Lake Trail

Operated by Plymouth Park and Recreation

"Plymouth Park and Recreation is devoted to promoting the importance of recreation and leisure and its life-enriching value by ensuring a wealth of opportunities for meeting the leisure needs of Plymouth residents. Plymouth has approximately 40 miles of paved trails and will eventually have about 65 miles. Special features include a connection with the Luce Line Trail and several sections of floating boardwalk." —Mary Bisek, Plymouth Park and Recreation.

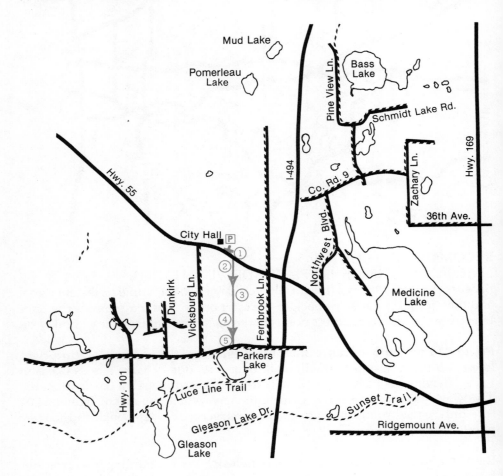

FACILITIES

- ✓ **Restrooms** are available at the swimming beach at Parker's Lake during summer hours. Portable units are available year-round.
- ✓ **Water** is available in the beach concession building.
- ✓ **Public telephones** are available at the beach.

49

DIRECTIONS: Parker's Lake Trail is northwest of Minneapolis in Plymouth. **Public transportation** is available. Call Metrolink at 612/827-7733 or, for local transportation, call Plymouth Dial-A-Ride at 612/559-5057. **From Interstate 494:** Proceed west on State Highway 55, north on Plymouth Boulevard to City Hall. **Park** in the City Hall parking lot.

INFORMATION: Call the Plymouth Park and Recreation Department at 612/550-5130. The trail (sidewalk) is available year-round. There is no admission fee.

HIGHLIGHTS: • Parkers Lake • Plymouth City Hall • Swimming beach, picnic area • Playground.

TIPS FOR WALKERS: • Street clothes are recommended. • You may want to carry water. • Be careful crossing Highway 55. • The City of Plymouth has a Plymouth Pedestrians Hiking Club ($5 annual membership) that offers incentives to walkers. • The City of Plymouth sponsors an annual Volksmarch in October.

RECOMMENDED ROUTE: 2.4 K (1.5 miles)
PAVED SURFACE. LEVEL. UNSHADED.
From the City Hall parking lot, cross ① **Plymouth Boulevard** and follow the sidewalk south all the way to ② **Highway 55.** As you are walking, you will see part of a trail to your right, but it runs parallel with the sidewalk, so just stay on the sidewalk to avoid bikers. Cross the highway and resume the trail along Niagara Lane. This is an industrial area, so you will see many businesses and warehouses. You will pass the ③ **Plymouth water tower** on your left. A few blocks before reaching the lake you will pass a ④ **large apartment complex** on your right. At ⑤ **Parker's Lake** you may want to walk around the lake; however, the trails are not marked or measured. Retrace your steps back to City Hall.

GIVING BACK: Direct your inquiries about volunteer opportunities and financial donations to Plymouth Park and Recreation, 3400 Plymouth Boulevard, Plymouth, MN 55447, or call 612/550-5130.

French Regional Park

Operated by Hennepin Parks

"In 1962, Hennepin County Park Reserve District owned 400 acres of land. We knew if we wanted to reach our goal of a park reserve within a thirty-minute drive of every resident in the county that we would have to move fast to beat both the shrinking availability of good park reserve sites and sharply rising land costs due to pressure from residential and commercial development."

—Clifton French, Former Superintendent of Hennepin Parks. Today, Hennepin Parks offers more than 24,000 acres of park reserves, regional parks, and special use areas.

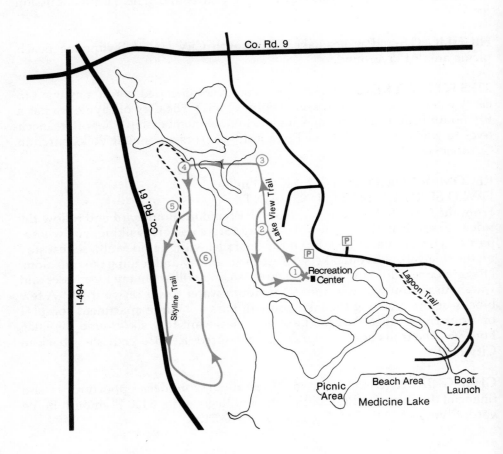

50

DIRECTIONS: French Regional Park is located northwest of Minneapolis in Plymouth. **Public transportation** information is available through Plymouth Dial-A-Ride at 612/559-5057. **From Interstate 494:** Proceed east on County Road 9 (Rockford Road) 1 mile to the park entrance. **Park** in the lot near the Recreation Center.

INFORMATION: Call the Recreation Center at 612/559-8891 for seasonal hours and events. The park and trails are open from 5 A.M. to sunset. *Trail maps are available at the Recreation Center.* The parking fee is $16 annually, or $3.25 daily. Hennepin Parks has reciprocal parking agreements with Anoka, Carver, and Washington counties.

HIGHLIGHTS: • 2.6 miles of turf hiking trails • Paved beach trail • Accessible creative play area, boat launch, fishing area, picnic grounds, beach • Equipment rentals • Group picnic area can accommodate up to 150 people for a walking event • Recreation Center • Shuttle transportation to beach and picnic areas.

TIPS FOR WALKERS: • You may want to bring a walking stick. • Trail clothes are recommended. • Major trails are identified with wooden signs. • Some portions of the trail may be flooded after a significant rainfall. • Trails are not shared with any other users. • *Trails are closed to walkers in the winter.*

RECOMMENDED ROUTE: 3.8 K (2.4 miles)
TURF/WOOD-CHIP SURFACE. HILLY. MOSTLY UNSHADED.
The walking trail begins behind the ① **Recreation Center.** Keep to the right. At the next ② **trail junction,** keep to the right. Turn left at the next ③ **trail junction** with a sign with arrows indicating Challenge Hill Trail and Skyline Trail. At the next ④ **trail junction,** take a left and proceed to the Skyline Trail. At the next ⑤ **trail junction,** ignore the Challenge Hill sign and keep walking until you see the Skyline Trail sign. Follow the trail into the woods. Keep on the main path; don't take any side trails. Complete the loop. Eventually, you will arrive at the top of a hill that provides a ⑥ **scenic view** of the park and surrounding areas. When you return to junction ②, **keep to the right** until you reach the Recreation Center.

GIVING BACK: To volunteer, call 612/559-9000. Direct your financial donation to the Hennepin Parks Foundation, 12615 County Road 9, Box 47320, Plymouth, MN 55447-0320.

Fish Lake Regional Park

Operated by Hennepin Parks

"Life isn't a spectator sport. Get out there and get involved! The more I do, the more involved I become as a volunteer, the more exciting life gets. I want to look back on my life and be glad that I took the time to do the things that I really wanted to do."

—Bill Tevogt, Hennepin Parks volunteer.

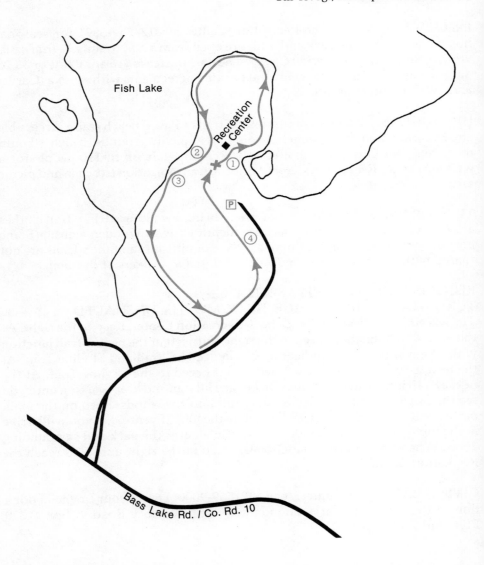

Fish Lake

Recreation Center

Bass Lake Rd. / Co. Rd. 10

FACILITIES

✓ **Restrooms** (accessible) are available at the Recreation Center.
✓ **Water** is available at the Recreation Center.
✓ **Public telephones** are available at the Recreation Center.

51

DIRECTIONS: Fish Lake Regional Park is located north of the metro area in Maple Grove. **Public transportation** is not available. **From Interstate 494:** Proceed west on County Road 10 (Bass Lake Road) one mile to the entrance. **Park** near the Recreation Center.

INFORMATION: Call the Recreation Center at 612/420-3423 for seasonal hours and events. The park and trails are open from 5 A.M. to sunset. *Trail maps are available in the Recreation Center.* The parking fee is $16 annually, or $3.25 daily. Hennepin Parks has reciprocal parking agreements with Anoka, Carver, and Washington counties.

HIGHLIGHTS: • 1 mile of paved, accessible walking trails • 2 miles of turf hiking trails • Accessible picnic area, beach, fishing area, boat launch • Equipment rentals.

TIPS FOR WALKERS: • Street clothes are recommended. • The length of the trails and the paved, level surface make this an excellent place to start a walking program for children. • Paths are shared with bikers, so keep to the right. • *Trails are closed to walkers in the winter.*

RECOMMENDED ROUTE: 2.4 K (1.5 miles)
PAVED SURFACE. LEVEL. MOSTLY SHADED.
The trail begins behind the Recreation Center. Take the trail to the right marked ① **Bay Point Trail.** Continue walking until you return to the Recreation Center. Walk along the ② **beach area** and resume the trail near the ③ **boat rental area.** The trail winds through the woods and ends at the first ④ **parking lot.** Take a left and walk back to the start point.

GIVING BACK: To volunteer, call 612/559-9000. Direct your financial donation to the Hennepin Parks Foundation, 12615 County Road 9, Box 47320, Plymouth, MN 55447-0320.

City of Maple Grove Trails/
Elm Creek Special Use Park and Arboretum

Operated by the City of Maple Grove

"Within the solitude of a natural environment, the Maple Grove trails provide walkers with an opportunity to discover beautiful things in nature. The trails are a nice, peaceful retreat for people who work in a busy city, with busy schedules."

—Patty Anderson, Administrative Management Aide, City of Maple Grove.

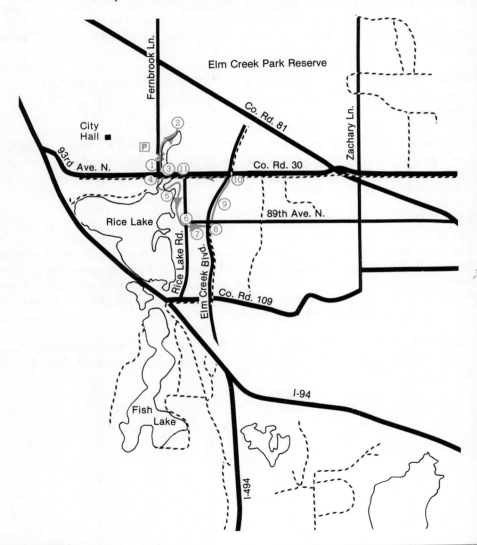

52

DIRECTIONS: Elm Creek Special Use Park is located northwest of the metro area in Maple Grove. **Public transportation** is not available. **From Interstate 94:** Take the 95th Avenue exit. Proceed east (it becomes 93rd Avenue). Turn left (north) on Fernbrook Lane and immediately turn right. **Park** in the lot provided.

INFORMATION: Call Maple Grove Parks and Recreation at 612/420-4000. The park is open from 6 A.M. to 11 P.M. *A trail map is available through the City of Maple Grove.* There is no admittance fee.

HIGHLIGHTS: • Maple Grove City Hall (across the street from the park) • Accessible trails and picnic tables • City Arboretum • Picnic area with grill.

TIPS FOR WALKERS: • Paths are shared with bikers, so keep to the right. • Carry water. • Street clothes are recommended. • The first part of the recommended route is ideal for children because it's a short walk.

RECOMMENDED ROUTE: 6.6 K (4.1 miles)
PAVED SURFACE. LEVEL. UNSHADED.
From the parking lot, as you face the creek, proceed to the paved trail to the left. Walk past the bridge (do not cross). You will pass a ① **picnic shelter** on the left, and on the right you'll eventually pass some steps down to the creek (do not take them). Notice the City Arboretum and the signs that describe the different types of trees. When you reach the end of the trail you'll come to a ② **dam** and a scenic view of Elm Creek. Retrace your steps back to the parking lot. Then, proceed on the path ③ **under the 93rd Avenue Bridge** and you will come to a sign that says "Rice Lake Trails." Stay on the trail and turn left at the next ④ **trail junction.** Houses will be on your right and a small portion of the lake will be on the left. Stay left at the next fork. At the next junction, go left across a ⑤ **wooden bridge.** Continue along the shoreline through a residential area, keeping to the right at the first and second trail junctions. Follow the trail up to a ⑥ **residential street, 88th Place North.** Cross the street, and turn left, and head toward the brick building at the end of the street. Follow the paved trail as it turns right for a bit, then ⑦ **cross the street (Rice Lake Road)** and continue on the paved trail through the play fields. At the next junction, keep walking straight ahead past Rice Lake School, through a parking lot, and then ⑧ **turn left on the sidewalk** and walk along Elm Creek Boulevard past the ⑨ **Kerber Playfields.** Turn left at ⑩ **County Road 30/93rd Avenue North** and continue walking until you cross a ⑪ **pedestrian bridge** across the creek. Turn left and go under the 93rd Avenue Bridge to return to the parking lot.

GIVING BACK: For information about Arboretum Tree Sponsorship or the Maple Grove Wish List, call 612/420-4000.

Elm Creek Park Reserve/
Eastman Nature Center

Operated by Hennepin Parks

"The Eastman Nature Center trails are along Rush and Elm creeks. As you walk in the cool, damp woods you hear small animals skittering back into the forest. It's a wonderful walk in the fall because you're in a basswood and sugar maple forest where the leaves turn brilliant colors."

—Lee Ann Landstrom, Outdoor Education Supervisor, Eastman Nature Center.

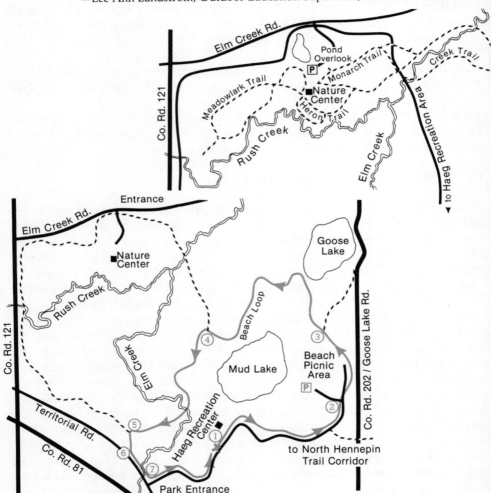

FACILITIES

- ✓ **Restrooms** (accessible) are located in the Eastman Nature Center and Recreation Center.
- ✓ **Water** is available in the Eastman Nature Center, Recreation Center, and beach house.
- ✓ **Public telephones** are available in the Eastman Nature Center, Recreation Center, and beach house.

53

DIRECTIONS: Elm Creek Park Reserve is located north of Minneapolis between the communities of Osseo, Champlin, Dayton, and Maple Grove. **Public transportation** is not available. **From County Road 81:** Turn right on Territorial Road, turn right at the park sign for the Haeg Recreation Center. Proceed past the gatehouse to the Recreation Center. **Park** in the Recreation Center lot.

INFORMATION: Call the Recreation Center at 612/424-5511 or the Eastman Nature Center at 420-4300 for seasonal hours and events. The park and trails are open from 5 A.M. to sunset. *Trail maps are available at the Recreation Center and Eastman Nature Center.* The parking fee is $16 annually, or $3.25 daily. Hennepin Parks has reciprocal parking agreements with Anoka, Carver, and Washington counties.

HIGHLIGHTS: • 9.1 miles of paved walking trails • 8.9 miles of wood-chip hiking trails • Accessible picnic area, beach area, group campgrounds • Largest park reserve in Hennepin County with over 5,000 acres • Eastman Nature Center • Creative play area • The paved trails at Elm Creek Park Reserve join the 7-mile North Hennepin Regional Trail Corridor that leads to the Coon Rapids Dam Regional Park • Large picnic shelter can hold three hundred people for a walking event.

TIPS FOR WALKERS: • Paved trails are shared with bikers and skaters, so stay to the right. • "You are here" maps are posted at most trail junctions. • *Most trails are closed to walkers during the winter months but Eastman Nature Center trails are open year-round.* • Street clothes are recommended.

RECOMMENDED ROUTE: 7.8 K (4.9 miles)
PAVED SURFACE. HILLY. MOSTLY UNSHADED.
From the parking lot at the Recreation Center, proceed to the ① **outdoor Gamefield Exercise Court** that contains useful information about various forms of exercise. Turn left on the paved trail that runs parallel to the entrance road. When you arrive at the ② **picnic area,** cross the road and continue on the paved trail. At the next ③ **trail junction,** keep to the left. You'll be able to catch views of Mud Lake as you continue to the next ④ **trail junction.** Keep to the left. The trail winds past a creek and through a wooded area. At the next ⑤ **trail junction,** keep left. You'll walk just a short distance and then come to ⑥ **Territorial Road.** Take a left onto the road and walk on the shoulder to the ⑦ **entrance road.** Turn left at the entrance road and the trail will take you back to the Haeg Recreation Center.

GIVING BACK: To volunteer, call 612/559-9000. Direct your financial donation to the Hennepin Parks Foundation, 12615 County Road 9, Box 47320, Plymouth, MN 55447-0320.

North Hennepin/
Regional Trail Corridor

Operated by Hennepin Parks

"When you become a park volunteer, you meet people with similar interests and you become good friends. Volunteering is time well-spent." —Bob Iverson, Hennepin Parks volunteer.

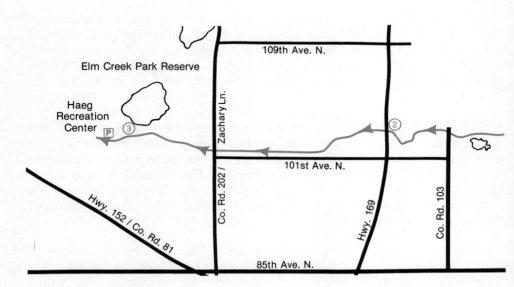

DIRECTIONS: The North Hennepin Regional Trail Corridor is north of Minneapolis in Maple Grove and Brooklyn Park. It can be accessed from Elm Creek Park Reserve, Coon Rapids Dam Regional Park, or Oak Grove City Park (located in the center of the trail). **Directions to Oak Grove City Park from County Road 81:** Proceed east on 85th Avenue North (County 109), north (left) on Zane Avenue (County 14) to the entrance to Oak Grove City Park on the left. Follow the entrance road to the picnic area. **Park** near the picnic shelter.

INFORMATION: Call the Coon Rapids Dam at 612/757-4700 for information about special events. The trail is open from 5 A.M. to sunset. *Trail maps are available at Coon Rapids Dam or Elm Creek Park.* The parking fee is $16 annually, or $3.25 daily. Hennepin Parks has reciprocal parking agreements with Anoka, Carver, and Washington counties.

HIGHLIGHTS: 7.5 miles of paved, accessible walking trail • Bicycle rentals.

TIPS FOR WALKERS: • The trail is shared with bikers, so keep to the right. • This is a linear trail, so you may want to walk segments of the trail in different seasons. • *This trail is closed to walkers in the winter.*

54

FACILITIES

✓ **Restrooms** are available at Elm Creek Recreation Center, Coon Rapids Dam Visitor Center, Coon Rapids Dam Comfort Station, and Oak Grove City Park (summer only).

✓ **Water** is available at the same facilities as the restrooms.

✓ **Public telephones** are available at Elm Creek Recreation Center, Coon Rapids Dam Visitor Center, and Coon Rapids Dam Comfort Station.

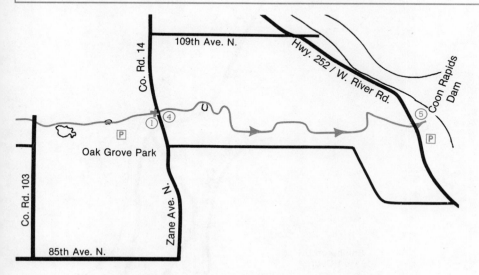

RECOMMENDED ROUTE TO ELM CREEK: 13.4 K (8.4 miles)

PAVED SURFACE. LEVEL. MOSTLY UNSHADED.

From the Oak Grove parking lot, proceed along the entrance road back to Zane Avenue. You will see a paved trail that runs parallel to the entrance road. The ① **trail to the left** will take you through wooded areas and open fields, across a ② **footbridge** over U.S. 169, through residential areas, and finally to the ③ **Haeg Creek Recreation Center** (with a concession stand and equipment rentals). From the Recreation Center, follow the trail back to your start point.

TO COON RAPIDS DAM: 13.4 K (8.4 Miles)

PAVED SURFACE. LEVEL. MOSTLY SHADED.

From the Oak Grove parking lot, proceed along the entrance road back to Zane Avenue. You will see the paved trail that runs parallel to the entrance road. The ④ **trail to the right** will take you through wooded areas and open fields. At the end of the trail you will cross West River Road. At the entrance gate, turn left and follow the path to the ⑤ **Coon Rapids Dam.** The path across the dam leads to the Visitor's Center with information displays and equipment rentals. From the Visitor's Center, follow the trail back to the start point.

GIVING BACK: To become a Hennepin Parks volunteer, call 612/559-9000. Direct financial donations to Hennepin Parks Foundation.

City of Brooklyn Park Trails/
Edinburgh USA Golf Course

Operated by the City of Brooklyn Park

"We appreciate the trails in Brooklyn Park because of their proximity, and our young children enjoy the outdoor experience. Walking gives us all a chance to have some quality time together at the end of the day and get some exercise at the same time."

—Nancy and Bill Freeman, residents of Brooklyn Park.

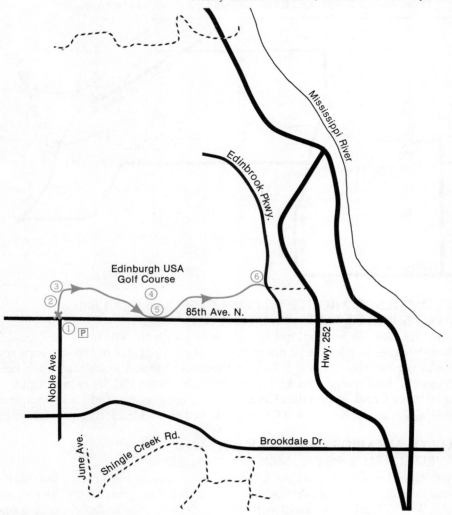

FACILITIES

✓**Restrooms** (accessible) are available in the Edinburgh Clubhouse during regular hours.

✓**Water** is available in the Edinburgh Clubhouse during regular hours.

✓**Public telephones** are available in the Edinburgh Clubhouse during regular hours.

55

DIRECTIONS: The City of Brooklyn Park trails are located about 12 miles northwest of Minneapolis. **Public transportation** is not available. **From Interstate 694:** Proceed north on State Highway 252, west (left) on 85th Avenue North, north (right) on Noble Avenue and make a quick right turn into the shopping center parking lot. **Park** in the shopping center lot.

INFORMATION: Call the Brooklyn Park Parks and Recreation Department at 612/424-8017 for information. *A trail map is available for $1 from the Parks and Recreation Department.* The trails are open from dawn to dusk throughout the year. There is no admission fee.

HIGHLIGHTS: • Edinburgh USA Golf Course designed by Robert Trent Jones II • Lots of greenery and well-landscaped areas.

TIPS FOR WALKERS: • Wear street clothes. • The path is shared with bikers and joggers so keep to one side. • As you pass through the golf course, watch for players. They may signal you to stop walking for a minute while they take a shot.

RECOMMENDED ROUTE: 3.2 K (2 miles)
PAVED SURFACE. LEVEL. MOSTLY UNSHADED.
From the shopping center parking lot, proceed ① **north on Noble Avenue** for about one block. Just after you ② **cross Edinbrook Terrace,** watch for the beginning of a paved trail to the right. Turn right onto the ③ **paved trail** and you will walk through a residential area along Edinbrook Channel. Eventually you will enter the ④ **Edinburgh USA Golf Course.** To visit the Clubhouse, turn left at the entrance road (Edinburgh Crossing) and enter the large castlelike brick building at the end of the road. To continue on the trail, proceed on the paved path past the ⑤ **fountains and gardens** along 85th Avenue North. Continue through a wooded area to ⑥ **Edinbrook Parkway.** Turn around and retrace your steps back to the start point.

GIVING BACK: For volunteer positions, call the Parks and Recreation Department. The City of Brooklyn Park has a Memorial Rose Garden near the Brooklyn Park Community Center. Donations of $20 or more given in memory of a birthday, anniversary, special event, or a loved one are used to purchase and plant a community rose bush. A commemorative plaque in the Community Center acknowledges the gift and the event. Gifts can be forwarded to the Brooklyn Park Parks and Recreation Department, Memory Rose Garden Program, 5600 85th Avenue North, Brooklyn Park, MN 55443.

City of Brooklyn Center Trails/ _____

Shingle Creek Trailway/Palmer Lake Nature Area

Operated by the City of Brooklyn Center

"One of the best things Brooklyn Center ever did was put in a trail system. People use the trails every day, during every season. Right now there are 12 miles of trails, but our long-term plans call for up to 22 miles of paved and on-road trails."

—Arnie Mavis, Superintendent of Brooklyn Center Parks and Recreation.

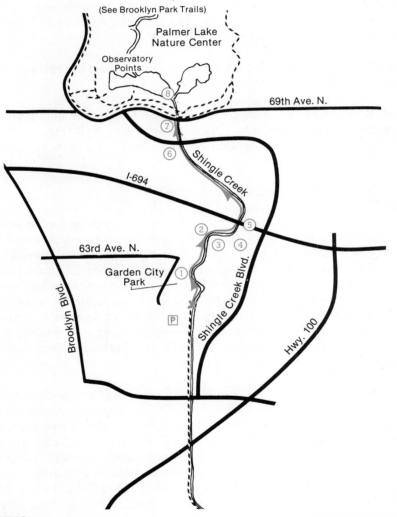

FACILITIES

✓**Restrooms** (portable) are available at Central Park behind the Brooklyn Center City Hall and at Palmer Lake just off 69th Street.

✓**Water** is not available.

✓**Public telephones** are not available.

56

DIRECTIONS: Shingle Creek Parkway is northwest of the metro area in Brooklyn Center. **Public transportation** is not available. **From Interstate 694:** Proceed south on Brooklyn Boulevard, east (left) on 63rd Avenue, south (right) on Brooklyn Drive. Proceed about one block and then turn left into Garden City Park. **Park** in the entrance lot.

INFORMATION: Call Brooklyn Center Parks and Recreation at 612/569-3400. The trail is open from 6 A.M. to 10 P.M. There is no admission fee.

HIGHLIGHTS: • The 5.5 miles of Shingle Creek trails in Brooklyn Center link with the Minneapolis greenways • Well groomed, paved trails • Outdoor exercise course • Quiet walk along historic Shingle Creek • Close to shopping centers, restaurants.

TIPS FOR WALKERS: • Street clothes are recommended.

RECOMMENDED ROUTE: 6.4 K (4 miles)
PAVED SURFACE. LEVEL/ONE BRIDGE. UNSHADED.
From the parking lot, proceed to the beginning of the trail (the children's playground and basketball court should be to your right). Turn left onto the trail. (There is another paved trail close to the creek for bikers.) Along the trail you'll see the first ① **exercise station.** You will continue to see these fitness centers along the way. You will pass ② **tennis courts** on your left just before crossing a ③ **wooden bridge** across Shingle Creek. On the right you will see ④ **Brooklyn Center City Hall and Civic Center.** Cross the ⑤ **pedestrian bridge** over I-694 (and nine lanes of traffic). At the next trail junction, stay to the left and follow the trail along the creek. After passing under ⑥ **two bridges,** continue along the trail until you see the ⑦ **city maintenance buildings** to the right. When you reach 69th Avenue, you may turn around and retrace your path back to the start point or you may walk the 2.9-mile walking path around ⑧ **Palmer Lake Nature Area** or another 2 miles of wood-chip nature trails. Add these to your mileage if you decide to walk them.

GIVING BACK: Direct inquiries about volunteer opportunities and financial donations to the City of Brooklyn Center, Department of Parks and Recreation, 6301 Shingle Creek Parkway, Brooklyn Center, MN 55430, or call 612/569-3400.

City of Robbinsdale Trails/
Sochacki Community Park

Operated by the City of Robbinsdale

"Sochacki Park is a thirty-three-acre, nature-oriented passive park with two wildlife viewing decks, a picnic shelter and numerous birdhouses. The park was named after Red Sochacki (pronounced so-hockey), who was the mayor of Robbinsdale, a former school board member, a physical education teacher and coach, and a very civic-minded resident."

—Russ Fawbush, Director of Parks, Recreation, and Forestry.

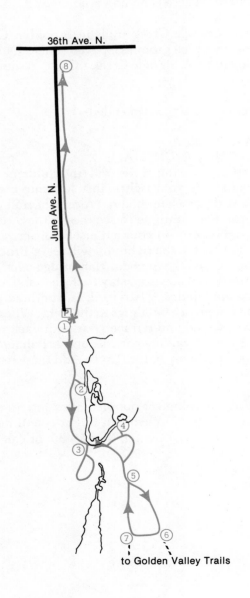

36th Ave. N.

June Ave. N.

to Golden Valley Trails

FACILITIES

✓**Restrooms**
are not available.
✓**Water**
is not available.
✓**Public telephones**
are not available.

57

DIRECTIONS: Robbinsdale is northwest of the metro area. **Public transportation** is available on MTC Routes #14 and 9. **From State Highway 100:** Proceed east on 36th Avenue North and south (right) on June Avenue to the first entrance on the right. **Park** in the main lot at the very end of the road.

INFORMATION: Call Robbinsdale Parks and Recreation at 612/537-4534. The park is open from 8 A.M. to 10 P.M. daily. *A trail map is available through the city.* There is no admission fee.

HIGHLIGHTS: • Wildflowers • Observation decks • Wetlands • Prairie grass • Wildlife.

TIPS FOR WALKERS: • The trails are shared with bikers and mountain bikers. • Street clothes are recommended. • The northern part of the trail parallels June Avenue, a wide, quiet stretch of road, and a perfect place for kids to ride bikes or skate beside a walking parent.

RECOMMENDED ROUTE: 3.2 K (2 miles)
ASPHALT/LIMESTONE/WOOD-CHIP. LEVEL. MOSTLY SHADED.
From the parking lot, proceed ① **south on the limestone trail.** You may want to stop and enjoy the ② **overlook.** Continue to the ③ **wood-chip nature trail** that in the summer offers a fairy-tale patch of Queen Anne's Lace. At the next trail junction, take a left to another ④ **overlook,** and then follow the wood-chip trail back to the paved trail. At the next trail junction, ⑤ **keep to the left on the paved trail,** and follow the trail around a loop to an ⑥ **asphalt trail.** At this point you may extend the walk by proceeding south along the asphalt trails of Golden Valley, or continue your tour of Sochacki Park by taking a right at the ⑦ **wood-chip trail.** Follow the paved trail north past the picnic area to the ⑧ **northern-most point,** and then turn around. For a change, you may want to walk back along June Avenue on the wide, paved path, instead of the limestone path.

GIVING BACK: For information about volunteer and donation opportunities, contact the City of Robbinsdale, 4221 Lake Road, Robbinsdale, MN 55422, or call 612/537-4534.

City of Golden Valley Trails

Operated by the Golden Valley Park and Recreation Department

"We have over 40 miles of trails in Golden Valley. Some are street trails, others are limestone or asphalt trails or sidewalks. Using the trails is an outstanding and inexpensive way to maintain physical fitness and cope with the stresses of today."

—Rick Jacobson, Director of Park and Recreation.

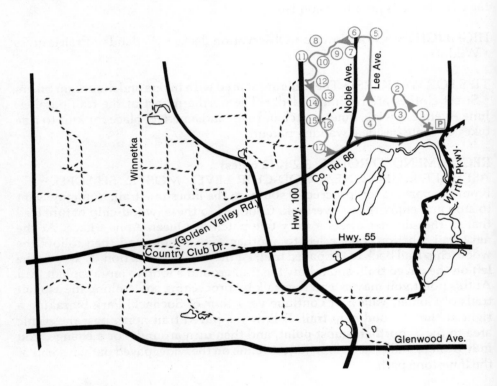

58

DIRECTIONS: Golden Valley is northwest of the metro area. **Public transportation** is available on MTC Route #19. **From State Highway 100:** Proceed east on the Duluth Street exit (County Road 66/Golden Valley Road), past Courage Center, and turn left on Bonnie Lane (just past the fire station). **Park** at the end of this dead-end street near the trailhead.

INFORMATION: Call Golden Valley Park and Recreation at 612/544-5218. Parks and trails are open from dawn to dusk. *A trail map is available through the city.* There is no admission fee to parks or trails.

HIGHLIGHTS: • 40 miles of walking/biking trails in Golden Valley • Rice Lake Nature Area • Papoose Park • Gearty Park • Scheid Park.

TIPS FOR WALKERS: • Street clothes are recommended. • Trails are shared with bikers.

RECOMMENDED ROUTE: 6.4 K (4 miles)
PAVED/LIMESTONE SURFACE. LEVEL. MOSTLY UNSHADED.
Proceed to the ① **Mary Hills trailhead** along the road. You will walk through a wooded area. At the Sochacki Park sign, you may take a detour and walk another two miles through this Robbinsdale park (see map # 57). The Golden Valley trail leads to ② **Dresden Lane cul-de-sac.** Walk on the road to ③ **Basset Creek Drive.** Turn right and walk on a crushed limestone path past Rice Lake Nature Area before you make a sharp right turn at the end of the limestone path and walk on the road. At ④ **Lee Avenue** turn right (there's a jog in the road early on) and walk on the road north about a mile. At ⑤ **Adell Avenue** turn left (notice Papoose Park on the right) and at ⑥ **Noble Avenue** turn left again. Then, cross the street and turn ⑦ **right on Lowry Terrace,** which has two jogs in the road (right on Orchard Avenue, left on Lowry Terrace again, left on Quail Avenue North, right on Lowry Terrace), and you will arrive at ⑧ **Gearty Park.** Turn ⑨ **left at Regent,** walk along the road by the park, then turn ⑩ **right at Triton Drive** and then ⑪ **left on Scott Avenue** (the road curves). Just past ⑫ **Dawnview Terrace** the crushed limestone trail resumes and will lead you to another wooded area parallel to Highway 100. When you get to the ⑬ **fork in the path,** turn right, and then at the end of the trail ⑭ **turn left onto Unity Avenue.** Walk south to ⑮ **Minnaqua Drive** and turn left, then turn ⑯ **right on Toledo** (watch street signs). At ⑰ **Duluth Street,** cross the street and turn left onto the asphalt trail. Notice Scheid Park on the right. Follow the trail back to the fire station and your start point.

GIVING BACK: For information about volunteer and donation opportunities, call 612/544-5218 or write City of Golden Valley Park and Recreation, 8200 Wayzata Boulevard, Golden Valley, MN 55426.

Bunker Hills Regional Park

Operated by Anoka County Parks

"People come to Bunker Hills for the variety it offers. From the wave pool to the horse stables to campgrounds and archery, the park offers something for everyone in the family."
—Jeanne Masloski, Co-caretaker, Bunker Hills Park.

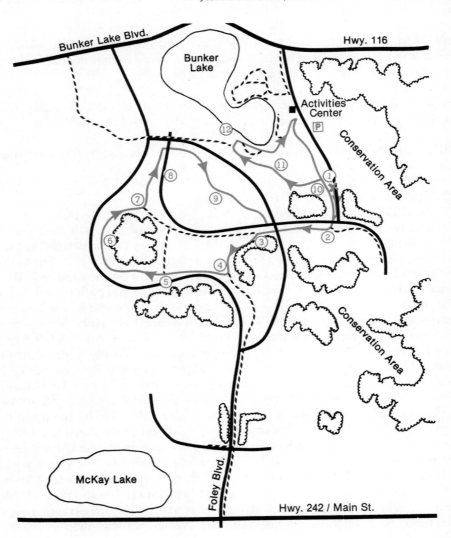

FACILITIES

- ✓ **Restrooms** (accessible) are available at the Activities Center, wave pool, picnic areas, and at campsites.
- ✓ **Water** is available at the Activities Center, wave pool, picnic areas, and campsites, but not along the trail.
- ✓ **Public telephones** are available at the Activities Center during regular hours.

59

DIRECTIONS: Bunker Hills Park is located north of the metro area in Coon Rapids. **Public transportation** information is available through Anoka County Traveler at 612/464-8883. **From Interstate 694:** Proceed north on University Avenue (State Highway 47), take the Foley Boulevard exit. Turn left onto Foley Boulevard and drive 3 miles to the park entrance. **Park** at the Activities Center (follow the signs).

INFORMATION: Call Anoka County Parks at 612/757-2390 or the Bunker Hills caretaker at 612/755-4165. *A trail map of the park is available at the Activities Center or through Anoka Parks.* The park is open from 7:30 A.M. to 9:30 P.M. year-round. No admittance fee is charged.

HIGHLIGHTS: • 5.5 miles of trails • Nature trails • Activities Center (available for seminars, social events, family gatherings) • Wave pool for swimming • Archery range and building • Picnic tables, grills, shelters • Veterans War Memorial • Golf course • Riding stables that offer trail rides, hay and sleigh rides, carriage rides, pony rides • Campgrounds.

TIPS FOR WALKERS: • Street clothes are recommended. • The trail is shared with bikers, so keep to the right.

RECOMMENDED ROUTE: 5.6 K (3.5 miles)
PAVED/DIRT SURFACE. MOSTLY LEVEL. SHADED/UNSHADED.
From the front of the Activities Center, take the paved trail to the left and remain on it, passing the unpaved nature trail to the right. Watch for horses in the pasture to the left. At the ① **first trail junction,** keep to the left. Cross the entrance road and ② **proceed to the right** on the paved trail. Cross another entrance road, keeping to the left, then ③ **turn left at the trail junction.** Eventually you will walk through an avenue of pines and wildflowers. Take a right at the next junction and you will pass the ④ **wave pool.** Continue on the trail past the parking lot. At the next ⑤ **paved trail junction,** keep to the left and you will walk through an ⑥ **open prairie area.** Turn left at the next ⑦ **paved trail junction** and walk past the ⑧ **children's playground area and ball park.** Continue on the path past the ⑨ **Veterans Memorial** (restrooms are to the right) and **picnic area.** At the next paved trail junction, cross the road, turn left, and cross another road. Follow this familiar paved path to the ⑩ **next junction.** Turn left and follow the path that leads to the overlook. Along the way stop and rest on the ⑪ **covered benches** to the right. At the next junction, take a right and proceed to the ⑫ **overlook.** Walk down the stairs to the dirt path, turn left, and walk along the dirt trail back to the Activities Center.

GIVING BACK: Direct financial donations to Anoka County Parks, 550 Bunker Lake Boulevard Northwest, Andover, MN 55304. Please designate what park or project you'd like the money used for.

City of Coon Rapids Trails/____
Sand Creek/Coon Creek Trail

Operated by the City of Coon Rapids Park and Recreation Department

"I walk the trails to get some exercise and walk my dog, Bambi. After being cooped up inside all winter, walking in the woods on a summer day is really great."

—Dan Nelson, Coon Rapids resident.

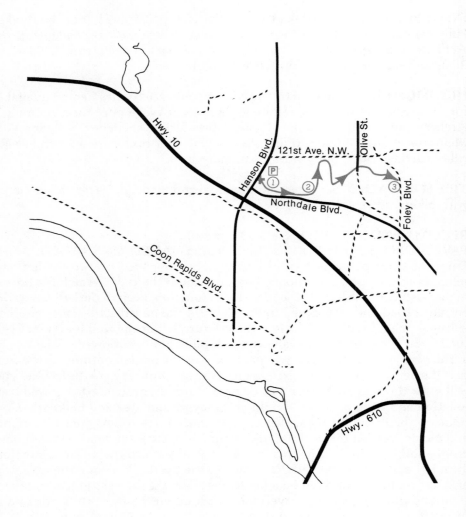

FACILITIES ____

- ✓**Restrooms** are not available.
- ✓**Water** is not available.
- ✓**Public telephones** are not available.

60

DIRECTIONS: Coon Rapids is north of the metro area. **Public transportation** is available on MTC Route #24E and through the Anoka County Traveler at 612/464-8883. **From U.S. Highway 10:** proceed north on Hanson Boulevard/ County Road 11 past Northdale Boulevard to Lions Coon Creek Park on the right. **Park** in the main lot.

INFORMATION: Call Coon Rapids Park and Recreation at 612/755-2880. The trails are open from sunrise to sunset year-round. *A map of the Coon Rapids park system is available through the city.* There is no admission fee.

HIGHLIGHTS: • Lions Coon Creek Park • Mallary Park • Sand Creek.

TIPS FOR WALKERS: • Street clothes are recommended. • Carry water. • Trails are shared with bikers, so keep to the right. • There are plenty of benches along the way. • The trail goes through a residential area along a creek. One segment of the trail involves a detour over some railroad tracks. • Coon Rapids is developing a system of trails that will eventually connect most residential areas with city parks.

RECOMMENDED ROUTE: 7.2 K (4.5 miles)
PAVED SURFACE. LEVEL. MOSTLY SHADED.
From the parking lot, walk to the ① **footbridge.** After you cross the bridge, turn right onto the paved path. Follow the path and you will eventually cross a side street (Xeon Boulevard). Keep walking until you come to ② **Xeon Street.** Turn left, walk to 121st Avenue, and turn right. Just beyond the railroad tracks the paved trail continues. Turn right onto the trail and follow it along the tracks and then left into the woods. Eventually you will cross Olive Street. Continue walking until you reach the end of the trail at ③ **Foley Boulevard** (Burr Oak development). Retrace your steps back to the start point.

GIVING BACK: For information about volunteer and donation opportunities, contact the City of Coon Rapids Park and Recreation Department at 1313 Coon Rapids Boulevard, Coon Rapids, MN 55433-5397, or call 612/755-2880.

Coon Rapids Dam Regional Park————

Operated jointly by Hennepin Parks and Anoka County

"There is a half-mile trail on Dunn's Island, named after the man who donated the land. He used to graze his sheep there. You can also walk over the Mississippi on a dam that was built in 1914. This is a great park for walking because there are trails along both sides of the river."

—Karen Kobey, Naturalist.

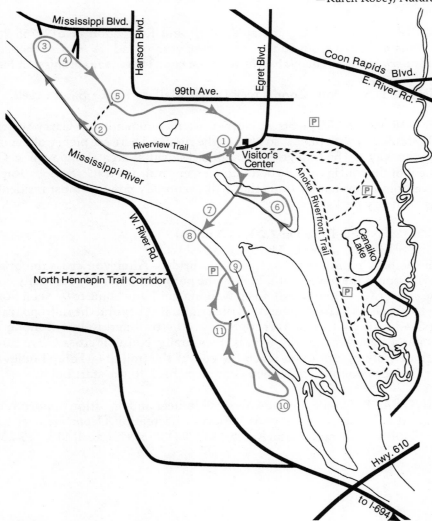

FACILITIES————

- ✓ **Restrooms** (accessible) are available in the Visitor Center and at the Comfort Station on the west side of the river.
- ✓ **Water** is available in the Visitor Center and the Comfort Station on the west side of the river.
- ✓ **Public telephones** are available outside the Visitor Center and at the Comfort Station on the west side of the river.

61

DIRECTIONS: Coon Rapids Dam Regional Park is located on the Mississippi River between Coon Rapids and Brooklyn Park. **Public transportation** is available to the park via MTC Routes #26 and 27. **From Interstate 694:** Proceed north on East River Road (County Road 1), west on Egret Boulevard .3 mile to the park entrance. **Park** in the lot close to the Visitor Center.

INFORMATION: Call the Visitor Center at 612/757-4700 for seasonal hours and events. The park and trails are open from 5 A.M. to sunset. *Trail maps are available in the Visitor Center.* The parking fee is $16 annually or $3.25 daily. Hennepin Parks has reciprocal parking agreements with Anoka, Carver, and Washington counties.

HIGHLIGHTS: • 4 miles of dirt/woodchip hiking trails • 1.5 miles of paved, accessible trail • Accessible picnic area, fishing area, boat launch • Accessible walkway across the dam • Visitor Center with displays • Equipment rental • Dunn's Island • The North-Hennepin Trail Corridor joins Coon Rapids Dam and Elm Creek Regional Park.

TIPS FOR WALKERS: • Some trails wind through grassy areas so trail clothes are recommended. • There are some wooden directional signs with trail names. • *Trails are closed to walkers in the winter.*

RECOMMENDED ROUTE: 6.7 K (4.2 miles)
MOSTLY DIRT/WOOD-CHIP SURFACE. LEVEL. SHADED/ UNSHADED.
From the Visitor Center, follow the path past the boat launch area to ① **two wooden posts** that mark the beginning of a wide dirt trail. Follow the trail past picnic area A. As you approach ② **picnic area B,** stay on the main trail, not the dirt trail off to the right. When you get to the next ③ **trail junction,** continue on the wide dirt path to the right. At the next ④ **junction,** keep right. When you arrive at an ⑤ **"Autumn Hiking Program"** sign keep straight ahead; don't turn right. The trail juts to the left near Kildeer Street. Don't take the footpaths to the right. Follow the trail back to the Visitor's Center and take the path around ⑥ **Dunn's Island.** Cross over the ⑦ **Coon Rapids Dam.** Follow the ⑧ **dirt trail** (near the water fountain) into the woods along the river. Proceed through an ⑨ **open field.** Keep to the left. You will enter a woods and arrive at the ⑩ **Cottonwood Canoe camp.** Follow the semi-circular trail along the river that leads up into a wide grassy path. Stay on the main path. At the ⑪ **trail juncture,** take the path to the left. Cross the large open picnic area and follow the path back across the dam to the start point.

GIVING BACK: To volunteer, call 612/559-9000. Direct your financial donation to the Hennepin Parks Foundation, 12615 County Road 9, Box 47320, Plymouth, MN 55447-0320.

Springbrook Nature Center _____

Operated by the City of Fridley

"Walkers at Springbrook will enjoy the floating boardwalks through the low-lying wetlands that are full of wildlife, and the serene, quiet paths through the oak forest. Our nature center has video footage from the tornado that struck here in 1986 and information about our tornado restoration project." —Karen Shanberg, Naturalist.

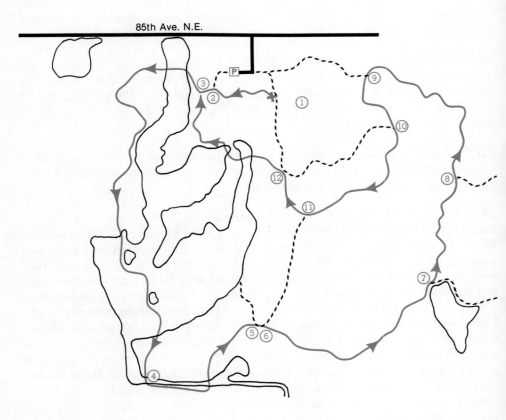

FACILITIES _____

  ✓**Restrooms** (accessible) are available in the Nature Center.
  ✓**Water** is available in the Nature Center.
  ✓**Public telephones** are not available. The Nature Center phone is available for emergency use only.

62

DIRECTIONS: Springbrook Nature Center is located north of the metro area in Fridley. **Public transportation** is available on MTC Route #27. **From Interstate 694:** Proceed north on University (Highway 47), left on 85th Avenue Northeast. The entrance is on the left. **Park** in the main lot.

INFORMATION: Call the Nature Center at 612/784-3854 for seasonal events. The trails and the Interpretive Building are open from 9 A.M. to 9 P.M. daily. *A trail map is available in the Interpretive Building.* There is no admission fee.

HIGHLIGHTS: • 3 miles of trails (with 1 mile of paved accessible trails with overlooks) • Earth-sheltered Interpretive Center with one-of-a-kind tornado information, lab, classroom, auditorium • Outdoor amphitheater, picnic area • Classes for children and adults.

TIPS FOR WALKERS: • Street clothes are recommended. • Bring binoculars to observe wildlife. • Springbrook Nature Center has a Volkssport Club for walkers and sponsors an annual volksmarch.

RECOMMENDED ROUTE: 3.5 K (2.2 miles)
PAVED/BOARDWALK/WOOD-CHIP SURFACE. LEVEL.
SHADED/UNSHADED.
From the ① **Interpretive Building,** proceed to the paved trail to the right. You will walk over a boardwalk. At the ② **first junction,** keep to the left (the other paved trail leads back to the parking lot). At the next junction, take a ③ **right on the wood-chip Hiking Trail.** You will walk through a marsh on a long, sturdy boardwalk. When you pass over the ④ **bridge** with the iron railings, take a left, and the path will lead to a similar bridge and through some woods. Take the ⑤ **dead-end trail to the observation deck** that leads to a cedar pentagon shelter overlooking a marsh. Proceed back to the main trail, turn left, and you will come to a junction. Take the ⑥ **Hiking Trail** to the right through the forest. There are plenty of benches along the way. At the ⑦ **next junction, turn left.** Note the long, thin tubes that say "Caution—tree growing." Keep to the left over the wooden deck. ⑧ **At the next junction,** keep straight ahead, do not take the deck to the right. You will come to another junction and turn left at the ⑨ **Oak Savanna Trail.** Continue on the trail, then turn left at the ⑩ **Springbrook Trail.** At the next junction, ⑪ **turn right over the bridge.** Continue on the trail, then ⑫ **turn left at the Beaver Pond Trail.** Note the accessible overlook. At the next trail junction, turn left back to the parking lot.

GIVING BACK: Call the Springbrook Nature Center at 612/784-3854 for information about volunteer opportunities and financial donations.

Rice Creek West Regional Trail

Operated by Anoka County Parks

"I usually walk my dog early in the morning. Sometimes I'll listen to the radio, but most of the time I take off my earphones and just listen to the sounds around me. Walking is very relaxing and enjoyable." —Kim Flesner, Ramsey resident.

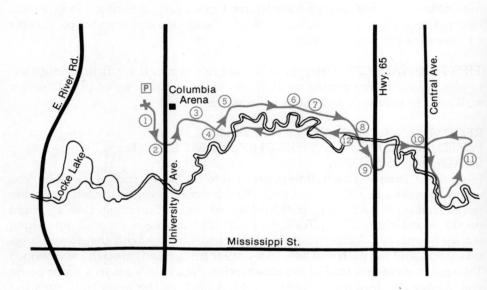

FACILITIES

✓**Restrooms** (accessible) are available along the trail at the end of the loop.
✓**Water** is available along the trail (a drinking fountain and hand pump).
✓**Public telephones** are available at the Columbia Arena during regular hours.

224

63

DIRECTIONS: Rice Creek Trails are located in Fridley about fifteen minutes north of the metro area. **Public transportation** is available on MTC Route #10. **From Interstate 694:** Proceed north on University Avenue (Highway 47), turn left on 69th Avenue. At the dead end, turn right. **Park** in the first lot.

INFORMATION: Call Anoka County Parks at 612/757-3920. The trail is open from 7:30 A.M. to 9:30 P.M. year-round. *A large map of the Anoka County Parks system is available through the County Parks office at 612/757-3920.* There is no admission fee.

HIGHLIGHTS: • Paved trails through densely wooded areas along Rice Creek • Archery range • Horseshoe pits • Picnic areas.

TIPS FOR WALKERS: • Trail clothes are recommended. • Be careful when you cross Highway 65 because there isn't a stop light. • *Trails are available for walking during the winter.*

RECOMMENDED ROUTE: 8 K (5 miles)
PAVED/LIMESTONE SURFACE. LEVEL/FEW STEEP HILLS. SHADED.
From the parking lot, proceed south on the trail along University Avenue past a ① **small pond.** Cross ② **University Avenue** and continue along the trail. Do not veer to the right on the bike trail. Follow the trail past the ③ **Columbia Arena.** Notice the ④ **soccer field** on your right and the archery range just past that. Soon you will pass a ⑤ **horseshoe pit** on your left. You may want to sample the water from the hand pump. Continue straight ahead and you will pass a trail junction, then a lovely ⑥ **park shelter** with a fireplace, water, and restrooms (to your left). The trail winds down to the right, closer to the creek. Notice the ⑦ **NSP transformers** that tower above and along the trail. The next point of interest is a ⑧ **wooden walking bridge** that takes you over the creek. When you come out of the woods, ⑨ **cross Highway 65** and proceed left on the trail past the Sunliner Motel. After you cross the next bridge over the creek, you will go up a steep hill. Cross ⑩ **Central Avenue** and proceed right to the gravel trail and walk down along the creek. Follow the trail to the ⑪ **restrooms** and follow the road out to 69th Avenue. Cross the street and turn left onto the trail and follow it back to Central Avenue. Follow the trail back into the woods. At the next ⑫ **trail junction,** cross the wooden bridge and turn an immediate left onto the limestone path that follows the creek. Stay on the limestone until it ends at the original paved trail. Take a left and follow the paved trail back to the parking lot.

GIVING BACK: Direct financial donations to Anoka County Parks, 550 Bunker Lake Boulevard Northwest, Andover, MN 55304. Please direct your donation to a specific park or project.

Islands of Peace

Operated by Anoka County Parks

"People from nursing homes and group centers say finding Islands of Peace Recreation Center is like finding a pot of gold at the end of the rainbow."

—Evelyn Oxley, Anoka County Parks Receptionist.

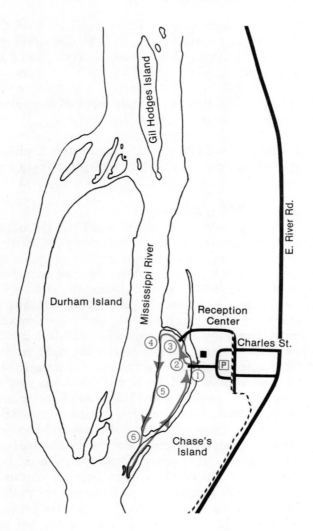

FACILITIES

✓ **Restrooms** (accessible) are located at the Reception Center and a portable unit is available during the summer on the trail.
✓ **Water** is available at the Reception Center.
✓ **Public telephones** are not available. A phone at the Reception Center is available for emergency use during park hours.

64

DIRECTIONS: Islands of Peace park is located north of the metro area in Fridley. **Public transportation** is available on MTC Route #27. **From Interstate 694:** Proceed north about .75 mile on East River Road and turn left (west) on Charles Street. Follow the signs to the park. **Park** in the lot by the Reception Center.

INFORMATION: Call the Reception Center at 612/571-6855. The park is open from sunrise to 10 P.M. The Reception Center is staffed from 8 A.M. to 10 P.M. year-round. • *A large map of the Anoka County Parks system is available at the Reception Center or through the County Parks office at 612/757-3920.* There is no admission fee.

HIGHLIGHTS: • Barrier-free park along the Mississippi • The Reception Center (with a kitchen and cozy fireplace) is open year-round and is available to groups • Accessible picnic and fishing areas • Vehicles equipped for transporting people in wheelchairs can drive directly onto the island to the trailhead.

TIPS FOR WALKERS: • Street clothes are recommended. • This is an ideal place to walk with children who are ready to walk a mile or longer. • You may want to bring a fishing rod and try your luck.

RECOMMENDED ROUTE: 2 K (1.25 miles)
PAVED. LEVEL. SHADED.
From the parking lot, proceed left to the large wooden sign where the trail begins. Follow the ramp down to the island. Once you are on the island, you will cross a ① **foot bridge** over a small lagoon. Turn right after crossing the bridge. On your left you will see a ② **picnic shelter** and then the ③ **driveway** for vehicles equipped for transporting people with handicaps. An ④ **access for fishing** is located along the Mississippi River. You will come to another ⑤ **picnic area** and then you will ⑥ **turn left** and walk along the edge of the lagoon back across the bridge to the start point.

GIVING BACK: Financial donations may be directed to the Foundation for Islands of Peace, Inc., 200 Charles Street Northeast, Fridley, MN 55432.

*Anoka County Riverfront Park*_____

Operated by Anoka County Parks

"I have to push myself to get out for a walk. My husband Jack and I walk hard and fast, so we usually come home drenched in sweat, and I don't like that part of exercising. But after I walk, I feel like I've accomplished something and I feel better. I've tried other forms of exercise and I've found that walking is the only form of recreation that doesn't hurt me."

—Kathy Sparks, Anoka resident.

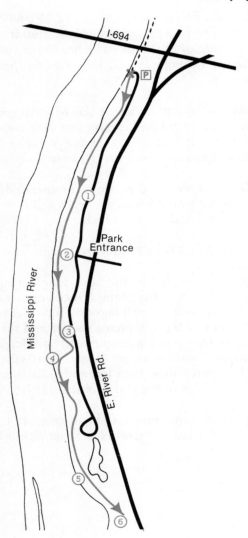

FACILITIES ———————————————————————

✓**Restrooms** (accessible) are located at both picnic shelters.
✓**Water** is available at both picnic shelters.
✓**Public telephones** telephones are not available.

65

DIRECTIONS: Anoka County Riverfront Park is located north of the metro area in Fridley. **Public transportation** is available on MTC Route #27. **From Interstate 694:** Proceed south on East River Road for about .5 mile. The park entrance is on the right. At the white house, turn right and follow the entrance road to the end. **Park** in the lot near the bridge.

INFORMATION: Call Anoka County Parks at 612/757-3920. The trail is open from 7:30 A.M. to 9:30 P.M. year-round. *A large map of the Anoka County Parks system is available through the County Parks office at 612/757-3920.* There is no admission fee.

HIGHLIGHTS: • Picnic shelters and areas with grills, water, and restrooms • Trail under the bridge near the parking lot connects to Islands of Peace park • Playground.

TIPS FOR WALKERS: • Street clothes are recommended. • This is a linear trail that is ideal for fitness walking because there aren't any junctions or other trail users.

RECOMMENDED ROUTE: 5.6 K (3.5 miles)
PAVED. LEVEL/SLIGHT HILLS. MOSTLY UNSHADED.
From the parking lot, proceed to the paved trail marked for walkers. You will come to a ① **picnic shelter,** restroom, and parking lot on your left. Continue walking past the ② **park entrance** and a large white house (this house can be used for meetings, social events, and family gatherings). Just ahead to the left is another ③ **picnic area.** After you reach the site for a ④ **proposed scenic overlook** continue past the site of the ⑤ **proposed arboretum** to the end of the trail by the ⑥ **Minneapolis Waterworks.** (The trail ends abruptly at a fence.) Turn around and follow the trail back to the beginning.

GIVING BACK: Direct financial donations to Anoka County Parks, 550 Bunker Lake Boulevard Northwest, Andover, MN 55304. Please designate what park or project you'd like the money used for.

Kordiak Park

Operated by Anoka County Parks

"Kordiak Park is located in an older, residential area. The lake is being aerated and cleared of sediment and restocked with fish; we're reclaiming the lake."

—Ron Cox, Anoka County Park Planner.

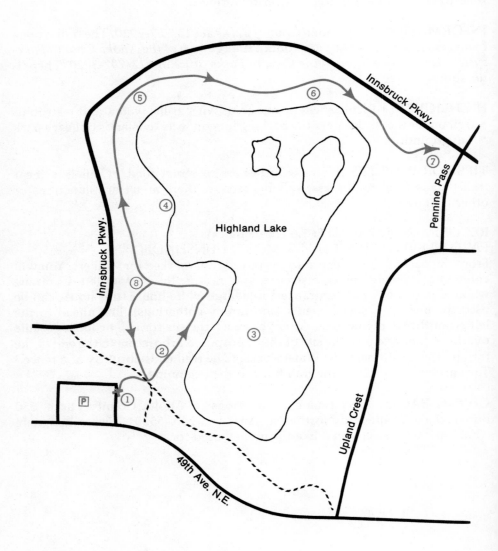

Highland Lake

FACILITIES

✓ **Restrooms** are along the south shore of the lake.
✓ **Water** is available at the drinking fountain in the park.
✓ **Public telephones** are not available.

66

DIRECTIONS: Kordiak Park is located north of the metro area in Columbia Heights. **Public transportation** is available on MTC Route #18D. **From Interstate 694:** Proceed south on Central Avenue (State Highway 65). Turn left (east) on 49th Avenue and the entrance to the park is on the left, about three blocks. **Park** in the lot.

INFORMATION: Call Anoka County Parks at 612/757-3920. The trail is open from 7:30 A.M. to 9:30 P.M. year-round. *A large map of the Anoka County Parks system is available through the County Parks office at 612/757-3920.* There is no admission fee.

HIGHLIGHTS: • Peaceful, well-kept park in a residential neighborhood • Geese and ducks roam about the park • Waterfall • Picnic shelter and tables • Highland Lake • Playground.

TIPS FOR WALKERS: • This is a short, flat trail that is ideal for fitness walking or racewalking training. • This is also an ideal trail to walk with young children. • Street clothes are recommended.

RECOMMENDED ROUTE: 2.4 K (1.5 miles)
PAVED. FLAT. MOSTLY SHADED.
From the parking lot, proceed to the trail to the right. At the ① **first trail junction,** take a right and then a quick left. Notice the ② **children's playground** and picnic shelter and waterfall. You will see ③ **Highland Lake** to the right. The path becomes wooded and shaded for a short distance and then you will pass a ④ **pump house** that is being used to aerate the lake. The lake is also being cleared of sediment and stocked with fish so that it can eventually be used for recreational fishing. After coming out of the wooded section you will walk along a ⑤ **residential street.** After crossing the ⑥ **wooden bridge** you will proceed along the trail until you come to ⑦ **tennis courts.** Turn around. At the ⑧ **trail junction,** follow the path to the right back to the parking lot.

GIVING BACK: Direct financial donations to Anoka County Parks, 550 Bunker Lake Boulevard Northwest, Andover, MN 55304. Please direct your donation to a specific park or project.

Long Lake Regional Park

Operated by Ramsey County Parks and Recreation

"At Long Lake Regional Park, the New Brighton Area Historical Society is restoring a Soo Line railroad depot built in 1887. Bulver Junction, as it was called, was established so that the trains could be stopped to accommodate traffic to and from what was then the Minneapolis stockyards. The depot provided complete living quarters for the family of the depot manager, and we're restoring the depot exactly as it was over one hundred years ago. We're also adding interpretive information so that people can take self-guided tours of the old stockyards site and learn about history as they walk."

—Gayle Bromander, New Brighton Area Historical Society.

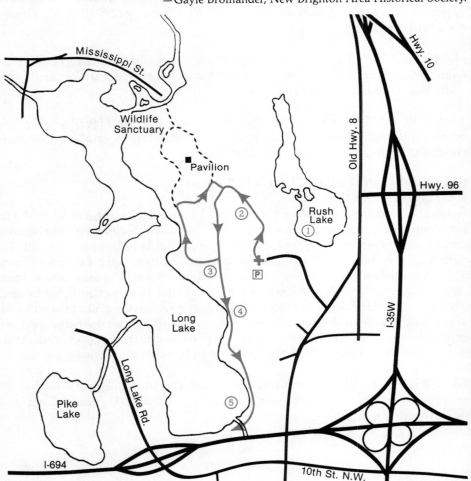

FACILITIES

✓ **Restrooms** (accessible) are available in the seasonal beach house and the Depot Museum.

✓ **Water** is available at the seasonal beach house and the Depot Museum.

✓ **Public telephones** are available at the seasonal beach house and the Depot Museum.

67

DIRECTIONS: Long Lake Regional Park is located north of Saint Paul in New Brighton. **Public transportation** is not available. **From Interstate 694:** Proceed north on Interstate 35W, west on State Highway 96, and south on Old Highway 8. The entrance is on the right side of the road. **Park** in the first parking lot to your left.

INFORMATION: Call Ramsey County Parks and Recreation at 612/777-1707. The park is open daily from one-half hour before sunrise to one-half hour after sunset. There is no admittance fee.

HIGHLIGHTS: • 3 miles of paved walking paths • Large picnic pavilion can accommodate over three hundred people for a walking event • Beach area and beach house with shower facilities (open June through August) • Playground • Fishing • Boat launch.

TIPS FOR WALKERS: • Street clothes are recommended. • Paved paths are shared with bikers, so keep to the right. • Paths are not available to walkers in the winter.

RECOMMENDED ROUTE: 4.8 K (3 miles)
PAVED SURFACE. LEVEL. SHADED/UNSHADED.
From the parking lot, take the paved trail into the woods (not the one that crosses the road). As you walk through the woods, you can see ① **Rush Lake** to your right. Follow the path to the historic ② **Soo Line Depot** exhibit. When you cross the railroad track, take a left at the trail junction. The paved trail runs parallel with the railroad tracks. Eventually you will cross a road. The trail picks up again just beyond the parking area. Proceed left on the trail to the ③ **beach house** and fenced area with a playground. This segment of the walk is linear—it doesn't go around the entire lake. On the left you'll see mounds of ④ **gravel** (accessible walkways just waiting to be built!). You may also see some of the parked railroad boxcars that carry inscriptions from "King Ed, Tramp," who records each trip with a date of passage. On the right you'll see ⑤ **Long Lake.** As you near the end of the path near the large concrete highway barrier, look for the bird house in the tree. Follow the path back to the beach house and then take the trail to the left. You'll walk through lovely pines. At the junction near the big hill, keep to your left. Cross the road and continue back to your start point, passing the Soo Line depot.

GIVING BACK: For information about volunteer and financial donation opportunities, call Ramsey County Parks and Recreation at 612/777-1707, or write to the New Brighton Area Historical Society at 2872 18th Street Southwest, New Brighton, MN 55112.

Village of Arden Hills Trails/
Perry Park

Operated by the Village of Arden Hills

"The paths are beautiful and they go right by our house, so we take walks and look for raccoons, pheasants, and turtles."
— Kathy Menge, Arden Hills resident.

"I can walk 'til my mom gets tired and my legs don't even hurt."
— Tara Menge, Arden Hills resident.

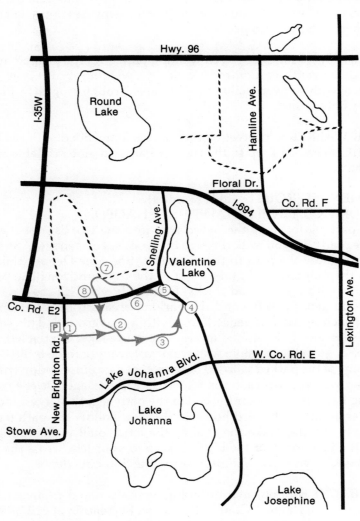

FACILITIES

✓ **Restrooms** are not available.
✓ **Water** is not available.
✓ **Public telephones** are not available.

68

DIRECTIONS: Arden Hills is located north of the metro area. **Public transportation** is not available. **From Interstate 35W:** Proceed east on County Road D, north (left) on Cleveland Avenue, east (right) on County Road E, north (left) on New Brighton Road. The entrance to Perry Park is on the right. Proceed down the entrance road. **Park** in the lot at the end of the road, near the woods.

INFORMATION: Call the City of Arden Hills at 612/633-5676. The parks and trails are open from one-half hour after sunrise to one-half hour after sunset. *A trail map is available through the city.* Trail start points are marked with wooden posts with a hiker symbol. There is no admission fee. Security is provided by the City of Arden Hills.

HIGHLIGHTS: • Rustic trail experience within an urban setting • Swinging benches • Picnic area • Playground • Wildlife • Footbridges.

TIPS FOR WALKERS: • Carry water. • Trail clothes are recommended. • You may want to bring binoculars.

RECOMMENDED ROUTE: 5.6 K (3.5 miles)
DIRT/GRASS SURFACE. HILLY. MOSTLY SHADED.
From the parking lot, proceed to the ① **wooden steps** and take the trail to the left. The trail winds down a hill, through woods. At the next junction, take the trail to the right that leads to a wooden footbridge over a marsh. Watch your footing. At the gravel road, turn left. At the trail post, take the ② **path to the right.** Proceed up the hill. Watch your footing on the short stretch of land that is at an uncomfortable angle. You will pass a viewing bench, walk across a small open field, and then the trail continues to the left up a hill (a bench is at the top). Houses will be to your left, and the woods will be on your right. At the next junction, turn right. Again, houses will be to your left as the trail winds in and out of the woods. You'll be able to see railroad tracks through the trees to your right. Continue through this residential area, keeping close to the woods. The trail winds up a hill. You will pass a ③ **pond** with another viewing bench. The trail juts to the right under a power line, then curves a short distance through a residential area. Eventually, the trail will exit on the ④ **street.** Turn left, and the trail resumes just a few feet beyond McCrachen Lane. Follow the trail past a ⑤ **pond and a wooden footbridge.** Keep to the right at all trail junctions. The trail leads to ⑥ **Valentine Hills School.** Cross the street, resume the trail. At the first junction, take the ⑦ **trail to the left.** Continue straight ahead, eventually turning left across a wooden footbridge. Cross the ⑧ **street** to the gravel road. Proceed back to the start point.

GIVING BACK: For information about volunteer or donation opportunities, call the Village of Arden Hills at 612/633-5676.

City of Roseville Trails/
Central Park

Operated by the City of Roseville

"We enjoy walking at Central Park because it has everything—water, all kinds of wildlife. What more could you want? The city founders should be complimented for thinking ahead and providing something this beautiful for the City of Roseville."

—Nina and Al Ahlf, Roseville residents.

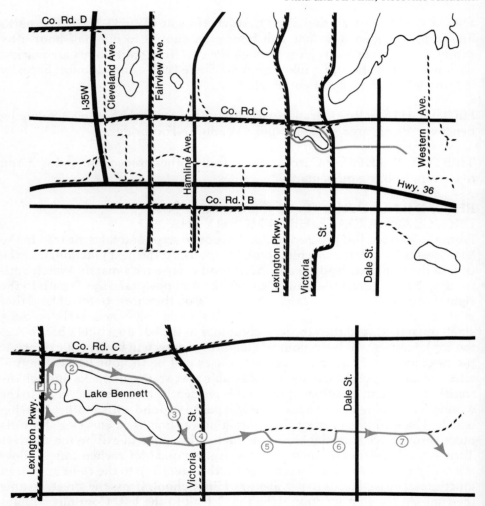

FACILITIES

✓ **Restrooms** (portable units) are available along the trail. Accessible restrooms are available in the Interpretive Center during regular hours and in the picnic shelters from May through October.

✓ **Water** is available at fountains in each of the park segments.

✓ **Public telephones** are available at the Interpretive Center.

69

DIRECTIONS: Central Park is located north of the Saint Paul downtown area. **Public transportation** is available on MTC Route #17 and Roseville Circulator #103. **From State Highway 36:** Proceed north on Lexington Parkway. Just beyond County Road B-2 you will come to the park entrance on the right. **Park** in the main lot.

INFORMATION: Call the City of Roseville at 612/490-2280. Trails and parks are open daily from 5 A.M. to 10 P.M. Call for open hours of the new Harriet Alexander Interpretive Center. *A free booklet (with walking trails) titled* Discover the Pleasures of Roseville's Parks *is available through the Parks and Recreation Department.* There is no admission fee.

HIGHLIGHTS: • 1.1 miles of boardwalk and trails • Fishing pier, band shell, playground, swinging benches, softball field, picnic shelter, football field, horseshoe courts • Wetland with abundant wildlife • Interpretive Center.

TIPS FOR WALKERS: • Trail clothes are recommended. • Trails are shared with bikers.

RECOMMENDED ROUTE: 7.2 K (4.5 miles)
PAVED. LEVEL. SHADED/UNSHADED.
This trail covers three interconnecting segments of Central Park. From the parking lot, proceed to ① **Lake Bennett** and take the trail to the left (past the pier and volleyball field). Note the ② **swinging bench.** Continue around the lake. ③ **Just before the playground,** take a left on the paved trail. Walk past the tennis courts on your right to ④ **the pedestrian crossing** on Victoria Street. The paved trail resumes on the other side of the street. Walk around the baseball fields (the trail curves to the right) until you approach the parking lot on the south side of the fields. ⑤ **Turn left onto the paved path** and you will walk through a wooded area. A football field will be on your left, some homes on the right. The walking trail curves to the left as you approach the ⑥ **pedestrian crossing at Dale Street.** The trail continues on the other side. Walk through the parking lot, past the tennis courts, and proceed up the paved trail to the ⑦ **Harriet Alexander Interpretive Center.** From the Center, take the steps down to the road, turn left and then right onto the dirt trail. Proceed on the board walks, making a right turn at every junction, and you will exit at the dirt road. Turn right and retrace your steps back to Lake Bennett. When you get to the children's playground, turn left and walk along the south shore of the lake, past the bandshell to the parking lot.

GIVING BACK: For information about volunteer opportunities and financial donations, contact the City of Roseville Parks and Recreation Department, 1114 Woodhill Drive, Roseville, MN 55113, or call 612/490-2280.

Bald Eagle–Otter Lakes Regional Park/
Tamarack Nature Center

Operated by Ramsey County Parks and Recreation

"This park is one of the largest nature preserves in Ramsey County, and it is located in a growing urban area. When the land was acquired by the Ramsey County Board of Commissioners in the early 70s, the area was undeveloped. Today, there is a school across the street from the Tamarack Nature Center and all residents of the east metro area are within easy access to a truly natural experience."
— Kevin Finley, Director of Operations.

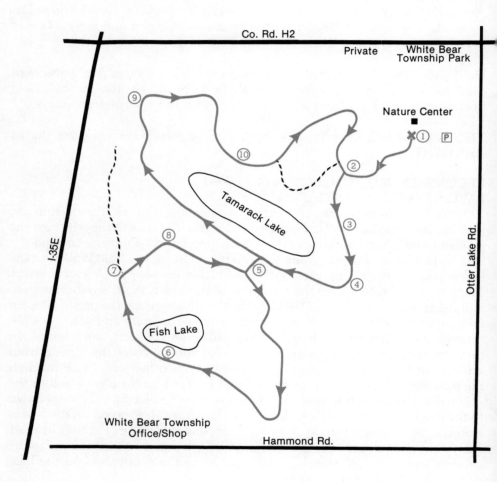

FACILITIES

✓**Restrooms** (accessible) are available at the Nature Center during regular hours.
✓**Water** is available at the Nature Center during regular hours.
✓**Public telephones** are not available. The Nature Center phone is available for emergency use only.

70

DIRECTIONS: Tamarack Nature Center is north of Saint Paul in the town of White Bear. **Public transportation** information is available through White Bear Lake Area Transit at 612/464-8876. **From Interstate 35E:** Proceed east on State Highway 96, north on Otter Lake Road to the entrance on the left. **Park** near the Nature Center.

INFORMATION: Call the Nature Center at 612/429-7787. Tamarack Nature Center is open Monday through Saturday from 8:30 A.M. to 5 P.M., Sundays noon to 5 P.M. Call for holiday hours. *A trail map is available at the Nature Center.* There is no admittance fee.

HIGHLIGHTS: • 3 miles of wood-chip and boardwalk paths • Weekend programs include bird banding, snowshoeing, and maple syrup making • There are plenty of trail benches.

TIPS FOR WALKERS: • Trail clothes are recommended. • Watch your step on the boardwalks. • *The trail around Tamarack Lake is open in the winter.* • You may want to bring binoculars. • Phenology information (the relationship between climate and wildlife) is available on the large bulletin board just inside the nature center.

RECOMMENDED ROUTE: 4.8 K (3 miles)
WOOD-CHIP/BOARDWALK SURFACE. SOME HILLS.
SHADED/UNSHADED.
After browsing through the Nature Center, proceed past the ① **wooden information kiosk** just outside the entrance. Follow the trail to the far left (as you face the information kiosk). When you get to the open field, turn right and follow the grassy path to the ② **first trail junction.** Follow the path to the left that goes across an open field into the woods. At the ③ **next trail junction,** proceed straight ahead to the boardwalk that overlooks Tamarack Lake. Return to the junction and take the trail to the right that winds around the shoreline. Follow the ④ **boardwalk** to a wood-chip path down to the trail. At the next trail junction with a map post, follow the ⑤ **path around Fish Lake.** Birds are plentiful along this loop. You may want to stop at the ⑥ **observation bench** and enjoy the view. Continue on the path until you come to a ⑦ **trail to the right (marked for skiers)** that leads up a dirt hill to another ⑧ **observation bench** that offers a nice view of the lake. At the information post, take the trail to the left. Take another left to a shoreline dirt trail that leads to another ⑨ **boardwalk.** Follow the wood-chip trail to the right, not the path that leads to a residential area. Just beyond another ⑩ **boardwalk and bench,** follow the path to the right. At the next junction, follow the path to the left back to the Nature Center.

GIVING BACK: Volunteer opportunities require no past experience, only a love of nature and a few hours of time. For information about volunteer and financial donation opportunities, call the Nature Center at 612/429-7787.

City of White Bear Lake Trails

Operated by the City of White Bear Lake

"I live a couple of blocks from the lake and my husband and I use the trail to walk or run or bike as individuals or with our three children. It's a beautiful area with the lake and parks and all the sights and sounds of nature. It's about ten miles if you go around the entire lake. It makes it easy to get out for your exercise with an established trail here. I see many people enjoying this trail daily! I would encourage residents as well as visitors to try this delightful trail."

—Wendy Fitzsimmons, White Bear Lake resident.

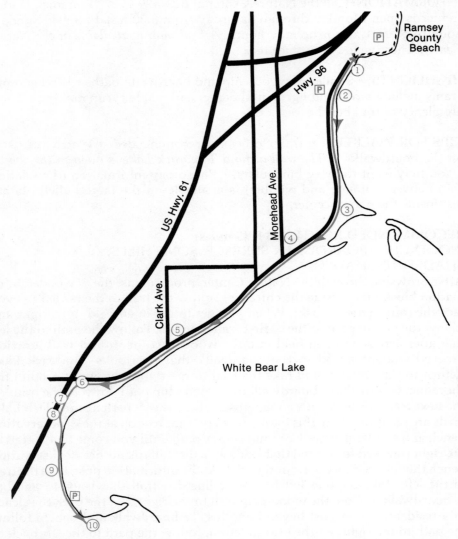

FACILITIES

✓ **Restrooms** (accessible) are available at the Ramsey County beach house.
✓ **Water** is available at the Ramsey County beach house.
✓ **Public telephones** are available at the West Park park building (outside).

71

DIRECTIONS: White Bear Lake is north of downtown Saint Paul. **Public transportation** is available on MTC Route #15 or White Bear Lake Area Transit at 612/464-8876. **From Interstate 35E:** Proceed east on State Highway 96, north on U.S. Highway 61, and then turn right to continue on State Highway 96. Just as the road curves to the left you'll find the entrance to the Ramsey County Beach. **Park** near the beach.

INFORMATION: Call the City of White Bear Lake at 612/429-8526. The parks and trails are open from dawn until dusk throughout the year. *Trail maps are not available.* There is no admission fee.

HIGHLIGHTS: • 3.5-mile roadside trail along White Bear Lake • Ramsey County Beach, West Park, Matoska Park, Lion's Park • Historic Fillebrown House (tours are every Sunday 1 P.M. to 4 P.M., admission $2 per adult).

TIPS FOR WALKERS: • Street clothes are recommended. • The trail is part of the road and is defined by a white line. Car traffic is one-way (south). • The trail is shared with bikers and skaters. • A nature preserve with walking trails at Rotary Park at Birch Lake will open in 1991. Facilities, including an Interpretive Center and shelters, will be constructed in 1992. Call for more details.

RECOMMENDED ROUTE: 9.6 K (6 Miles)
PAVED SURFACE. LEVEL. MOSTLY SHADED.
From the parking lot, proceed to the paved trail to the right. Pass through the ① **gates** and you will walk through a residential development (tennis courts to your left, living units to the right). Continue on the path to ② **West Park** where there will be picnic areas to your right and a playground and park building to your left. Proceed south, noting the lakeshore homes to your right and the lake and private lakeshore docks and beach houses to the left. At ③ **Matoska Park,** you'll find plenty of picnic areas, a playground, and a large monument explaining the history of White Bear Lake with a quote from Mark Twain. Continue on the roadside trail, keeping to the left. On the corner of Morehead Avenue you'll see the ④ **Fillebrown House,** one of the few remaining examples of American Picturesque architecture. As you continue walking along the trail, note the variety of vegetable gardens, flower gardens, landscaped yards, and architectural details. You will pass ⑤ **Clark Avenue,** a tree-lined boulevard that leads to stores in the down-town area. To your left is the White Bear Lake Park Bench overlook. Eventually, you will begin walking on ⑥ **sidewalk.** Note the impressions in the cement as you near the corner. Turn left and ⑦ **walk along Highway 61.** At ⑧ **Lake Avenue South,** turn left onto the pathway. Walk past the ⑨ **marina and stores** to ⑩ **Lion's Park,** a great place for a picnic before heading back.

GIVING BACK: For information about volunteer and donation opportunities, call the City of White Bear Lake at 612/429-8526, or write 4701 Highway 61, White Bear Lake, MN 55110.

Pine Point Park

Operated by Washington County Parks

"Pine Point has over 325 acres with walking trails through hardwood forests, pines, and prairie areas. From the trails you can see some great views of the lakes and lots of wildlife including deer raccoons, wild geese, owls, and hawks. People use the trails for hiking, skiing, and horseback riding. The State Trail passes through the park, and the Gateway Segment of the Willard Munger Trail now makes it possible to walk from Downtown Saint Paul 17 miles north to Pine Point."

—Lee Gohlike, Outing Lodge at Pine Point.

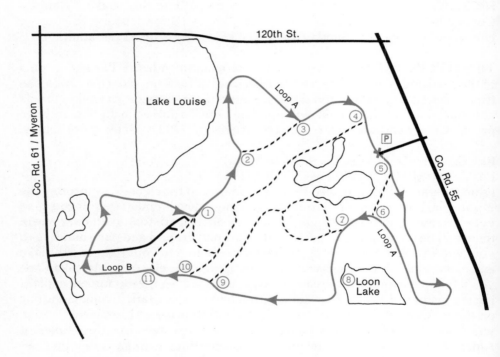

72

DIRECTIONS: Pine Point Park is located northeast of Saint Paul. **Public transportation** is not available. **From State Highway 36:** Proceed north on County Road 15 (Manning Avenue), turn east (right) onto Trunk Highway 96, then turn north (left) on County Road 55 to the park entrance. **Park** in the lot.

INFORMATION: Call Washington County Parks at 612/731-3851. The park is open from 7 A.M. to one-half hour after sunset. *A trail map is available through Washington County.* An annual motor permit costs $12 and a daily pass $2. Hennepin Parks vehicle permits are honored.

HIGHLIGHTS: • 5 miles of grass/dirt walking trails • Majestic pine trees • Open fields • Minnesota-Wisconsin State Boundary Trail.

TIPS FOR WALKERS: • Trail clothes are recommended. • Trail junctions are marked with numbers or letters. • Trails are shared with horseback riders. • Washington County offers a "Take a Hike" program for walkers. • Outing Lodge provides services to groups interested in walking from Saint Paul to Pine Point.

RECOMMENDED ROUTE: 4.8 K (3 miles)
GRASS/DIRT SURFACE. HILLY. MOSTLY SHADED.
Note: The junction numbers are the same as the signs you'll see in the park—the first junction will be 5 and the last junction will be 4. From the parking lot, proceed to the main trail to the left and cross over the Minnesota-Wisconsin Boundary Trail. Follow the path up into the woods. At the next ⑤ trail junction, take the path to the left. Keep to the left. Don't follow any small footpaths or a path that leads through a fence. Proceed along the fence line and you will eventually see Loon Lake on your left. When you come out of the woods, stay on the path to the left. At the next ⑥ trail junction, take the path to the left. This is a hilly stretch. When you come to another ⑦ trail junction, take the far left trail up a hill and you will be able to see another view of ⑧ Loon Lake. At the next ⑨ trail junction, cross the road and go up the trail to the next ⑩ trail junction; take the trail to the left. When you arrive at the next ⑪ trail junction, take the left trail marked "B." You will eventually cross the entrance road and the "B" trail resumes on the other side. At the next junction, ① follow the wide path to the far left. At the next ② trail junction, follow the path to the left into the woods toward Lake Louise. When the path splits, don't turn left. Follow the path that crosses the corn field and leads into the woods. At the next ③ trail junction, follow the path to the left and walk along the tree line. Enter the woods, and eventually a field will be on your left. At the next ④ trail junction, keep going straight along the field (don't take the path into the woods). Return to your start point.

GIVING BACK: If you are interested in becoming a park volunteer, call the Washington County Park Office at 612/731-3851.

William O'Brien State Park

Operated by the Minnesota Department of Natural Resources

"We are a people park. We have 125 campsites and two large picnic grounds. Our trails are for walkers and cross-country skiers."
—George Terzich, Park Manager

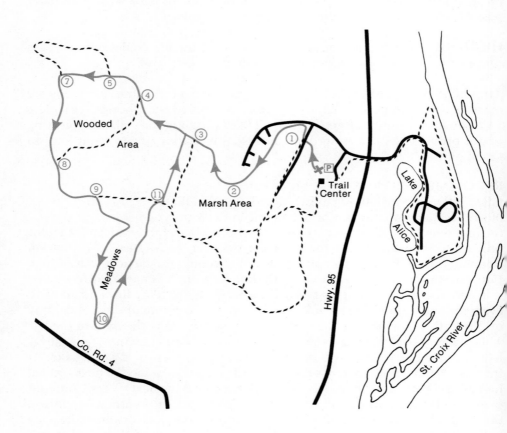

FACILITIES

✓ **Restrooms** (accessible) are available at the Trail Center. Portable units are located along the walking trail.

✓ **Water** is available at the park office, Trail Center, and beach area.

✓ **Public telephones** are available at the park office.

73

DIRECTIONS: William O'Brien State Park is located north of Stillwater. **Public transportation** is not available. **From Interstate Highway 35E:** Proceed east on State Highway 36 to Stillwater, and then north (13 miles) on State Highway 95 to the park entrance on the left (west) side of the highway. **Park** in the lot near the Trail Interpretive Center, which is about a quarter mile from the entrance.

INFORMATION: Call the park at 612/433-2421. The park is open daily from 8 A.M. to 10 P.M. The Trail Center opens at 8 a.m and closes at 4 P.M. during the week and at 6 p.m on the weekends (10 P.M. during the summer). *A trail map is available at the Interpretive Center.* An annual motor vehicle permit or a daily permit is required.

HIGHLIGHTS: • 9.5 miles of hiking trails • 2.5 miles of paved accessible trails • Trail Interpretive Center with information, displays, and presentations • Beach, recreation, and picnic areas • Trail shelters along the trail • Wildflowers, restored prairie, marshes, St. Croix River, Lake Alice, assortment of trees (maple, oak, pine, beautiful coloring in the fall), deer, beaver, fox, and birds.

TIPS FOR WALKERS: • Trail clothes are recommended. • Paved trails are shared with bikers. • Walkers do not share the dirt trails with any other users. • Trail junctions are well marked with numbers. • You may want to bring your camera or binoculars. • *Trails are closed to walkers in the winter.* • If the recommended route is too difficult, you may alter your route at post signs 4 or 9.

RECOMMENDED ROUTE: 8 K (5 miles)
GRASS SURFACE. ROLLING HILLS. MOSTLY SHADED.
From the trail center, go out the back door (near the restrooms) and take the trail to your right. At the first ① **junction, turn right** and you will enter a ② **marsh area** with a boardwalk. At the next two **junctions** ③,④ continue straight ahead. Keep to the **left at the next two junctions** ⑤,⑦ and **keep to the right at the next two junctions** ⑧,⑨. At post 9, after you turn right, you will enter open meadows with steep hills. At **post** ⑩ you are at the **highest point of the park,** overlooking the St. Croix River valley, one of the most picturesque spots in Minnesota, especially during the fall when the leaves are fully colored. At **junction** ⑪ continue straight ahead (north) to the next trail junction. Turn right toward **junction** ③ and return to the trail center.

GIVING BACK: To volunteer, call the park office at 612/433-2421. Direct financial donations to Minnesota Parks and Trails Council, E-1311 First National Bank Building, St. Paul, MN 5510, or call 612/291-0715 or 800/289-1930.

Lake Elmo Park Reserve

Operated by Washington County Parks

"Of the 2,165 acres in Lake Elmo Park Reserve, 80 percent will remain in a natural state so that the park can support a variety of wildlife including pheasants, weasels, red fox, woodpeckers, cardinals, cottontail rabbits, squirrels, and white-tailed deer. The other 20 percent is for recreational use. We offer bike trails, play structures, swimming, fishing, boating, horseback riding, camping, and winter skiing so there's something for everyone."

— Mike Polehna, Washington County Parks Department.

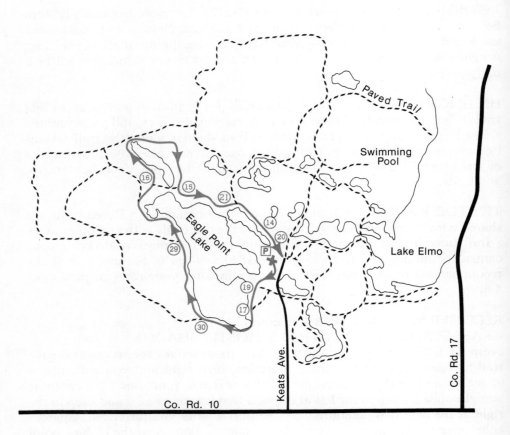

FACILITIES

✓**Restrooms** (accessible) are available during the summer at the swim facility and picnic shelter. Portable units are available at the parking lots, campgrounds, and boat launch.

✓**Water** is available during the summer at the picnic area and swim facility.

✓**Public telephones** are available during the summer at the swim facility and campground. An office phone is available for emergency use only.

74

DIRECTIONS: Lake Elmo Park Reserve is located northeast of Saint Paul. **Public transportation** is not available. **From Interstate 94:** Proceed north on County Road 19 (Keats Road) to the entrance to Lake Elmo Park Reserve. After you pass the office, proceed to the first parking lot on the left. **Park** in the lot near the green shelter.

INFORMATION: Call Washington County Parks at 612/731-3851. The park is open from 7 A.M. to one-half hour after sunset. *A trail map is available through Washington County.* An annual motor vehicle permit costs $12 and a daily pass $2. Hennepin Parks vehicle permits are honored.

HIGHLIGHTS: • 8.1 miles of grass walking trails • 3 miles of paved trails that are shared with bikers • Natural prairie.

TIPS FOR WALKERS: • Trail clothes are recommended. • Trail junctions are marked with numbers or letters. • Trails are shared with horseback riders. • Washington County offers a "Take a Hike" program for walkers. • Paths are almost 10 feet wide, ideal for walking groups.

RECOMMENDED ROUTE: 4.8 K (3 miles)
GRASS/DIRT SURFACE. SOME HILLS. UNSHADED.
Note: The junction numbers are the same as the signs you'll see in the park—the first trail junction will be 19 and the last junction will be 20. From the parking lot, proceed in the direction of the green shelter. Proceed to the trail marked **Ski Shelter Trail Patrol.** Follow the trail marked "A/C" into the woods. At the ⑲ **trail junction,** take the path to the right marked "A." Continue on the path around **Eagle Point Lake** until you come to another ⑰ **trail junction** and keep to the right. At the next ㉚ **trail junction,** keep to the right, following the trail into the woods. You will travel along the lakeshore (keeping to the right at all trail junctions) past an old silo and picnic shelter into an open field. Note the wooden birdhouses. At the next ㉙ **trail junction,** keep to the right (straight ahead), following the "A" trail. At the next ⑯ **junction,** take the middle trail lined with wooden birdhouses. Continue following the wide trail along the lakeshore and prairie. The path leads along a treeline (a field will be on your left). At the next ⑮ **trail junction,** stay to the left, following the treeline around the field. At ㉑ **trail junction,** veer right. At the next ⑭ **trail junction,** take a right. At the final ⑳ **trail junction,** take a left and you will eventually follow the paved bike path (right) back to the parking lot.

GIVING BACK: If you are interested in becoming a park volunteer, call the Washington County Parks Office at 612/731-3851.

Maplewood Nature Center

Operated by the City of Maplewood

"Because it's located in an urban area, the Maplewood Nature Center is a great place to come for an hour-long walk in the quiet, peaceful woods. It's also a great place for families because young children can walk one of the shorter segments of trail and feel like they've walked through an entire forest."
— Ann Hutchinson, Naturalist.

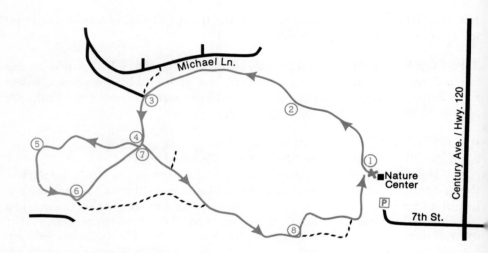

✓**Restrooms** (accessible) are available at the Nature Center during regular hours.
✓**Water** is available at the Nature Center during regular hours.
✓**Public telephones** are not available.

75

DIRECTIONS: The Maplewood Nature Center is east of downtown Saint Paul in Maplewood. **Public transportation** is available on MTC Route #12 that will take you to the corner of Minnehaha and Century Avenue. You'll have to walk a quarter of a mile north to East Seventh Street and turn left. Or, call Northeast Suburban Transit at 612/227-6378. **From Interstate 94:** Proceed north 1.25 miles on Century Avenue and west (left) on East Seventh Street to the entrance. **Park** near the Nature Center Building.

INFORMATION: Call the Nature Center at 612/738-9383 for seasonal events. The Nature Center is open Monday through Saturday from 8:30 A.M. to 4:30 P.M. and Sundays (April—October) 12:30 P.M. to 5:30 P.M. The trails are open every day of the year from one-half hour before sunrise to one-half hour after sunset. *A large wooden trail map is available at the entrance. A trail map brochure is available through the Maplewood Nature Center.* There is no admission fee.

HIGHLIGHTS: • Green Heron Marsh • Maturing oak forest with woodland birds and gray squirrels • Restored prairie • Floating boardwalk • Interpretive building with exhibits • Nature classes • Butterfly Garden • Jim's Prairie—a virgin prairie remnant (available by making arrangements with a naturalist).

TIPS FOR WALKERS: • Trail clothes are recommended. • You may want to bring binoculars or a camera.

RECOMMENDED ROUTE: 2.4 K (1.5 miles)
LIMEROCK/BOARDWALK SURFACE. MOSTLY LEVEL. SHADED.
Proceed through the gate near the Nature Center to the ① **trail to the right.** Follow the trail around the shoreline of the marsh to the first ② **overlook** where you will be able to observe the marsh. At the ③ **trail junction,** keep to the left. At the ④ **next junction, turn right.** The trail narrows as you walk through dense, heavy brush. You'll eventually walk across a ⑤ **footbridge.** Continue along the trail and you'll walk over another ⑥ **footbridge** bordered by a beautiful, mature silver maple. At the next ⑦ **junction,** take a right and follow the path and take the ⑧ **floating boardwalk** back to the nature center.

GIVING BACK: Volunteers are needed to assist with ongoing and seasonal events. For information about volunteer opportunities or financial donations, call the Maplewood Nature Center at 612/738-9383.

Battle Creek Regional Park

Operated by Ramsey County Parks and Recreation

"Ramsey County Parks and Recreation manages four large regional parks and a number of smaller county parks. All of our parks are located in an urban area so people use them at all hours of the day. Battle Creek is a very popular place to walk during all seasons. Over the next ten years, we hope to add more trails throughout the entire park system."

—Larry Holmberg, Supervisor of Planning and Development.

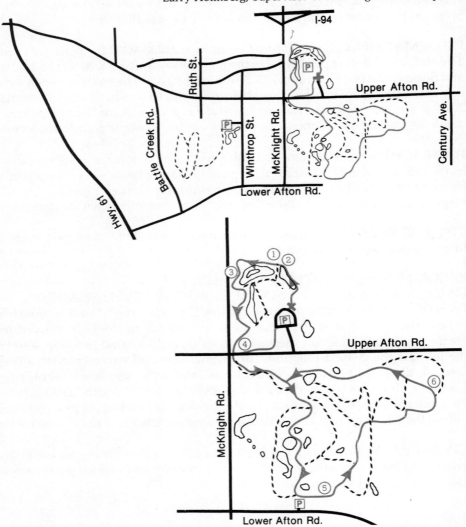

FACILITIES

✓ **Restrooms** are located in the large seasonal pavilion. Portable units are available during the winter outside the pavilion and at the parking lot on Lower Afton Road.

✓ **Water** is available in the seasonal pavilion.

✓ **Public telephones** are located in the seasonal pavilion.

76

DIRECTIONS: Battle Creek Regional Park is located east of Saint Paul. **Public transportation** is available on MTC Routes #49 and 3K. **From Interstate 94:** Proceed south on McKnight Road, east on Upper Afton Road (about one block). **Park** in the lot near the pavilion.

INFORMATION: Call Ramsey County Parks and Recreation at 612/777-1707. The park is open daily from one-half hour before sunrise to one-half hour after sunset. There is no admittance fee.

HIGHLIGHTS: 4 miles of paved trails and 5 miles of grass/wood-chip trails • A large picnic pavilion (open May through October) can accommodate up to five hundred people for a walking event.

TIPS FOR WALKERS: • Street clothes are recommended. • The paths are shared with bikers, so keep to the right. • *The trails near the pavilion are cleared for walkers in the winter.*

RECOMMENDED ROUTE: 4.8 K (3 miles)
PAVED SURFACE. ROLLING HILLS. SHADED/UNSHADED.
From the parking lot, proceed to the northeast side of the pavilion. On this urban part of the walk you'll see the ① **3M Company** buildings on the skyline as you walk over ② **footbridges.** You may want to spend some time looking at the water control system that was built in the 1980s. Because the park was built on a flood plain, a system was developed to prevent flooding and to slow down the excessive water flow from Battle Creek to the Mississippi River. You see only about 5 percent of the water above ground—the rest is channeled under McKnight Road to the Mississippi. You can observe the underground channel through a ③ **covered grate** along McKnight Road. Follow the path to the corner of Upper Afton Road and McKnight Road and ④ **cross the street.** The paved trail continues on the other side of Upper Afton Road. At the first junction, turn right. When you get to the parking lot on Lower Afton Road, look for activity in the ⑤ **wooden birdhouses** nestled in the trees. Continue to follow the trail until you reach a ⑥ **trail junction.** Take the trail to the left past some very wide oaks. Continue following the path until you reach another junction, turn right, and follow the path back to Upper Afton Road. Cross the street, take the paved trail to the right and continue back to the parking lot.

GIVING BACK: For information about volunteer and financial donation opportunities, call Ramsey County Parks and Recreation at 612/777-1707.

City of Woodbury Trails/
Ojibway Park

Operated by the City of Woodbury

"Ojibway Park is a beautiful, natural preserve with unspoiled beauty. We walk these trails often because walking is the best exercise there is— it's relatively easy and not strenuous."

—June and Harvey Henry, Woodbury residents.

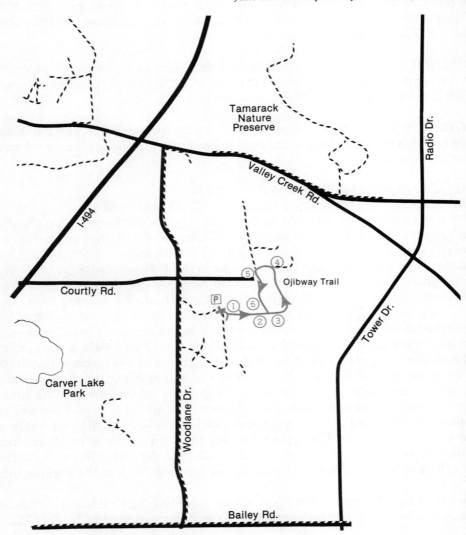

77

DIRECTIONS: Woodbury is located southeast of downtown Saint Paul. **Public transportation** is available on MTC Route #3W. **From Interstate 94:** Proceed south on Interstate 494, east (left) on Valley Creek Road, right on Woodlane Drive, left on Courtly Road, right on Ojibway Drive (Wyndham Way is to the left). **Park** at the main lot.

INFORMATION: Call the City of Woodbury at 612/739-5972. Woodbury parks and trails are open daily from 6 A.M. to 10 P.M. *A very large trail map with city information on the back is available through the Park and Recreation Department.* There is no admission fee.

HIGHLIGHTS: • Woodbury has over 30 miles of off-road and on-road trails throughout the city, connecting parks, retail centers, and schools • Ojibway Park facilities include ballfields, soccer fields, volleyball courts, horseshoe courts, picnic facilities, park building, and amphitheater.

TIPS FOR WALKERS: • Street clothes are recommended. • The nature trails (wood-chip paths to the side of the paved trail) are unmarked. • The recommended route is a rectangular loop.

RECOMMENDED ROUTE: 2.4 K (1.5 miles)
PAVED. LEVEL. SHADED/UNSHADED.
From the parking area, proceed past the wooden sign to the ① **paved trail and turn left.** Follow the trail across an open field. At the ② **first junction,** take the trail to the right. You will enter a shaded oak/aspen woods. Notice the ③ **nature trails** that are to your left and right. The paved trail eventually curves to the left through an open area. You will pass bird houses on the right, soccer fields on the left. ④ **Turn left at the next junction.** When you come to a ⑤ **parking lot area,** turn left and walk along the parking lot. The paved trail continues at the end of the parking lot, beside a house. Continue walking. There will be woods and swamp on the left and ballfields on the right. Part of the ballfields are in a small prairie area. At the next ⑥ **trail junction,** turn right. Proceed back to the start point.

GIVING BACK: For information about volunteer opportunities or financial donations, contact the Woodbury Park and Recreation Department at 8301 Valley Creek Road, Woodbury, MN 55125, or call 612/739-5972.

Afton State Park

Operated by the Minnesota Department of Natural Resources

"It's a great place to go just for the day, to get out of town. People from the cities come here in the evenings and star gaze. It's also a great place to come and try out the new camping equipment and hiking boots." —Calvin G. Kontola, Park Manager.

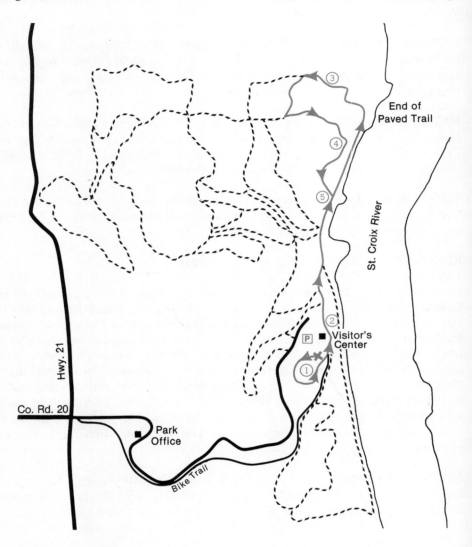

FACILITIES

✓**Restrooms** (accessible) are available in the Visitor's Center. Pit toilets are available in the picnic areas.
✓**Water** is available at the park office, parking lots, picnic areas, and outside the Visitor's Center.
✓**Public telephones** are available outside the Visitor's Center.

78

DIRECTIONS: Afton State Park is southeast of Saint Paul in Washington County. **Public transportation** is not available. **From Interstate 94:** Proceed south on County Road 15 (it becomes State Highway 95) and east on County Road 20. **Park** near the Visitor's Center.

INFORMATION: Call the park at 612/436-5391 for seasonal events. The park is open from 8 A.M. to 10 P.M. daily. The Visitor's Center opens at 8:30 A.M. and closes at 5 P.M. in the winter and 9 P.M. in the summer. *A trail brochure and Plant Checklist is available at the Visitor's Center.* A yearly motor vehicle pass or a daily pass is required.

HIGHLIGHTS: • 18 miles of hiking trails • 4 miles of accessible paved trails • Visitor's Center with displays, information • Walk-in beach and picnic area • Bird migration route for warblers in the spring, hawks and eagles in the fall • Wildflowers, restored prairie, beavers, white-tailed deer, woodcocks, and fox.

TIPS FOR WALKERS: • Trail clothes are recommended. • You may want to bring a compass and walking stick. • Some paths are shared with bikers and horseback riders. • *Trails are closed to walkers in the winter.* • Carry water.

RECOMMENDED ROUTE: 6.7 K (4.2 miles)
PAVED/DIRT SURFACE. STEEP HILLS. SHADED AND UNSHADED.
Caution: There are three steep hills on this route. Take a few minutes to browse through the displays at the Visitor's Center, then follow the trail on the south side of the building to the ① **Self-guided Prairie Walk.** This grassy, plowed "getting acquainted" trail will introduce you to prairie grasses, wildflowers, and farming equipment. Follow the paved path behind the Visitor's Center, past the shelter building. Before taking the steps down to the river, stop and enjoy the ② **scenic overlook** (just to the right of the stairs). Take the stairs, then follow the trail north, turn left before the second bridge, and proceed up the steep path. Once you get to the top of the bluff, take the short trail to the ③ **north scenic overlook** to view the St. Croix River. Return to the main trail. Turn left at the next two trail junctions and follow the trail along the ④ **terraced prairie.** Turn right onto the ⑤ **paved trail** and return to the Visitor's Center.

GIVING BACK: Volunteers are needed to assist with resource management programs. Applications are available through the park office. Direct financial donations to the Minnesota Parks and Trails Council, E-1311 First National Bank Building, St. Paul, MN 55101, or call 612/291-0715 or 800/289-1930.

Cottage Grove Ravine Regional Park

Operated by Washington County

"Cottage Grove is great for hiking because there are lots of hills, and you really get a good workout. I've seen foxes, deer, rabbits, squirrels, all kinds of wildlife along the trail. It's a great place to work up an appetite."
— Dick Roberts, Washington Parks volunteer.

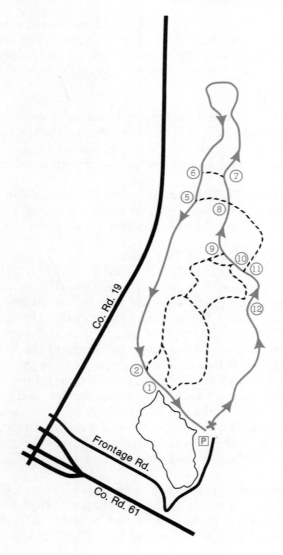

79

DIRECTIONS: Cottage Grove Ravine Regional Park is southeast of downtown Saint Paul. **Public transportation** is not available. **From Interstate 94:** Proceed south on U.S. Highway 61/County Road 10. Exit at Chemolite Road. Proceed east on Chemolite Road, then turn right onto Frontage Road/Pt. Douglas and turn left into the park entrance. Follow the road to the right. **Park** in lot 2.

INFORMATION: Call Washington County Parks at 612/731-3851. The park is open from 7 A.M. to one-half hour after sunset. *A trail map is available through Washington County.* An annual motor permit costs $12 and a daily pass $2. Hennepin Parks vehicle permits are honored.

HIGHLIGHTS: • 150-foot elevation changes • Natural meadows • White oak, burr oak, red oak, aspen, maple, basswood, birch, and cherry trees • Watch for pileated woodpeckers, grouse, and ermine.

TIPS FOR WALKERS: • Trail clothes are recommended. • Trails are for hiking only. • Washington County offers a "Take a Hike" program for walkers.

RECOMMENDED ROUTE: 4.8 K (3 miles)
GRASS/WOOD-CHIP SURFACE. VERY HILLY. SHADED/UNSHADED.
Note: The junction numbers are the same as the signs you'll see in the park — the first trail junction will be marked 12 and the last one will be marked 1. From the parking lot, proceed to the trail head to the right of the picnic shelter (next to the large brown sign) and follow the wide, wood-chip path. Continue walking until you reach the ⑫ **first trail junction** and take a right as you walk through the woods. At the ⑪ **next trail junction,** proceed straight ahead. You will come to another ⑩ **trail junction;** keep on the main path (don't take the path to the left). Continue walking straight ahead at the ⑨ **next junction.** The trail winds through pine trees and prairie. At the next ⑧ **trail junction,** keep straight ahead, and at the next ⑦ **junction,** take the trail to the right. When you get to a fork in the path, follow the trail up a hill into the woods. Follow the path around a loop until you arrive at the next ⑥ **junction** and follow the middle path with the blue arrow. At the next ⑤ **trail junction,** take the path to the right. You will come to another ② **trail junction;** follow the path straight ahead, not to the left. Follow the next ① **trail junction** around the lake shore and you will arrive at a playground across the street from the parking lot where you began.

If you are interested in the scenic overlook at the other end of the park, you may want to drive. From the dead-end lookout point you can see the City of Hastings.

GIVING BACK: If you are interested in becoming a park volunteer, call the Washington County Park Office at 612/731-3851.

Carpenter Nature Center

Operated by the Thomas and Edna Carpenter Foundation

"We're the best-kept secret in the valley. We have 15 miles of trails. Walkers enjoy the mile-long river bluff trail that overlooks the St. Croix Wild and Scenic River, as well as the oak savanna, the restored native tall grass prairie, the riparian bluffs, and the flood plain peninsula along the St. Croix."
—Jim Fitzpatrick, Executive Director.

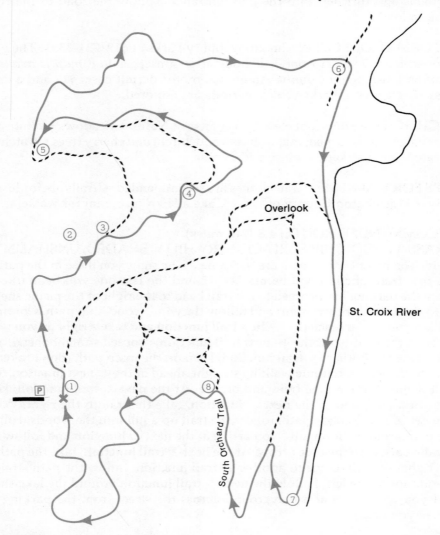

FACILITIES

✓ **Restrooms** (accessible) are available at the Interpretive Center.
✓ **Water** is available at a fountain between the Interpretive Center and maintenance building.
✓ **Public telephones** are not available. An office phone is available for emergency use only.

80

DIRECTIONS: Carpenter Nature Center is located in Hastings. **Public transportation** is not available. **From Interstate 94:** Proceed southeast on State Highway 61/10. Stay on Highway 10 toward Prescott for 3 miles and turn left at County Road 21 for 1 mile. The entrance to the Nature Center is on the right. **Park** in the lot.

INFORMATION: Call the Nature Center at 612/437-4359 for seasonal events. The trails and Nature Center are open from 8 A.M. to 4:30 P.M. seven days a week. The trails and Nature Center are closed on Easter, Thanksgiving, Christmas, and New Years Day. The trails are not open after hours. *A trail map is available at the Nature Center.* There is no admission fee.

HIGHLIGHTS: • 15 miles of walking trails • Bridges • River view • Interpretive Center • Apple orchard • Trails pass through thick woods and open areas.

TIPS FOR WALKERS: • Trail clothes are recommended. • You may want to bring a tape recorder to preserve bird calls or binoculars to observe birds and animals.

RECOMMENDED ROUTE: 4 K (2.5 miles)
PAVED/WOOD-CHIP SURFACE. ROLLING HILLS/ONE STEEP HILL. MOSTLY SHADED.
Just inside the entrance to the park, there are ① **two paved trails.** Take the left one a short distance. At the next trail junction, take the path to the left across a bridge past a ② **farm complex.** Turn right at the ③ **North Orchard Trail.** At the next junction, turn right onto the ④ **North Lookout Trail.** This wood-chip trail winds back around to the blacktopped Orchard Trail. At the trail junction, turn right onto the ⑤ **North River Bluff Descent.** This wood-chip path offers a variety of terrain. You'll cross a couple of bridges, then turn right, away from the red pine forest and descend toward the ⑥ **old railroad bed.** Cross over the sand path and follow the railroad bed along the St. Croix for a good stretch until you come to another ⑦ **wood-chip trail.** Climb the steps to your right. After a steep climb, you'll be on blacktop again, heading back to the nature center. Turn left on the ⑧ **paved trail,** which will take you back to the start point.

GIVING BACK: The Nature Center is entirely privately funded. Memberships are $10 (individual) and $25 (family) per year. The money is used to teach children about nature and wildlife and to rehabilitate wounded animals. Send membership fees and donations to: Carpenter St. Croix Valley Nature Center, 12805 St. Croix Trail, Hastings, MN 55033.

O.L. Kipp State Park

Operated by the Minnesota Department of Natural Resources

"O.L. Kipp State Park is located on a bluff that provides breathtaking panoramic views of the Mississippi River, its basin, and the bluffs that surround it. The colorful wildflowers on the side hill prairie bluffs during the summer and the dramatic changing of the leaves in the fall provide year-round natural wonders."
                                                        —John Wilzbacher, Park Manager.

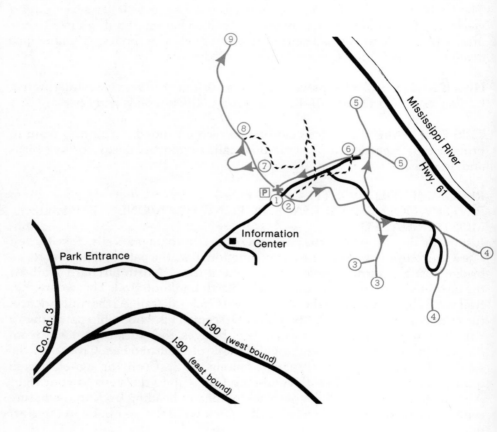

FACILITIES

   ✓ **Restrooms** (pit toilets) are available at campsites and picnic areas.
   ✓ **Water** is available at campsites and picnic areas. Showers and flush toilets are available at the campground.
   ✓ **Public telephones** are not available.

DIRECTIONS: O.L. Kipp State Park is located 20 miles southeast of Winona. **From Interstate 90:** Proceed north on County Road 12 and right on County Road 3/Apple Blossom Drive. After you stop at the Information Office, continue on the entrance road. **Park** in the lot to the left for trail hiking.

INFORMATION: Call the park at 507/643-6849. The park is open daily from 8 A.M. to 10 P.M. *A trail map is available at the park office.* An annual motor permit or a daily pass is required.

HIGHLIGHTS: • 6 miles of hiking trails • Eight scenic overlooks • Camping area • Interpretive trail.

TIPS FOR WALKERS: • Trail clothes are recommended. • Excellent scenic views without having to climb steep hills. • Many of the scenic views are within driving distance.

RECOMMENDED ROUTE: 11.2 K (7 Miles)
GRASS/DIRT SURFACE. LEVEL. MOSTLY UNSHADED.
From the parking lot, proceed to the ① **trail on the north side of the lot,** and turn right. At the ② **next junction,** turn right. At the next two junctions, keep to the right and continue until you reach the ③ **two overlooks** that offer scenic views of bluffs and valleys. Return to the main trail and turn right and you will come to ④ **another set of overlooks** that provide great views of the Mississippi River and valley. Follow the trail back, and then take a right to ⑤ **another set of overlooks** that offers terrific views of the Mississippi River basin, bluffs, and islands. Walk back to the main trail and ⑥ **turn right.** At the parking lot, turn right and you will begin the ⑦ **Interpretive Trail** with plenty of information posts along the way that describe the geological foundation, plant life, and wildlife in the area. Stay left at each junction and you will come to ⑧ **another scenic overlook.** Walk a little farther and you will reach yet another ⑨ **scenic overlook.** Retrace your steps back to the parking lot.

GIVING BACK: For information about volunteer opportunities, call the park office. Direct financial donations to Minnesota Parks and Trails Council, E-1311 First National Bank Building, St. Paul, MN 55101, or call 612/291-0715 or 800/289-1930.

...iver Trail is along a bird migration route so there is plenty to see when you walk ....spring and fall. You can also catch glimpses of deer, wild turkey, and beaver as you walk through hardwood forests and prairies."

—Leslie Udenberg, Trail Technician.

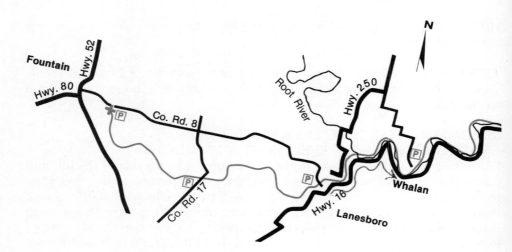

DIRECTIONS: The Root River State Trail is located in southeastern Minnesota, just east of U.S. Highway 52 between Fountain and Rushford. There are six entrances to the trail: 1) **Fountain,** 1.2 miles east on County Road 8; 2) **Isinours Unit,** farther east on County Road 8, south on County Road 17; 3) **Lanesboro,** at the junctions of County Road 8 and State Highway 16; and three entrances along State Highway 16, 4) **Whalan,** 5) **Peterson,** 6) **Rushford.** The recommended route begins in Lanesboro.

INFORMATION: Contact the Root River Trail Center at 507/467-2552 or the Root River Trail Towns, Box 411, Lanesboro, MN 55949, or call the Lanesboro Chamber of Commerce at 507/467-3335 or Rushford Committee on Tourism at 507/864-2444, or call the Minnesota Department of Natural Resoures at 800/652-9747. *Trail maps are available through the Minnesota Department of Natural Resources.* There is no admission fee.

HIGHLIGHTS: • 28.5 miles of paved, accessible trails and 6.5 miles of dirt trails along the Root River • Trail centers at Lanesboro and Rushford • Picnic areas along the trail • Biking • Canoeing • Historic walking tours • Food and lodging along the trail.

FACILITIES

- ✓ **Restrooms** (accessible) are available at the trail centers in Lanesboro and Rushford. Portable units are available at the trail entrance on County Road 8 and at the Isinours Unit just outside the town of Whalan.
- ✓ **Water** is available at the trail centers in Lanesboro and Rushford and in the picnic areas of Peterson and the Isinours Forestry Unit.
- ✓ **Public telephones** are available in Fountain, Lanesboro, Whalan, Peterson, Rushford.

TIPS FOR WALKERS: • Street clothes are recommended. • Trails are shared with bikers. • Mile markers are placed along the way. • This is an excellent trail for long distance aerobic walking or walking from inn to inn. For a list of lodge owners, call the local tourism offices and make arrangements to have your luggage transported as you walk from one point to another. **Round-trip mileages are: Fountain to Highway 17** (8 miles), **Fountain to Lanesboro** (20 miles), **Lanesboro to Whalan** (9 miles), **Peterson to Rushford** (9 miles).

RECOMMENDED ROUTE: 14.4 K (9 miles)
PAVED SURFACE. LEVEL/ROLLING HILLS. SHADED/UNSHADED.
This is only one of many ways to experience the Root River Trail. From the trail center in Lanesboro, proceed east 4.5 miles to the town of Whalan. You may want to stop for a picnic and walk around the town a bit before you head back. This walk offers scenic views of the Root River, limestone bluffs, wildflowers, wildlife, and old railroad bridges.

GIVING BACK: For volunteer opportunities, call the Root River Trail Center, Box 376, Lanesboro, MN 55949, or call 507/467-2552. Direct financial donations to Minnesota Parks and Trails Council, E-1311 First National Bank Building, St. Paul, MN 55101, or call 612/291-0715 or 800/289-1930.

Forestville State Park

Operated by the Minnesota Department of Natural Resources

"Forestville State Park has a wide diversity of attractions, including Mystery Cave (Minnesota's largest cave from soluable rock), the historic 19th-century Meighen General Store, an abundance of wildflowers, trout-filled streams and rolling wooded hills with deer, wild turkeys, and other wildlife."
—Mark White, Park Manager.

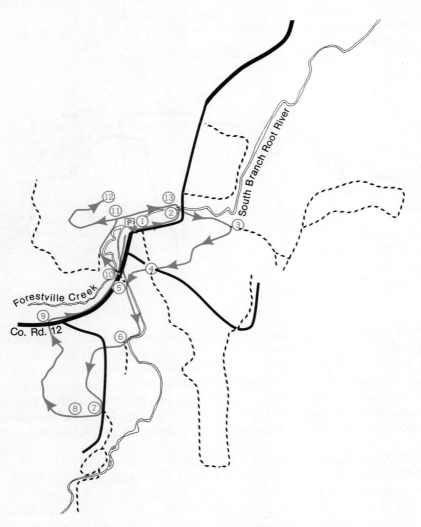

FACILITIES

✓**Restrooms** (accessible) are available at the Information Center and picnic area. Portable units are available at the cave and campgrounds.
✓**Water** is available at the Information Center, picnic area, and campground.
✓**Public telephones** are available at the Information Center.

83

DIRECTIONS: Forestville State Park is in southeastern Minnesota between Spring Valley and Preston. **From State Highway 16:** Proceed south on County Road 5, and then follow the signs to either starting point—the Mystery Cave or the State Park. If you select the State Park, follow the entrace road to the picnic area. **Park** in the main lot.

INFORMATION: Call the park office at 507/352-5111. The park is open daily from 8 A.M. to 10 P.M. *Trail maps are available at the Information Center.* An annual motor vehicle permit or a daily permit is required. Daily cave tours are available from Memorial Day through Labor Day. Call for current tour fees and schedules.

HIGHLIGHTS: • 16 miles of hiking trails • Picnic and camping areas • Interpretive Center. • Big Spring • Naturalist-led cave tours cover approximately .5 mile underground and last approximately one hour • Historic general store.

TIPS FOR WALKERS: • Trail clothes are recommended. • Bring a jacket because the temperature in the cave is 48 degrees. • Trails are muddy in the lower areas after a storm. • There is fast-moving water across streams, so watch your footing. • Many of the trails are shared with horseback riders. • Wear rubber boots or old shoes for muddy areas and low-level streams.

RECOMMENDED ROUTE: 4 K (2.5 miles)
DIRT/WOOD-CHIP SURFACE. HILLS (ONE STEEP GRADE). SHADED.
From the parking lot proceed ① **north to the trail** and then turn right (east). Walk a bit, then ② **take a left,** then a right going across the road and joining the trail that heads west. At the ③ **next junction,** turn right and follow the trail through open prairie. At the ④ **next junction,** keep straight ahead, crossing a road, then a river. At the ⑤ **next junction,** take a left, then ⑥ **turn right** at the next junction. Continue on the trail to the ⑦ **next junction.** (To add 4 more miles to your walk, you may want to veer left and walk to Big Spring, two miles there and two miles back. The trail will take you through wooded areas to a limestone cliff that has a lovely view of a stream from a cave. Then return to the main trail.) On the main trail, keep to the right, and you will ascend a ⑧ **very steep grade** that leads into a hardwood forest. Walk back down the hill and you will eventually cross County Road 12. The trail continues on the ⑨ **other side of the road. At the** ⑩ **next junction,** turn left, cross the river, and walk along the shoreline. At the ⑪ **next junction,** take a left, then a right to the next junction to the ⑫ **Scenic Overlook.** Return back along the scenic trail, keeping to the left, and proceed to the ⑬ **bridge.** Take a right, cross the bridge, and then make another right turn and follow the trail back to the parking lot.

GIVING BACK: For volunteer opportunities, call the park office. Direct financial donations to Minnesota Parks and Trails Council, E-1311 First National Bank Building, St. Paul, MN 55101, or call 612/291-0715 or 800/289-1930.

Whitewater State Park

Operated by the Minnesota Department of Natural Resources

"The absence of mosquitoes, excellent trout fishing, magnificent overlooks on the hiking trails and one of the nicest inland beaches in the area make Whitewater a great place to spend the day."

—Jerry Bachman, Assistant State Park Manager.

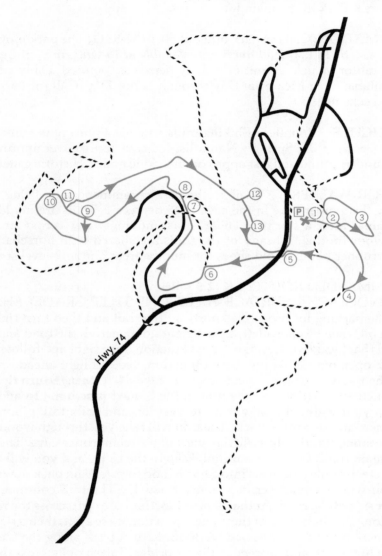

Hwy. 74

FACILITIES

✓ **Restrooms** (accessible) are available at the Information Center and the beach.
✓ **Water** is available at the Information Center, beach, and campgrounds.
✓ **Public telephones** are available at the Information Center.

84

DIRECTIONS: Whitewater State Park is east of Rochester. **From U.S. Highway 52:** Proceed east on Interstate 90 to the St. Charles exit, north on Highway 74 for about 8 miles. The Information Center will be on the left side. After you receive your permit and map, go back out on State Highway 74, turn right, then right again about .5 mile down the road where the beach, picnic area, and Chimney Rock Geological Center are located. **Park** near the Geological Center.

INFORMATION: Call the park office at 507/932-3007. The park is open from 8 A.M. to 10 P.M. May through October and from 8 A.M. to sundown November through March. *Trail maps are available at the Information Center.* An annual motor vehicle pass or a daily permit is required.

HIGHLIGHTS: • 11 miles of hiking trails • Scenic views of bluffs • Wild turkeys • Swimming beach • Picnic and campgrounds • Interpretive Center.

TIPS FOR WALKERS: • Trail clothes are recommended. • Unless you are an experienced hiker, stay off the bluffs and steep slopes.

RECOMMENDED ROUTE: 5.6 K (3.5 miles)
DIRT /ROCK SURFACE. SOME HILLS. MOSTLY SHADED.
At the ① **east end of the parking lot** the trail begins. If you are an experienced hiker, ② **turn left and cross the river** and hike the bluff incline and the descent along the looped Chimney Rock Trail. The ③ **scenic overlook is worth the hike.** If you are not an experienced hiker and would prefer to stay on level ground, keep to your right and avoid the steep loop trail. At the ④ **next junction,** take a sharp right. Follow the trail back to another parking lot. Walk through the lot to the ⑤ **self-guided trail to the left** across Highway 74. Follow the trail until you ⑥ **cross the bridge and turn left.** The trail leads through meadows and along the Whitewater River. At the ⑦ **next junction,** continue straight ahead. At the ⑧ **next junction,** turn left, and turn left again at ⑨ **the next junction.** At the end of the loop, you'll see a bridge and a park road. Do not cross the bridge. Take the ⑩ **trail to the right.** At the ⑪ **next junction,** if you want to stay on level ground, keep to the right, and then turn left at all the next intersections back across Highway 74, and then walk along the road back to the parking lot. If you want to hike the bluffs, turn left onto the Dakota Trail and keep to the right at the next junction. Stop at ⑫ **Ice Cave Point** and ⑬ **Coyote Point.** Follow the trail to Highway 74 and follow the road back to the parking lot.

GIVING BACK: For volunteer opportunities, call the park office. Direct financial donations to Minnesota Parks and Trails Council, E-1311 First National Bank Building, St. Paul, MN 55101, or call 612/291-0715 or 800/289-1930.

Carley State Park

Operated by the Minnesota Department of Natural Resources

"Walkers enjoy this park because the trails run along the stream. From just about every point you can see water, or birds, or wildflowers. I especially enjoy the quiet long grass, and all the wonderful smells."
—Kris Mueller, Building and Grounds.

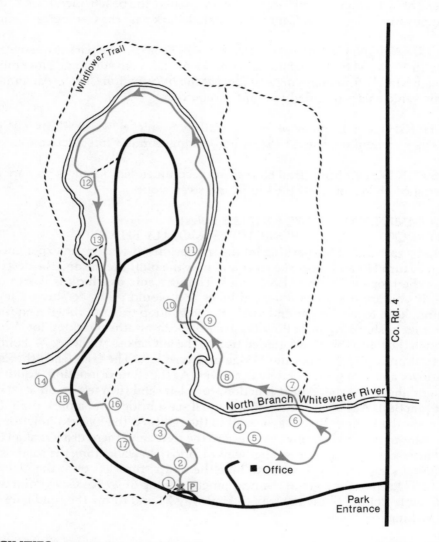

FACILITIES

- ✓ **Restrooms** (vault toilets) are located at the campgrounds.
- ✓ **Water** is available at the campgrounds and a handpump is available near the park office.
- ✓ **Public telephones** are not available. The office phone is available during regular office hours for emergency use only.

85

DIRECTIONS: Carley State Park is located in the southeastern part of Minnesota, northeast of Rochester. **From State Highway 63:** Proceed east on State Highway 247, south on State Highway 42 about .5 mile, then turn left on County Road 4 and follow it to the park entrance. **Park** in the lot near the historic monument.

INFORMATION: Call the park office at 507/534-3400 for seasonal hours and events. Information is also available through Whitewater State Park at 507/932-3007. The park is open from 8 A.M. to 10 P.M. year-round. *A trail map is available in the park office.* An annual motor vehicle permit or daily pass is required.

HIGHLIGHTS: • 5 miles of hiking trails • Wildflower Trail • Bluebell Festival • Hardwood forest • Picnic grounds • Campgrounds • White pine preservation area • Ruffed grouse, ruby-throated hummingbird, red-tailed hawk • Fall colors • Spring wildflowers.

TIPS FOR WALKERS: • You may want to bring binoculars and a walking stick. • Trail clothes are recommended.• Some portions of the trail may be flooded after a significant rainfall. • There is one very steep climb up log stairs at the end of the trail. Watch your footing!

RECOMMENDED ROUTE: 3 K (1.9 miles)
DIRT SURFACE. HILLY/ONE VERY STEEP CLIMB. SHADED.
Proceed from the ① **"Scenic Overlook 1/4 Mile"** sign to the trailhead to the left of the monument. At the first ② **trail junction,** take the path to the right. At the ③ **"Scenic Overlook" sign** take a right and proceed down the stairs to the ④ **overlook.** As you leave the overlook, take the ⑤ **trail to the left (on the same level as the overlook).** You will eventually cross a cement ⑥ **footbridge.** Just a short distance away, take a ⑦ **left at the trail junction.** Note the ⑧ **bench** overlooking the river. Take a ⑨ **left at the next trail junction,** go down some log steps, across the stream, and up some wooden steps, and you'll come to a ⑩ **peaceful picnic area.** Cross the open area, and the ⑪ **Wildflower Trail** begins in the woods (to the left) along the shoreline. At the next ⑫ **trail junction,** keep to the right. You'll come to a ⑬ **bench and then you'll ascend steep wooden stairs** to a narrow footpath on the bluff. Continue on this path (don't take steps up to the campground) until you come to a ⑭ **dirt road.** Proceed left to the open road. The ⑮ **trail resumes** across the road. After you cross a ⑯ **footbridge,** take the trail to the right. At the next junction, ⑰ **keep right** and enjoy the bed of pine needles underfoot as you make your way back to your start point.

GIVING BACK: For volunteer opportunities, call the park office. Direct financial donations to the Minnesota Parks and Trails Council, E-1311 First National Bank Building, St. Paul, MN 55101, or call 612/291-0715 or 800/289-1930.

City of Rochester Trails/
Bear Creek Trail

Operated by the City of Rochester Park and Recreation Department

"There are so many beautiful areas to walk in Rochester! My sister from Seattle was here for a visit and she was very impressed with all the trails we have."

—Carol Keehn, Rochester resident.

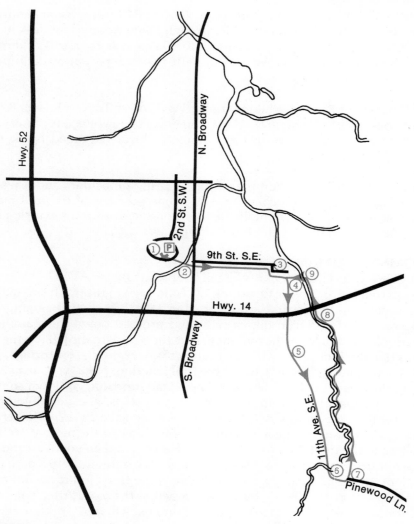

FACILITIES

- ✓ **Restrooms** (accessible) are available at Soldiers Memorial Park, Slatterly Park, and Bear Creek Park.
- ✓ **Water** is available at Soldier's Memorial Park, Slatterly Park, and Bear Creek Park.
- ✓ **Public telephones** are available at Soldier's Memorial Park.

86

DIRECTIONS: Rochester is in southeastern Minnesota. **Public transportation** information is available through Rochester City Lines at 507/288-4353. **From U.S. Highway 52:** Proceed east on U.S. Highway 14. Turn left at the first stop light (Apache Mall will be on your right). Follow the signs to Soldier's Memorial Field. As you enter the park, the road curves to the right. Follow the road past the playground to the golf clubhouse. **Park** in the lot near the clubhouse.

INFORMATION: Call Rochester Parks and Recreation at 507/281-6160. The trails are open from sunrise to sunset year-round. *A Rochester On Foot —Walk, Jog, Run booklet is available through the Rochester Area Chamber of Commerce, 507/288-1122. The booklet features five different walking routes, warm-up exercises, and safety tips.* There is no admission fee.

HIGHLIGHTS: • Soldiers Memorial Field Monument • Public golf course • Slatterly Park • Mayo High School • Bear Creek Park • Bear Creek Trail.

TIPS FOR WALKERS: • Street clothes are recommended. • If you want a short walk, there is a 2.5-mile paved path around the perimeter of Soldiers Memorial Field. • Bear Creek Trail is shared with bikers and there are many curves, so listen for oncoming traffic. • This trail is through a residential area, then secluded woods.

RECOMMENDED ROUTE: 10 K (6.2 miles)
PAVED SURFACE. LEVEL. UNSHADED/SHADED.
From the parking lot, proceed to the ① **paved bike path** between the clubhouse and the maintenance building. The trail follows along a fence line past the golf course. Cross ② **South Broadway** and walk along Ninth Street Southeast. When the ③ **road dead-ends,** turn right for one block, then turn left on 9½ Street and you will be at ④ **Slatterly Park.** Turn right and follow the road along 11th Avenue Southeast. First there is a paved trail, then you walk on the road, then along the sidewalk past ⑤ **Mayo High School.** You'll walk about 2 miles along 11th Avenue Southeast. At 16th Street Southeast cross the street and the sidewalk continues on the other side. You will eventually cross over a river (just beyond 20th Street Southeast). After you cross a small bridge, turn left at the ⑥ **pedestrian crossing.** Cross 11th Avenue Southeast and walk east along Pinewood Lane for about a block where you will see the ⑦ **paved bike trail** across the street. Follow this trail (keeping on the main trail with the dividing lines) all the way to ⑧ **Bear Creek Park.** At the park, take the path to the right and then turn left onto the entrance road. The trail continues beyond the playground at the end of the parking lot. The trail will take you back to Slatterly Park. Cross the ⑨ **bridge** and retrace your steps back to Soldiers Memorial Field.

GIVING BACK: For information about volunteer and donation opportunities, contact the Rochester Parks and Recreation Department at 507/281-6160.

Douglas State Trail

Operated by the Minnesota Department of Natural Resources

"The Douglas Trail is unique for a number of reasons. It is the shortest (12.5 miles) state trail and is linked with a large urban area, so there is a significant amount of local use by the residents of Rochester. It has two parallel treadways, one paved for biking and snowmobiling and the other grassy for horseback riding. Both may be used for hiking. It passes through many diverse landscapes including wooded hills, river valleys, pasture, and cropland."

—Joel Wagar, Supervisor.

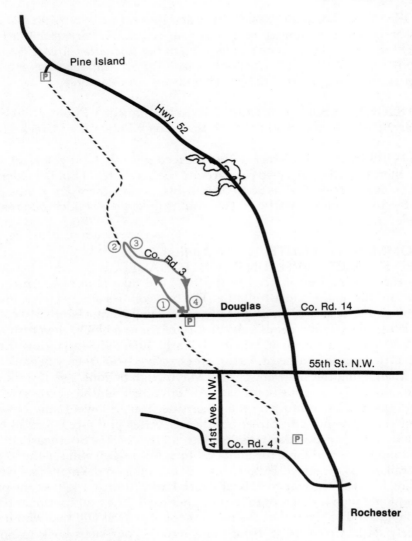

FACILITIES

✓**Restrooms** (pit toilets) are available at all three entrance points.
✓**Water** is available at all three entrance points.
✓**Public telephones** are not available.

87

DIRECTIONS: The Douglas Trail is a "rails to trails" conversion along State Highway 52, just north of Rochester. **Public transportation** information is available through Rochester City Lines at 507/288-4353. There are three entry points: **Pine Island Entrance** (18 miles north of Rochester): From State Highway 52 go west on County Road 11 just a few yards. The park entrance is on the left, near a picnic shelter and small open area. Turn left on Northeast First Avenue, and left into the park. **Douglas Entrance** (10 miles north of Rochester): From State Highway 52 go west on County Road 14 (about 2.4 miles) past County Road 3. Turn left into the Douglas Trail Park area. **Rochester Entrance:** From State Highway 52 proceed west on 55th St. Northwest, south on 41st Avenue, then east on County Road 4 (Valleyhigh Drive Northwest). Watch for the signs to the left. **Park** in the entrance lot.

INFORMATION: Call the DNR Trails and Waterways Unit at 507/285-7176. *A trail map is available through the DNR.* There is no fee for using the trail.

HIGHLIGHTS: • Small log cabin rest area at trailhead • 12.5 miles of mixed use trails • Minnesota farms.

TIPS FOR WALKERS: • Street clothes are recommended. • You will probably be walking this trail in segments, so plan your walk in hours rather than miles and turn around at your half-way point. • The trail is shared with bikers and horses, so keep to the right.

RECOMMENDED ROUTE: 7.2 K (4.5 miles)
PAVED SURFACE. LEVEL. SHADED/UNSHADED.
This is just an introduction to the trail. At some point, you may want to walk the other segments or walk the entire trail and back again (26 miles) when you're a marathon walker! From the Douglas Entrance cross the street and enter the ① **Douglas Trail.** Eventually, you will see a dirt road to your left that runs parallel with the trail. When the ② **dirt road crosses the trail** you will have a number of options. You may continue walking on the trail and turn around when you're at your own halfway point. Or, you may ③ **turn right and walk along County Road 3.** County Road 3 is a paved road that winds past farms and homes and offers an opportunity to feast your senses on the sights, sounds, and smells of Minnesota farms. Walk with extreme caution along the road. When you come to County Road 14 (the main street), ④ **take a right,** walk a few blocks, and you will be back at the trailhead.

GIVING BACK: Direct financial donations to the Minnesota Parks and Trails Council, E-1311 First National Bank Building, St. Paul, MN 55101, or call 612/291-0715 or 800/289-1930.

Frontenac State Park

Operated by the Minnesota Department of Natural Resources

"Frontenac offers moderately challenging walking trails with great year-round, panoramic, scenic vistas of Lake Pepin and the Mississippi River Valley."

—Harry Roberts, Park Manager.

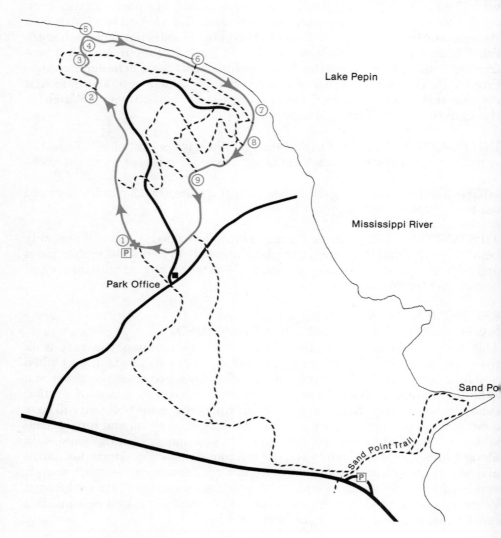

Lake Pepin

Mississippi River

Sand Po

Sand Point Trail

Park Office

88

DIRECTIONS: Frontenac State Park is located 10 miles southeast of Red Wing. **Public transportation** via Greyhound is available to the community of Frontenac, 1 mile from the park entrance. **From U.S. Highway 61:** Proceed north on County Road 2 one mile to the entrance. Turn left immediately past the park office onto a small gravel road to the trail center. **Park** anywhere in the large lot and proceed to the northwest corner of the lot (near the trail center).

INFORMATION: Call the park at 612/345-3401. The park is open daily from 8 A.M. to 10 P.M. *A trail map is available at the Park Office.* An annual motor vehicle permit or a daily permit is required.

HIGHLIGHTS: •15 miles of hiking trails • Excellent bird watching in spring and fall • Bald Eagles • In-Yan-Teopa rock overlook • Wildflowers, ferns.

TIPS FOR WALKERS: • Trail clothes are recommended. • The recommended route is steep and challenging. If you typically walk a fifteen-minute mile, plan on walking one mile per hour on the first part of the walk because of the rocks and hills. But it's well worth it! • There are less challenging routes available (talk with the park supervisor).

RECOMMENDED ROUTE: 6.4 K (4 miles)
ROCK/DIRT SURFACE. STEEP HILLS. SHADED/UNSHADED.
From the parking lot start up the ① **Hill Trail.** Bear left at the first junction and then turn right at the ② **second junction.** Follow this trail into the campground then turn left onto the campground road and follow it past C lane to the "In-Yan-Teopa Rock" sign. Take the trail past this sign into the woods and turn left at the first sign and follow the narrow path along a steep, wooded bluff to the ③ **first overlook.** Continue on the path until you come to In-Yan-Teopa Rock, once used by the Dakota and Fox Indians to view their sacred land. You may proceed up the steps and take a relatively flat walk along the bluff or continue with the recommended route and take the ④ **path off the overlook** and down the wooded bluff. Proceed very cautiously down this graded steep path over steps and rocks. At the ⑤ **trail sign,** do not follow the path down to the river but turn right and follow the main trail, which is much easier walking for a while. At the ⑥ **next trail junction,** continue on the main trail. There is a ⑦ **steep ascent** at the end before you reach the ⑧ **self-guided trail.** Take the left fork at the junction and stay on the mostly horizontal trail until it "Ts" into a ⑨ **wide, grassy trail.** Go left at the "T" and follow this trail down the hill and into the prairie. Continue on this trail across the park entrance road back to the trail center.

GIVING BACK: If you are interested in volunteer opportunities, call the park office. Direct financial donations to the Minnesota Parks and Trails Council, E-1311 First National Bank Building, St. Paul, MN 55101, or call 612/291-0715 or 800/289-1930.

City of Red Wing Trails/
Barns Bluff Park

Operated by the City of Red Wing

"You can take a historic walking tour of the downtown area, or you can join all the fitness walkers over at Bay Point Park on Levee Street, or you can challenge yourself by climbing the bluffs. Red Wing offers an interesting experience for every type of walker."

—Ron Bucholz, Superintendent, Public Services Department.

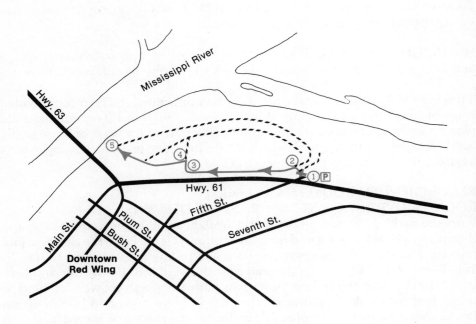

89

DIRECTIONS: Red Wing is in southeastern Minnesota along the Mississippi River. **From U.S. Highway 61:** Proceed to downtown Red Wing. Turn south onto Bush Street (away from the river), turn left on Fifth Street, and follow Fifth Street through a residential area until you pass under the Highway 61 bridge. **Park** on the right side of the road just past the bridge (across from Barns Bluff).

INFORMATION: Call the City of Red Wing at 612/388-6796. The park is open from dawn until dusk throughout the year. *Two booklets,* Explore Pretty Red Wing *and* Footsteps Through Historic Red Wing *are available through the Red Wing Chamber of Commerce at 612/388-4719.* There is no admission fee.

HIGHLIGHTS: • 2-mile trail on the large bluff overlooking the city of Red Wing • Scenic views of the Mississippi River, Red Wing, Hastings, Lake Pepin • Kiwanis Stairs • Carlson kiln.

TIPS FOR WALKERS: • Trail clothes are recommended. • The Quarry Trail is for experienced hikers only because it is on a narrow footpath along cliffs. • The Bluff Trail requires climbing two sets of very steep stairs. • *If you are afraid of heights, do not even attempt this walk.* Instead, try Bay Point Park—it's paved, level, and very scenic (3 laps = 2 miles)—it's an ideal place to take young children to walk. Bay Point Park is off Main Street in downtown Red Wing. From Main Street, turn onto Broad Street heading toward the river, then turn left on Levee Road and follow it to Bay Point Park (about six blocks away).

RECOMMENDED ROUTE: 3.2 K (2 miles)
DIRT/WOOD-CHIP SURFACE. VERY STEEP HILLS. MOSTLY SHADED.
From the side parking lot on Fifth Street, proceed across the street to the ① **Kiwanis Steps.** You may want to read the memorial that describes the history of the bluff and an interesting fact about Henry David Thoreau. Proceed up the steps. *The more walkable Bluff Trail is to the left of the stairs.* Follow the ② **Bluff Trail** to the ③ **Kiwanis Stairway.** Proceed up the stairs. Follow the ④ **trail to the left** for the "Northwestern View" of the City of Red Wing and the Mississippi River. You will walk through grasslands and eventually arrive at the ⑤ **top of the bluff.** Once you reach the summit, retrace your steps back to your start point.

If you want an extremely challenging hike, begin by following the signs for the "Primitive Trail" that leads to the "Quarry Trail" to the right. For most of the trail, a rocky bluff will be on your left and the Mississippi River will be off to the distance on your right. At the end of the trail you'll climb an incredible set of stairs up to the summit to view the city. Follow the Bluff Trail back to the start point.

GIVING BACK: For information about volunteer or donation opportunities, call the City of Red Wing at 612/388-6796.

Cannon Valley Trail

Operated by the cities of Cannon Falls and Red Wing and Goodhue County

"The Cannon Valley Trail is from the old grade of the Chicago North Western railroad line that connected the towns of Cannon Falls, Welch, and Red Wing. The trail goes through a diverse environment of beautiful heavy woods, farm lands, marsh areas, and along the Cannon River that provides a sanctuary for a multitude of wildlife."

—Bruce Blair, Trail Manager.

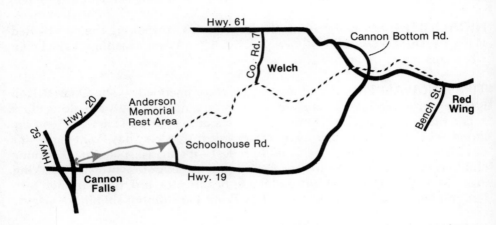

FACILITIES

✓ **Restrooms** (accessible) are available in Cannon Falls, Welch, Red Wing, and at the Schoolhouse Road/trail intersection.
✓ **Water** is available at Cannon Falls, Welch, and Red Wing.
✓ **Public telephones** are available at Cannon Falls, Welch, and Red Wing.

90

DIRECTIONS: The Cannon Valley Trail passes through the cities of Cannon Falls, Welch, and Red Wing. **Cannon Falls access:** From U.S. Highway 52, proceed east on State Highway 19 across the Canon River to the public parking lot on the left. **Park** in the public lot. **Welch access:** Follow U.S. Highway 61 to County Road 7 south through Welch and then .25 mile beyond. Turn right and **park** in the public lot. **Red Wing access:** Follow U.S. Highway 61, turn south on Bench Street (County Road 1) and the trail begins at Old West Main Street. **Park** in the public lot.

INFORMATION: Call any of the following numbers for information: Cannon Valley Trail 507/263-3954; Red Wing Chamber of Commerce 612/388-4719; Cannon Falls Chamber of Commerce 507/263-2289. *A trail map is available by calling any of these numbers.* The trail is open from sunrise to 10 P.M. every day. There is no admission fee, but there are donation boxes along the trail.

HIGHLIGHTS: • 19.7 miles of trails (13.5 miles paved) • Picnic area • Anderson Memorial Rest area • Cannon Falls Historical Museum • Goodhue County Historical Society Museum in Red Wing.

TIPS FOR WALKERS: • Street clothes are recommended. • This is an excellent trail for long fitness walks because the trail is flat. • The trail is shared with bikers, so keep to the right. • Round-trip distances: Cannon Falls to Anderson Rest Area (7.2 miles); Welch to Schoolhouse Road (9.6 miles); Welch to Cannon Bottom Road (11.2 miles); Red Wing to Cannon Bottom Road (8.4 miles).

RECOMMENDED ROUTE: 15.4 K (9.6 miles)
PAVED SURFACE. LEVEL. SHADED/UNSHADED.
(Cannon Falls to Schoolhouse Road): From the public parking area, walk to the Anderson Memorial Rest area (you may want to expore the .5 mile loop trail off the main trail) and then on to Schoolhouse Road. You may want to have a picnic at the rest area and then walk back to Cannon Falls.

GIVING BACK: For information about volunteer and donation opportunities, contact the Cannon Valley Trail Manager, City Hall, 306 West Mill Street, Cannon Falls, MN 55009, or call 507/263-3954.

Nerstrand Big Woods State Park _____

Operated by the Minnesota Department of Natural Resources

"I call it the 'Magic Woods' because the trees form a canopy over the trails that creates a very special, magical walking experience. Nerstrand Woods has over 150 species of wildflowers—there's always something wonderful to look at."

—Kathryn Cassem, Naturalist.

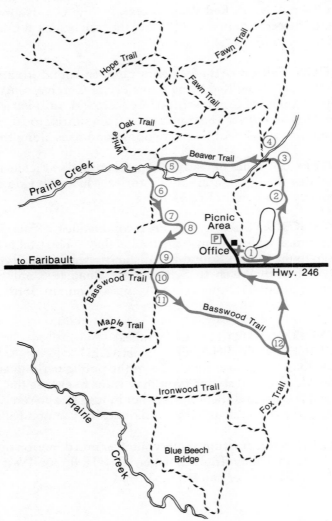

FACILITIES

- ✓**Restrooms** (pit toilets) are available year-round in the building between the picnic shelter and group campground, located along the walking trail.
- ✓**Water** is available at the picnic shelter and campgrounds. A hand pump is located near the office.
- ✓**Public telephones** are not available. The office phone is available during office hours for emergency use only.

91

DIRECTIONS: Nerstrand Big Woods is located south of the metro area in Nerstrand. **From Interstate 494:** Proceed south on U.S. Highway 52, south on State Highway 56, west on State Highway 246, and follow the state park signs. **Park** in the lot just beyond the park office.

INFORMATION: Call the park at 507/334-8848 for seasonal office hours and events. The park is open daily from 8 A.M. to 10 P.M. *A trail map is available at the park office.* A yearly motor vehicle pass or a daily pass is required.

HIGHLIGHTS: • 13 miles of hiking trails • Large picnic area and shelter • Group campsites • One of the last "Big Woods" parks featuring sugar maple, basswood, elm, green ash, and ironwood trees • Wildflowers, ferns, mushrooms • Hidden Falls • Bird watching • Oaks.

TIPS FOR WALKERS: • Trail clothes are recommended. • Carry a compass. • You may want to bring a walking stick, tape recorder, and binoculars.

RECOMMENDED ROUTE: 4.8 K (3 miles)
DIRT/GRASS SURFACE. ROLLING/STEEP HILLS. SHADED.
From the parking lot, proceed to the park office. Follow the marked ① **hiking trail** that begins behind the park office. At the first ② **trail junction,** turn right and walk down a steep path. Continue on the trail and listen for the ③ **Hidden Falls.** Follow any of the small footpaths that lead down to the falls for a closer look. Cross the ④ **cement bridge** and follow the Beaver Trail to the left. As you walk the Beaver Trail, look for the tree with a chair (a flat piece of wood) nestled between two limbs. At the next ⑤ **trail junction,** turn left, cross the Oak Bridge and ascend up a steep hill. At the next ⑥ **trail junction,** take a left (do not go up to the picnic grounds). At the next ⑦ **trail junction,** take the trail to the left and at the ⑧ **next junction,** the trail to the right. Eventually you will come to a ⑨ **dirt road.** Cross the road and proceed to the nearest "no parking any time sign" (to the right about 30 feet as you face the woods) and you'll find a small footpath. Follow the ⑩ **footpath** into the woods and turn left onto Beaver Trail. At the first junction, take a left to the ⑪ **Basswood Trail** that turns into a stone path and winds past the park ranger's residence. Continue to the next trail junction and take a left on ⑫ **Fox Trail.** Proceed north on Fox Trail, across the dirt road, and back to the parking lot.

GIVING BACK: If you're interested in volunteering, talk with park personnel. Volunteers include naturalists, storytellers, carpenters, and trail guides. Direct financial donations to Minnesota Parks and Trails Council, E-1311 First National Bank Building, St. Paul, MN 55101, or call 612/291-0715 or 800/289-1930.

City of Lakeville Trails

Operated by the City of Lakeville

"Starting at Aronson Park, this trail leads to beautiful downtown Lakeville, past the recently dedicated Pioneer Plaza and ends at historic Antlers Park at Lake Marion. Walk, jog, or bike this stretch of trail and enjoy the beauty of the Lakeville parks or the special atmosphere of the Lakeville downtown area."

—Steve Michaud, Director of Parks and Recreation.

FACILITIES

- ✓ **Restrooms** (accessible) are available at Aronson Park, downtown Lakeville, and Antlers Park.
- ✓ **Water** is available at Aronson Park, downtown Lakeville, and Antlers Park.
- ✓ **Public telephones** are available in downtown Lakeville.

92

DIRECTIONS: Lakeville is south of the metro area. **From Interstate 35:** Proceed east on State Highway 70 (the Lakeville/Farmington Exit), north on Holyoke (15), east (right) on 202nd Street, and turn right into Aronson Park. **Park** in the lot near the playground.

INFORMATION: Call the Lakeville Park and Recreation Department at 612/ 469-4431. Parks and trails are open from 6 A.M. to 10 P.M. *A large trail map is available through the city.* There is no admission fee.

HIGHLIGHTS: • 22 miles of walking trails within the City of Lakeville • Aronson Park • Antler Park • Picnic area • Playground (Antler Park) • Marion Lake • Beach area • Picnic area.

TIPS FOR WALKERS: • Street clothes are recommended. • This is a great trail to walk in August at the height of the corn season. • The trails are shared with bikers. • The trails in Lakeville connect with the trails in Apple Valley making it possible to walk from Lakeville to the Minnesota Zoo.

RECOMMENDED ROUTE: 7.2 K (4.5 miles)
PAVED. LEVEL. UNSHADED.
From the parking lot, proceed to the paved trail that begins near the picnic shelter. Follow the trail around the ball field, past the ① **Lakeville Grove Cemetery,** and past a corn field. Turn right onto the dirt road and turn left on ② **Holt Avenue,** and walk on the side of the street until you reach 206th Street, then walk on the sidewalk. You will pass stores and a senior center. Turn right on 208th Street (notice the large oak) and as you enter ③ **downtown Lakeville,** cross Holyoke at the pedestrian crossing. Turn left and walk along Holyoke, turn right at 208th Street Southwest. Continue on the sidewalk straight ahead, cross the road, and keep walking to the ④ **trailhead by the railroad tracks** (there will be large grain elevators to your right). You will walk through an open field with houses to your right. Cross ⑤ **Dodd Boulevard** and continue walking across an open field. At the ⑥ **trail junction, turn right.** Follow the path to the pedestrian crossing at ⑦ **202nd Street** to ⑧ **Antlers Park and Marion Lake.** You may want to swim or rest before retracing your steps back to the start point. On the way back, walk along the east side of Holyoke, ⑨ **turn right on 205th Street,** and follow the trail back to the park.

GIVING BACK: For information about future volunteer or donation opportunities, call the City of Lakeville Parks and Recreation Department at 612/469-4431.

Sakatah Singing Hills State Trail _____

Operated by the Minnesota Department of Natural Resources

"The Sakatah Singing Hills State Trail is a 39-mile-long old railroad grade from Mankato to Faribault that has a diversity of hardwoods, farmlands, marshes, prairies, and lakes. The trail also goes through the beautiful Sakatah Lake State Park that has a swimming beach, picnic grounds, and fishing, so there's something for everyone."

—Randy Schoeneck, Trail Manager.

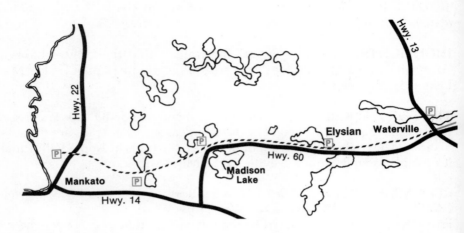

DIRECTIONS: Sakatah Singing Hills State Trail is located in southeastern Minnesota. **From Interstate 35:** Proceed west on State Highway 60. There are a number of entrances to the trail along Highway 60: Faribault (at the exit near Dairy Queen), Warsaw, **Sakatah Lake State Park** (take this one for the recommended walking route), Waterville, Elysian, Madison Lake, and north of Mankato off of State Highway 22 on Lime Valley Road. At Sakatah Lake State Park, continue on the entrance road to the picnic and beach area. **Park** in the lot near the picnic area.

INFORMATION: Call the trail office at 507/267-4772 or Sakatah Lake State Park at 507/362-4438. The park and state trail is open daily from 8 A.M. to 10 P.M. *Trail maps are available at the Information Office.* There is no admission fee if you use a public entrance along Highway 60. In the state park, an annual motor vehicle permit or a daily pass is required.

HIGHLIGHTS: • 39 miles of paved, accessible limestone walking trails • Trail is linked with Mankato City Trail System • Campgrounds • Picnic and rest areas along the trail • Wildlife.

TIPS FOR WALKERS: • Street clothes are recommended. • The trails are shared with bikers. • This is a great trail for aerobic walking because it is level and paved. • There are 5 more miles of hiking trails in Sakatah Lake State Park.

FACILITIES

✓ **Restrooms** (accessible) are available at Mankato, Madison Lake, Elysian, Waterville, Sakatah Lake State Park, Fairbault, Morristown, and Warsaw.
✓ **Water** is available at at all the above locations.
✓ **Public telephones** are available at all the above locations.

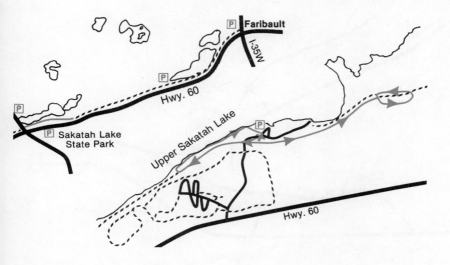

RECOMMENDED ROUTE: 6.4 K (4 miles)
LIMESTONE. LEVEL. MOSTLY UNSHADED.

From the parking lot near the picnic area, walk back along the entrance road to the entrance to the Sakatah Singing Hills State Trail. You can take a 4-mile walk in either direction or do both loops for a total of 8 miles.

If you proceed east, you will walk 2.25 miles through a tranquil wooded area until you come upon a walking trail to your right. Take the trail to the right and you will walk a half-circle loop of wildflowers and tall grasses. When you come back to the main trail, turn left and return to your start point.

If you proceed west, you will walk 1.5 miles through a wooded area and you will eventually come to a walking trail to the right. Take the trail to the right and walk back along the beautiful Sakatah Lake to the picnic and beach area where you parked.

GIVING BACK: For volunteer opportunities, call the park office. Direct financial donations to Minnesota Parks and Trails Council, E-1311 First National Bank Building, St. Paul, MN 55101, or call 612/291-0715 or 800/289-1930.

Minneopa State Park

Operated by the Minnesota Department of Natural Resources

"People are attracted to Minneopa because of its beautiful waterfalls. Minneopa means water falling twice and when you see the falls, you'll see a small waterfall leading into a bigger one. People also enjoy bird watching."
—David Pribbenow, park worker.

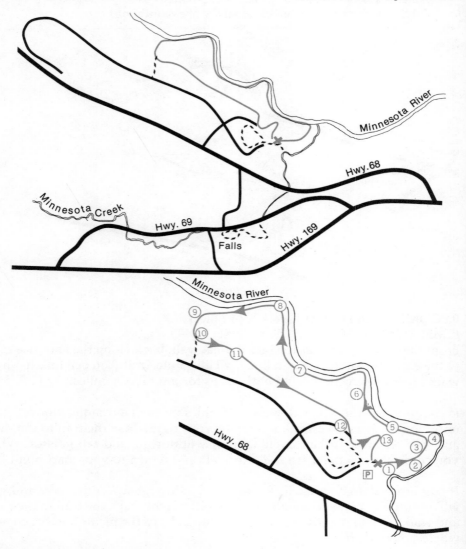

FACILITIES

✓ **Restrooms** (pit toilets) are located in the campground at the beginning of the trail and in the Red Fox Campground near the end of the trail.

✓ **Water** is available at the beginnning of the trail and at the Red Fox Campground near the end.

✓ **Public telephones** are available at the Red Fox Campground.

94

DIRECTIONS: Minneopa State Park is located south of Mankato. **From U.S. Highway 169 in Mankato:** Proceed south for 3 miles, west on State Highway 68 for 2 miles. You will pass a sign that says "waterfall" to the left but do not turn here. Turn right into the park where the sign says "Campgrounds." Continue past the ranger station and turn right at the first four-way intersection. Follow the road around to the group campground and picnic area. **Park** in the picnic area lot.

INFORMATION: Call the park at 507/625-4388. Minneopa State Park is open from 8 A.M. to 10 P.M. all year. *A trail map is available at the office.* An annual motor vehicle pass or a daily permit is required.

HIGHLIGHTS: • 5 miles of hiking trails through river bottom hardwoods and prairie savanna adjacent to the Minnesota River • Three picnic areas • Campgrounds • Grist mill that dates back to 1864 • Bluebird houses • Waterfalls.

TIPS FOR WALKERS: • If you want to see the waterfalls and mill, you will have to drive to them because they are not on the walking trail. • Trail clothes are recommended. • You may want to bring a walking stick and binoculars.

RECOMMENDED ROUTE: 6.4 K (4 miles)
DIRT SURFACE. LEVEL/ONE STEEP HILL. SHADED/UNSHADED.
From the campground, follow the trail that looks like a ① **primitive road** to the east. The first trail marker will be a blue sign with a white arrow pointing to follow the trail straight ahead. At the first junction, keep to the right. You will come to a ② **trail map.** Continue on the trail and you will come to a ③ **small, sandy hill.** You will now be down at the Minnesota River floodplain. This is a lovely walk in the fall. On the right you will notice a ④ **railroad bridge.** Soon you will come to an ⑤ **opening in the tree-lined trail** that provides a scenic view of the river. Next you will cross a ⑥ **wooden bridge** and then ⑦ **another wooden bridge** across a small stream. Continue on the trail to the next ⑧ **trail map.** The trail winds around under a ⑨ **railroad bridge.** At the ⑩ **next junction,** turn left. You will come to another ⑪ **trail map,** and then you will walk across virgin prairie land. Notice the bluebird restoration project along the way. When you come to the ⑫ **gravel road,** turn left to the Red Fox Campground and follow the road until you come to a ⑬ **trail sign.** Turn right and follow the trail back to the start point.

GIVING BACK: To volunteer, call the park office at 507/625-4388. Direct financial donations to Minnesota Parks and Trails Council, E-1311 First National Bank Building, St. Paul, MN 55101, or call 612/291-0715 or 800/289-1930.

Lake Hanska County Park

Operated by Brown County Park Department

"The word 'hanska' is a Dakota word that means long and narrow. The lake is very long and narrow, and it's the largest lake in southern Minnesota. Walkers talk about how they enjoy the variety of trees and the walk along the lakeshore." —Gary Olson, Park Caretaker.

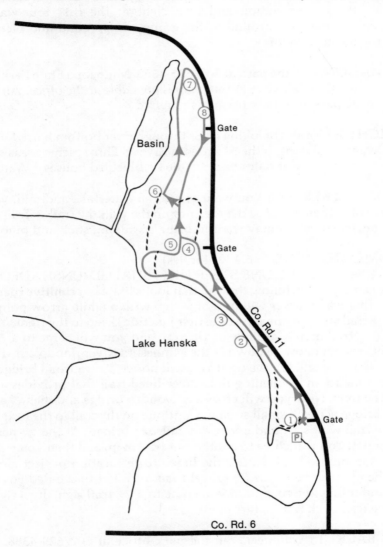

FACILITIES

✓**Restrooms** (pit toilets) are available in the summer. Flush toilets available at the seasonal campground.
✓**Water** is available at all areas of the park.
✓**A public telephone** is available at the seasonal campground.

95

DIRECTIONS: Lake Hanska park is located in rural Hanska. **From New Ulm:** Proceed 12 miles south of New Ulm on County Road 13, then 5 miles west on County Road 6. Turn right (north) onto County Road 11, then turn left at the first park sign. **Park** at the picnic area.

INFORMATION: Call the park coordinator at 507/359-7900 ext. 24 or the park caretaker at 507/439-6411. The park is open all year from 8 A.M. to 10 P.M. *A trail map/brochure is available at the Campground building.* There is no admission fee.

HIGHLIGHTS: • 5 miles of walking trails • Campgrounds • Picnic area • Original log cabin and Fort Hill.

TIPS FOR WALKERS: • Trail clothes are recommended. • You may want to bring a camera.

RECOMMENDED ROUTE: 8 K (5 miles)
DIRT/GRASS SURFACE. LEVEL. MOSTLY SHADED.
From the ① **picnic shelter,** proceed north along the grassy shoreline trail. Continue along the trail until you reach the ②**second picnic area.** At the ③**first trail junction,** take a right. You'll walk past an authentically restored ④ **log cabin** and the park caretaker's home. You will also walk past ⑤ **Fort Hill.** At the trail junction, take a right. At the next trail junction, take a left and then ⑥ **turn right.** The trail follows along a basin that provides access for boats to the campground. Follow the trail around the ⑦ **campground.** The trail continues on the other side of the ⑧ **park gate** (look for sign). Continue on the straight path back to Fort Hill again. At all the next trail junctions, keep right and you will eventually return to the picnic area.

GIVING BACK: Volunteers are needed to help with the restoration of the Log Cabin and other park facilities. Direct financial donations to Brown County Park Department, Brown County Courthouse, Center and State Streets, New Ulm, MN 56073.

Flandrau State Park

Operated by the Department of Natural Resources

"The natural beauty of the Cottonwood River Valley draws people to Flandrau."
—Archie Daleiden, Park Manager.

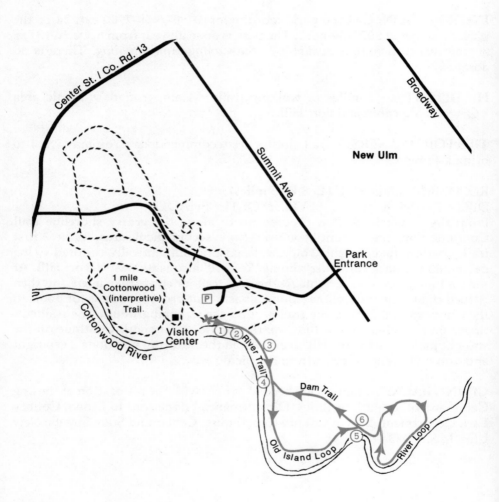

96

DIRECTIONS: Flandrau State Park is located adjacent to and partially within the city of New Ulm. **From U.S. Highway 14 in New Ulm:** Turn south on Broadway, right (west) on Center Street, left (south) on Summit Avenue to the park entrance on the left. **Park** in the lot by the beach house and swimming pool.

INFORMATION: Call the park office at 507/354-3519. The park is open from 8 A.M. to 10 P.M. year-round. *A trail map is available in the park office.* An annual motor vehicle permit or a daily pass is required.

HIGHLIGHTS: • 8 miles of dirt hiking trails • 1.5-mile self-guided interpretive trail • Accessible beach house • Cottonwood River • Abundant wildlife • Broad-winged hawks, indigo buntings, and northern orioles • Beach and beach house • Group center and mess hall • Ninety campsites • Picnic grounds.

TIPS FOR WALKERS: • Carry water. • Trail clothes are recommended. • You may want to bring a walking stick, compass, and a camera. • Call ahead for trail conditions. Some portions may be flooded after a significant rainfall.

RECOMMENDED ROUTE: 5.1 K (3.2 miles)
DIRT/GRASS SURFACE. MOSTLY LEVEL/ONE STEEP HILL. UNSHADED. Proceed from the parking lot to the beach. As you face the beach, proceed to the① **trail to the left** (look for an open area of grass). At the② **first junction,** take a right onto the River Trail. You'll come to a③ **steep hill,** the only really difficult part of the trail. At the④ **next junction,** take a right along Old Island Loop. At the ⑤ **next junction,** take a right, then a left and follow the River Loop. Halfway around the loop you'll be able to hear river falls, once the site of a dam that was destroyed by flood waters. Continue around the River Loop. At the next junction, take a right along the⑥ **Dam Trail.** Continue walking along the River Trail back to the start point.

GIVING BACK: Direct donations to the Friends of Flandrau, 1300 Summit Avenue, New Ulm, MN 56073.

Fort Ridgely State Park———————————

Operated by the Minnesota Department of Natural Resources

"Walkers at Fort Ridgely will have an opportunity to see hawks and bald eagles, a restored Oak Savanna in progress, and displays prepared by the Minnesota Historical Society."

—Mark Tjosaas, Assistant Park Manager.

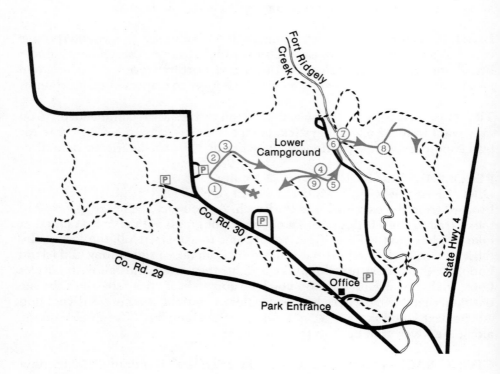

FACILITIES ————————————

✓ **Restrooms** (pit toilets) are located at the picnic grounds, and flush toilets (not accessible) are available at the Interpretive Center.

✓ **Water** is available along the trails.

✓ **Public telephones** are available at the picnic grounds where the trail begins. The park office phone is available for emergency use only.

97

DIRECTIONS: Fort Ridgely State Park is located in southwestern Minnesota 6 miles south of Fairfax. **From State Highway 4:** Proceed west on County Road 29 to the park entrance. **Park** near the picnic area just beyond the cemetery.

INFORMATION: Call the park office at 507/426-7840 for Interpretive Center hours and events. The park is open from 8 A.M. to 10 P.M. throughout the year. *A trail map is available at the Interpretive Center.* An annual motor vehicle permit or a daily pass is required.

HIGHLIGHTS: • 11 miles of walking trails through wooded ravines and open prairie meadows • Interpretive Center with historical displays • Self-guided interpretive trail • Nine-hole golf course • Group campsite • Prairie wild-flowers and grasses • Amphitheater • Playground.

TIPS FOR WALKERS: • Trail junctions are well marked. • Trail clothes are recommended. • You may want to bring a walking stick and camera. • Some of the trails are shared with horses. • Winter hikers are reminded not to destroy the cross-country ski tracks.

RECOMMENDED ROUTE: 4 K (2.5 miles)
DIRT/GRASS SURFACE. LEVEL/ONE STEEP HILL.
SHADED/UNSHADED.
From the picnic area, go left on the grass trail to the ① **Old Fort site.** Explore the ruins of the military post that occupied the land in the 1850s. From the Interpretive Center, turn right and proceed to the ② **trail that begins in the woods.** At the ③ **first junction,** keep left. At the ④ **next junction,** keep left. You will enter a campground. Proceed past the restrooms and take the wooden steps down to the ⑤ **lower campground.** Follow the ⑥ **road to the right** and take the bridge across Fort Ridgely Creek. At the next ⑦ **trail junction,** turn right (follow the sign to Upper Valley Trail). At the next ⑧ **trail junction,** keep left and follow the sign to Airplane Hill Trail. This is a very steep hill. Once you've made it to the top, work your way back down the hill, take the trail to the right, cross the creek to the lower campground, and walk back up the hill. When you get to the next ⑨ **trail junction,** turn left. You will exit by the Amphi-theater at the picnic grounds.

GIVING BACK: Direct financial donations to the Minnesota Parks and Trails Council, E-1311 First National Bank Building, St. Paul, MN 55101, or call 612/291-0715 or 800/289-1930.

Blue Mounds State Park

Operated by the Minnesota Department of Natural Resources

"Blue Mounds is the largest virgin prairie park in the state of Minnesota. We also have abundant wildlife including a small herd of bison, coyotes, and white-tail deer."

—Merlin Johnson, Park Manager.

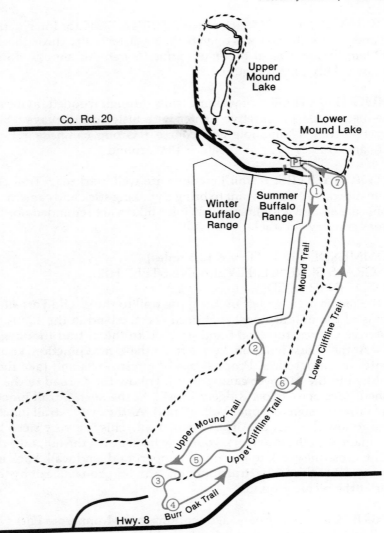

98

DIRECTIONS: Blue Mounds State Park is located in southwestern Minnesota. **From Interstate 90:** Proceed to Luverne, then proceed north 6 miles on U.S. Highway 75, east on County Road 20 to the park entrance. **Park** in the lot at the very end of the road in the beach parking area.

INFORMATION: Call the park at 507/283-4892. The park is open from 8 A.M. to 10 P.M. year-round. The Interpretive Center is open during the summer. *A trail map is available at the park office.* An annual motor vehicle permit or a daily pass is required.

HIGHLIGHTS: • 13 miles of trails • Quartzite rock • Beautiful prairie with hundreds of different types of grasses and wildflowers • Prickly pear cacti • Bison • Cliffline for viewing the farmscapes of Iowa and South Dakota.

TIPS FOR WALKERS: • Trail clothes are recommended. • Be careful along the cliffs.

RECOMMENDED ROUTE: 6.4 K (4 miles)
DIRT SURFACE. LEVEL. UNSHADED.
From the parking lot, cross the road and proceed to the ① **Mound Trail.** Walk south along the summer bison range. At the ② **trail junction,** turn left onto the Upper Mound Trail. Follow the trail to the ③ **Interpretive Center.** From the Interpretive Center proceed to the ④ **Burr Oak Trail,** the only heavily wooded area in the park. You will also see huge quartzite boulders. At the trail junction, turn right onto the ⑤ **Upper Cliffline Trail.** Keep to the right at the next junction. At the fork, take the ⑥ **Lower Cliffline Trail,** the trail to the right. Keep to the right at the next junction, ⑦ **veer left just before Lower Mound Lake,** and follow the trail back to the parking lot.

GIVING BACK: For information about volunteer and donation opportunities, call the park at 507/283-4892. Donations may also be directed to the Minnesota Parks and Trails Council, E-1311 First National Bank Building, St. Paul, MN 55101, or call 612/291-0715 or 800/289-1930.

Upper Sioux Agency State Park

Operated by the Minnesota Department of Natural Resources

"The Yellow Medicine River Valley and the Minnesota River Valley provide a beautiful, natural, soothing retreat that heals and energizes the human spirit. In this park, the Yellow River joins the Minnesota River and then the Minnesota River continues for 330 miles through central Minnesota on its way to the Mississippi River."
—Richard Tjosaas, Park Manager.

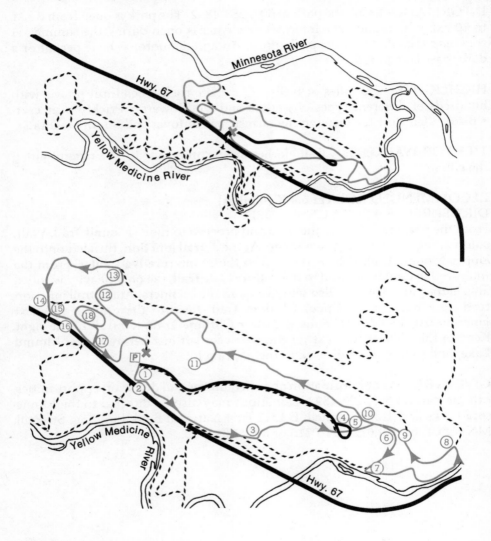

99

DIRECTIONS: The Upper Sioux Agency State Park is located in southwestern Minnesota. **On State Highway 67:** Proceed 8 miles southeast of Granite Falls. The entrance to the park is on the left. **Park** in the lot near the picnic area.

INFORMATION: Call the park at 612/564-4777. The park is open from 8 A.M. to 10 P.M. year-round. *A trail map is available at the park office and the Interpretive Center.* An annual motor vehicle permit or a daily pass is required.

HIGHLIGHTS: • 8 miles of hiking trails • Interpretive Center. • Picnic area • Historic Upper Sioux Agency site • River fishing.

TIPS FOR WALKERS: • Trail clothes are recommended. • Some of the trails are shared with horses. • You may want to bring binoculars for viewing wildlife.

RECOMMENDED ROUTE: 5.6 K (3.5 miles)
DIRT SURFACE. LEVEL. SHADED/UNSHADED.
From the parking lot, ① **cross the road** past the first trail junction, then ② **turn left onto the Prairie Trail.** You will walk through prairie bluffs overlooking the Yellow Medicine River valley. At the ③ **next junction,** turn left and cut through the prairie to the dirt road that is on the other side of the ④ **lookout over the junction of the rivers.** Pick up the trail on the ⑤ **east side of the turn-around loop of road** and proceed on the trail, turning ⑥ **right at the next junction,** walking downhill, crossing a road, then ⑦ **turning left** along the trail that follows along the Yellow Medicine River. At the next ⑧ **trail junction,** turn left, cross the road, and follow the trail into a wooded area. At the ⑨ **next junction, keep to the left,** but then bear right at the ⑩ **next junction.** Follow the trail through a wooded area. Wildlife is abundant in this area. About .5 mile along the trail, veer to the left to visit the ⑪ **Upper Sioux Agency site.** Proceed back to the main trail, keeping to the right at the next junction. You will cross a road and then ⑫ **turn right at the trail junction,** then ⑬ **turn left,** working your way down to the Minnesota River. Continue on the trail that starts circling uphill, keeping to the ⑭ **right at the junction** and then ⑮ **left at the next junction** where you will pass the ⑯ **contact station** and ⑰ **the Interpretive Center.** Be sure to walk the ⑱ **self-guided Interpretive Trail.** Proceed on the main trail back to your start point.

GIVING BACK: For information about volunteer or donation opportunities, call the park office at 612/564-4777. Donations may also be directed to the Minnesota Parks and Trails Council, E-1311 First National Bank Building, St. Paul, MN 55101, or call 612/291-0715 or 800/289-1930.

Collinwood County Park

Operated by Wright County Parks System

"A lot of people come to Collinwood to watch the birds. We even have pelicans up here, and not many people get a chance to see them anywhere else." —John Dolloff, Park Manager.

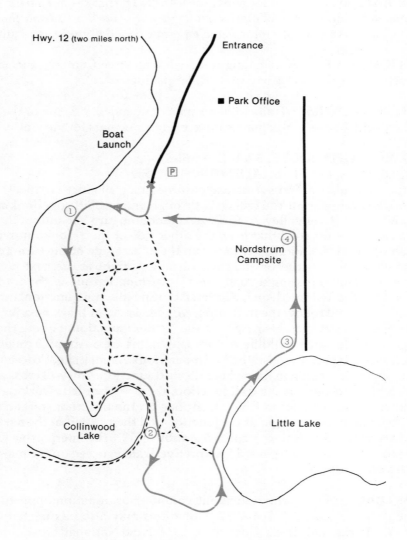

100

DIRECTIONS: Collinwood County Park is located 3 miles southwest of Cokato. **From State Highway 12:** Once you reach Cokato, continue on Highway 12 about 3 miles west. Turn left at the "Collinwood County Park" sign and follow the road 2 miles to the park entrance. The entrance road winds around past the manager's house and a concession stand. **Park** in the south lot (not the boat launch lot).

INFORMATION: Call the park manager at 612/286-2801. The park is open from 6 A.M. to 9 P.M. The office/concession stand is open from May through September from 8 A.M. to 9 P.M. *Trail maps are available at the concession stand.* There are no admission fees for walking the trails. Camping and boat launch fees are posted.

HIGHLIGHTS: • 5 miles of walking trails • Individual and group camping facilities • Picnic area with shelter and toilets • Swimming beach • Creative play area • Boat launch.

TIPS FOR WALKERS: • Trail clothes are recommended. • You may want to use a walking stick. • Bring binoculars for bird watching.

RECOMMENDED ROUTE: 8 K (5 miles)
DIRT SURFACE. ONE STEEP HILL. SHADED/UNSHADED.
From the parking lot, proceed to the large wooden trail sign near the southeast corner of the lot. The trail begins just beyond the sign. The first part of the shoreline trail is quite hilly, providing excellent views of ① **Collinwood Lake.** You will walk past some campsites. When you come to the play area, continue walking along the treeline until you see the continuation of the dirt trail. You will proceed down a steep hill, and up another one. **At all the trail junctions, keep to the right.** You will find viewing benches along the way. The second part of the trail will take you through open, grassy fields. When you come to the ② **major trail junction** at the south end of the park, take the trail to the far right. The trail winds along a bay, then through a campsite. The trail resumes on the other side of the campsite. Keep to the right, following the Little Lake shoreline. It's a pleasant walk with an open field and tall grasses to your left. Keep to the right. The trail ends at the ③ **Little Lake Group Campsite,** so follow the dirt road. When you get to the ④ **Nordstrum Group Campsite,** find the trail at the northwest corner of the campsite and proceed west on this trail back to your start point.

GIVING BACK: Direct financial donations to the Wright County Parks System, Public Works Building, Route 1, Box 97B, Buffalo, MN 55313.

Lake Maria State Park

Operated by the Minnesota Department of Natural Resources

"Lake Maria is one of the few state parks that was designed for hikers, backpackers and horseback riders looking for beauty and solitude in a wilderness experience."

—Mark Crawford, Park Manager.

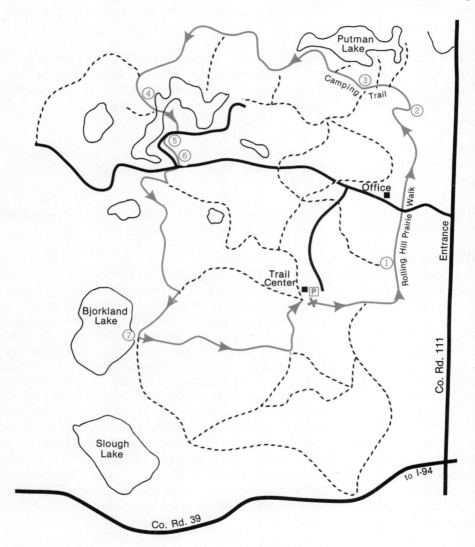

FACILITIES

✓ **Restrooms** (accessible) are available in the Trail Center. Pit toilets are available in the picnic areas.
✓ **Water** is available at the park office and campsites.
✓ **Public telephones** are available at the park office.

300

101

DIRECTIONS: Lake Maria State Park is located in Wright County, 45 miles northwest of Minneapolis. **From Interstate 94:** Take the Monticello exit and proceed south .5 mile on State Highway 25, west 6 miles on County Road 39, north 2 miles on County Road 111 to the park entrance on the left. **Park** in the lot near the Trail Center.

INFORMATION: Call the park at 612/878-2325 for information. The park is open daily from 8 A.M. to 10 P.M. *A trail map is available at the Trail Center.* A yearly motor vehicle permit or a daily pass is required.

HIGHLIGHTS: • 14 miles of walking trails • Trail Center with information displays • Boating and canoe access to Lake Maria and Bjorkland Lake • Campsites • 205 species of birds • Deer, beaver, fox, reptiles.

TIPS FOR WALKERS: • Trail clothes are recommended. • Some paths are shared with horseback riders. • Carry water. • You may want to bring binoculars. • Trails are well marked. • *Trails are closed to walkers in the winter.*

RECOMMENDED ROUTE: 7.2 K (4.5 miles)
DIRT/GRASS SURFACE. ROLLING HILLS (ONE STEEP HILL WITH A BYPASS). MOSTLY SHADED.
Take a few minutes to browse through the displays and the trail map in the Trail Center. The trail begins on the south side of the building. Most of the first part of the trail is a ① **rolling hill prairie walk** that introduces you to wildflowers and prairie grasses. Toward the end of the prairie walk you will come to ② **Anderson Hill,** the highest point of the park that overlooks the rolling hills and wooded areas. To walk the hill, take the trail to the right. To bypass the hill, take the trail to the left. From Anderson Hill, you will walk down into a totally shaded, woody terrain. Along this part of the trail, stay to the right. You may want to veer off onto one of the small dead-end trails that are designated as ③ **individual campsites,** which provide a beautiful view of Putman Lake. After getting on the main trail again, you will enter a ④ **wooded marsh area** filled with sounds of birds and reptiles. You will eventually come upon a ⑤ **gravel road.** Turn right. At the ⑥ **intersection, turn right.** After about 100 yards, look for the first opening in the woods to the left, and take this trail, keeping to the right. Eventually, you will come to ⑦ **Bjorkland Lake** where you may observe loons and other waterfowl. Take a left on the trail designated for hikers and stay to the left as you make your way back to the Trail Center.

GIVING BACK: Lake Maria State Park is always in need of volunteers to help keep the park facilities in top condition. Call the park office at 612/878-2325 for volunteer opportunities. Direct financial donations to Minnesota Parks and Trails Council, E-1311 First National Bank Building, St. Paul, MN 55101, or call 612/291-0715 or 800/289-1930.

Harry Larson Memorial County Forest

Operated by Wright County Parks System

"Harry Larson Memorial County Forest provides a wonderful walking experience through a hardwood forest. People who walk or ski through the park enjoy the wildlife and rolling hills."
—Bruce Thielen, Parks Administrator.

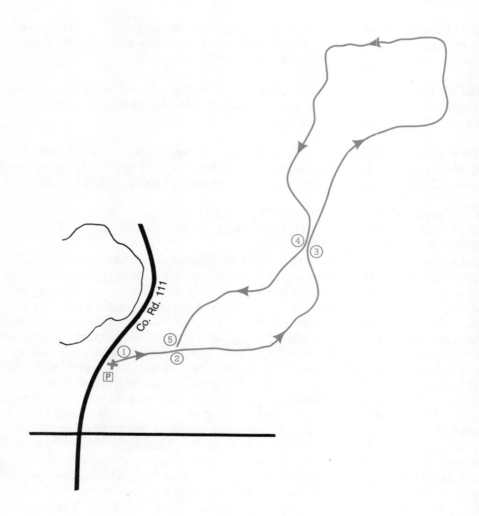

102

DIRECTIONS: Harry Larson Memorial County Forest is near Monticello, northwest of the metro area. **From Interstate 94:** Take the Monticello exit and proceed south on State Highway 25, west on County Road 39 and north on County Road 111 to the park entrance. **Park** in the lot on the east (right) side of the street.

INFORMATION: Call the Wright County Parks at 800/362-3667 (ext. 7693) or (metro) 612/339-6881. The park is open during the spring, summer, and fall months from 6 A.M. to 11 P.M. *A brochure is available on the Wright County Parks System.* There is no admission fee.

HIGHLIGHTS: • 170 acres of rolling terrain • Picnic area • Oak, aspen • Wildlife.

TIPS FOR WALKERS: • Trail clothes are recommended. • You may want to bring binoculars to observe deer and birds. • This is an ideal trail for people (especially children) who can walk more than a mile and need a challenging workout.

RECOMMENDED ROUTE: 3.2 K (2 miles)
DIRT SURFACE. ROLLING HILLS. SHADED.
From the parking lot, proceed to the ① **trailhead.** At the ② **first junction,** keep to the right. This segment of the trail is level. At the ③ **next junction,** keep to the right until you make a full circle. At the ④ **next junction,** take a right. The rolling hills make this segment of the walk more challenging. Continue along the trail, past a ⑤ **deer feeding area** where you may be able to observe deer in their natural habitat. Retrace your steps to the start point.

GIVING BACK: For information about volunteer or donation opportunities, contact the Wright County Parks System, Public Works Building, Route 1, Box 97B, Buffalo, MN 55313.

City of St. Cloud Trails/____

Heritage Park

Operated by the City of St. Cloud and the Stearns County Historical Society

"This is such an exciting place! My kids loved the wildlife area. Even my one-year-old could look and learn but there were enough barriers so that he couldn't hurt anything. I'd love to come back again."

—Krista Hoffman, with Quinn and Logan Hoffman and Alyssa Wenberg, residents of Sauk Rapids.

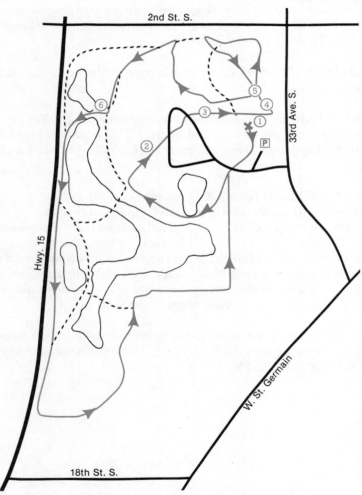

- ✓ **Restrooms** (accessible) are available in the Nature Center and Museum.
- ✓ **Water** is available in the Nature Center and Museum.
- ✓ **Public telephones** are available in the Nature Center and Museum.

103

DIRECTIONS: Heritage Park is located in St. Cloud. **Public transportation** information is available through the St. Cloud Metro Transit Commission at 612/253-2420. **From Interstate Highway 94:** Proceed north on State Highway 15, turn east onto Second Street South, turn right (south) onto 33rd Avenue South. The entrance to the park is on the right side of the road. **Park in the lot near the Nature Center.**

INFORMATION: Call St. Cloud Parks and Recreation at 612/255-7256 or the Heritage Nature Center at 612/255-7255 or the Heritage Center Museum at 612/253-8425. The trails in the park are open from sunrise to sunset year-round. *A trail map is available at the Nature Center. The city also offers a map to the parks of St. Cloud.* The Nature Center is open on Fridays (10 A.M. to 4 P.M.), Saturdays (9 A.M. to 4 P.M.), and Sundays (noon to 8 P.M.). Weekday hours vary with the season. There is no admission fee to the Nature Center. The **Heritage Center Museum** is open on Friday and Saturday (10 A.M. to 4 P.M.) and Sundays (noon to 4 P.M.). Weekday hours vary with the season. There is an admission fee ($2.50 for adults, children under 5 years admitted free).

HIGHLIGHTS: • 3.5 miles of trails • 2 miles of paved accessible trails • Heritage Center Museum (Indian and pioneer dwellings, granite quarry replica, minor league baseball memorabilia) • Heritage Nature Center (displays, day and evening classes).

TIPS FOR WALKERS: • This is a great place for a family outing. • Street clothes are recommended.

RECOMMENDED ROUTE: 4.8 K (3 miles)
PAVED/DIRT SURFACE. LEVEL. UNSHADED.
From the parking lot, proceed to the ① **Nature Center.** Then take the paved path that leads across the street and around to the ② **Museum.** After a tour of the Museum, proceed out the front door across the parking lot to the paved trail that leads past the ③ **pioneer house** and winds behind the Nature Center. Follow the trail. Keep to the right at all trail junctions. When you come to a ④ **wide wood-chip trail,** follow it into the woods. (It crosses a paved path, then leads back to the V-shaped fork, then back across a paved trail, and back to the main trail again.) At the ⑤ **next junction,** turn right. Follow the paved trail until you near the museum. At the ⑥ **junction,** turn right and follow the wide wood-chip trail around the perimeter of the park back to the Nature Center.

GIVING BACK: For information about volunteer and donation opportunities, contact the City of St. Cloud Parks and Recreation Department, City Hall, 400 Second Street South, St. Cloud, MN 56301 or the Stearns County Historical Society at 235 South 33rd Avenue, Box 702, St. Cloud, MN 56302-0702.

Charles A. Lindbergh State Park ___

Operated by the Minnesota Department of Natural Resources

"Walkers enjoy this park because the trails are heavily wooded, very scenic, and they follow Pike Creek. There's plenty of wildlife and flowers to see, and it's a great way to relax and enjoy the peace and quiet of the woods." —Ron Jones, Park Manager.

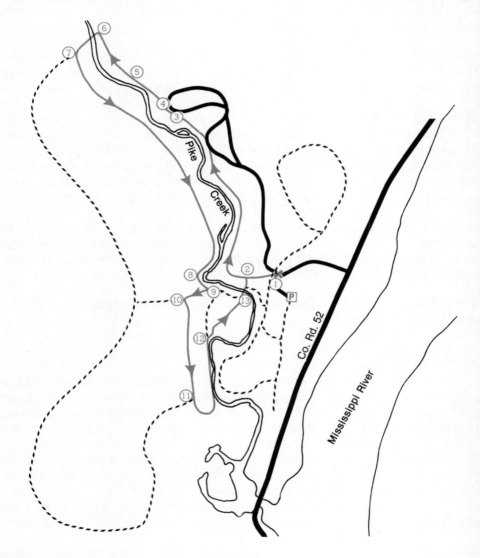

FACILITIES

✓**Restrooms** (accessible) are located in the Interpretive Center. Restrooms are also located at the picnic area and campgrounds.

✓**Water** is available at the campgrounds.

✓**Public telephones** are available.

104

DIRECTIONS: Charles A. Lindbergh State Park is located south of Little Falls. **From U.S. Highway 10:** Proceed west on State Highway 27, then south on County Road 52 (Lindbergh Drive). The entrance to the park is on the right. **Park** in the picnic area to the left of the park office.

INFORMATION: Call the park at 612/632-9050. The park is open year-round from 8 A.M. to 10 P.M. The Lindbergh Interpretive Center and Lindbergh family home (across the street) are open from 10 A.M. to 5 P.M. May 1 through Labor Day. Admission is $2 for adults, $1 for children. *Trail maps are available at the park office.* An annual motor vehicle permit or daily pass is required.

HIGHLIGHTS: • 6 miles of walking trails • Interpretive Center • Lindbergh House • Weyerhauser Museum.

TIPS FOR WALKERS: • You may want to bring binoculars. • Trail clothes are recommended.

RECOMMENDED ROUTE: 3.2 K (2 miles)
DIRT SURFACE. HILLY/STEPS. SHADED.
From the parking lot, proceed to the ①**trail** that begins near the junction of the paved roads. At the ②**first junction, turn right.** Proceed along the creek until you come to the ③ **campground.** Take the ④ **wooden steps** down and follow the narrow, dirt foot path along the shoreline. The wide trail continues at the ⑤**"you are here" map.** Take a ⑥**left over the bridge** and another ⑦**left at the junction.** You will cross a footbridge. Continue walking and you will come to a bench at a ⑧**scenic overlook.** At the ⑨**next junction, take a right,** then take a ⑩ **left,** then another ⑪ **left.** Stay on the main path, keeping to the left at every junction. You'll pass the first set of stone steps, but don't take them. Proceed to the ⑫ **overlook** and walk down the **second set of stone steps** (each step is different, so watch your footing). At the base of the steps, turn left. At the next junction, turn left. Proceed over the ⑬ **bridge,** turn left and then right and follow the path back to the parking lot.

GIVING BACK: Direct financial donations to Minnesota Parks and Trails Council, E-1311 First National Bank Building, St. Paul, MN 55101, or call 612/291-0715 or 800/289-1930.

Lake Carlos State Park

Operated by the Minnesota Department of Natural Resources

"Lake Carlos State Park is in a wonderland of lakes and hardwood forests that was developed by the WPA in 1936 and established as a state park in 1937."

—David Dirks, Assistant Park Manager.

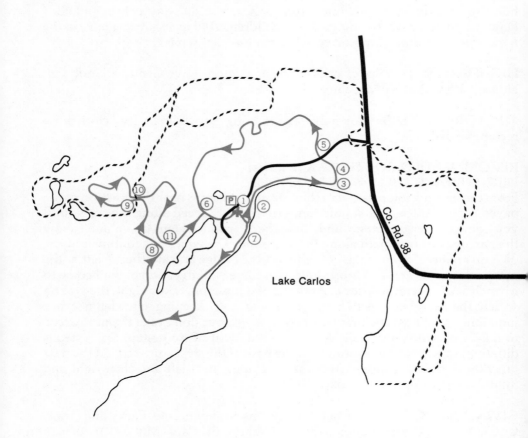

Lake Carlos

Co. Rd. 38

FACILITIES

- ✓ **Restrooms** (accessible) are available at the beach and campsite. Tip pan toilets are available at the picnic area.
- ✓ **Water** is available at the beach, campsite, and picnic area.
- ✓ **Public telephones** are available at the trailer dump station by the campsite.

105

DIRECTIONS: Lake Carlos is located in central Minnesota just north of Alexandria. **From State Highway 29:** From Alexandria, proceed north 10 miles. Follow the signs to the entrance to the park (County Road 38). **Park** in the lot near the beach and picnic area.

INFORMATION: Call the park at 612/852-7200. The park is open from 8 A.M. to 10 P.M. year-round. *A trail map and a* Maple-Basswood Nature Trail *booklet is available at the park office and the Interpretive Center.* During the summer a naturalist is available to provide evening programs for campers and hikers. An annual motor vehicle permit or a daily pass is required.

HIGHLIGHTS: • 13 miles of hiking trails • Interpretive Center and Trail • Swimming • Fishing • Boating (Lake Carlos connects with four other lakes) • Campgrounds.

TIPS FOR WALKERS: • Trail clothes are recommended. • You may want to bring a camera.

RECOMMENDED ROUTE: 8.5 K (5.3 miles)
DIRT/GRAVEL/SAND SURFACE. ROLLING HILLS. MOSTLY SHADED.
From the parking lot, take the ① **trail south** and proceed down to the ② **beach** and take a left on the trail along the shoreline, through a campground to the ③ **boat launch** where you will turn left on the road that leads to the ④ **Interpretive Center.** After visiting the Interpretive Center, continue along the road, crossing the main road, where the ⑤ **Maple-Basswood Trail begins,** using your booklet as a guide. At the ⑥ **next junction,** keep to the left and return to the picnic and beach area. Proceed to the lake and this time take the ⑦ **trail to the right.** Follow the trail along the lake; it becomes Hidden Lake Trail. You will walk through wooded areas and marshes. After making a half-circle around Hidden Lake you will be turning ⑧ **left onto Red Oak Trail,** which is hilly but provides you with an incredible view of the trees. At the next two intersections ⑨, ⑩, **proceed straight ahead.** You will eventually come back to Hidden Lake Trail where you will take a ⑪ **left.** At the junction with Maple-Basswood Trail, take a right and follow it back to your start point.

GIVING BACK: For information about volunteer and donation opportunities, call the park at 612/852-7200. Donations may also be directed to the Minnesota Parks and Trails Council, E-1311 First National Bank Building, St. Paul, MN 55101, or call 612/291-0715 or 800/289-1930.

Crow Wing State Park

Operated by the Minnesota Department of Natural Resources

"Our trails offer people a chance to learn about Minnesota history and forest and prairie eco-systems while they walk along the scenic Mississippi River." —Paul Roth, Park Manager.

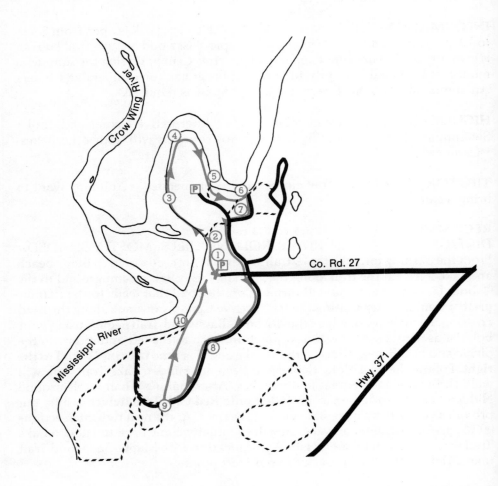

FACILITIES

✓ **Restrooms** (accessible) are available at the Information Center, picnic shelter, and the campgrounds.
✓ **Water** is available at the park office and campgrounds.
✓ **Public telephones** are available at the park office.

106

DIRECTIONS: Crow Wing State Park is located 9 miles south of Brainerd. **From U.S. Highway 371:** Proceed west on County Road 27 (the road leads directly to the park entrance). **Park** in the lot near the picnic area (straight ahead, past the office).

INFORMATION: Call the park at 218/829-8022. The park is open from 8 A.M. to 10 P.M. year-round. *A trail brochure is available in the office.* An annual motor vehicle permit or a daily pass is required.

HIGHLIGHTS: • 14 miles of walking trails • Picnic shelter • Campsites • Canoe and boat rentals • Information center.

TIPS FOR WALKERS: • Trail clothes are recommended. • You may want to bring a camera and binoculars.

RECOMMENDED ROUTE: 6.4 K (4 miles)
DIRT SURFACE. LEVEL (ONE SET OF STEPS). SHADED/UNSHADED.
From the parking lot, proceed to the picnic shelter and the ①**information kiosk** behind the shelter that provides a brief history of the park, the Red River Trade, and the Chippewa Indians. A paved trail begins down by the river. Turn right onto the trail. The paved trail turns into a dirt trail. The ② **Old Crow Wing Town Site** has a number of information posts. At the next two ③,④ **trail junctions** keep to the left. As you follow the trail along the Mississippi River, ⑤ **turn left at the Episcopal Cemetery sign.** At the next junction, turn right and you will come to a bench. Do not take the Historic Trail—keep to the right on the main trail. You will come to the ⑥ **Chippewa Lookout** and then take the stairs down to the boat launch area. Follow the ⑦ **paved road back to the park office.** Cross the entrance road and continue walking along the dirt road past a ⑧ **prairie.** At this point you may take the ⑨ **trail through the woods** with lots of wildflowers or continue along the road to the campground and the ⑩ **Indian Rifle pits.** As you walk along the Mississippi shoreline, look to your right for signs of the picnic area, and you will be back at your start point.

GIVING BACK: To volunteer, call the park office at 218/829-8022. Direct financial donations to Minnesota Parks and Trails Council, E-1311 First National Bank Building, St. Paul, MN 55101, or call 612/291-0715 or 800/ 289-1930.

Paul Bunyan Arboretum

A partnership of land owners managed by the Paul Bunyan Arboretum, Conservation and Nature Center

"Jack Pine Savanna Preserve is a 160-acre area comprised of sand dunes, wetlands, and fores. It is an island of sand dunes covered by tallgrass prairie and jackpines; jackpine and hardwood forest; and tamarack bog. Only a few acres of Jack Pine Savanna remain in the state of Minnnesota. It is a rare site."

—The Nature Conservancy

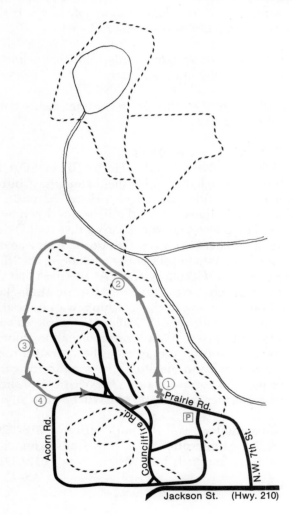

FACILITIES

- ✓ **Restrooms** (pit toilets) are available along Acorn Road.
- ✓ **Water** is available.
- ✓ **Public telephones** are not available.

107

DIRECTIONS: The Paul Bunyan Arboretum is located in Brainerd and Baxter. **Public transportation** is available through Brainerd Dial-a-ride at 218/ 829-7077. **From State Highway 371:** Proceed west on State Highway 210, north on Northwest Seventh Street. The Arboretum gate is at the end of the street. **Park** in the lot to the left.

INFORMATION: Call the Arboretum at 218/829-8770. The Arboretum is open during the summer from 8 A.M. to dusk and during the winter from 8 A.M. to 9 P.M. (to 10 P.M. on Fridays and Saturdays). *Trail maps are available.* Admission is $2 per person over 16 years of age during the summer season and $5 during cross-country ski season. Annual memberships are available.

HIGHLIGHTS: • 19 miles of hiking and cross-country ski trails • Fruit trees • Test gardens • Wildflower Garden • Deer, black bear, beaver • Wagon rides for group tours • Conservation demonstration areas • Clubhouse.

TIPS FOR WALKERS: • Trail clothes are recommended. • This beginning arboteum offers a pleasant walk through woods and wildlife. • The trails are marked.

RECOMMENDED ROUTE: 4.8 K (3 miles)
DIRT SURFACE. HILLY. SHADED/UNSHADED.
From the parking lot proceed across Prairie Road to the left to the beginning of the ① **Little Ben trail.** At the first junction, keep to the left. Continue until you reach a major junction and proceed on the ② **Potlatch Trail.** At the junction, follow the Acorn Trail to the right. After you cross the Ox Cart Trail, you will arrive at the ③ **Fitness Trail.** Keep to the right and walk half of the fitness loop. Follow the trail to Amphitheater Road and turn left. Continue along the road to ④ **Prairie Road** and return to your start point.

GIVING BACK: For information about volunteer and donation opportunities, call 218/829-8770, or write to Paul Bunyan Arboretum, Box 375, Brainerd, MN 56401.

Crow Wing State Forest/
Bass Lake Nature Trail

Operated by the Minnesota Department of Natural Resources

"The Bass Lake Nature Trail is a good example of ecological diversity because it shows the natural changes that result from fire, logging, and artificial regeneration (tree planting). The timber and lakeshore provide a variety of aesthetic pleasures." —Mark Mortensen, Forest Supervisor.

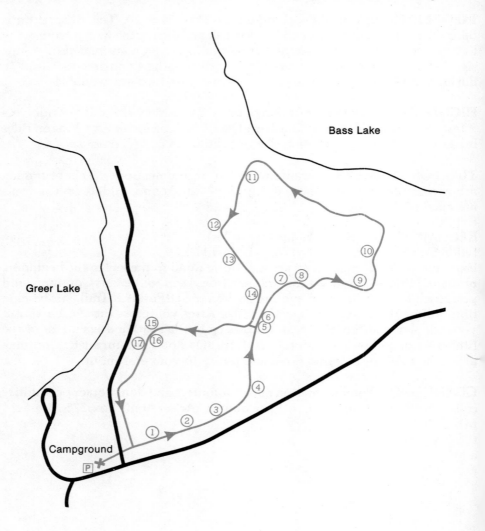

FACILITIES

✓**Restrooms** (pit toilets) are available at the campground.
✓**Water** is available at the campground.
✓**Public telephones** are not available.

108

DIRECTIONS: Crow Wing State Forest is located 20 miles northeast of Brainerd. **From State Highway 6 out of Crosby:** Proceed west on County Road 36. Follow the signs to Greer Lake Campgrounds (you will proceed south on County Road 114 to the entrance road). Follow the entrance road to the campgrounds. **Park** near the information sign.

INFORMATION: Call the Brainerd Area Forest Supervisor at 218/828-2565. The forest is open from 8 A.M. to 10 P.M. year-round. *Before you visit, obtain a self-guided trail map from the DNR.* There is no vehicle fee, but if you are going to camp, there is a $6 per night camping fee.

HIGHLIGHTS: • Self-guided interpretive trail • One-hundred-year-old Jack Pine tree. • Campground • Beach • Boat landing • Fishing.

TIPS FOR WALKERS: • Trail clothes are recommended. • You may want to bring binoculars. • This could be a camping/walking experience for families with young children because of the trail length and the valuable information along the trail (how to identify poison ivy, how to measure the age of a tree).

RECOMMENDED ROUTE: 2.8 K (1.75 miles)
DIRT SURFACE. LEVEL. SHADED.
From the parking area, proceed to the beginning of the nature trail to the right of the information sign. There is a short and a long loop to this trail. Highlights along the trail, also noted in the self-guided tour brochure provided by the DNR, are a ① **dead paper birch** (the tree died because the bark was peeled off); an example of ② **Eastern gall rust** (notice the black swellings—galls—on the trees), a disease that spreads between red oak and Jack pine; a ③ **Norway pine** (Minnesota state tree) grove, naturally seeded from the virgin Norway pine that originally inhabited the state; a④ **lightning-struck Norway pine,** a⑤ **Civilian Conservation Corps plantation** from 1936; an exhibit that shows the⑥ **age and growth of a tree** (count the rings); an enormous⑦ **Grandfather Jack pine** (Happy one hundred years in 1991!); a⑧ **pitch pine stump** (with a short lesson about the origin and properties of pitch); a⑨ **poison ivy plant** (a close-up look at the plant and its berries); a ⑩ **Norway pine plantation** (hand planted); the **Bass Lake rest stop** (with scenic views of the lake and a bit of history); a ⑪ **Norway pine plantation** (machine planted); a ⑫ **tamarack swamp** (a close-up look at this familiar bog tree); a ⑬ **plantation release area** (that shows how forest trees are thinned); an example of ⑭ **white pine blister** (a disease that kills White pine). **Note:** When you get to the road, don't cross it. Turn left to view a ⑮ **paper birch,** ⑯ **bur oak,** and ⑰ **scrub oak.**

GIVING BACK: For information about donation opportunities, contact the Brainerd Area Forest Supervisor, 1601 Minnesota Drive, Brainerd, MN 56401, or call 218/828-2565.

North Country National Scenic Trail

Operated by the National Park Service, U.S. Department of the Interior

"From the shores of Lake Champlin in New York, the route of the trail extends westward approximately 3,200 miles to the Missouri River in North Dakota where it meets the Lewis and Clark Trail that goes all the way to the west coast. The trail exists as much for the enjoyment of the afternoon casual walker as it does for the long-distance backpacker."

—Roderick MacRae, North Country Trail Association Coordinator, Minnesota segment.

FACILITIES

✓ **Restrooms** (accessible) are available in the towns of Walker, Longville, and Remer. Latrines are at designated campsites along the trail.

✓ **Water** is available in Walker, Longville, and Remer and at selected trailheads.

✓ **Public telephones** are available in Walker, Longville, and Remer.

109

DIRECTIONS: The recommended route of the North Country Trail is located in the Chippewa National Forest in northern Minnesota. **From State Highway 371:** Proceed north to Walker. Then proceed south on State Highway 34 to the Shingobee Recreation Area. **Park** in the lot.

INFORMATION: Call Roderick MacRae, North Country Trail Association Coordinator, at 612/377-0130, or write 1210 West 22nd Street, Minneapolis, MN 55405. *Trail maps are also available through the NCT Trail Manager, Chippewa National Forest, HCR 73, Box 15, Walker, MN 56484.* The trail is open throughout the year for hiking and skiing. There is no admission fee.

HIGHLIGHTS: • Of the 390 designated miles in Minnesota, 68 are completed in the Chippewa National Forest where you will see meadows, lakes, and ponds with an abundance of wildlife. • The trail runs through old logging sites and over old railroad grades and stands of two-hundred-year-old white pine.

TIPS FOR WALKERS: • Carry water and a compass. • Trail clothes are recommended. • There are seven campsites along the trail. • The NCT is well marked with a gold star on a blue triangle sign. However, the trail intersects with numerous small forest, ski trails, and some confusing intersections. • There is lodging in Hackensack and Walker. Motels and NCTA members may be able to provide shuttles for hikers. Call the NCT Association for further information.

GRASS/DIRT SURFACE. ROLLING HILLS. MOSTLY SHADED.
Note: The following text was provided by Roderick MacRae, Trail Coordinator:

RECOMMENDED ROUTE #1: (4—8 miles)

From the parking lot, walk .25 miles north to the start of the trail. Proceed **westbound** on the NCT for 2 miles to junction Country Road 12, or 4 miles to the western end of the trail. The route passes through mature hardwood forest, plantation pine forest, some open fields, Ten Lake (which is part of a chain of lakes), and some scattered virgin Norway Pines near the end of the trail. There is one moderate hill near Ten Lake. Return to your start point.

RECOMMENDED ROUTE #2: (4—14 miles)

From the parking lot, walk .25 miles north to the start of the trail. Proceed **eastward** for 2.5 miles to the junction with County Road 50 as it crosses the Shingobee River. Or continue another 5 miles to Lake Erin Trailhead on Highway 371. The route includes the famous Shingobee Vista that overlooks the Chippewa Forest. The route continues along the Shingobee River and then climbs a high ridge before leveling out into mixed forest and field. Return to your start point.

GIVING BACK: For volunteer and donation opportunities, contact the NCT Manager, Chippewa National Forest, HCR 73, Box 15, Walker, MN 56484.

Heartland State Trail

Operated by the Minnesota Department of Natural Resources

"The Heartland State Trail has been developed from a once-used railroad line that stretches 50 miles from Park Rapids, to Walker, to just south of Cass Lake. The trail passes through peaceful, picturesque farms, lakes, ponds, and woods."

—Dick Kimball, Area Trails and Waterways Supervisor.

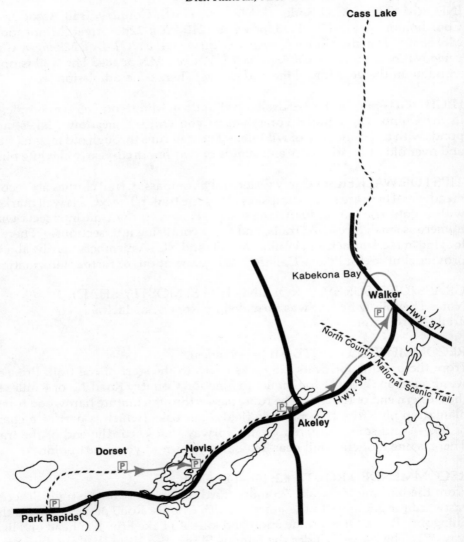

FACILITIES

- ✓ **Restrooms** (bulk toilets) are available in park and rest areas. There are accessible public restrooms in each town.
- ✓ **Water** is available in the towns along the trail.
- ✓ **Public telephones** are available in the towns along the trail.

110

DIRECTIONS: The Heartland Trail is along State Highway 34 between Park Rapids and Walker, and along State Highway 371 between Walker, Kabekona Bay, and Cass Lake. Trail access, parking, and rest areas are available in the following locations: Park Rapids, Dorset, Nevis, Akley, Walker, and Kabekona Bay.

INFORMATION: Call the DNR at 612/296-6699 or the Heartland Trail Headquarters at 218/652-4054 for a *Heartland State Trail* map and a *Heartland State Trail Area Services Guide* that includes the phone numbers of lodging, gas, food, and emergency service locations at each site. There is no admission charge for using the trail.

HIGHLIGHTS: • 28 miles of paved, accessible paths between Park Rapids and Walker • 23 miles of unpaved trails from Walker to Cass Lake • Eventually, the Paul Bunyan Trail out of Brainerd will join the Heartland Trail just south of Walker.

TIPS FOR WALKERS: • Trail clothes are recommended. • This is an ideal trail to walk in segments. Call ahead for reservations if you plan on walking from lodge to lodge. Talk with lodge owners to see if they would be willing to transport your luggage as you walk from point to point. You may want to keep your car at your point of departure until you return. • Carry water. • The trail is shared with bikers and horseback riders between Park Rapids and Walker. • The Heartland Trail also intersects with the North Country Trail south and west of Walker.

RECOMMENDED ROUTES:
PAVED/DIRT SURFACE. LEVEL. MOSTLY UNSHADED.
If you want to sample a portion of the trail, then you may want to try the following segments and walk from lodge to lodge:

• **Dorset to Nevis (5 miles one way, 10 miles round trip)**
• **Akeley to Walker (8.5 miles one way, 17 miles round trip)**
  These portions of the trail will take you through farms, pastures, lakes, ponds, marshes, and plenty of wooded areas.
• **Walker to Kabekona Bay (3 miles one way, 6 miles round trip)**
  The Walker to Kabekona Bay segment is the "Walker Bypass," an off-rail grade trail that goes through heavily wooded areas of glacial moraine. At Highway 371 the trail connects with a trail back to Walker that is partially on and partially off the rail grade. This trail is shared with mountain bikers, so use caution.

GIVING BACK: Direct financial donations to Minnesota Parks and Trails Council, E-1311 First National Bank Building, St. Paul, MN 55101, or call 612/291-0715 or 800/289-1930.

Maplewood State Park

Operated by the Minnesota Department of Natural Resources

"Maplewood State Park is a rolling glacial moraine of hills, lakes, prairie, and hardwood forest. It is set in the transitional area between the eastern forest and western prairie."

—Robert Hanson, Park Manager.

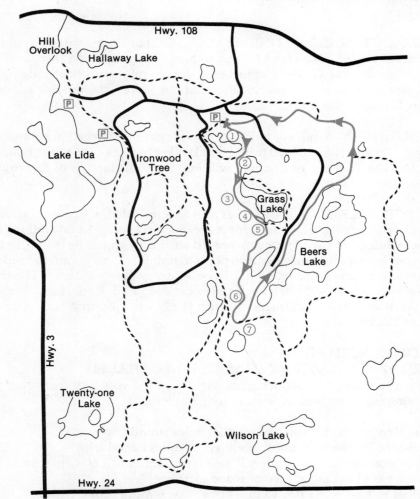

FACILITIES

✓ **Restrooms** (vault toilets) are available at the Trail Center, picnic area, camping areas. Accessible restrooms are available year-round at the Information Center and during the summer at the vehicle campgrounds, picnic area, and beach area.

✓ **Water** is available year-round at the Information Center and during the summer at the campgrounds.

✓ **Public telephones** are available at the vehicle campgrounds and Information Center.

111

DIRECTIONS: Maplewood State Park is located near Pelican Rapids. **From Pelican Rapids:** Proceed east for 7 miles on Trunk Highway 108. The entrance will be on the south (right) side of the road. **Park** in the main lot beyond the park office.

INFORMATION: Call the park at 218/863-8383. The park is open daily from 8 A.M. to 10 P.M. The Information Center opens at 8 A.M. and closes at 4:30 P.M. in the winter and at 10 P.M. during the summer. *A trail map is available at the Information Center. Also, pick up a* Grass Lake Interpretive Trail *pamphlet.* An annual motor vehicle permit or a daily pass is required.

HIGHLIGHTS: • 25 miles of walking trails along woods and prairie • Two self-guided interpretive trails • Largest Ironwood tree in the state • Beach area • Picnic area • Horseback riding trails • Boating • Canoe campgrounds • Backpacking campgrounds • Vehicle camping sites • Abundant wildlife.

TIPS FOR WALKERS: • Trail clothes are recommended. • You may want to drive to Hill Overlook and the Largest Ironwood tree, park in the lot or along the entrance road, and then walk to each site.

RECOMMENDED ROUTE: 10 K (6.2 miles)
GRASS/DIRT SURFACE. ROLLING HILLS. SHADED/UNSHADED.
From the ① **parking lot,** walk south to the trail that descends into a wooded area. You will walk along the shoreline of Cataract Lake. About a quarter of the way around the lake you will take the② **trail to the left to Grass Lake.** At the next junction, take a③ **right onto the Grass Lake Interpretive Trail** and use the pamphlet to guide you from station to station. You will walk through a ④ **camping area.** Stay to the right. As you leave the camping area, take the ⑤ **trail to the right heading south.** When you eventually come to a wide multi-use trail, ⑥ **veer left.** At the⑦ **next junction,** veer left again. Follow this trail for the next 3 miles through wooded, prairie, and lake areas back to the parking lot.

GIVING BACK: Volunteers are needed to help maintain the park. Financial donations are needed to complete projects in progress. For information about volunteer and donation opportunities, call the park office at 218/863-8383. Donations may also be directed to the Minnesota Parks and Trails Council, E-1311 First National Bank Building, St. Paul, MN 55101, or call 612/291-0715 or 800/289-1930.

Buffalo River State Park

Operated by the Minnesota Department of Natural Resources

"Buffalo River State Park is made up of natural prairies that allow you to enjoy a clean, fresh-smelling sensation, an assortment of beautifully colored wildflowers, and an inland sea of prairie grasses that look like waves when the wind is blowing." —Bernie Dohlmann, Park Manager.

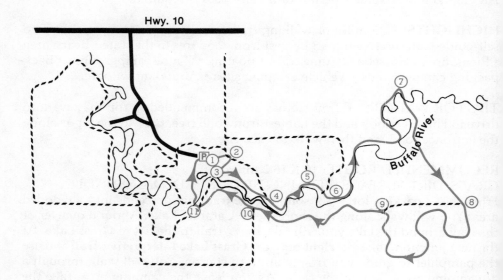

✓**Restrooms** (pit toilets) are located at the campgrounds and the picnic area. Accessible restrooms are available at the picnic area during the summer.
✓**Water** is available during the summer at the picnic area and campground.
✓**Public telephones** are located at the registration station.

112

DIRECTIONS: Buffalo River State Park is located 12 miles east of Moorhead. **From Moorhead:** Proceed east on U.S. Highway 10. Turn south (right) into the park and proceed .5 mile to the registration station. Proceed along the entrance road for another mile. **Park** in the lot near the picnic area.

INFORMATION: Call the park at 218/498-2124. The park is open from 8 A.M. to 10 P.M. year round. *A trail map is available at the registration station or Interpretive Center. Also pick up a* Savanna Cutoff Interpretive Trail *pamphlet.* An annual motor vehicle permit or a daily pass is required.

HIGHLIGHTS: • 12 miles of walking trails • Buffalo River winds through the park • Beach • Picnic area • Campgrounds • Interpretive Center • Self-guided interpretive trail.

TIPS FOR WALKERS: • Trail clothes are recommended. • "You are here" maps and trail name signs are at some trail junctions.

RECOMMENDED ROUTE: 7.2 K (4.5 miles)
DIRT/GRASS SURFACE. LEVEL. MOSTLY UNSHADED.
From the parking lot proceed to the ① **trail to the east.** At the ② **next two trail junctions, turn right.** Turn left onto the ③ **Savanna Cutoff Interpretive Trail** and use the pamphlet to guide you from station to station. At the next two trail junctions ④,⑤, **turn right.** The trail winds along the river. Eventually you will ⑥ **turn right onto the River View Trail.** You may want to stop and enjoy the river along the way. You will eventually cross a ⑦ **bridge that leads to the Prairie View Trail.** At the ⑧ **next junction, keep to the left** and you will walk beside prairie wildflowers and very tall prairie grasses. At the next trail junction, ⑨ **keep to the left** and at the next junction, ⑩ **keep to the right.** Continue walking along the trail until you come to a ⑪ **bridge.** Cross the river and, at the next trail junction, take a right back to the parking lot.

GIVING BACK: Volunteers are needed to help maintain the park. Financial donations are needed to complete projects in progress. For information about volunteer and donation opportunities, call 218/498-2124. Donations may also be directed to the Minnesota Parks and Trails Council, E-1311 First National Bank Building, St. Paul, MN 55101, or call 612/291-0715 or 800/289-1930.

Old Mill State Park

Operated by the Minnesota Department of Natural Resources

"Welcome to an oasis of hardwoods and prairie grass in the northwest farmland country of Minnesota where we have an autumn tradition of catching twelve falling leaves before they hit the ground for good luck during the next year. Come join us in this beautiful tradition at our state park, or any of the other state parks." —Chris Weir-Koetter, Assistant Park Manager.

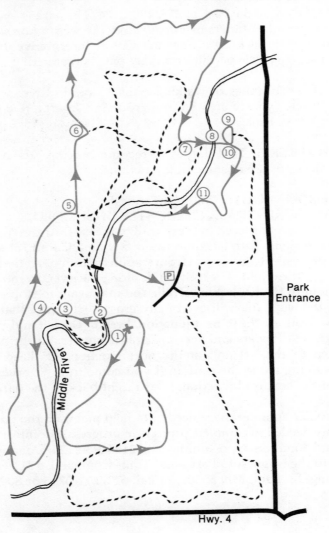

Park Entrance

Middle River

Hwy. 4

113

DIRECTIONS: Old Mill State Park is located in northwestern Minnesota. **From U.S. Highway 59:** Proceed west from Newfolden on Highway 4. Follow the signs to the entrance road, and proceed straight ahead. **Park** near the beach and picnic area.

INFORMATION: Call the park at 218/437-8174. The park is open from 8 A.M. to 10 P.M. year-round. *A trail map is available at the park office. Also, pick up a self-guided tour brochure.* An annual motor vehicle permit or a daily pass is required.

HIGHLIGHTS: • 7 miles of hiking trails • WPA stone buildings and a swinging bridge across the river • Lars Larson's old grist mill that was powered first by water, then by a steam engine • Beach and picnic area • Larson brought seeds from Sweden and planted Scotch pines that are now over one hundred years old.

TIPS FOR WALKERS: • Trail clothes are recommended. • As you walk you will probably encounter an abundance of wildlife including moose, deer, and beaver along the river and in wooded areas. • You may want to bring binoculars because the park is along the migration route of many bird species.

RECOMMENDED ROUTE: 4.8 K (3 miles)
GRASS SURFACE. LEVEL. MOSTLY SHADED.
From the parking lot, walk to the south end of the lot where you will find the ① **beginning of the Agassiz Self-guided Trail.** Follow the trail with the help of the self-guided brochure, as you complete the loop and return to the parking lot. Stay to the left and ② **proceed down the hill to the swinging bridge** on the left side of the swimming pond. Cross the river and proceed straight ahead. At the ③ **trail junction, keep to the right.** At the ④ **next trail junction, turn left.** Follow the trail along the river and through the wooded areas. Be on the lookout for wildlife on this portion of the trail. At the next two **trail junctions** ⑤,⑥**, keep to the left.** Watch for wildlife when you get near the river. You will come to a ⑦ **campsite** where you will take another left and cross ⑧ **a road bridge.** After crossing the bridge, take an immediate left and visit ⑨ **Lars Larson's grain mill and home.** Return back to the main trail by crossing the main entrance road in front of the home. The trail resumes on the other side of the road, near the road bridge. Turn ⑩ **left onto the trail** as it follows the road for a while. You will eventually come upon a ⑪ **mound** that overlooks the river and park. Continue on the trail along the river back to the picnic area. Cross through the picnic area back to your start point.

GIVING BACK: For information about volunteer and donation opportunities, call the park at 218/437-8174. Donations may also be directed to the Minnesota Parks and Trails Council, E-1311 First National Bank Building, St. Paul, MN 55101, or call 612/291-0715 or 800/289-1930.

Itasca State Park

Operated by the Minnesota Department of Natural Resources

"Itasca State Park was established in 1891 and has a well-developed hiking trail system of over 30 miles. From the Prehistoric Schoolcraft Trail to the newly developed Crossover Trails, all parts of the 32,000-acre park are accessible by the hiking trail system. All major trails were developed during the depression era Civilian Conservation Corps program and many of these trails have rustic backpacking sites. Comments regarding our hiking trail system are encouraged."

—Ben Thoma, Naturalist.

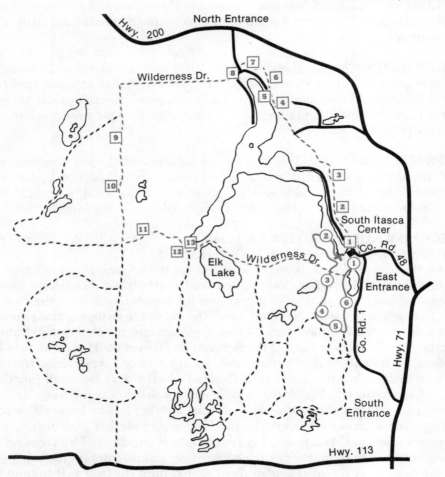

FACILITIES

- ✓**Restrooms** (accessible) are available at the campgrounds, Douglas Lodge, Brower Inn, and both Interpretive Centers.
- ✓**Water** is available at the same locations as the restrooms, and along the bike trail between the headwaters and the beach.
- ✓**Public telephones** are available at the campgrounds, outside of Douglas Lodge, and at park headquarters.

114

DIRECTIONS: Itasca State Park is located north of Park Rapids. **From Park Rapids:** Proceed north on U.S. Highway 71 to the south entrance, and proceed 3 miles north on the entrance road to the South Itasca Center. **Park** in the South Itasca Center Lot.

INFORMATION: Call the park at 218/266-3654. The park is open from 8 A.M. to 10 P.M. During the winter, the Forest Inn is the only major facility that remains open. *A trail map is available at the Forest Inn.* From Memorial Weekend through the first week in October, you may pick up *Dr. Robert's Interpretive Trail* booklet at Douglas Lodge. An annual motor vehicle permit or a daily pass is required.

HIGHLIGHTS: • Mississippi headwaters • Oldest state park in Minnesota • Historic buildings • Beach • Boat area • Picnic areas • Amphitheater • Lodges, cabins • Food service • Interpretive Center • Bicycle rental.

TIPS FOR WALKERS: • There is so much to do that you may want to plan on spending at least two days. • The first recommended route is by car, with short walking jaunts to points of interest. The second route is a walking trail.

CAR ROUTE: Proceed to ⬜ **Forest Inn,** the Interpretive Center. Take County Road 48 north along Itasca Lake and stop at the following sites: ② **Preacher's Grove,** ③ **Peacepipe Vista, Pioneer Cemetery,** ④ **Brower Inn and Natural History Museum,** ⑤ **Wildlife Museum,** ⑥ **Wegmann Cabin,** ⑦ **Indian mounds,** ⑧ **Interpretive Center** and **headwaters of the Mississippi.** Continue on Wilderness Drive and visit the ⑨ **Wilderness Area Orientation** (with a 1-mile trail), the ⑩ **Forestry Demonstration Area,** the state's ⑪ **largest white pine,** the state's ⑫ **largest red pine,** the ⑬ **Bison Kill Site** (they don't kill Bison there), on to the Observation Tower and back to South Itasca Center.

RECOMMENDED WALKING ROUTE: 9.6 K (6 miles)
GRASS/DIRT SURFACE. ROLLING HILLS. MOSTLY SHADED.
From ① **Douglas Lodge,** proceed to ② **Dr. Robert's Trail** at the bottom of the hill by Itasca Lake. Use the booklet to guide you from station to station. Return to the south side of Douglas Lodge and follow the sign to the ③ **Deer Park Trail.** At the trail junction, turn left to the ④ **Red Pine Trail** and left again to the ⑤ **Crossover Trail.** Continue until you reach the ⑥ **Ozawindib Trail.** Take the trail north (left) back to South Itasca Center.

GIVING BACK: For information about volunteer and donation opportunities, call 218/266-3654. Donations may also be directed to the Minnesota Parks and Trails Council, E-1311 First National Bank Building, St. Paul, MN 55101, or call 612/291-0715 or 800/289-1930.

Lake Bemidji State Park

Operated by the Department of Natural Resources

"Lake Bemidji has numerous walking trails along with our famous 440-foot boardwalk that extends into a Spruce Tamarack bog. Among the flowers you'll find are the state flower, the Showy Ladyslipper that blooms in abundance in late June, Sundew, and pitcher plants. The park has over two hundred species of birds, and a portion of our old logging trail is a favorite of bird watchers'. We give guided tours on a regular basis and would love to show you around and answer any questions you may have." —Paul Mork, Manager, and John Fylpaa, Naturalist.

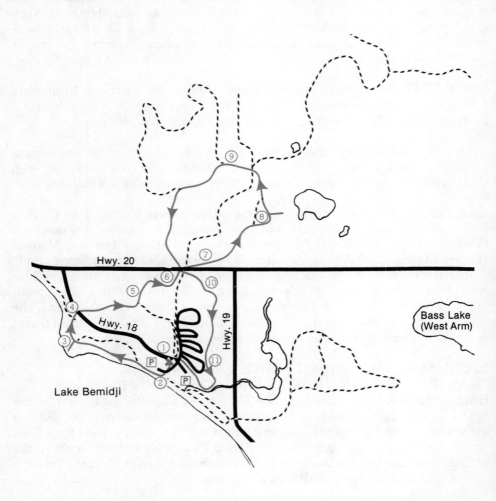

115

DIRECTIONS: Lake Bemidji is located just north of Bemidji. **From Bemidji:** Proceed north on State Highway 21 for 5 miles. Turn east on Highway 20. Watch for the entrance on the south (right) side of the road just past the golf course on Highway 18. Proceed on the entrance road for .75 mile to the park office/Vistor Center. **Park** in the lot near the picnic area.

INFORMATION: Call the park at 218/755-3843. The park is open from 8 A.M. to 10 P.M. The Visitor Center is open during the same hours as the park in the summer, but closes at 4:30 P.M. in the winter. *A trail map is available at the Visitor Center.* An annual motor vehicle permit or a daily permit is required.

HIGHLIGHTS: • 14 miles of walking trails • 1.5 miles of paved accessible trail (Rocky Point) • Self-guided interpretive trails • Visitor Center • Picnic area • Campground • Beach • Boat ramp • Fifty species of mammals, two hundred species of birds.

TIPS FOR WALKERS: • Trail clothes are recommended. • Some of the trails are shared with mountain bikers.

RECOMMENDED ROUTE: 8.3 K (5.2 miles)
PAVED/GRASS/BOARDWALK SURFACE. LEVEL. SHADED/UNSHADED.
From the picnic area, proceed to the ① **Visitor Center** and enjoy a twelve-minute movie on park vegetation and wildlife. Proceed south from the center to the lakefront. At the lake, ② **take a right to Rocky Point Trail.** Follow the trail along the beach, and eventually it turns into an interpretive trail with a ③ **scenic overlook of Lake Bemidji.** Stay to your right and you will come to the ④ **Homestead Trail.** Watch for ant mounds along the trail. Stay to the left and you will come to the ⑤ **Balsam Trail** and then turn left onto the ⑥ **Pinewood Trail** before crossing Highway 20. After crossing the highway, stay to your right and follow the ⑦ **Bog Trail,** which will lead you to the famous ⑧ **Bog Boardwalk,** a self-guided interpretive trail that will introduce you to bog wildlife and vegetation. Return to the Bog Trail, turn right, and you will come to the ⑨ **Old Logging Trail.** Stay to the left along Pinewood Trail. Turn right, cross Highway 20, and then ⑩ **turn left onto the Balsam Trail.** Stay to the left all the way back to the ⑪ **Bass Creek Trail,** an interpretive trail with a scenic overlook. Follow the trail back to the campgrounds and then back to the Visitor Center.

GIVING BACK: For information about volunteer opportunities, call 218/755-3843. Direct financial donations to the Minnesota Parks and Trails Council, E-1311 First National Bank Building, St. Paul, MN 55101, or call 612/291-0715 or 800/289-1930.

Taconite and Arrowhead State Trails

Operated by the Minnesota Department of Natural Resources

"The two trails have a combined length of over 300 miles through national forests, state forests, and state parks, with an abundance of isolated lakes and streams."
—Ron Potter, Manager of the Taconite Trail and the Arrowhead Trail.

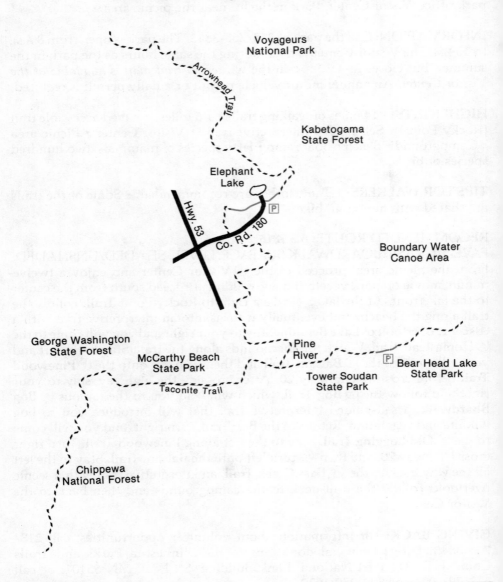

FACILITIES

✓ **Restrooms** (accessible) are available in the towns along the trails.
✓ **Water** is available in the towns along the trails.
✓ **Public telephones** are available in the towns along the trails.

116

DIRECTIONS: The Taconite Trail and the Arrowhead Trail are located in northern Minnesota. State Highway 169 is the main highway along the Taconite Trail from Grand Rapids through Hibbing, Chisholm, Virginia, Tower, and Ely. U.S. Highway 53 is the main highway along the Arrowhead Trail from Cook to International Falls. **Directions to the Taconite Trail (Bear Head Lake State Park):** From State Highway 169 proceed south on County Road 128 for 4 miles to Bear Head Lake State Park. **Park** near the information office. **Directions to the Arrowhead Trail (Elephant Lake):** From U.S. Highway 53 proceed north to Cusson, east on County Road 180, past the first access point to the Arrowhead Trail. **Park** off the road on the left side near the second access point.

INFORMATION: Call the trail manager at 218/753-6256. The trail is open year-round. *A trail map is available through the Department of Natural Resources at 800/652-9747.* There is no admission fee.

HIGHLIGHTS: • Wilderness walking • Campsites • Scenic vistas • Jack and Red pine forest • Rustic wayside rests and picnic facilities.

TIPS FOR WALKERS: • Trail clothes are recommended. • Carry food and water. • Hike with other people because these trails are in a very remote, unpopulated area of the state. Let someone else know about your itinerary. • Bring warm clothes in the spring and fall.

BOTH RECOMMENDED TRAILS: DIRT SURFACE. HILLY. SHADED.

RECOMMENDED ROUTE #1: Taconite Trail: 9.6 K (6 miles)
From the parking lot, follow the trail north past Cub Lake, then turn left at the first junction. Continue on the trail until you reach the Taconite Trail. At this point you have two options. Turn left onto the trail and walk 3 miles west to the Camp Shelter on beautiful Star Lake, rest, then return to your start point. Or, for a longer route (12 miles), turn right onto the trail and walk 6 miles to the camp shelter on Purvis Lake, rest, and return back to your start point.

RECOMMENDED ROUTE #2: Arrowhead Trail: 9.6 K (6 miles)
From the road, proceed to the trail. You have two options. You may turn right and walk 3 miles to the first shelter which is also a scenic overlook, rest, and return to your start point. Or, you may turn left and walk 5 miles along the trail to the first shelter, passing a lookout tower and scenic overlook on the way. Rest, and return to your start point.

GIVING BACK: For information about volunteer opportunities, contact the Ranger Station at 1201 East Highway 2, Grand Rapids, MN 55744, or call 218/753-6256. Direct financial donations to the Minnesota Parks and Trails Council, E-1311 First National Bank Building, St. Paul, MN 55101, or call 612/291-0715 or 800/289-1930.

Superior National Forest/
Caribou Rock/Split Pine Trail

Operated by the U.S. Forest Service, U.S. Department of Agriculture

"Welcome to the picturesque walkways of the Boundary Waters in the Superior National Forest! The trails are heavily wooded, and multiple waterways provide solitude and an abundance of wildlife on both the land and lakes." —Becky Spears, Ranger.

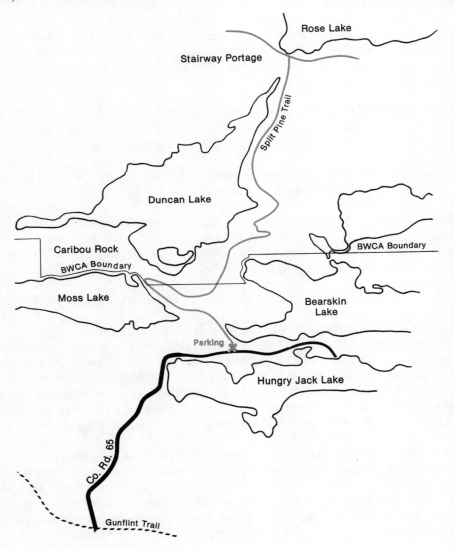

FACILITIES

✓**Restrooms** (accessible) are available in Grand Marais.
✓**Water** is available in Grand Marais.
✓**Public telephones** are available in Grand Marais.

117

DIRECTIONS: The Caribou Rock/Split Pine Trail is located approximately 28 miles north of Grand Marais. **From the Gunflint Ranger Station in Grand Marais:** Proceed north on the Gunflint Trail (County Highway 12). Turn right onto County Road 65 and continue about 2 miles to the sign for the Caribou Rock Trail. **Park** in the space provided near the "Caribou Rock Trail" sign.

INFORMATION: Call the Ranger Station at 218/387-1750. *A trail map is available at the Ranger Station. A "Hiking Trails" brochure is also available for the Eastern Superior National Forest, Cook County, MN.* There is no admission fee for the trail. If you will be camping overnight, you will need a free Boundary Waters Canoe Area (BWCA) permit. Also, since the trail is in the BWCA, be sure to obtain a brochure from the DNR that describes the wilderness rules and regulations that apply.

HIGHLIGHTS: • Caribou Rock provides a scenic overlook of the lakes in the Boundary Waters • Split Pine Trail is heavily wooded, with numerous lakes and the Stairway Portage Waterfalls.

TIPS FOR WALKERS: • This is a five- or six-hour hike. • Trail clothes are recommended. • Carry water and food and check trail conditions. • You may want to carry a walking stick.

RECOMMENDED ROUTE: 6.4 K (4 miles)
ROCK/DIRT SURFACE. STEEP. SHADED.
Note: The following text has been furnished by the U.S. Department of Agriculture Forest Service: Those interested in a short, steep walk on a firmly-packed trail may hike to Caribou Rock overlook and then turn back, for a total distance of less than .5 mile. Those prepared for a strenuous day hike can hike the Split Pine Trail, a steep, demanding, 3.5-mile trail that begins at Caribou Rock and ends when it adjoins the Border Route Trail near Rose Lake. Plan at least five hours for the hike to Rose Lake and back to County Road 65; allow extra time for rests, lunch, and relaxation.

The walk from County Road 65 to Caribou Rock overlook follows a short, gradual upgrade. The rock, which is about 150 feet above the water, provides a wonderful vantage point from which to scan Bearskin Lake and the surrounding area. From Caribou Rock, Split Pine Trail leads toward Rose Lake, popping out of the Forest periodically for views of Moss, Duncan, and Daniels lakes along the route. The intersection of the Split Pine and Border Route Trails is near "Stairway Portage" between Duncan and Rose Lake. The portage area sports a beautiful waterfall and makes a nice lunch spot before the return hike.

GIVING BACK: For information about volunteer and donation opportunities, contact the Superior National Forest Gunflint Ranger District, Grand Marais, MN 55604, or call 218/387-1750.

Superior Hiking Trail

Operated by the Superior Hiking Trail Association

"This trail is so soft in some parts that it feels like you're walking on a couch of pine needles. From the trail you can see spectacular views of valleys, rivers, inland lakes, rocky ridges, and Lake Superior and its bays. It's an experience that gives a glimpse of the past and lets you come as close to nature as you can."

—Bill Anderson, Board Member, Superior Hiking Trail.

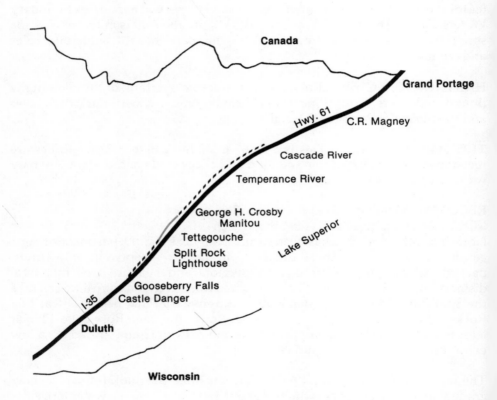

FACILITIES

✓ **Restrooms** are available at state parks, towns, and lodges along the trail. Portable units are available at some trailheads. Back woods latrines are available at campsites.

✓ **Water** is available at state parks, towns, and lodges along the trail. Water from streams or rivers must be boiled, filtered, or treated.

✓ **Public telephones** are available at state parks, towns, and lodges along the trail.

118

DIRECTIONS: The Superior Hiking Trail runs parallel to Highway 61 along Lake Superior between the towns of Castle Danger (3 miles south of Gooseberry State Park) on the south to Judge C. R. Magney State Park on the north. (Segments of this trail are still being completed). The Superior Hiking Trail currently connects with 6 state parks and numerous county roads that join Highway 61. Both of the recommended walking routes begin from Tettegouche State Park.

INFORMATION: Call the Superior Hiking Trail Association at 218/834-4436 or write to Box 4, Two Harbors, MN 55616. *Trails maps are available through the Superior Hiking Trail Association.* For the recommended routes, request two maps: *Gooseberry Falls to Tettegouche* and *Tettegouche to Lutsen Ski Hill.* There is no admission fee if you enter the trail from county roads. If you enter the trail from a state park, an annual motor vehicle permit or a daily pass is required. *A Lodge-to-Lodge Packages brochure is available through the Lutsen-Tofte Tourism Association at P.O. Box 2248, Tofte, MN 55612, or call 218/663-7804.*

HIGHLIGHTS: • 130 miles of wilderness trail (Eventually, the trail will cover 250 miles from Jay Cooke State Park just south of Duluth to Grand Portage on the Canadian border) • Spectacular views of Lake Superior • Campgrounds.

TIPS FOR WALKERS: • Trail clothes are recommended. • The trail is basically broken up into 12-mile segments. There is lodge-to-lodge hiking with shuttle service available (call the Lutsen-Tofte Tourism Association). • Plan on walking no more than 2 miles per hour. • Carry a map, compass, and plenty of water. Protect yourself against mosquitoes and black flies. • Be prepared for sudden weather changes off of Lake Superior (temperature shifts and storms).

DIRT/ROCK/PINE NEEDLE SURFACE. RUGGED HILLS. SHADED.

ROUTE #1 (Tettegouche to Wolf Lake): 16 K (10 miles). From the parking lot near the Information Office in Tettegouche State Park, proceed northeast along the north side of the Baptism River on the spur trail to the Superior Hiking Trail (SHT). The trail will join the SHT, veer off from the river, and proceed north. You will pass State Highway 1 on your way to Wolf Lake campsite. Proceed back to your start point.

ROUTE #2: (Tettegouch to Bear Lake) 19.2 K (12 miles). From the parking lot near the campgrounds in Tettegouche State Park, proceed north on the spur trail to the Superior Hiking Trail, west on the SHT and then south, passing Mount Trudee and Round Mountain bluffs until you reach the campsite area at Bear Lake. Proceed back to the start point.

GIVING BACK: For membership, volunteer, and donation opportunities, contact the Superior Hiking Association, Box 4, Two Harbors, MN 55616, or call 218/834-4436.

Tettegouche State Park

Operated by the Minnesota Department of Natural Resources

"This 'Jewel of the North' has breathtaking sights of Lake Superior, northland forests, and inland lakes from mountain and cliff peaks. There is a feeling of going back in time as you hike through a wonderment of color along Tettegouche's trails."

—Jim Bischoff, Buildings and Grounds Worker.

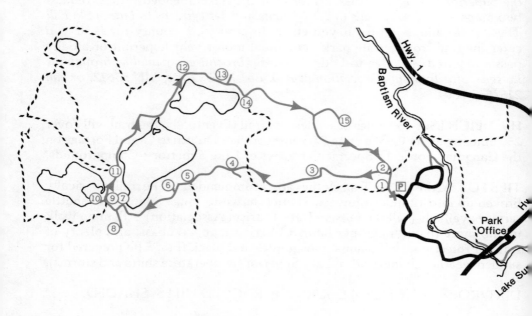

FACILITIES

✓ **Restrooms** (accessible) are available at the Information Office and HDA campsites. Pit toilets are available at the parking areas and Tettegouche Camp.
✓ **Water** is available at the Information Office, picnic areas, and HDA campsites.
✓ **Public telephones** are available at the Information Office.

119

DIRECTIONS: Tettegouche State Park is located north of Silver Bay along Lake Superior. **From U.S. Highway 61:** Proceed 4.5 miles northeast of Silver Bay. The entrance to the park is shared with the Baptism River Rest Area. **Park** near the Information Office (to the right as you enter the park).

INFORMATION: Call the park at 218/226-3539. The park is open seven days a week from 8 A.M. to 10 P.M. Office hours vary. *A trail map is available at the Information Office.* An annual motor vehicle permit or a daily pass is required.

HIGHLIGHTS: • 17 miles of hiking trails • Picnic areas • Self-guided interpretive trail • Fishing • Waterfalls • Camping • Superior Hiking Trail • Lakes.

TIPS FOR WALKERS: • Trail clothes are recommended. • Bring a compass. • Some trails are closed to walkers in the winter. Alternate routes include: Shovel Point's Self-guided Interpretive Trail (1.5 miles) with views of Lake Superior, and the High Falls Trail (1 mile) to see one of the highest waterfalls in Minnesota.

RECOMMENDED ROUTE: 8 K (5 miles)
GRASS/DIRT SURFACE. VERY STEEP HILLS. SHADED.
From the Information Office, walk along the road going under Highway 61 and stay to your right until you come to a parking area. Just north of the parking area there will be a wide trail going northwest. At the ①**first junction, turn right.** At the next junction, turn left onto the ② **Superior Hiking Trail.** This trail is narrow and steep and you will be stepping over rocks in some locations. Continue along the trail and you will come to **mountain peaks** ③,④ that provide incredible views of forest areas, inland lakes, and Lake Superior. At the ⑤ **next junction the Superior Hiking Trail turns south,** but you will continue straight ahead on the main trail. Take the ⑥**trail to see the Conservancy Pines.** Continue along the trail, and ⑦**keep left at the next junction.** Turn ⑧**left at the next junction to see the Palisade Valley lookout.** Return to the trail and at the next junction ⑨**turn right;** then take a ⑩ **left to see Floating Bog Bay.** Return to the trail and proceed north to ⑪ **Tettegouche Camp,** a picturesque old lodge on Mic Mac Lake. You have to hike to it—there are no roads. Stay on the north trail going away from the lodge. At the ⑫ **next junction, stay to the right.** Continue to the ⑬ **Papasay Ridge overlook.** At the ⑭ **next junction, keep to the left.** You will come to the ⑮ **Lake Superior overlook** and then follow the trail back to the start point.

GIVING BACK: Direct financial donations to the Minnesota Parks and Trails Council, E-1311 First National Bank Building, St. Paul, MN 55101, or call 612/291-0715 or 800/289-1930.

Split Rock Lighthouse State Park

Operated by the Minnesota Department of Natural Resources

"Enjoy the walking trail along the shoreline where you have a panoramic view of Lake Superior—its cliffs, pebble stone beaches, and the historic Split Rock Lighthouse that used to protect ships from coming into contact with the North Shore." —Mark Kovacovich, Park Manager.

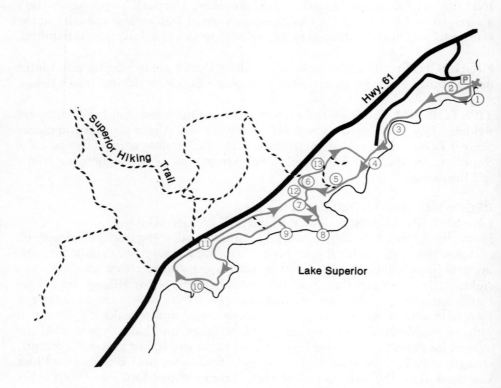

DIRECTIONS: Split Rock Lighthouse State [...] bors. **From U.S. Highway 61:** Proceed 20 mil[...] the park on the east side of the highway and fo[...] Follow the entrance road to the left. **Park in th[...]**

INFORMATION: Call the park at 218/226-3065 [...] Society at 218/226-4372. The park is open from [...] *A trail map is available at the park office.* An annua[...] daily pass is required.

HIGHLIGHTS: • 12 miles of hiking trails • Histori[...] [...]ck Lighthouse • Superior Hiking Trail • Picnic area • Fishing.

TIPS FOR WALKERS: • Trail clothes are recommended. • You may want to bring a camera and walking stick.

RECOMMENDED ROUTE: 4.8 K (3 miles)
GRAVEL/DIRT SURFACE. ROLLING HILLS. MOSTLY SHADED.
From the parking lot, proceed east toward the lake and ① **Split Rock Lighthouse** and staff quarters, built in 1909. Turn south and follow the ② **Two Harbors Trail** along Lake Superior. The trail will take you down from the cliff to the ③ **shoreline.** At the trail junction, turn left onto the ④ **Day Hill Trail;** at the next three trail junctions ⑤,⑥,⑦, **keep to the left** as you begin walking on the Corundum Mine Trail. There are **two overlooks** ⑧,⑨ along the trail that provide views of the jagged, rocky cliffs of the north shore. As you come around ⑩ **Split Rock Point,** the Corundum Mine Trail eventually turns into an ⑪ **old road.** Keep to your right on the old road trail. Follow the road back to the ⑫ **junction** and turn left. At the next junction, bear left; at the next junction, bear right; at the next junction, bear left onto the ⑬ **Day Hill Trail.** Proceed to the lookout. Follow the trail back to the start point.

GIVING BACK: For volunteer opportunities, call the Minnesota Historical Society at 218/226-4372. Direct donations to the Minnesota Parks and Trails Council, E-1311 First National Bank Building, St. Paul, MN 55101, or call 612/291-0715 or 800/289-1930.

"...is actually five different waterfalls at different levels, plunging down to Lake ... The park has beautiful scenic overlooks of the falls, Lake Superior, and the forest ...ng Gooseberry River. A cool Lake Superior breeze makes hiking and camping very ...able during the summer."

—Jenny Herschbach, Student Worker.

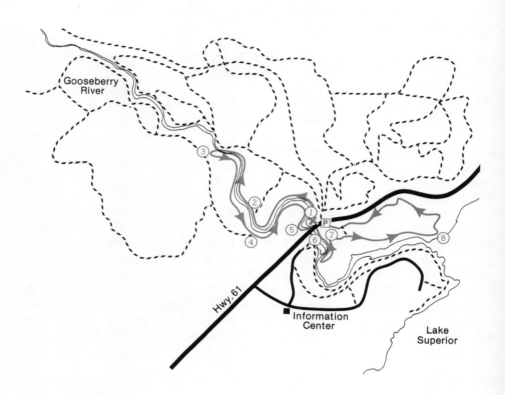

FACILITIES

✓**Restrooms** (accessible) are available at the Information Office, Interpretive Center, campgrounds, and picnic areas.

✓**Water** is available at the Information Office, Interpretive Center, Campgrounds, and picnic areas.

✓**Public telephones** are available at the Information Office.

DIRECTIONS: Gooseberry Falls State Park is northeast of Two Harbors. **From U.S. Highway 61:** Proceed north 12 miles past Two Harbors. Watch for park signs. After you visit the park office on the right side of the highway, continue on the highway over the bridge and turn left. **Park** near the Interpretive Center.

INFORMATION: Call the park at 218/834-3855. The park is open from 8 A.M. to 10 P.M. *A trail map is available at the park office and the Interpretive Center.* An annual motor vehicle permit or a daily pass is required.

HIGHLIGHTS: • 12 miles of hiking trails • Camping and picnic areas • Self-guided interpretive trail • Several overlooks of the falls and Lake Superior.

TIPS FOR WALKERS: • Trail clothes are recommended. • You may want to bring a camera and walking stick.

RECOMMENDED ROUTE: 4.8 K (3 miles)
DIRT/ROCK SURFACE. LEVEL/STEEP HILLS AROUND FALLS.
MOSTLY SHADED.
From the parking lot, the Interpretive Center will be to your right and the ① **Voyageur Interpretive Trail** will be to the left, heading northwest. Follow the trail, staying left at each junction along the Gooseberry River. At the ② **first junction, keep to the left** as you start walking along the **Fifth Falls Trail.** Stay along this trail until you reach the falls. There are two viewpoints—from the bottom along the rocks, and from the top on the bridge. Cross the ③ **bridge** and immediately turn left. Halfway back you will reach an ④ **overlook** with a view of the Gooseberry River, forest areas, Lake Superior, and the falls. Stay to your left and follow the trail back to Highway 61. ⑤ **Cross the highway,** turn left, and cross the bridge, and start walking down the path along the falls. There will be ⑥ **three areas where you can stop and view the falls.** At the bottom of the falls, take a left and follow the trail back up to the Gitchi Gummi Trail. At the ⑦ **trail junction,** turn right and stay to your right along the trail. You will come upon an ⑧ **overlook** that offers views of Lake Superior and the cliffs along the shoreline. Follow the trail back to the highway and return to your start point.

GIVING BACK: For information about volunteer opportunities, call the park. Direct financial donations to Minnesota Parks and Trails Council, E-1311 First National Bank Building, St. Paul, MN 55101, or call 612/291-0715 or 800/289-1930.

City of Duluth Trails/
Park Point Trail

Operated by the City of Duluth Parks and Recreation Department

"Enjoy the historic sights of the old lighthouse and boathouse along the trail; be overwhelmed by man-made grain elevators and the iron ore rail car system in Duluth Harbor and the majestic view of the waves and cool air breeze off of Lake Superior."

—Tim Howard, Associate Director, Parks and Recreation Department.

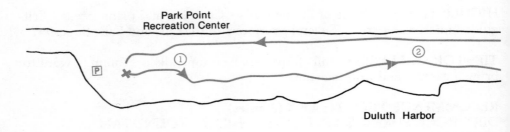

DIRECTIONS: Park Point is in downtown Duluth. **Public transportation** information is available through the Duluth Transit Authority at 218/722-7283. **From downtown Duluth:** Proceed south on Lake Avenue (toward Lake Superior) across the Aerial Lift Bridge and continue driving to the end of the island until you reach Park Point Recreation Center. You will make a half-circle around the Recreation Center. **Park** outside the fence at Sky Harbor Airport.

INFORMATION: Call the Duluth Parks and Recreation Department at 218/723-3337. The park is open daily from sunrise to sunset. There is no admission fee. *A Hiking the Hills of Duluth brochure that describes eight different walking trails throughout the city is available through the Parks and Recreation Department.* Another excellent source of information about Duluth is the Duluth Convention and Visitors Bureau, 100 Lake Place Drive, Duluth, MN 55802. If you are calling from Minnesota or Iowa, call toll free at 800/4—DULUTH or 218/722-4011.

HIGHLIGHTS: • 4-mile sandy trail • Duluth Harbor with international ships and loading areas • Pine trees • Swimming beach along Lake Superior.

TIPS FOR WALKERS: • Trail clothes are recommended. • The trail is sandy, so it will take you longer to walk. • You may want to bring a sweatshirt or jacket due to cool winds off Lake Superior. • Excellent location for birdwatching and photography. • Poison ivy is along this trail. Beware of this three-leaved plant.

FACILITIES

✓**Restrooms** (accessible) are available at Park Point Recreation Center.
✓**Water** is available at the Park Point Recreation Center.
✓**Public telephones** are available at the Park Point Recreation Center.

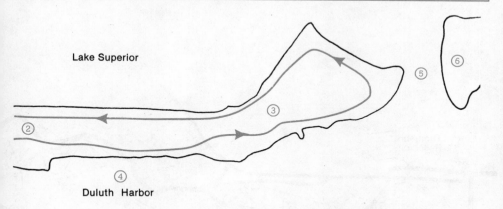

• Another highly recommended walk is "Downtown Lakewalk" which begins along the boardwalk on the west side of the Aerial Lift Bridge and extends along the Lake Superior shoreline to Fitger's (1.5 miles one-way). It is scheduled to extend to 26th Avenue East (2.5 miles one-way) by 1992. Lakewalk features a winding boardwalk with bike and carriage paths, period lampposts, benches, and other amenities.

RECOMMENDED ROUTE: 6.4 K (4 miles)
SAND SURFACE. LEVEL. MOSTLY UNSHADED.
From the parking lot enter the ① **airport gate** and follow the gravel road behind the hangers to the sandy trail along the Duluth Harbor side. You will pass a ② **historic lighthouse** and a ③ **boathouse** as you view ships, grain elevators, and iron ore train docks in the ④ **Duluth Harbor.** As you circle the boathouse you will see the ⑤ **Superior Shipping entry point** and ⑥ **Wisconsin's entry point** on the other side. Continue on the trail around the boathouse and start back toward the airport through a wooded area. At this point you have the option of staying on the wooded trail or walking along the beach of Lake Superior back to the airport.

GIVING BACK: For information about volunteer and donation opportunities, contact the Duluth Parks and Recreation Department, City Hall, Duluth, MN 55802, or call 218/723-3337.

Jay Cooke State Park

Operated by the Minnesota Department of Natural Resources

"The beautiful St. Louis River runs through the park, a river that seems like a hundred different rivers in one. In the middle there are high slate and graywacke rocks that forced the early French fur traders to portage up the river. The park has an abundance of wildlife and an old growth forest of yellow birch that you cannot get your hands around." —Amy Rager, Park Worker.

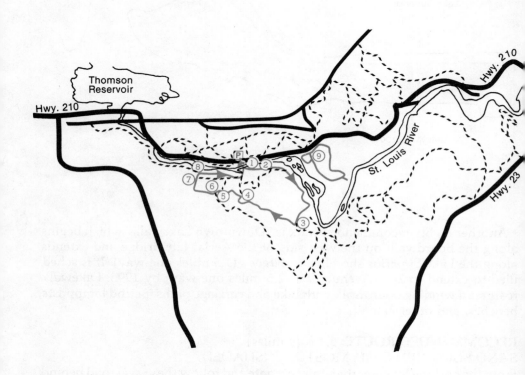

FACILITIES

- ✓ **Restrooms** (accessible) are available at the park headquarters and picnic areas.
- ✓ **Water** is available at the park headquarters and picnic areas.
- ✓ **Public telephones** are available at park headquarters.

123

DIRECTIONS: Jay Cooke State Park is southeast of Duluth. **From Interstate 35:** Proceed east on State Highway 210 (follow the signs). **Park** in the lot near the Park Headquarters.

INFORMATION: Call the park at 218/384-4610. The park is open from 8 A.M. to 10 P.M. throughout the year. *A trail map is available at the park headquarters.* An annual motor vehicle permit or a daily pass is required.

HIGHLIGHTS: • 50 miles of hiking trails • Swinging bridge over the St. Louis River • Largest hydroelectric plant in Minnesota • Thomson Dam • Grand Portage Trail • Willard Munger Trail.

TIPS FOR WALKERS: • Trail clothes are recommended.

RECOMMENDED ROUTE: 7.2 K (4.5 miles)
DIRT/GRASS SURFACE. ROLLING HILLS. SHADED.
The trail begins on the southeast side of park headquarters where you will walk across the St. Louis River on the ① **swinging bridge.** Take an immediate left after you cross the bridge and ② **keep to the left at the trail junction.** The trail follows the course of the river. At the ③ **next trail junction, turn right.** You may see deer along this trail. At the ④,⑤ **next two junctions, turn left.** At the ⑥ **next junction, turn right;** then turn ⑦ **left at the next junction.** Take a ⑧ **right onto the Carlton Trail** that goes along the St. Louis River back to the swinging bridge and your start point.

If you want to walk further, try the ⑨ **Ogantz Trail** (one mile). Proceed east on Highway 210 about a mile. Watch for the park sign and park in the lot near the picnic area. It's a very scenic loop trail that offers views of the St. Louis River valley.

GIVING BACK: If you are interested in volunteer opportunities, call the park at 218/384-4610. Direct financial donations to the Minnesota Parks and Trails Council, E-1311 First National Bank Building, St. Paul, MN 55101, or call 612/291-0715 or 800/289-1930.

*Willard Munger State Trail/*_____
Carlton to West Duluth

Operated by the Minnesota Department of Natural Resources

"When completed, the Willard Munger Trail will be a complex system of interconnecting paved and dirt trails that will stretch from Saint Paul to Duluth, offering plenty of opportunities for hiking, bicycling, snowmobiling, ski touring, and horseback riding."

—Kevin Arends, Moose Lake Area Trails and Waterways Supervisor.

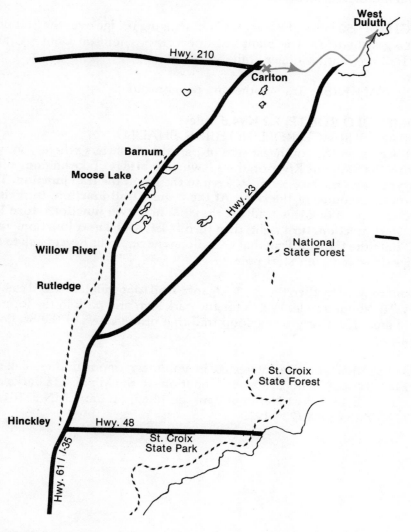

FACILITIES

- ✓ **Restrooms** (accessible) are available in Carlton, Thomson, and West Duluth.
- ✓ **Water** is available in Carlton, Thomson, and West Duluth.
- ✓ **Public telephones** are available in Carlton, Thomson, and West Duluth.

124

DIRECTIONS: The recommended route of the Willard Munger State Trail is located 20 miles west of Duluth. **From U.S.61/Interstate 35:** Proceed south on State Highway 45 to Carlton. **Park** in the lot for the Willard Munger Trail on the left side of County Highway 1, one block south of the stop sign.

INFORMATION: Call the trail manager at 218/485-8647. The trail is open year-round. *A trail map is available through the Department of Natural Resources (call toll-free at 800/652-9747).* There is no admission fee.

HIGHLIGHTS: • Scenic views of Jay Cooke Park • St. Louis River Gorge • Creeks • Indian Point Park • Duluth Zoo • St. Louis Bay and the twin ports of Duluth, Minnesota, and Superior, Wisconsin.

TIPS FOR WALKERS: • Trail clothes are recommended. • Trails are shared with bikers. Expect heavy bicycle traffic in the summer and snowmobile traffic in the winter. • This is an ideal trail for walking from one lodge or motel to another. • If you are walking one-way from Carlton to West Duluth (14 miles), you may want to arrange transportation back to your start point, or have your luggage transferred to your new destination. For information about lodging opportunities, contact the Carlton Area Chamber of Commerce, Box 526, Carlton, MN 55718, or call 218/384-4987; or write the Duluth Area Chamber of Commerce at 325 Harbor Drive, Duluth, MN 55802, or call 218/722-5501.

RECOMMENDED ROUTE: 22.4 K (14 miles—one way)
PAVED SURFACE. LEVEL. SHADED/UNSHADED.
Starting at Carlton, follow the paved trail through beautiful Jay Cooke State Park. Since it's a well-marked linear trail, you won't have to make any trail junction decisions. You will walk along the tree-lined path for 14 miles. In the summer, walk single file since you cannot hear bicycles approaching from behind. The trail ends near Indian Point Park (with a campground) to your right and the Duluth Zoo across the highway to your left.

GIVING BACK: For information about volunteer and donation opportunities, contact the Department of Natural Resources, Route 2, 701 South Kenwood, Moose Lake, MN 55767, or call 218/485-8647. You may also direct financial donations to the Minnesota Parks and Trails Council, E-1311 First National Bank Building, St. Paul, MN 55101, or call 612/291-0715 or 800/289-1930.

St. Croix State Park

Operated by the Minnesota Department of Natural Resources

"St. Croix State Park is the largest state park in Minnesota with 127 miles of hiking trails going through 33,000 acres of forest, meadows, marshes, and streams along two large rivers—the St. Croix and the Kettle. It's relatively flat country, which makes for easy walking, and the extensive trail system lets you walk as long and as far as you want."

—Jack Nelson, Park Manager.

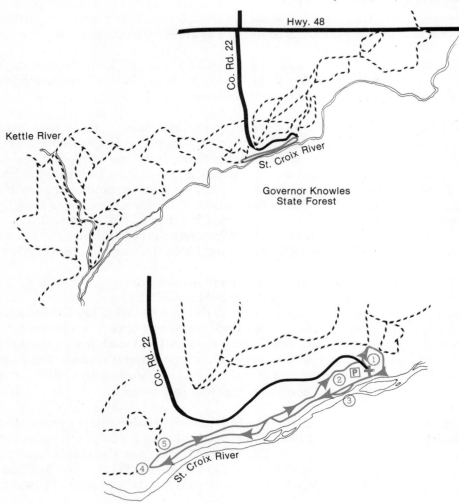

FACILITIES

- ✓**Restrooms** (accessible) are available at the Interpretive Center, campground, and beach. Pit toilets are at designated places throughout the park.
- ✓**Water** is available at the Interpretive Center, campground, and beach.
- ✓**Public telephones** are available at the St. Croix Lodge, and there is a phone booth between the Interpretive Center and park headquarters.

125

DIRECTIONS: St. Croix State Park is north of the metro area along the St. Croix River. **From Interstate 35:** Take the Hinckley exit and proceed east on State Highway 48 for 16 miles to the park entrance, then south on County Road 22 to the park headquarters. **Park** near the picnic area and phone booth.

INFORMATION: Call the park office at 612/384-6591. The park is open daily from 8 A.M. to 10 P.M. *Trail maps and a self-guided leaflet of the Sundance Trail are available at the Interpretive Center.* An annual motor vehicle permit or a daily permit is required.

HIGHLIGHTS: • 127 miles of hiking trails • Swimming • Boating and canoeing • Bike and horseback trails • Numerous and varied campsites can accommodate over six hundred campers • Souvenier shop • Daily nature classes • Wildlife • 6 miles of paved, accessible trails.

TIPS FOR WALKERS: • Trail clothes are recommended. • Paved trails are shared with bikers. • There are so many trails in this park that you might want to spend a few days camping on-site to explore some of the more scenic routes. The recommended route is just a very small sample of what the park has to offer.

RECOMMENDED ROUTE: 9.6 K (6 miles)
DIRT /GRASS SURFACE. LEVEL. MOSTLY SHADED.
From the parking lot proceed to the ① **self-guided Sundance Trail** (to the left as you face the Interpretive Center). The loop will take you back to the Interpretive Center where you will continue on the ② **River Bluff Trail** (to the right as you face the Interpretive Center). You may want to take the ③ **River Edge Trail** that runs parallel with the River Bluff Trail along the river. Continue along the River Bluff Trail. Continue to walk on the dirt/grass trail as it approaches the paved trail. At the ④ **next junction, turn right** and proceed to the biking/hiking path. ⑤ **Turn right on the paved path** and follow it back to the Interpretive Center as you walk through forests and meadows.

GIVING BACK: For volunteer opportunities, call the park office. Direct financial donations to Minnesota Parks and Trails Council, E-1311 First National Bank Building, St. Paul, MN 55101, or call 612/291-0715 or 800/289-1930.

Wild River State Park

Operated by the Minnesota Department of Natural Resources

"The park is a contrast of marshes, prairies, and hardwood forests along the St. Croix River that provides an ideal sanctuary for a variety of wildlife. The colorful wildflowers and the changing colors of the prairie grasses in the late summer make it an ideal place to walk."

—Kathy Teryll, Interpretive Center.

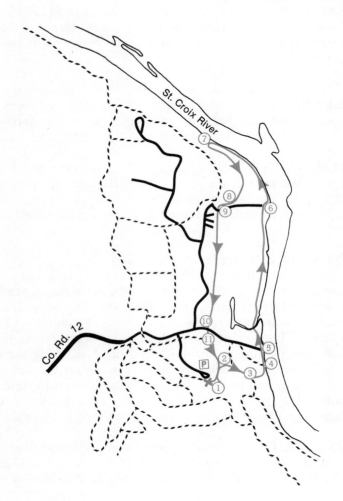

FACILITIES

- ✓**Restrooms** (accessible) are available at the Interpretive Center, Trail Center, and picnic grounds.
- ✓**Water** is available at the Information Office, Interpretive Center, picnic grounds, and campgrounds.
- ✓**Public telephones** are available at the Information Office.

126

DIRECTIONS: Wild River State Park is north of the metro area along the St. Croix River. **From Interstate 35:** Take the State Highway 95 exit, proceed east to Almelund, and then north on County Road 12. After you stop at the Information Office, follow the road to the right. **Park** near the Interpretive Center.

INFORMATION: Call the park office at 612/583-2125. The park is open daily from 8 A.M. to 10 P.M. during the summer months. *Trail maps are available at the Information Office.* An annual motor vehicle permit or a daily pass is required.

HIGHLIGHTS: • 35 miles of walking trails (20 of the 35 miles are shared with horseback riders) • Campgrounds • Nevers Dam site • Wildlife • Deer/bird watching • Interpretive Center.

TIPS FOR WALKERS: • Trail clothes are recommended. • You may want to bring binoculars. • You may want to carry water. • The trails on the recommended route are for hikers only.

RECOMMENDED ROUTE: 7.2 K (4.5 miles)
DIRT /GRASS SURFACE. LEVEL. SHADED/UNSHADED.
From the parking lot, proceed to the Interpretive Center. At the trail junction, you can proceed ahead to the Interpretive Center or turn left onto the ① **Mitigwaki Trail.** At the ② **next junction,** turn right, and at the next junction, also keep to the right. At the ③ **next junction,** turn left just before you reach the river and then ④ **keep to the right** as you walk along wildflowers and prairie grasses on your left and the river on your right. You will cross a ⑤ **boat launch road.** Continue along the River Trail until you reach the ⑥ **Old Nevers Dam site.** Keep to the right and continue along the ⑦ **River Terrace Loop,** making a sharp left at the north end of the loop. At the ⑧ **next junction,** take a right onto the Nevers Dam Trail; after passing through the picnic area, take a left onto the ⑨ **Old Logging Trail.** You'll walk through a forest and cross a ⑩ **road.** At the ⑪ **next junction,** keep to the left along the Mitigwaki Trail, then turn right and return to the start point.

GIVING BACK: For volunteer opportunities, call the park office. Direct financial donations to the Minnesota State Parks Gift Account, 500 Lafayette Road, St. Paul, MN 55155-4039. Or, contact the Minnesota Parks and Trails Council, E-1311 First National Bank Building, St. Paul, MN 55101, or call 612/291-0715 or 800/289-1930.

Downtown Saint Paul Skyway

Operated by the Saint Paul Downtown Council and the Saint Paul Merchants Association

"The skyway system is a great way to experience the historic beauty of Saint Paul in all kinds of weather. Walkers use the skyway early in the morning and later in the evening to get their exercise."
—Ronnie Brooks, Marketing Consultant.

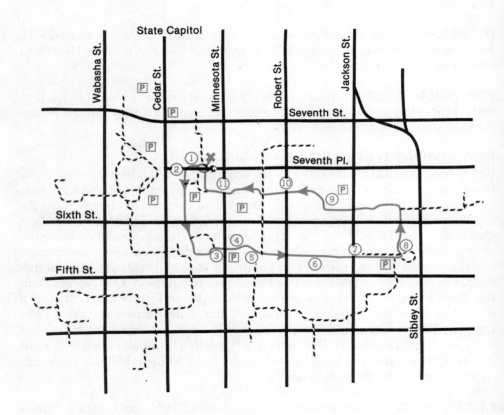

DIRECTIONS: The skyway system is located in downtown Saint Paul. **Public transportation** is available on most MTC Routes including #1, 6, 7, 8, and 11. **From Interstate 94:** Exit on any of the downtown exits and proceed to Cedar Street between Sixth and Seventh streets. **Park** in the Town Square parking lot. (Parking lots are marked with blue circular signs with the letter "P.")

INFORMATION: Call the Saint Paul Downtown Council during regular business hours at 612/297-6899. The skyway is open from 6 A.M. to 2 A.M. every day throughout the year. • *Skyway maps are available at the Information Center in Town Square.* Maps are also posted throughout the skyway system. There is no admission fee.

HIGHLIGHTS: • The Saint Paul skyway system is the largest publicly-owned skyway system in the world • More than 4 miles of indoor walking paths • Town Square, Galtier Plaza retail centers • Historic Cafesjian Carousel in Town Square • Minnesota Office of Tourism.

TIPS FOR WALKERS: • There is no place to check coats, so wear a jacket that can be tied around your waist as you walk. • Some doors linking sections of the skyway are electronic, others are hand-operated. • *The skyway is open for walkers year-round.*

RECOMMENDED ROUTE: 1.6 K (1 mile)
PAVED. LEVEL. SHADED.
Proceed to the skyway level of Town Square near the elevators—the escalators to the Garden Level should be directly in front of you. Proceed to the ① **Norwest Center** skyway to the right. Turn left at the ② **first junction.** At the Norwest Center lobby turn left and proceed to the ③ **American National Building** skyway. ④ **Veer to the left** (do not take the escalator to the right). You will come to a main corridor with three skyway junctions. Take the center skyway to ⑤ **Farm Credit Services.** The ⑥ **Minnesota Office of Tourism** will be on your right (open during regular business hours). There is lots of free literature in the lobby. Note the wooden mural on the wall of the administration office. Continue walking to ⑦ **Galtier Plaza.** Keep to the right and proceed to the second set of elevators. Turn left and proceed to the ⑧ **YMCA/Mears Park Place** skyway. Don't take the stairs; turn left on the carpeted walkway. Proceed to the ⑨ **Minnesota Mutual Life** center skyway around the lobby. Note the waterfall sculpture. Proceed to the ⑩ **Twin City Federal** building. At the next junction, take a right through the doors, and then a quick left. Follow the signs to ⑪ **Saint Paul Center** (make a quick left, then right). Turn right at the library and you're back at the start point.

GIVING BACK: Direct financial donations to the Saint Paul Downtown Council, 600 North Central Tower, St. Paul, MN 55101. Volunteer opportunities are available.

Minneapolis/Saint Paul

International Airport

Operated by the Metropolitan Airports Commission

"This self-guided tour developed by the Metropolitan Airports Commission provides a great walking alternative when it's too hot or too cold to walk outside, or when you have at least a 45-minute wait for a plane."
— Tom Nieszner, Airport Tour Guide.

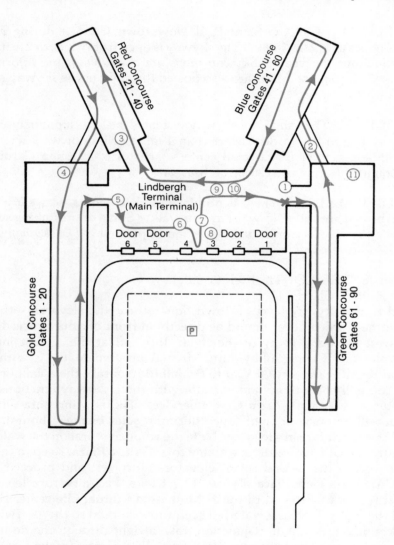

FACILITIES

✓**Restrooms** (accessible) are available in all the concourses.
✓**Water** is available in all the concourses.
✓**Public telephones** are available in all the concourses.

DIRECTIONS: The Minneapolis/Saint Paul International Airport is located south of the metro area. **Public transportation** is available on MTC Routes #7 and 15. **From Interstate 494:** Take the airport exit to the main terminal. **Park** in the short-term section of the parking ramp.

INFORMATION: Call the Tour Office at 612/726-5515. The airport concourses are open daily from 5:30 A.M. to about 10 P.M. (depending on the last scheduled flight). *A tour brochure is available at the Tour Office (Room 336) on the second floor above the ticket area during regular business hours.* There is no admission fee.

HIGHLIGHTS: • Observation deck • Climate-controlled environment • Historic displays.

TIPS FOR WALKERS: • Concourses are not available for walking when airport security is increased. Call ahead to check on public access. • Rent one of the lockers just inside the green concourse. Carry only ID and pocket change—this makes it much easier to pass through security. • One-way mileage for each concourse is as follows: Green (.3 miles); Blue (.2 miles); Red (.2 miles); and Gold (.4 miles). • Street clothes are recommended.

RECOMMENDED ROUTE: 4.8 K (3 miles)
PAVED. LEVEL. SHADED.
From the parking ramp, proceed to the main terminal, ticket level, Green Concourse. Enter through the security checkpoint at the ① **Green Concourse.** Lockers are available just beyond the security gate. Take the walkway to the ② **Blue Concourse** and walk to the farthest point and back again. Walk back into the lobby area over to the security checkpoint for the ③ **Red Concourse.** Walk to the farthest end and back again. Take the walkway over to the ④ **Gold Concourse** and walk the full length and back again. Proceed to the main lobby ticket area. Observe the replica of the ⑤ **Spirit of St. Louis,** the plane that was used during the first solo flight across the Atlantic Ocean by Minnesota native Charles Lindbergh. Look down on the terazzo floor and observe the two ⑥ **world maps.** The star on the map is your current location. You may want to talk with the ⑦ **Foreign Currency Exchange** to see what your dollar is worth in other parts of the world. On the walls, look for the ⑧ **dedication plaques** marking the opening of Chamberlain Field in 1923. Take the walkway between the ticket counters to the shopping side of the lobby. Observe the ⑨ **Police Memorial** and the ⑩ **Architect's model** showing plans for future expansion of the airport. If you have time, take the elevator downstairs to the Fireman's sculpture. Proceed back upstairs to the Green Concourse. Walk to Gate 65 and walk up the steps to the ⑪ **Observation Deck.** Then proceed back to your start point.

West Saint Paul

Signal Hills Center: Located at South Robert Street and Butler Avenue in West Saint Paul, Signal Hills Center is open to walkers on Monday through Friday from 8 A.M. to 9 P.M., Saturday from 7 A.M. to 5:30 P.M., and Sunday from 11 A.M. to 5 P.M. One lap around Signal Hills Center equals .6 mile. A walking program, co-sponsored with Divine Redeemer Hospital, offers regular seminars and occasional health screenings. For additional information, call 612/457-0589.

Downtown Minneapolis

Minneapolis Skyway: An extensive skyway system in downtown Minneapolis links a signficant portion of the retail and business sectors. Large maps of the skyway system are posted in strategic locations along the route. The skyway is owned and operated by the businesses along the route. All segments are open during regular business hours but only a few segments are open on the weekends. A brochure containing a map of the skyway system is available through the Greater Minneapolis Convention and Visitors Association at 612/348-4313.

Metrodome: From November to March the Minnesota Distance Runners Association (MDRA) coordinates a running and walking program in the Metrodome. The Metrodome is located between Chicago Avenue and 11th Avenue South along Fifth Street South. Two and one-half laps equal 1 mile. An annual schedule is published by the MDRA. Hours vary per season but are usually from 5 P.M. to 8 P.M. on Tuesday and Thursday evenings. The admission is $1 per session. Call for entry door information. Someone will be inside the door to explain the program and provide you with a brochure. Restrooms are available for changing clothes. Lockers are not available. For more information, contact Rick Recker at 612/375-0805. (See Chapter 8 for more information about the MDRA.)

Bloomington

Mall of America: Scheduled to open in the fall of 1992, the Mall of America will be the largest fully enclosed retail and family entertainment center in the United States. The Mall of America will be located near the airport on Interstate 494 between 24th Avenue South and Cedar Avenue (Highway 77). One lap around one of the floors will equal .9 mile. The top floor will have a track for walkers and runners. The Mall of America will also feature an eighteen-screen cinema complex, a hotel, a 1.2 million gallon walk-through aquarium, four hundred specialty stores, high tech and adventure miniature golf courses, and Knott's Camp Snoopy, a seven-acre complex with twenty-six rides and attractions including Peanuts characters. For updated information about the Mall of America, call the Bloomington Convention and Visitor's Bureau at 612/888-8810 or 800/346-4289 ext. 92.

Burnsville _____ F

Burnsville Center: Burnsville Center is located at the junctions of 35W and 35E at County Road 42. Mall walking hours are from 7 A.M. to 9 P.M. Monday through Friday, 8 A.M. to 6 P.M. on Saturday, and 10:30 A.M. to 5 P.M. on Sunday. The distance around one level is .5 mile. Walkers need to register for the walking program. Burnsville Center also offers "Inside Track to Good Health" seminars on health topics and occasional health screenings on the first Wednesday of every month, October through May. Professionals from Fairview Ridges Hospital are available from 7 A.M. to 8:30 A.M. to provide information and answer questions. Refreshments are provided. A brochure with a registration form is available at Burnsville Center or by calling 612/435-8182.

Edina _____ G

Edinborough Park: This unique indoor park is owned and operated by the City of Edina Parks and Recreation Department. Facilities at the park include a pool, an ice skating rink, a Great Hall for open basketball, and a three-lane track for walkers and runners. It's an ideal location for indoor walking in any kind of weather. The park is open Monday through Thursday from 9 A.M. to 9 P.M., Friday and Saturday from 9 A.M. to 5 P.M., and Sunday from noon to 9 P.M. The track is on the second floor of the park. Track hours are Monday through Thursday from 6 A.M. to 9 P.M., Friday from 6 A.M. to 5 P.M., Saturday from 9 A.M. to 5 P.M., and Sunday from noon to 9 P.M. Walkers use the inside lane. Seventeen laps around the track equal 1 mile. There is a $2.50 admission fee to use the track. Free lockers are available. For information about special hours for walkers, call City Line at 612/645-6060 Category #7275.

Edina _____ H

Southdale Center: Southdale, the first enclosed climate-controlled shopping mall in the United States, offers a comprehensive walking program that serves up to three hundred people per day. Southdale is located at 66th and France Avenue South between Crosstown 62 and Interstate 494. Southdale is open to walkers Monday through Friday from 7:30 A.M. to 9:30 P.M., Saturday from 7:30 P.M. to 6 P.M., and Sunday from 10:30 A.M. to 5 P.M. Holiday hours may vary. Walkers need to register for the walking program at the Customer Service Center. On the first level, two and one quarter laps equal 1 mile and on the second level, two and three quarter laps equal 1 mile. Southdale and Fairview Southdale Hospital also offer the "Making Tracks for Health" program that provides seminars and health screenings on the fourth Tuesday of every month at 8:30 A.M. in the Southdale Community Room. Brochures are available at the Customer Service Center. For additional information about the walking program, call 612/925-7852.

Eden Prairie _____ I

Eden Prairie Shopping Center: Eden Prairie Shopping Center is located at Highway 169 and Interstate 494. The Center is open to walkers from 7 A.M. to 9 P.M. Monday through Friday, 7 A.M. to 6 P.M. on Saturday, and 7 A.M. to 5 P.M. on Sunday. A 1-mile course has been developed for walkers. "Eden Prairie Pacers" is a walking program co-sponsored by the Eden Prairie Shopping Center and Methodist Hospital. The program offers monthly seminars on the fourth Tuesday of the month at 9 A.M., except during the months of June, July, August, and December. In addition, walkers are invited to participate in community health education activities conducted by Methodist Hospital at 8 A.M. on the first, second, and third Tuesdays of each month. Programs feature physical therapists, dietitians, and registered nurses. An "Eden Prairie Pacers" brochure that includes warm-up activities is available at the shopping center or by calling 612/932-5041 or 612/941-7650.

St. Louis Park _____ J

Knollwood Mall: Located one block east of Highway 169 on Highway 7 in St. Louis Park, Knollwood Mall's doors open at 7 A.M. Monday through Sunday for mall walking. Two laps around the mall equals 1 mile. Knollwood's walking program is co-sponsored by Methodist Hospital. Health education activities are offered the first Thursday of each month at 8 A.M. in the Court Cafes. The activities are presented by physical therapists, dietitians, and registered nurses. In addition, there are special quarterly events held at 9 A.M. on the first Thursday of February, May, September, and November. All people participating in the walking program are required to sign a release form at the Knollwood Mall Management Office prior to beginning a regular walking program at the Mall. A "Walking Program" brochure that includes warm-up exercises and a map of the mall is available at Knollwood Mall by calling 612/933-8041 or 612/932-5041.

Minnetonka _____ K

Ridgedale Center: Located on the south side of Highway 394, Ridgedale Center opens for walkers at 7 A.M. Monday through Saturday and at 9 A.M. on Sunday. Walkers are encouraged to use the facility before the stores open at 10 A.M. on weekdays, 9:30 A.M. on Saturday, and noon on Sunday. Lockers are available. "Step Into Fitness With the Morning Milers" is a walking program that is co-sponsored by Ridgedale Center and Methodist Hospital. The program offers monthly seminars every third Wednesday from 8 A.M. to 10 A.M. on the Lower Level. Seminars are not scheduled in June, July, August, or December. On the first, second, and fourth Wednesdays a nurse is available to test blood pressure. A program brochure is available at Ridgedale Center or by calling 612/541-4864 or 612/932-5041.

Brooklyn Center

Brookdale Center: Located at the intersection of Highways 100 and 152/ Brooklyn Boulevard, Brookdale opens its doors to walkers at 7 A.M. Monday through Saturday and at 10 A.M. on Sunday. Walkers may use the facility before and during regular store hours. The shopping center's regular hours are from 10 A.M. to 9:30 P.M. Monday through Friday, 9:30 A.M. to 6 P.M. on Saturday, and noon to 5 P.M. on Sunday. Holiday hours may vary. "Keeping Pace" is a walking program that is co-sponsored by Brookdale Center and Investors Savings Bank. The program sponsors health seminars on the third Tuesday of each month from 8 A.M. to 9 A.M. On other Tuesdays, blood pressure and cholesterol screenings are available from 8 A.M. to 10:30 A.M. A "Keeping Pace" brochure is available at Brookdale Center or by calling 612/569-2604.

Blaine

Northtown Mall: Located at the intersection of Highway 10 and University Avenue Northeast, Northtown Mall opens it doors to walkers every day from 7:30 A.M. to 9 A.M. All entrances are open Monday through Saturday. However, on Sundays only entrance #6 is open. All walkers are requested to register and sign a release form. Forms are available in the Management Office or the Security Office. Walkers are issued a button and are asked to wear the button when walking. One lap around the mall equals one mile. "Northtown Mall Walkers" is a walking program sponsored by Northtown Mall and Mercy & Unity Medical Centers. Participants in the program receive a monthly "Guide to Health" publication that lists upcoming seminars and programs. For more information about the "Northtown Mall Walker" program, call 612/786-9704.

St. Anthony

Apache Plaza Shopping Center: Located at the intersection of 38th Avenue Northeast and Silver Lake Road, Apache Plaza is available to walkers from 6:30 A.M. to 9 P.M. on Monday through Friday, 6:30 A.M. to 6 P.M. on Saturday, and 8:30 A.M. to 6 P.M. on Sunday. Hours vary during holidays and special events. For information, call the shopping center at 612/788-1666 during regular business hours.

Roseville

Rosedale Center: Located on the north side of Highway 36 between Fairview and Snelling Avenues, Rosedale is available to walkers from 7 A.M. to 9:30 P.M. Monday through Friday, 7 A.M. to 6 P.M. on Saturday, and 10 A.M. to 5 P.M. on Sunday. One lap around equals .6 of a mile.

Roseville

Har Mar Mall: Located on Snelling Avenue just south of Highway 36, Har Mar Mall is open to walkers from 6:30 A.M. to 9 P.M. Monday through Friday, 8 A.M. to 6 P.M. on Saturday, and 9 A.M. to 5 P.M. on Sunday. Holiday hours may vary. One lap around equals 1 mile. Mall maps and free parking stickers that allow walkers to park close to the entrance doors early in the morning are available from the Mall Management Office from 8:30 A.M. to 5 P.M. weekdays. For additional information, call the Har Mar Mall at 612/631-0340.

Maplewood

Maplewood Mall: Located at the intersection of Interstate 694 and White Bear Avenue, Maplewood Mall is available to walkers from 7:30 A.M. to 10 A.M. Monday through Friday, 7:30 A.M. to 9:30 A.M. on Saturday, and 9 A.M. to 11 A.M. on Sunday. Hours vary during holidays and special events. For information, call the Maplewood Mall at 612/770-5010. Lakewood Community College sponsors a walking club that is available to Maplewood Mall walkers. Information about the Lakewood Community College program is available in Chapter 8. For additional information about the Lakewood College program, call 612/779-3358.

Oakdale R

Oakdale Mall: Located at the junction of Interstate 694 and Highway 10, the Oakdale Mall opens to walkers at 8 A.M. on Monday through Saturday and at 10 A.M. on Sunday. Five laps around equals 1 mile.

Rochester

Indoor walking opportunities abound. Contact the Rochester Area Chamber of Commerce at 507/288-1122, or write 220 South Broadway, Suite 100, Rochester, MN 55904, for a free Visitor's Guide that includes a *Skyway and Subway Guide*—a map of both systems. Guides are also available at most downtown hotels.

Skyway System: The skyway extends from the Medical Sciences Building at Third Avenue Southwest and Third Street Southwest north four blocks to Center Street at Rochester Methodist Hospital, with extensions to the Baldwin Building, Harwick Building, Mayo Clinic, Kahler Plaza Hotel, Kahler Hotel, Damon West, and the Clinic View Inn.

Subway System: The subway extends from the Holiday Inn and Marquette Bank at Second Street Southeast and First Avenue Southeast north one block to the Radisson Centerplace Hotel, west one block to the Galleria Shopping Mall and the Kahler Plaza Hotel, and then south to the First Bank Building.

Apache Mall: The mall, located at the intersection of U.S. Highway 14 East and U.S. Highway 52 South, is open to walkers at 7:30 A.M. every day of the week before the stores open at 10 A.M. There are no fees or registration forms. For more information, call 507/288-8056.

Saint Cloud

Haws Civic Center: The Civic Center, located downtown at 10 Fourth Avenue South, is the site of an indoor walking program sponsored by St. Cloud Park and Recreation Department. A carpeted track is available to walkers for an annual fee of $15 or a daily fee of $2 payable at the door; eight laps around the track equal 1 mile. Showers and lockers are usually available. For a monthly schedule of walking hours, call 612/255-7277 or 612/225-7256.

Halenbeck Hall, St. Cloud State University: The indoor track is located south of 10th Street on the east side of the building along the river. Walkers may purchase a Recreation User ID card for $24 per quarter, or pay a $2 daily fee at the door; eight laps around the track equal 1 mile. Family and young adult rates are available, as are special discounts for people affiliated with SCSU. Lockers are available. There is also a comprehensive adult fitness program available through the Human Performance Lab. For additional information about the walking or fitness program, call the Lab at 612/255-3105 or 612/255-3637.

District 742 Community Education: There are a number of St. Cloud schools that are open to walkers from October through May. Stop in at 628 Roosevelt Road, St. Cloud, MN 56301 to sign up for the winter walking program and obtain a schedule and walker's badge. This program is free. Call Community Education at 612/251-1733 for more information.

Alexandria

Walk of the Town: This popular Alexandria program is sponsored by Lakes Community Recreation at 1401 Jefferson, Alexandria, MN 56308. For a $10 annual fee, walkers receive: a map and a recordkeeping booklet, a sweatshirt seminars on health and safety, and occasional health screenings. Jefferson High School is open to walkers on Monday through Friday from 4:30 P.M. to 6:30 P.M., November through April. Three laps around all the hallways equal 2 miles. Walkers in the program are also eligible to win walking shoes and other prizes throughout the year. Walkers must register for the program. For more information, call 612/762-7747.

Viking Plaza Mall: The mall is located along Highway 29 in Alexandria Although there is no formal walking program, walkers are encouraged to use the facility. The doors to the mall open at 7 A.M. every day of the week. Walkers may also get their exercise during regular shopping hours from 10 A.M. to 9 P.M. Monday through Friday, 10 A.M. to 5 P.M. on Saturday, and noon to 5 P.M. on Sunday. If you have any questions, call the Viking Plaza Mall at 612/763-3800.

Brainerd

Westgate Mall: The mall is located at 1200 Highway 210 West in Brainerd in front of the Paul Bunyan Arboretum. The mall offers a carpeted walking surface along its corridor; three trips down the corridor equal 1 mile. The mall is open to walkers from 7 A.M. to 10 P.M. Monday through Friday, 8 A.M. to 10 P.M. on Saturdays, and 9 A.M. to noon on Sundays. Walkers who use the mall for exercise are asked to register in the mall office. For an annual fee of $5 walkers can join the Westgate Mall Walkers Club that offers breakfast and holiday socials, an annual meeting, and t-shirts. The Club plans to offer health seminars in the near future. For information, call the Westgate Mall at 218/828-1668.

Detroit Lakes

Washington Square Mall: The Washington Square Mall is located on the main street in Detroit Lakes. The Mall opens its doors to walkers every day of the week at 7 A.M. Walkers are asked to register at the office. Registered participants in the program are eligible to win prizes in a monthly drawing. For additional information about the program, call 218/847-1670.

Moorhead

Moorhead Center Mall: The Moorhead Center Mall is located at Fifth Street and Center Avenue. Doors open to walkers at 7 A.M. Monday through Friday, at 8 A.M. on Saturday, and at 10 A.M. on Sunday. Regular mall hours are from 10 A.M. to 9 P.M. Monday through Friday, 10 A.M. to 5:30 P.M. on Saturday, and noon to 5 P.M. on Sunday. For more information, call 218/233-6117.

Bemidji

Paul Bunyan Mall: Paul Bunyan Mall is located at 1201 Paul Bunyan Drive Northwest, Bemidji, MN 56601. The mall is available to walkers beginning at 7 A.M. Monday through Friday and at 8 A.M. on Saturdays and Sundays. Three laps equal 1 mile. Walkers need to register at the mall office. Free seminars and blood pressure checks are offered at 8 A.M. on the first Tuesday of the month (October through May) by employees of North Country Hospital. For further information, call the mall at 218/751-3195.

Duluth

There are two wonderful indoor facilities for walking in Duluth—the Duluth Skyway that extends from Downtown Duluth to the Civic Center and the Miller Hill Mall.

Duluth Skyway: The Duluth Skyway system extends through the downtown area across Interstate 35 to the Civic Center. The skyway is open from 7 A.M. to 8:30 P.M. Monday through Friday, and from 8 A.M. to 7 P.M. on Saturday. The skyway is closed on Sunday. A map of the skyway system is available through the Greater Downtown Council at 720 Medical Arts Building, Duluth, MN 55802 or by calling 218/727-8549.

Miller Hill Mall: The Miller Hill Mall opens for walkers at 8 A.M. Monday through Saturday and at 10 A.M. on Sunday. The mall is located at Highway 53 and Trinity Road. Maps showing walking routes are posted just inside the doors. Walkers use both the inside and outside of the mall. One lap around the inside of the mall is .75 mile and one lap along the outside of the mall is 1 mile. The walking route maps are provided by St. Mary's Hospital. For more information, call 218/727-8301.

The lead writer for *Walking Minnesota* was Mary Jo Malach, an avid walker, freelance writer, and part-time Communications Coordinator for Arc of Hennepin County, an organization that provides advocacy and support for people with developmental disabilities and their families. Mary Jo interviewed walking enthusiasts and walked most of the metro sites.

Jim Malach spent weeks on the road, walking most of the trails in outstate Minnesota. Jim is a sales consultant for Dayton's and is director of Walkeen Adventures, an organization that promotes the development of a healthy, productive, and enjoyable lifestyle through walking.

Two other writers walked some of the metro and outstate trails: Mary Steffl, a freelance writer and director of MAS Communications and Martha McNey, a writer, editor, and photographer and Communications Coordinator for Arc of Hennepin County.

All the maps and illustrations were developed by Karen Berry, a freelance illustrator, designer, and cartographer. And then Mary Walstrom, director of JEZAC Type & Design, put it all together.